Ultimate Transformer Models Using PyTorch 2.0

Master Transformer Model Development, Fine-Tune Pretrained Models, and Deploy AI Solutions with PyTorch 2.0

Abhiram Ravikumar

www.orangeava.com

First Published: August 2025

Published By: Orange Education Pvt Ltd, AVA®

Address: 9, Daryaganj, Delhi, 110002, India

275 New North Road Islington Suite 1314 London,
N1 7AA, United Kingdom

ISBN (PBK): 978-93-49888-50-0
ISBN (E-BOOK): 978-93-49888-99-9

Scan the QR code to explore our entire catalogue

www.orangeava.com

Dedicated To

My Dear Wife, Kshama

My Beloved Parents:
Mrs. Harini and Mr. Ravikumar

My Father-In-Law, Mr Girish

And

Every Teacher, Who Inspired My Love for Learning

About the Author

Abhiram Ravikumar is a Senior Data Scientist at Publicis Sapient, where he applies his extensive expertise in natural language processing, machine learning, and AI to solve complex business challenges. He holds a Master's degree in Data Science from King's College, London, and brings a wealth of academic and industry experience to this book on transformer models and PyTorch 2.0.

An experienced member of the Mozilla Tech Speakers program, Abhiram has presented at international tech conferences such as PyCon, MozFest, and CodeMash. His ability to communicate complex technical concepts is further evidenced by his LinkedIn Learning course on Rust Programming, which has reached over 60,000 learners. His talk on Clustering Topic Models at the Analytics Vidhya DataHour Forum Talk series attracted over 4,200 participants and received an impressive feedback rating of 4.6 out of 5.

Abhiram's background spans through both academia and industry. He has published many papers and posters at IEEE and ACM research conferences. His industry experience includes over four years at SAP Labs in Bengaluru, where he specialized in web development, computer vision, and Robotic Process Automation (RPA). He also worked as a Data Science and Cloud Machine Learning Engineer at Collinson's specialist Data Science team. At AI Palette, he built contextually relevant Small Language Models for niche retail use cases, and successfully deployed transformer-based models in production environments.

His exceptional contributions to the field have been recognized through prestigious awards, including the Best Consultant Award for high-impact Data Science projects from AI Palette in 2024. He also received the SAP Stellar Award for Nascent Intrapreneurship —an honor accompanied by a grant of ₹4,00,000—recognizing his outstanding work in research, product development, and innovation.

With hands-on experience in developing, testing, and deploying NLP products—including building contextually relevant Small Language Models for specialized retail applications, and applying advanced techniques such as BERTopic—Abhiram is uniquely positioned to guide readers through the intricacies of transformer models, and their implementation, using PyTorch 2.0. His proven track record of taking transformer models from development to production, particularly in the context of both Large Language Models (LLMs) and specialized smaller models, ensures that this book provides cutting-edge insights and practical knowledge for both beginners and experienced practitioners in AI and machine learning.

About the Technical Reviewer

Gautam Kumar is a seasoned professional with over 8 years of experience in designing and developing data-driven enterprise applications, both in on-premises and cloud environments. He has always been interested in applying AI and machine learning to existing business scenarios. Earlier in his career, he worked across multiple industries such as semiconductors, telecom, HRMS, energy, finance, and retail data. There, he worked to optimize data strategies and modernize application architectures with AI. Over the years, he has held various technical and leadership roles, helping teams deliver impactful solutions that drive business value monetization. He has primarily worked in the data science field, building and integrating AI/ML models into existing systems and optimizing system performance. His focus is always on developing scalable and maintainable solutions that meet business needs. He has worked for Accenture, HCLTech, and Ericsson.

He is currently working full-time as a Sr. Data Scientist in the AI and Automation domain at "Racanaa Energy Solution Pvt Ltd." His role and responsibility include working with global clients to develop intelligent AI systems that transform operations and help management make AI-driven decisions. He has extensive knowledge of data flows, cloud infrastructures, and AI adoption strategies, enabling organizations to make confident, data-driven decisions. He also supports teams in adopting GenAI LLM and other new technologies.

In addition to technical implementation, he is passionate about supporting young talent and fostering a collaborative culture that drives innovation. He believes in continuous learning in Data Science, Cloud Computing, and AI to stay at the frontier of the AI industry.

Acknowledgements

There are a few people I want to thank for the continued and ongoing support they have given me during the writing of this book.

First and foremost, I would like to thank my wife Kshama, and my beloved parents, Mrs. Harini and Mr. Ravikumar, for continuously encouraging me throughout this journey. Their unwavering belief in my vision, and patient understanding during countless late nights of writing, made this book possible. I could have never completed this endeavor, without their love and support.

I extend my heartfelt gratitude to my father-in-law, Mr. Girish S, whose wisdom and encouragement provided invaluable motivation during challenging moments of the writing process.

Special thanks to all the teachers and mentors, who have shaped my understanding of Artificial Intelligence and Machine Learning, throughout my academic and professional journey. Their dedication to knowledge-sharing inspired me to contribute to the learning community through this book.

I would like to express my sincere appreciation to the editorial team at Orange Education Pvt Ltd for their meticulous attention to detail, constructive feedback, and professional guidance that transformed my manuscript into a polished publication. Their expertise and patience made the entire publishing process seamless and enjoyable.

I am also deeply grateful to my friends, Anusha and Misha for generously devoting their time to review early drafts of the manuscript. Their thoughtful feedback, insights, and encouragement were instrumental in refining the content, and strengthening the clarity of the key concepts. Their support added immense value to this book, and I truly appreciate their willingness to be a part of this journey.

A special acknowledgement to the incredible team at Hugging Face for building and maintaining such an amazing transformers library. Their dedication to making cutting-edge AI accessible to practitioners worldwide is truly remarkable, as this book would not exist, without their groundbreaking contributions to the field.

Finally, I thank the broader AI and machine learning community for their open-source contributions, research papers, and collaborative spirit that continue to push the boundaries of what is possible with artificial intelligence.

Preface

Welcome to ***Ultimate Transformer Models Using PyTorch 2.0***! In this book, we embark on an exploration of one of the most powerful and transformative paradigms in modern artificial intelligence–transformer models. From their humble beginnings in Natural Language Processing (NLP) to their groundbreaking applications in vision, speech, and beyond, transformers have revolutionized the way machines understand and process data. This book is designed to guide you through the theory, application, and fine-tuning of transformer models, using PyTorch 2.0, equipping you with the knowledge and tools to leverage these models for various real-world tasks. Thus, whether you are a beginner eager to learn the foundations, or an experienced practitioner looking to master the intricacies of transformer architectures, this book is your ultimate, comprehensive guide.

Chapter 1. Understanding the Evolution of Neural Networks: We begin by tracing the historical evolution of neural networks, from the foundational concepts to the groundbreaking transformer models. In this chapter, we explore the rise of deep learning, with a focus on how innovations like Convolutional Neural Networks (CNNs), Recurrent Neural Networks (RNNs), and transformers reshaped the AI landscape. We then delve into the architecture of transformers, and how they outperformed previous models in handling complex tasks, especially in NLP.

Chapter 2. Fundamentals of Transformer Architecture: This chapter is dedicated to dissecting the transformer architecture in detail. We cover essential concepts, such as self-attention, positional encoding, and multi-head attention, which form the backbone of transformer models. Understanding these fundamental components is critical to grasping how transformers process sequences, and generate outputs, as well as lays the groundwork for understanding more complex architectures in later chapters.

Chapter 3. Getting Started with PyTorch 2.0: In this chapter, we introduce PyTorch 2.0, the powerful framework used for building and training transformer models. We walk through the process of setting up the PyTorch environment, understanding tensors, and using autograd for automatic differentiation. By the end of this chapter, you will be comfortable with the basics of PyTorch, and be ready to begin implementing more complex models.

Chapter 4. Natural Language Processing with Transformers: This chapter explores the use of transformers in NLP. We dive into tasks, such as text classification, named entity recognition, sentiment analysis, and machine translation. Through hands-on examples, you will also learn how to apply transformer models such as BERT, GPT, and T5 for a variety of NLP tasks, and understand how fine-tuning pre-trained models can boost performance on specific tasks.

Chapter 5. Computer Vision with Transformers: Here, we focus on the application of transformers in computer vision, an area, where CNNs traditionally dominated. We explore Vision Transformers (ViTs), and their applications in image classification, object detection, and segmentation. We also cover how transformers can be integrated into hybrid architectures, with CNNs, and discuss efficient transformer models for edge devices.

Chapter 6. Speech Processing with Transformers: Transformers have proven to be just as effective in speech processing as they are in NLP. In this chapter, we examine how transformers are revolutionizing Automatic Speech Recognition (ASR), Text-to-Speech (TTS) synthesis, and other speech-related tasks. We also look at advancements, such as Wav2Vec 2.0 and how transformers handle speech data in real-time scenarios.

Chapter 7. Advanced Transformer Models: In this chapter, we dive into cutting-edge transformer models, such as BERT, GPT, and T5. We examine their unique architectures, pre-training objectives, and applications. Through hands-on implementations and in-depth analysis, you will learn how to fine-tune and optimize these models for a range of complex tasks, from text generation to language translation, and beyond.

Chapter 8. Using HuggingFace with PyTorch: The Hugging Face library provides a rich ecosystem of pre-trained transformer models that integrate seamlessly with PyTorch. In this chapter, we cover the Hugging Face model hub, fine-tuning techniques, tokenization strategies, and efficient workflows for working with transformers in real-world applications. By the end of this chapter, you will be able to rapidly prototype and deploy the state-of-the-art transformer models.

Chapter 9. Training and Fine-Tuning Transformers: Training and fine-tuning transformer models can be complex and resource-intensive. This chapter focuses on the best practices for preparing datasets, optimizing hyperparameters, and fine-tuning pre-trained models for domain adaptation. We also cover advanced techniques, such as gradient accumulation, mixed precision training, and managing large-scale datasets, using distributed systems.

Chapter 10. Deploying Transformer Models: In this chapter, we shift the focus to the practical aspects of deploying transformer models in real-world environments. We explore strategies for optimizing models for efficient inference, scaling to meet demand, and deploying models to cloud, edge, or serverless platforms. The chapter also covers model monitoring, versioning, and troubleshooting deployment issues.

Chapter 11. Transformers in Real-World Applications: The final chapter highlights the versatility of transformer models, across various industries. We examine their applications in healthcare, finance, social media, creative industries, robotics, education, and much more. Through detailed case studies, we explore how transformers are transforming sectors, and driving innovation across industries. We also discuss the challenges and limitations faced, when deploying transformers in practical scenarios.

This book provides not only the theory behind transformer models, but also the practical skills needed to implement, fine-tune, and deploy them. By the end of this interesting journey, you will be well-equipped to work with the latest advancements in transformer-based AI systems, across various domains.

Get a Free eBook

We hope you are enjoying your recently purchased book! Your feedback is incredibly valuable to us, and to all other readers looking for great books.

If you found this book helpful or enjoyable, we would truly appreciate it, if you could take a moment to leave a short review with a 5 star rating on Amazon. It helps us grow, and lets other readers discover our books.

As a thank you, we would love to send you a free digital copy of this book, and a **30%** discount code on your next cart value on our official websites:

www.orangeava.com

www.orangeava.in (For Indian Subcontinent)

☑ **Here's how:**

Leave a review for the book on Amazon.

Take a screenshot of your review, and send an email to **info@orangeava.com** (it can be just the confirmation screen).

Once, we receive your screenshot, we will send you the digital file, within 24 hours.

Thank you so much for your support – it means a lot to us!

Downloading the code bundles and colored images

Please follow the links or scan the QR codes to download the ***Code Bundles and Images*** of the book:

https://github.com/ava-orange-education/Ultimate-Transformer-Models-Using-PyTorch-2.0

The code bundles and images of the book are also hosted on ***https://rebrand.ly/5181c7***

In case there's an update to the code, it will be updated on the existing GitHub repository.

Errata

We take immense pride in our work at **Orange Education Pvt Ltd,** and follow best practices to ensure the accuracy of our content to provide an indulging reading experience to our subscribers. Our readers are our mirrors, and we use their inputs to reflect and improve upon human errors, if any, that may have occurred during the publishing processes involved. To let us maintain the quality and help us reach out to any readers who might be having difficulties due to any unforeseen errors, please write to us at :

errata@orangeava.com

Your support, suggestions, and feedback are highly appreciated.

DID YOU KNOW

Did you know that Orange Education Pvt Ltd offers eBook versions of every book published, with PDF and ePub files available? You can upgrade to the eBook version at **www.orangeava.com** and as a print book customer, you are entitled to a discount on the eBook copy. Get in touch with us at: **info@orangeava.com** for more details.

At **www.orangeava.com**, you can also read a collection of free technical articles, sign up for a range of free newsletters, and receive exclusive discounts and offers on Print Books and eBooks.

PIRACY

If you come across any illegal copies of our works in any form on the internet, we would be grateful if you would provide us with the location address or website name. Please contact us at **info@orangeava.com** with a link to the material.

ARE YOU INTERESTED IN AUTHORING WITH US?

If there is a topic that you have expertise in, and you are interested in either writing or contributing to a book, please write to us at **business@orangeava.com**. We are on a journey to help developers and tech professionals to gain insights on the present technological advancements and innovations happening across the globe and build a community that believes Knowledge is best acquired by sharing and learning with others. Please reach out to us to learn what our audience demands and how you can be part of this educational reform. We also welcome ideas from tech experts and help them build learning and development content for their domains.

REVIEWS

Please leave a review. Once you have read and used this book, why not leave a review on the site that you purchased it from? Potential readers can then see and use your unbiased opinion to make purchase decisions. We at Orange Education would love to know what you think about our products, and our authors can learn from your feedback. Thank you!

For more information about Orange Education, please visit **www.orangeava.com**.

Table of Contents

CHAPTER 1
Understanding the Evolution of Neural Networks

Introduction

In this chapter, we embark on a journey through the development of neural networks, tracing their evolution from simple perceptrons to the cutting-edge transformer models that are reshaping the field of artificial intelligence today. This exploration delves into pivotal moments in deep learning history, including the rise of deep architectures, the impact of convolutional and recurrent neural networks, and the challenges that spurred key innovations. By understanding the foundational advancements that led to transformer models, readers will be well-prepared to explore their architecture and applications in the chapters to come.

Structure

In this chapter, we will cover the following topics:

- Foundations of Artificial Neural Networks
- The Rise of Deep Learning
- Convolutional Neural Networks (CNNs) and their Impact
- Recurrent Neural Networks (RNNs) and Sequential Data Processing
- Introduction to Attention Mechanisms
- The Transformer Architecture: A Paradigm Shift
- Key Innovations in Transformer Models
- The Impact of Transformers on Various AI Domains
- Comparing Transformers to Previous Architectures
- The Role of Hardware Advancements in Neural Network Evolution
- Ethical Considerations in the Development of Advanced Neural Networks

Foundations of Artificial Neural Networks

The journey toward modern Artificial Intelligence (AI) began with the foundational concept of Artificial Neural Networks (ANNs) that were designed to mimic the workings of the human brain. Early researchers were fascinated by how the brain processes information through its vast network of neurons, and they sought to replicate this process in machines. Though far simpler in design, artificial neural networks laid the groundwork for the transformative AI models which we use today.

Biological Inspiration

The inspiration behind ANNs comes from the structure and functioning of biological neurons. In the human brain, billions of neurons are interconnected, allowing us to perform complex tasks like recognizing faces, processing language, and solving problems. These neurons communicate through electrical signals, where each neuron receives inputs, processes them, and passes them on to other neurons.

This biological process served as the conceptual model for the first artificial neurons. In the 1940s, **Warren McCulloch and Walter Pitts developed the first computational model of a neuron** which would later become a key component of artificial neural networks. Their work introduced the idea of simple binary neurons that either "*fired*" or remained inactive, depending on the input signals they received.

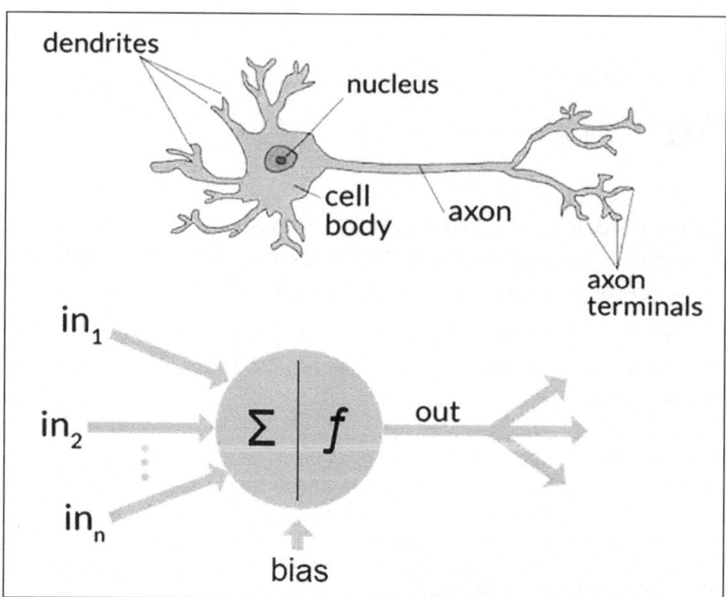

Figure 1.1: *A Biological and Artificial Neuron*

The preceding image (*Figure 1.1*) provides a comparison between a biological neuron, and an artificial neuron, emphasizing the similarities in their structure and function. At the top, we see a simplified diagram of a biological neuron which consists of several key components. The dendrites are branching structures that receive signals from other neurons. These signals are then passed to the cell body, also known as the soma, which contains the nucleus, and serves as the processing center for the incoming information. The signal is then transmitted through the axon, a long, thin projection that carries the signal away from the cell body. Finally, the signal reaches the axon terminals, where it is passed to other neurons, often through chemical neurotransmitters. The biological neuron, we see in the figure is schematic of an artificial neuron modelled after its biological counterpart.

In an artificial neuron, inputs (represented as in_1, in_2, ..., in_n) are analogous to the signals received by dendrites. These inputs are multiplied by their respective weights, and summed up in the summation unit, similar to how the cell body processes signals. A bias is also added to adjust the output independently of the input values. This sum is then passed through an activation function (*f*) that introduces non-linearity to the output, allowing the neuron to model more complex relationships in the data. Finally, the processed output is sent to the next layer of the network, just as the axon transmits the signal to other neurons in a biological network. This comparison illustrates how artificial neurons are designed, based on the biological principles of information processing, showcasing the inspiration drawn from the brain in the development of neural networks.

Early Developments

The first significant step toward modern neural networks came with the **invention of the *perceptron* in 1957 by Frank Rosenblatt.** The perceptron was a simple type of artificial neuron that could learn to classify inputs through a process of adjusting weights. It could handle linearly separable problems, but struggled with more complex, non-linear tasks. The inability of perceptrons to solve the XOR problem–a classic non-linear classification issue–caused a temporary stagnation in neural network research.

However, in the 1980s, neural networks saw a resurgence with the development of the Multi-Layer Perceptron (MLP) and the introduction of the backpropagation algorithm. The MLP allowed for more complex models by incorporating the hidden layers, enabling the network to learn non-linear relationships between inputs and outputs. Backpropagation provided an efficient method for adjusting the weights across all layers which significantly improved the training process for deep networks. This marked the beginning of modern neural networks as powerful computational models, capable of solving increasingly complex problems.

The Core Structure of Neural Networks

At its heart, an artificial neural network is composed of neurons arranged in layers.

These layers can be categorized into three types:

- **Input Layer:** The input layer is the entry point for the data. Each neuron, in this layer corresponds to one feature of the data being processed. For example, if the input is an image, each neuron might represent a pixel value.
- **Hidden Layers:** Hidden layers are where the magic happens. These layers contain neurons that take the input data, and apply transformations to extract useful features. As the network grows deeper (with more hidden layers), it can learn more abstract and complex patterns from the data.
- **Output Layer:** The final layer produces the network's prediction. In a classification task, this could be a set of probabilities, indicating which class the input belongs to.

The neural network learns by adjusting the weights and biases of each neuron through a process called *training*. During training, the network is fed with data, and its predictions are compared to the actual outcomes. Based on the errors, the weights are updated to improve the future predictions. This learning process is iterative, and continues until the network achieves a satisfactory level of accuracy.

Key Concepts: Activation Functions and Learning

To enable the network to model complex relationships, neurons use *activation functions* that introduce non-linearity into the network.

Some of the common activation functions include:

- **Sigmoid:** Useful for binary classification tasks, the sigmoid function maps input values to a range between 0 and 1.
- **ReLU (Rectified Linear Unit):** The most widely used activation function today, ReLU introduces non-linearity by outputting zero for any negative input and the input itself for positive values. This makes it efficient for deep networks.
- **Tanh:** The hyperbolic tangent function is similar to sigmoid but ranges from –1 to 1, making it effective in tasks where negative outputs are needed.

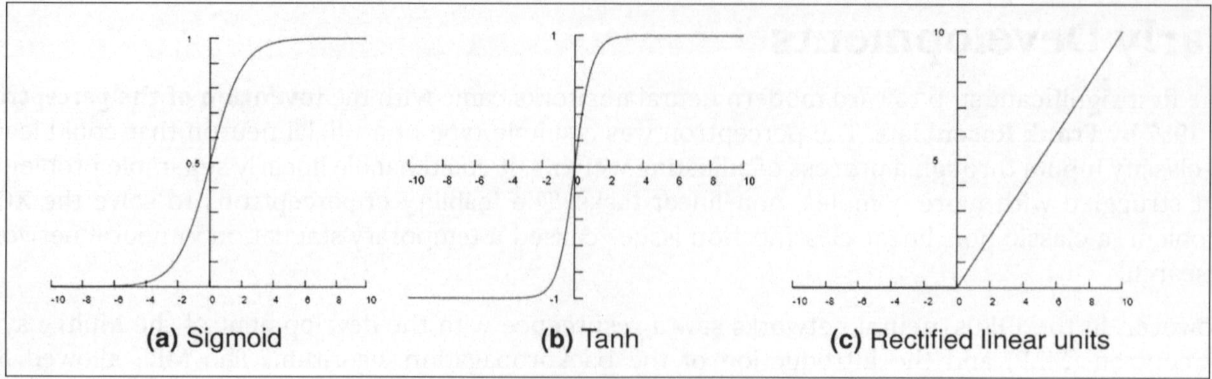

Figure 1.2: *Different Activation Functions*

Alongside activation functions, *loss functions* play a critical role in training. The loss function measures how far off the network's predictions are from the actual values, and backpropagation uses the gradient of the loss function to adjust the network's weights. This learning process allows the network to generalize better on unseen data, making it more accurate and reliable.

From Simple Models to Complex Architectures

The fundamental structure of ANNs, though simple, paved the way for the development of more complex and capable models. As researchers explored deeper architectures, the power of neural networks became increasingly evident. ANNs could now solve tasks that once seemed impossible, such as image recognition, voice synthesis, and even language translation. The foundational principles of artificial neural networks—layered structure, learning through training, and non-linear activation—remain the cornerstone of many modern AI systems. As we move into deeper architectures and more specialized networks, these core ideas continue to shape the evolution of Machine Learning Models (MLMs).

The Rise of Deep Learning

While artificial neural networks (ANNs) laid the groundwork for computational models inspired by the brain, it wasn't until the advent of *deep learning* that these models began to demonstrate their full potential. Deep learning refers to the use of neural networks with many layers—often called deep neural networks (DNNs)—that allow for the learning of increasingly abstract features from raw data. These deeper architectures have been instrumental in addressing complex tasks that were previously beyond the reach of machine learning systems.

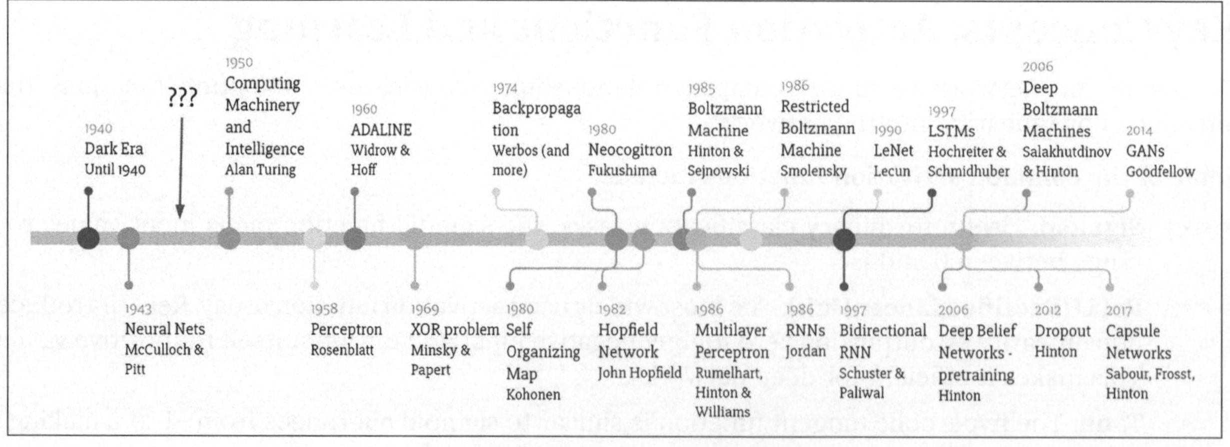

Figure 1.3: *Deep Learning Timetable*

Figure 1.3 presents a timeline highlighting key milestones in the development of artificial neural networks and the rise of deep learning. Starting from the 1940s, it captures significant moments in the evolution of neural networks, showing the progression of ideas and breakthroughs that have shaped the field.

- **1943 marks the foundational work of McCulloch and Pitts, who developed the first model of a neural network**, laying the theoretical groundwork for artificial neurons.
- **1958 introduces the perceptron, developed by Frank Rosenblatt, which was an early attempt at creating a trainable neural network**, but one that was limited to linearly separable problems.
- **1969 highlights the publication of "*Perceptrons*" by Minsky and Papert** which demonstrated the limitations of the perceptron and stalled progress in neural networks for more than a decade.
- **The timeline then picks up again in 1982 with the introduction of Hopfield networks** which played a role in revitalizing interest in neural networks.
- **In 1986, the development of the backpropagation algorithm, primarily credited to Geoffrey Hinton**, revolutionized neural networks by making it possible to train multi-layer networks efficiently, leading to the rise of multi-layer perceptrons (MLPs).
- Moving forward, **1997 marked the advent of Long Short-Term Memory (LSTM) networks, developed by Hochreiter and Schmidhuber** which addressed issues in training Recurrent Neural Networks (RNNs), and became crucial for handling sequential data.
- **In 2006, the concept of deep learning took center stage when Hinton and his collaborators introduced deep belief networks**, which paved the way for further advancements in training deep neural networks.
- **2012 was a pivotal year for deep learning, as the AlexNet Model won the ImageNet competition**, drastically reducing the error rate in image classification and bringing global attention to the potential of deep learning.
- Finally, the timeline stretches into 2017, marking the rise of transformer models, a paradigm shift in natural language processing, and a significant leap forward in deep learning architectures.

This timeline demonstrates how deep learning emerged from decades of incremental advancements in neural networks. Each milestone represents a crucial breakthrough that either solved a major challenge or introduced new architectures, ultimately leading to powerful deep learning models, we use today.

From Shallow to Deep Networks

Traditional neural networks, particularly those developed before the 2000s, typically had one or two hidden layers. These so-called *shallow networks* were limited in their ability to model highly complex relationships in data. Shallow networks struggled with tasks involving images, speech, or large datasets because they could not automatically extract hierarchical features–patterns within patterns.

The move to deeper networks began with breakthroughs in both algorithmic techniques and computational power. In a deep network, the layers of neurons are stacked, each layer learning more abstract representations than the last. For instance, in an image recognition task, lower layers may learn to detect edges or textures, while higher layers may combine these features to recognize entire objects like faces or animals. This hierarchy of feature learning gives deep networks their power to handle highly complex data.

Key Breakthroughs in Deep Learning

Several key developments were critical in the rise of deep learning as a dominant approach in AI research and industry.

- **The Backpropagation Algorithm**: While backpropagation was introduced earlier for training multi-layer perceptrons, its real potential was unlocked in deep learning. Backpropagation allowed deep networks to efficiently adjust weights layer by layer, minimizing prediction errors by propagating the gradient of the loss function backward through the network. This algorithm remains a cornerstone of neural network training today.
- **Improved Activation Functions**: The rise of the ReLU (Rectified Linear Unit) function played a major role in deep learning's success. Unlike earlier functions like sigmoid and tanh, which could cause the *vanishing gradient problem*—a situation where gradients become too small to update weights effectively—ReLU allowed deep networks to train faster and more accurately by avoiding these issues in large networks.
- **Hardware Advancements**: The explosion of deep learning in the 2010s was driven by the parallel processing capabilities of graphics processing units (GPUs). GPUs made it feasible to train large-scale neural networks on massive datasets in a reasonable amount of time, greatly accelerating research and industrial applications.
- **Availability of Big Data**: Deep learning thrives on data. Unlike traditional machine learning models that rely on handcrafted features, deep networks automatically learn features from raw data. The availability of massive datasets—especially in areas like computer vision, natural language processing, and speech recognition—enabled these networks to learn more robust and generalizable patterns.

The Importance of Depth

Why does *depth* matter? The answer lies in the network's ability to capture increasingly abstract patterns. In shallow networks, each hidden layer can only model a relatively simple function of the data. Deeper networks, however, stack these functions, creating compositions of functions that can model very complex, non-linear relationships. For example:

- In image processing, a shallow network may only detect low-level features like edges or color gradients, while a deep network can combine these features to recognize more sophisticated shapes and eventually entire objects.
- In natural language processing (NLP), shallow networks might identify simple word correlations, but deep networks can capture complex syntactic structures and even the meaning of sentences.

Depth allows the network to represent data in more compact and structured ways, which in turn leads to better performance on complex tasks.

Deep Learning's Explosive Impact

By the early 2010s, deep learning began to outshine traditional machine learning methods in several key domains. One of the most notable successes came in 2012 with the win of the *AlexNet* architecture in the ImageNet competition. ImageNet is a large-scale visual recognition challenge, and AlexNet—a deep convolutional neural network—demonstrated a significant leap in performance, reducing the error rate by nearly half compared to the previous best methods. This victory established deep learning as the go-to method for tasks like image classification, object detection, and segmentation.

Following this, deep learning models like *GoogleNet* and *ResNet* (Residual Networks) continued to push the boundaries of what was possible. Not only did these models achieve state-of-the-art results in computer vision, but they also had a profound impact on fields such as natural language processing, speech recognition, and reinforcement learning.

Beyond Supervised Learning

While deep learning initially thrived in supervised learning tasks—where the model is trained on labelled datasets—it has since expanded into other domains:

- **Unsupervised Learning**: Deep learning models have shown promise in learning useful representations from unlabeled data. Techniques like *autoencoders* and *generative adversarial networks* (GANs) allow for learning compact representations and generating new data from a given dataset.
- **Reinforcement Learning**: Deep learning has revolutionized reinforcement learning, particularly through the advent of *deep Q-networks* (DQNs). By combining deep learning's representation power with reinforcement learning's decision-making capabilities, agents like AlphaGo have outperformed human experts in complex tasks like the game of Go.

Challenges in Deep Learning

Despite its incredible success, deep learning is not without its challenges. Some of the most notable limitations include:

- **Data-Hungry:** Deep learning models require vast amounts of data to perform well. In areas where large datasets are unavailable, performance can suffer.
- **Black Box Nature:** Deep learning models are often criticized for being difficult to interpret. Unlike simpler machine learning models, which provide clear insights into how decisions are made, deep networks can seem opaque, making it hard to understand how they arrive at their predictions.
- **Computationally Intensive:** Deep learning models, particularly very large ones, require significant computational resources, which can be costly and time-consuming to train.

Despite these challenges, deep learning's rise has redefined the landscape of artificial intelligence. From vision to language to game-playing, deep networks continue to push the boundaries of what machines are capable of, driving innovation across industries and research fields.

Convolutional Neural Networks (CNNs) and Their Impact

As artificial neural networks advanced in complexity, it became clear that different types of data required specialized architectures. For example, traditional fully connected networks struggled with image data due to the high dimensionality and spatial complexity of images. This challenge led to the development of Convolutional Neural Networks (CNNs), a groundbreaking architecture designed specifically for tasks like image recognition and classification.

The Structure of CNNs

Convolutional Neural Networks are structured differently from traditional feedforward neural networks. They introduce convolutional layers that apply filters or kernels to the input data. These filters slide over the input image and detect patterns such as edges, textures, and shapes. The advantage of this approach is that it preserves the spatial relationships between pixels, allowing the network to understand the hierarchical structure of images.

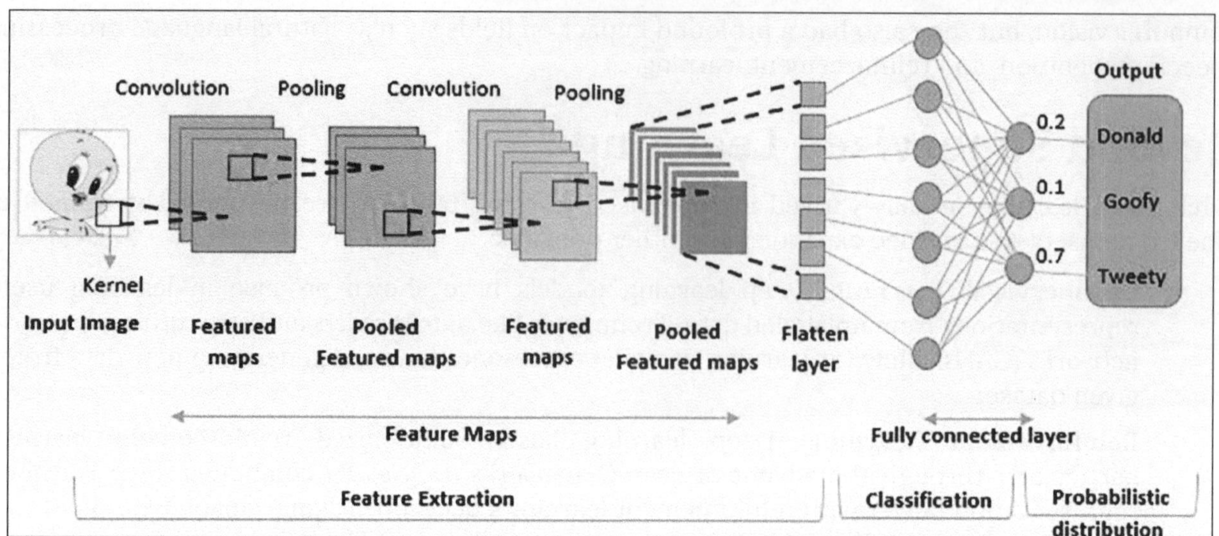

Figure 1.4: *A Typical Convolution Neural Network* (CNN)

As shown in *Figure* 1.4, CNN typically consists of several types of layers:

- **Convolutional Layers:** These layers apply a set of filters to the input image, creating feature maps that highlight important patterns.
- **Pooling Layers**: After convolution, a pooling layer reduces the dimensionality of the feature maps by downsampling them. This retains essential information while reducing computational complexity, making the model more efficient.
- **Fully Connected Layers:** Towards the end of the network, fully connected layers interpret the features extracted by the convolutional and pooling layers, leading to the final output (for example, class probabilities in an image classification task).

The hierarchical structure of CNNs allows them to learn low-level features (like edges) in the early layers and progressively more abstract, high-level features (like objects or faces) in the deeper layers. This structure makes CNNs highly effective for image processing tasks.

Key Innovations and Milestones in CNN Development

While convolutional networks were conceptualized earlier by researchers like Kunihiko Fukushima in the 1980s, it wasn't until the 1990s and early 2000s that CNNs began to gain momentum. A major breakthrough came in 1998 when Yann LeCun's LeNet-5 successfully demonstrated the effectiveness of CNNs for digit recognition. LeNet-5 was applied to the MNIST dataset, where it excelled at classifying handwritten digits for postal code recognition. This early success set the stage for the wider application of CNNs in image processing tasks.

CNNs truly entered the spotlight in 2012 when AlexNet, developed by Alex Krizhevsky, Ilya Sutskever, and Geoffrey Hinton, won the ImageNet Large Scale Visual Recognition Challenge (ILSVRC). AlexNet's deep architecture, combined with the use of GPUs for faster computation, achieved a significant reduction in error rates compared to previous models. This achievement not only validated CNNs but also ignited a wave of interest in deep learning, particularly for computer vision applications.

Following AlexNet, other innovations further advanced CNNs. Notable examples include:

- **VGGNet (2014):** This model used a simple but deep architecture, proving that increasing network depth could lead to better performance on image classification tasks.
- **GoogleNet (2014):** Also known as Inception, GoogleNet introduced the Inception module, which allowed for more efficient computation by processing data at multiple scales in parallel.

- **ResNet (2015):** Residual Networks (ResNet) addressed the issue of vanishing gradients in deep networks by introducing skip connections. These connections allowed gradients to bypass certain layers, enabling the training of extremely deep networks without performance degradation.

Impact of CNNs on Various Domains

The advent of CNNs revolutionized computer vision, and several other domains. The primary advantage of CNNs lies in their ability to automatically extract relevant features from images, eliminating the need for manual feature engineering, which was common in traditional machine learning models. Their impact can be seen in several areas:

- **Image Classification and Object Detection**: CNNs have become the standard model for image classification tasks, such as recognizing objects in images or detecting specific objects within images. This has practical applications in fields like medical imaging, autonomous driving, and security systems.
- **Facial Recognition**: CNNs are used extensively in facial recognition systems, where their ability to recognize faces from images with high accuracy is employed in security, identification, and even smartphone authentication.
- **Medical Image Analysis:** CNNs are widely used to analyze medical images such as X-rays, MRIs, and CT scans. Their ability to detect abnormalities, such as tumors or fractures, makes them invaluable in healthcare.
- **Video Analysis and Surveillance**: Beyond static images, CNNs have been adapted for use in video analysis, where they track objects, detect anomalies, and recognize activities in real-time surveillance footage.
- **Art and Creativity:** CNNs have also found a role in creative industries, particularly with the development of neural style transfer, where the style of one image can be applied to the content of another. This has led to a variety of artistic applications that blend technology and creativity.

Challenges and Limitations of CNNs

Despite their success, CNNs also come with some limitations. One of the primary challenges is the sheer amount of data required to train them effectively. CNNs rely on large, annotated datasets to learn meaningful features, which can be a hurdle in domains where labelled data is scarce or difficult to obtain.

Additionally, CNNs can be computationally expensive. Training a deep CNN with millions of parameters requires significant computational resources, including access to powerful GPUs or TPUs. This can limit the accessibility of CNNs for smaller research groups or businesses without substantial hardware infrastructure.

Another challenge is their black-box nature—CNNs, like other deep learning models, are often difficult to interpret. While they perform well in practice, understanding exactly how they arrive at a particular decision can be elusive, which is a concern in critical applications like healthcare or law enforcement, where interpretability is crucial.

The Broader Impact of CNNs

CNNs have had a profound impact on artificial intelligence, not just in computer vision but across a range of industries. Their ability to process and understand visual data has enabled breakthroughs in automation, surveillance, healthcare, and even entertainment. The efficiency and accuracy of CNNs in extracting meaningful features from images have set a high standard for future developments in AI and machine learning.

Furthermore, CNNs laid the groundwork for other architectures, such as Capsule Networks and Vision Transformers, which are further pushing the boundaries of what AI can achieve in the realm of vision and beyond. CNNs represent one of the most significant milestones in deep learning, and their influence continues to shape cutting-edge research and applications.

Recurrent Neural Networks (RNNs) and Sequential Data Processing

While Convolutional Neural Networks (CNNs) excel at processing spatial data such as images, they are not well-suited for tasks involving sequential data, where the order of inputs matters. This limitation led to the development of Recurrent Neural Networks (RNNs), a type of neural network specifically designed to handle sequences of data by incorporating memory of previous inputs. RNNs revolutionized the way deep learning models approached tasks involving time series, natural language, and other forms of sequential information.

The Structure and Function of RNNs

Unlike traditional feedforward neural networks, which assume that inputs are independent of each other, RNNs are designed to recognize patterns in sequences. The key innovation behind RNNs is the inclusion of recurrent connections that allow the network to maintain a hidden state, which serves as a memory of previous inputs. This hidden state is updated at each time step as the network processes the sequence, enabling the RNN to learn from the temporal dependencies between inputs.

Mathematically, the RNN takes an input **`xtx_txt`** at each time step **`ttt`** and produces an output **`yty_tyt`**. The hidden state **`hth_tht`** is updated based on both the current input and the previous hidden state: $h_t = f(W_x x_t + W_h h_{t-1} + b)$

where *f* is an activation function (such as tanh or ReLU), **`WxW_xWx`** is the weight matrix for the input, and **`WhW_hWh`** is the weight matrix for the hidden state. This recurrent structure allows RNNs to carry information from one time step to the next, making them ideal for sequence-based tasks.

Applications of RNNs

RNNs opened the door to a wide range of applications that required understanding and predicting sequences of data. Some of the most significant applications of RNNs include:

- **Natural Language Processing (NLP):** RNNs have been crucial in NLP tasks such as language modeling, machine translation, and sentiment analysis. In these tasks, understanding the order of words is essential for producing meaningful results. RNNs can remember previous words in a sentence to generate context-aware predictions, making them highly effective in tasks like text generation and speech recognition.
- **Time Series Analysis:** RNNs are widely used in time series forecasting, where data points are ordered in time. Examples include predicting stock prices, weather forecasting, or analyzing sensor data in IoT systems. The ability of RNNs to maintain a hidden state across time steps makes them well-suited for these tasks, where future values depend on previous patterns.
- **Speech Recognition:** In speech-to-text systems, RNNs process audio signals as sequences of sound waves, learning the temporal relationships between phonemes to transcribe spoken words accurately. They are also employed in voice assistants and real-time transcription services.

- **Music Generation:** RNNs have even been applied in creative fields such as music generation. By learning the patterns and structures in sequences of musical notes, RNNs can compose new music in various styles, generating sequences that adhere to musical rules and conventions.

The Challenges of Training RNNs

Despite their ability to handle sequential data, RNNs face significant challenges, particularly when dealing with long sequences. One of the primary issues is the vanishing gradient problem, where the gradients used to update the model's weights during training become extremely small, making it difficult for the network to learn long-term dependencies. As a result, RNNs often struggle with sequences that span many time steps.

To mitigate this issue, several innovations were introduced:

- **Long Short-Term Memory (LSTM):** In 1997, Hochreiter and Schmidhuber developed Long Short-Term Memory (LSTM) networks, a specialized type of RNN that addresses the vanishing gradient problem. LSTMs introduce memory cells that can store information for long periods, allowing the network to remember important details from earlier in the sequence while discarding irrelevant information. LSTMs use gates to control the flow of information, deciding when to keep or forget certain inputs, which enables them to model long-term dependencies more effectively than standard RNNs.
- **Gated Recurrent Units (GRUs):** Another variant of RNNs is the Gated Recurrent Unit (GRU), introduced in 2014. GRUs simplify the LSTM architecture by combining the forget and input gates into a single update gate, making them more computationally efficient while still retaining the ability to model long-term dependencies. GRUs are often preferred when faster training times are required without sacrificing too much performance.

Impact of RNNs on Sequential Data Processing

The introduction of RNNs, along with their LSTM and GRU variants, has had a profound impact on sequential data processing. RNNs allowed neural networks to extend their applicability to domains that require an understanding of temporal relationships, from language and speech to finance and sensor data. Some of the key contributions include:

- **Machine Translation:** RNNs made it possible to create machine translation systems that could process and generate sentences in one language and output them in another. Early machine translation systems, such as Google Translate, were built on RNN-based architectures before moving on to newer methods like the Transformer model.
- **Real-Time Applications:** RNNs are well-suited for real-time applications, such as live transcription and language interpretation. Their ability to process inputs in sequence, updating predictions as new information arrives, makes them invaluable in applications **that demand continuous output.**
- **Sequence-to-Sequence Learning: RNNs** are the foundation of sequence-to-sequence models, which are used in tasks like summarization, text translation, and video captioning. These models take one sequence as input (for example, a sentence in English), and produce another sequence as output (e.g., the same sentence translated into Spanish), relying on the RNN's capacity to understand and generate the sequential data.

Limitations and the Path to Attention Mechanisms

While RNNs and their variants like LSTMs and GRUs have transformed the way neural networks process sequential data, they are not without their limitations. Aside from the vanishing gradient problem, RNNs struggle with parallelization—since each time step must be processed sequentially, training RNNs can be slow, especially on long sequences. This lack of efficiency limits their scalability for very large datasets.

These limitations paved the way for the development of attention mechanisms, which alleviate some of the shortcomings of RNNs by allowing the model to focus on specific parts of the input sequence, regardless of their position. Attention mechanisms enable models to handle long-range dependencies more effectively, and process data in parallel, leading to the next wave of breakthroughs in neural network architectures.

Introduction to Attention Mechanisms

As deep learning models evolved, particularly in the realm of sequential data processing, researchers encountered significant challenges in dealing with long-range dependencies and efficiently processing large sequences. Recurrent Neural Networks (RNNs) and their variants, such as LSTMs and GRUs, made considerable strides in this area, but they still struggled with processing long sequences in parallel and often failed to capture global context efficiently. This gave rise to the concept of attention mechanisms, a pivotal innovation in the architecture of neural networks.

Attention mechanisms allow models to focus selectively on specific parts of the input sequence, weighting certain elements more heavily based on their relevance to the task at hand. Unlike traditional RNNs, which process sequences step by step, attention mechanisms can look at the entire sequence at once, capturing relationships between distant elements more effectively. This development proved to be a game changer, especially in natural language processing (NLP) and tasks involving sequential data.

The Motivation Behind Attention

RNN-based models process inputs sequentially, which means that information from earlier time steps can be lost or diluted by the time the model reaches the later time steps. While LSTMs and GRUs helped mitigate this problem to an extent by retaining longer-term dependencies, they still struggled with particularly long sequences. Additionally, RNNs inherently lack parallelism since they process data in sequence, limiting their efficiency when dealing with large datasets or longer inputs.

Attention mechanisms were introduced to solve these limitations. By allowing the model to assign different levels of importance to different parts of the input, attention mechanisms enable the network to focus on the most relevant pieces of information, regardless of their position in the sequence. This ability to "*attend*" to different parts of the sequence at once makes attention mechanisms highly effective for tasks where global context is critical.

The Attention Formula

At its core, attention is about computing a weighted sum of values based on the relevance (or attention score) between two elements–usually between an input sequence and an output sequence. The basic mechanism works as follows:

1. **Query:** The element from the target sequence that is being processed.
2. **Key:** Elements from the source sequence, each of which is compared to the query.
3. **Value:** The actual information from the source sequence that is aggregated based on the attention score.

The attention score between each query-key pair is computed as a similarity measure, such as a dot product or scaled dot product, followed by a softMax operation to normalize the scores into a probability distribution. This allows the model to attend to all positions in the input sequence, but with varying degrees of importance. The output is then computed as a weighted sum of the values, where each value is weighted according to its attention score.

Mathematically, the attention mechanism is often expressed as:

$$\text{Attention}(Q, K, V) = \text{softmax}\left(\frac{QK^T}{\sqrt{d_k}}\right)V$$

Where:

- Q represents the queries.
- K represents the keys.
- V represents the values.
- d_k is the dimension of the key vectors.

Figure 1.5: *Attention Mechanism Formula*

This formula captures the process of comparing the query to each key, computing attention scores, and then weighting the values accordingly.

Self-Attention and its Role in Transformers

A key innovation in the application of attention mechanisms is self-attention, which plays a central role in modern architectures like the Transformer model. Unlike traditional attention mechanisms that operate between two different sequences (for instance, a source and a target sequence in translation), self-attention operates within a single sequence, allowing each element of the sequence to attend to every other element.

In self-attention, every element of the input sequence generates a query, key, and value, and computes attention scores relative to all other elements in the sequence. This process enables the model to capture dependencies between any two positions, regardless of their distance from each other in the sequence. For example, in a sentence, the self-attention mechanism allows the model to understand relationships between words like "*dog*" and "*barked*," even if they are separated by several other words.

Self-attention offers several advantages:

- **Parallelization:** Unlike RNNs, which must process sequences sequentially, self-attention allows for parallel processing. Since each element of the sequence can be processed independently, self-attention significantly speeds up training, especially on long sequences.
- **Global Context**: By allowing each element to attend to every other element in the sequence, self-attention captures global context more effectively than traditional recurrent models, which are limited by the sequential nature of information flow.
- **Simplicity:** Self-attention simplifies the architecture by eliminating the need for recurrence, making it easier to train large-scale models on parallel hardware like GPUs and TPUs.

The Success of Attention in NLP

The attention mechanism initially gained widespread attention (pun intended) in the context of machine translation. In 2015, Bahdanau et al. introduced the attention-based encoder-decoder model for machine translation, which allowed the model to focus on different parts of the input sentence, when generating each word of the translated output. This approach dramatically improved the quality of translation, as it overcame the limitations of RNNs, which struggled with long sentences and complex word dependencies.

Since then, attention mechanisms have become a standard component of many deep learning models, particularly in NLP. Tasks such as text summarization, sentiment analysis, and question-answering all benefit from the ability of attention to capture relevant information from the input while disregarding irrelevant details.

Attention Beyond NLP

While attention mechanisms originated in NLP, their usefulness extends far beyond language-based tasks. In computer vision, attention models have been used for tasks such as image captioning, where the model generates a textual description of an image by attending to different regions of the image. In this case, the attention mechanism helps the model focus on the most important parts of the image, when describing each part of the scene.

Similarly, in reinforcement learning and sequence-to-sequence tasks, attention mechanisms enable the model to consider relevant parts of the input, when making decisions or generating outputs. This broad applicability makes attention a fundamental building block of modern neural networks.

The Transition to Transformer Models

The true breakthrough in the use of attention mechanisms came with the introduction of the Transformer architecture in 2017 which replaced RNNs entirely with self-attention mechanisms. Transformers leveraged the power of self-attention to handle sequential data without the need for recurrence, making them far more efficient and scalable. The Transformer model will be explored in greater detail in the next section, but it's important to note that the introduction of attention was the key innovation that made the Transformer possible.

The Transformer Architecture: A Paradigm Shift

The development of the Transformer architecture in 2017 by Vaswani et al. represents a significant turning point in the field of deep learning, particularly in natural language processing (NLP). Transformers introduced a new way of handling sequential data that completely eliminated the need for recurrence, relying solely on self-attention mechanisms. This innovation addressed many of the shortcomings associated with Recurrent Neural Networks (RNNs), such as slow training times and difficulty capturing long-range dependencies, and opened up new possibilities for scaling deep learning models.

The Transformer architecture's power and efficiency led to its rapid adoption across a wide range of applications, from machine translation to language modeling, and its influence has since extended far beyond NLP. By leveraging parallelism and attention mechanisms, Transformers have established themselves as the dominant architecture in modern AI systems, particularly with the rise of large-scale models like BERT, GPT, and T5.

The Core Components of the Transformer

The Transformer architecture is built entirely around self-attention mechanisms and the ability to process sequences in parallel, making it radically different from previous sequential models.

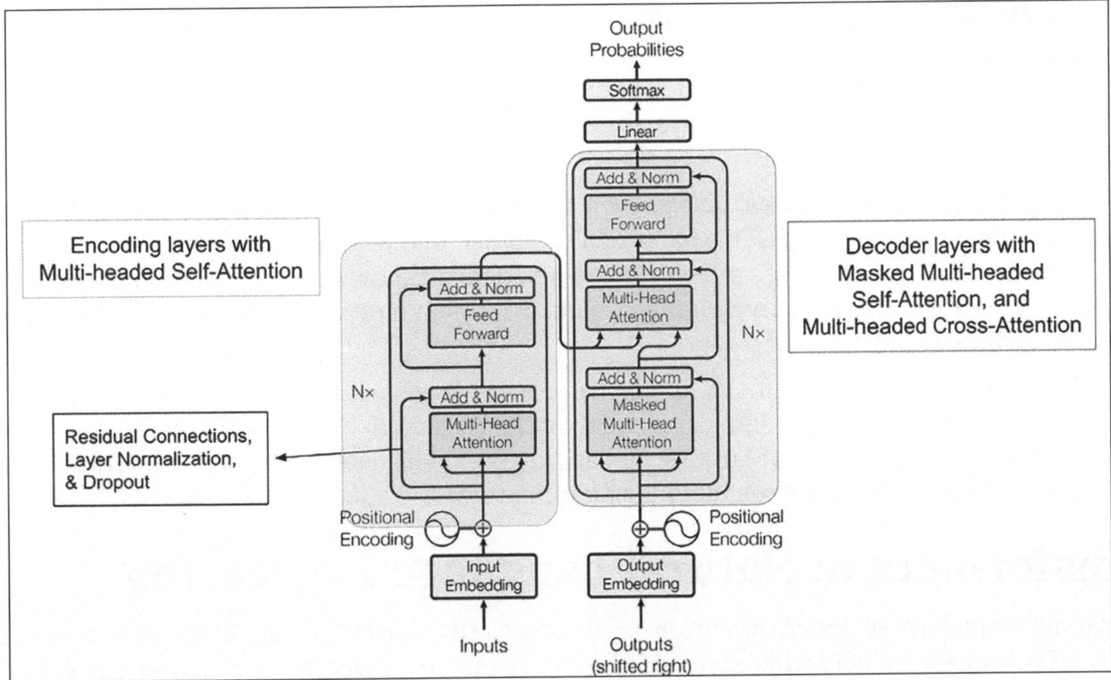

Figure 1.6*: Transformer Model Architecture*

The key components of the Transformer model, as shown in *Figure* 1.5 include:

- **Encoder-Decoder Structure:** The Transformer is built on an encoder-decoder framework, much like traditional sequence-to-sequence models. The encoder processes the input sequence, while the decoder generates the output sequence. However, unlike RNN-based encoder-decoders, the Transformer's encoder and decoder are both composed of layers of self-attention and feedforward neural networks, rather than recurrent connections.
- **Multi-Head Self-Attention:** One of the core innovations of the Transformer is multi-head self-attention. Instead of computing a single attention distribution over the input sequence, multi-head attention allows the model to compute multiple attention distributions in parallel, each attending to different parts of the sequence. This enables the model to capture various types of relationships in the input data at different levels of abstraction.
- **Positional Encoding:** Since the Transformer does not process sequences in order, it lacks the inherent positional information that RNNs naturally have through their sequential structure. To address this, the model uses positional encodings, which are added to the input embeddings to provide information about the order of the sequence. This allows the model to take positional relationships into account while processing the sequence in parallel.
- **Feedforward Neural Networks:** In addition to self-attention layers, each encoder and decoder layer includes a fully connected feedforward neural network applied independently to each position in the sequence. This allows the model to apply complex, learned transformations to the attended representations.
- **Layer Normalization and Residual Connections:** To improve stability and training speed, the Transformer makes use of layer normalization and residual connections. These techniques help maintain strong gradients during training, enabling the model to train deeper networks without suffering from issues like vanishing gradients.

Revolutionizing Sequence Modeling with Transformers

The introduction of the Transformer model addressed some of the most pressing challenges in sequential data processing that RNNs and their variants had faced:

- **Parallelism:** By processing the entire sequence at once using self-attention, Transformers allow for parallel computation. This is a major advantage over RNNs, which process data sequentially, making them much slower to train on long sequences. Transformers can take full advantage of modern hardware like GPUs and TPUs, leading to significantly faster training times.
- **Long-Range Dependencies:** RNNs, even with LSTM and GRU variants, struggled to capture dependencies between distant parts of a sequence due to the vanishing gradient problem. In contrast, the Transformer's self-attention mechanism allows each element in the sequence to directly attend to every other element, making it much more effective at capturing long-range dependencies.
- **Scalability:** The Transformer's ability to process large datasets efficiently made it scalable to much larger models and datasets than RNNs could handle. This scalability has been instrumental in the rise of large-scale language models like BERT and GPT, which consist of hundreds of millions or even billions of parameters.

Transformers in Natural Language Processing

The original Transformer paper, *Attention is All You Need* (Vaswani et al., 2017), demonstrated the model's effectiveness by achieving state-of-the-art results on machine translation tasks. However, the Transformer's flexibility and power quickly made it the architecture of choice for many other NLP tasks, such as text classification, question answering, and summarization.

The success of the Transformer in NLP was further solidified with the introduction of BERT (Bidirectional Encoder Representations from Transformers) in 2018 and GPT (Generative Pre-trained Transformer) in 2019. These models leverage the Transformer's ability to process language in both directions (in the case of BERT) or generate text (in the case of GPT), achieving state-of-the-art performance on a wide range of benchmarks.

- **BERT:** This uses the Transformer's encoder structure to process input sequences bidirectionally, allowing it to capture context from both the left and right sides of a word simultaneously. This made BERT, particularly effective at understanding the meaning of ambiguous words based on their context.
- **GPT:** This, on the other hand, uses the Transformer's decoder structure to generate text in an autoregressive manner, predicting the next word in a sequence based on the preceding words. GPT models, particularly GPT-3, demonstrated unprecedented performance in tasks like language generation, dialogue, and zero-shot learning.

Applications Beyond NLP

While the Transformer was originally designed for NLP, its success has led to its adoption in many other domains. In computer vision, models like Vision Transformers (ViT) have applied the Transformer architecture to image processing tasks, achieving competitive performance with traditional Convolutional Neural Networks (CNNs). Similarly, in speech recognition, Transformers have been used to process audio sequences, improving the quality of automatic speech transcription and synthesis.

The flexibility of the Transformer architecture has made it suitable for a wide range of sequential and non-sequential tasks, from time-series forecasting to reinforcement learning. Its ability to capture complex dependencies and process data in parallel has fundamentally changed how deep learning models are designed and deployed.

The Impact of Transformers on AI

The Transformer model has set a new standard for deep learning architectures, particularly in tasks involving large-scale data and complex relationships between inputs. By eliminating the need for recurrence and relying entirely on self-attention, Transformers have enabled the development of models that are faster, more scalable, and more capable of capturing global context than ever before.

The Transformer architecture marks a paradigm shift in the way we approach sequential data processing, and its influence will continue to shape the development of AI systems for years to come. In the following sections, we will dive deeper into the key innovations introduced by Transformers, and how they have impacted various AI domains, ultimately paving the way for the models that have become integral to modern machine learning.

Key Innovations in Transformer Models

The Transformer architecture introduced a series of groundbreaking innovations that not only reshaped how neural networks handle sequential data but also set the stage for the next generation of deep learning models. These key innovations contributed to the success and scalability of Transformer-based models across various domains, from natural language processing (NLP) to computer vision. In this section, we will explore the most impactful features that have made Transformer models so powerful and versatile.

Multi-Head Self-Attention

One of the fundamental innovations in Transformer models is multi-head self-attention. Unlike traditional attention mechanisms that focus on a single representation of the input sequence, multi-head attention allows the model to compute several attention distributions in parallel. Each "*head*" in the multi-head attention layer processes the sequence independently, capturing different aspects of the input.

For example, in a sentence, one head might focus on short-term relationships between adjacent words, while another head might capture long-range dependencies between words that are far apart in the sequence. By combining the outputs from all heads, the model can learn richer and more nuanced representations of the data. This multi-headed approach significantly improves the model's ability to capture complex dependencies and understand global context, which is crucial for tasks like machine translation and language modeling.

Mathematically, multi-head attention can be described as:

```
MultiHead(Q,K,V)=Concat(head1, head2, …, headh)WO
```

where each head computes its own attention using the same query (Q), key (K), and value (V) matrices, but with different learned projections. The outputs are concatenated and projected again, allowing the model to capture a variety of patterns within the input.

Positional Encoding

Unlike Recurrent Neural Networks (RNNs), which process data in a sequential manner and inherently account for the order of the sequence, Transformer models process all elements of a sequence in parallel. This raises a challenge: how can a Transformer model learn the positional relationships between different elements if it processes them all at once?

The solution comes in the form of positional encodings. These are added to the input embeddings to provide the model with information about the relative positions of tokens in a sequence. Positional encodings are designed to represent each position in the sequence as a unique vector, enabling the model to distinguish between different positions.

Typically, positional encodings use sine and cosine functions of different frequencies to create a fixed pattern for each position. This mathematical approach ensures that the encodings capture both short-term and long-term dependencies between elements. The use of positional encodings allows the Transformer to understand and preserve the order of elements in a sequence, which is critical for tasks like language translation and sentence generation.

Layer Normalization and Residual Connections

As deep learning models grow in depth, they often face challenges like vanishing gradients or instability during training. The Transformer model addresses these challenges by incorporating two key techniques: layer normalization and residual connections.

- **Layer Normalization:** This technique normalizes the output of each layer by adjusting its mean and variance. It helps stabilize the training process and ensures that each layer's outputs are well-scaled. Unlike batch normalization, which normalizes across the entire batch of data, layer normalization operates within each individual data sample, making it more suitable for sequential data.
- **Residual Connections:** Residual connections, first introduced in ResNet for computer vision, allow the output of a layer to bypass the layer and be added directly to the input. In Transformers, residual connections help preserve important information across multiple layers, ensuring that the model does not lose information as it processes deeper layers. These connections also help the model train more efficiently by mitigating the vanishing gradient problem, allowing the network to handle much greater depths.

Scalable Parallel Processing

One of the major limitations of traditional RNNs is their inability to process sequences in parallel due to their sequential nature. Transformers, by relying on self-attention instead of recurrence, allow for parallel processing of the entire input sequence. This not only speeds up training but also makes it possible to train much larger models on massive datasets.

This ability to scale up and parallelize computation has been crucial in the development of large-scale language models, such as BERT and GPT-3, which consist of hundreds of millions or even billions of parameters. Without the ability to process data in parallel, training models of this scale would be prohibitively slow and expensive.

Transfer Learning and Pre-Training

Another key innovation facilitated by Transformer models is the widespread adoption of transfer learning in NLP. Prior to Transformers, most models in NLP were trained from scratch on specific tasks, limiting their generalization to new tasks or domains. However, the architecture of Transformers, combined with large-scale pre-training, enabled models to learn general-purpose language representations that could be fine-tuned for a wide range of downstream tasks.

This approach became widely known with the introduction of BERT (Bidirectional Encoder Representations from Transformers), which was pre-trained on a massive corpus using a masked language model objective. After pre-training, BERT could be fine-tuned on specific tasks like sentiment analysis, question answering, or named entity recognition with minimal additional training data.

Similarly, GPT models (Generative Pre-trained Transformers) showed the power of pre-training large models on extensive datasets, allowing them to generate coherent text, answer questions, and even engage in conversations without needing task-specific training data. These models demonstrated that pre-training on general knowledge, followed by task-specific fine-tuning, was a highly effective way to leverage large-scale Transformer models.

The Emergence of Transformer Variants

While the original Transformer model introduced several key innovations, its success also inspired the development of various Transformer variants that have expanded its capabilities:

- **BERT:** Focuses on bidirectional context, allowing the model to capture dependencies from both the left and right sides of a sequence simultaneously. This made BERT highly effective for understanding context in language tasks.
- **GPT:** A unidirectional Transformer model that generates text by predicting the next word in a sequence. GPT models, particularly GPT-3, have demonstrated impressive language generation capabilities, from writing coherent essays to answering factual questions.
- **T5 (Text-to-Text Transfer Transformer):** A model that reframes all NLP tasks as text generation tasks, from translation to summarization. This unification of tasks under a single framework simplified fine-tuning for multiple tasks and improved performance across the board.
- **Vision Transformer (ViT):** A model that applies the Transformer architecture to image data, competing with and often surpassing traditional Convolutional Neural Networks (CNNs) on tasks like image classification.

Transformers as a Foundation for Future Models

The key innovations introduced by Transformers have not only revolutionized NLP but also created a foundation for models across various domains. The ability to scale, capture complex dependencies, and process large amounts of data in parallel has enabled the development of increasingly powerful models, opening up new possibilities in machine learning.

As we look forward, it is clear that the Transformer architecture and its variants will continue to influence the evolution of deep learning. Whether in natural language processing, computer vision, or even reinforcement learning, **Transformers have become the backbone of many state-of-the-art models, setting the stage for future innovations in AI.**

The Impact of Transformers on Various AI Domains

The introduction of the Transformer architecture was a watershed moment not just for natural language processing (NLP) but for the broader field of artificial intelligence (AI). What started as an innovation aimed at improving machine translation quickly evolved into a versatile tool that transformed numerous AI domains. From text generation to computer vision, and even areas like reinforcement learning, Transformers have pushed the boundaries of what deep learning models can achieve. This section explores the profound impact Transformers have had across different fields of AI.

Natural Language Processing (NLP)

Transformers were originally designed to tackle complex tasks in NLP, and their influence in this field has been nothing short of revolutionary. Before the advent of Transformers, traditional models like Recurrent Neural Networks (RNNs) and their variants, such as Long Short-Term Memory (LSTM) networks, were the go-to architectures for NLP tasks. However, these models struggled with long-range dependencies, parallelization, and scalability. Transformers addressed all of these limitations, enabling significant advancements in various NLP tasks, including:

- **Machine Translation:** The Transformer was first applied to machine translation tasks, where it set a new standard for accuracy and fluency in translating between languages. It outperformed traditional sequence-to-sequence models like RNNs, offering more accurate translations while handling longer sentences more effectively.

- **Text Generation:** The rise of models like GPT (Generative Pre-Trained Transformer) demonstrated the Transformer's remarkable capability in generating coherent and contextually appropriate text. GPT models, particularly GPT-2 and GPT-3, have shown that Transformers can generate human-like text, write essays, answer questions, and even compose poetry, opening up new possibilities for natural language generation.
- **Question Answering and Summarization:** Models like BERT (Bidirectional Encoder Representations from Transformers) excel at tasks that require deep contextual understanding, such as question answering and text summarization. BERT's ability to process text bidirectionally–capturing context from both the left and right sides of a word–has significantly improved performance on these tasks.
- **Named Entity Recognition (NER) and Sentiment Analysis:** Transformers have also proven highly effective in traditional NLP tasks like named entity recognition and sentiment analysis. The attention mechanism allows these models to identify key phrases and entities in a text while understanding the broader context in which they appear, resulting in more accurate classifications.

In just a few years, Transformers have become the backbone of state-of-the-art NLP models, and their ability to handle large datasets and long-range dependencies has paved the way for unprecedented advancements in the field.

Computer Vision

Initially, the Transformer architecture was designed with sequential data in mind, particularly text. However, researchers soon realized that the core principles of self-attention and parallelization could also be applied to image data. This led to the development of the Vision Transformer (ViT), a model that applies the Transformer architecture to image classification tasks.

- **Vision Transformers:** Traditionally, image processing tasks were dominated by Convolutional Neural Networks (CNNs), which excelled at extracting spatial features from images through the use of convolutional layers. However, Vision Transformers demonstrated that self-attention could be applied directly to image patches, treating each patch of the image as a token, much like words in a sentence. Vision Transformers have been shown to achieve competitive results with CNNs on image classification tasks, especially when trained on large datasets.
- **Advantages over CNNs:** While CNNs are highly effective at extracting local features (e.g., edges, textures), Vision Transformers excel at capturing global relationships within an image. By allowing each part of the image to attend to every other part, Vision Transformers can better understand the holistic structure of the image, which is particularly useful for tasks involving complex scenes or long-range dependencies between objects.
- **Image Generation and Captioning:** Beyond classification, Transformer models have been adapted for tasks like image generation (for example, DALL-E) and image captioning. In these cases, the attention mechanism allows the model to generate detailed and contextually accurate descriptions of images or even generate new, realistic images from text prompts.

The success of Vision Transformers has spurred further research into applying Transformers to other areas of computer vision, such as object detection, segmentation, and video analysis.

Speech Recognition and Synthesis

Transformers have also made significant strides in the field of speech recognition and synthesis. Traditionally, speech-to-text and text-to-speech systems relied on RNNs or CNNs to model the temporal dependencies in audio sequences. However, with the introduction of Transformers, these tasks saw a marked improvement in both accuracy and efficiency.

- **Speech-to-Text (Automatic Speech Recognition - ASR):** Transformers have been applied to automatic speech recognition systems, where they process audio inputs as sequences and translate them into corresponding text. The ability of Transformers to capture long-range dependencies has proven particularly useful in speech recognition, where understanding the entire audio context is crucial for accurate transcription.
- **Text-to-Speech (TTS):** In text-to-speech systems, models like Tacotron 2 and Transformer TTS leverage the Transformer architecture to generate highly natural-sounding speech from text inputs. By attending to the entire input sequence, these models can generate speech that is fluid, coherent, and contextually appropriate.
- **Speech Synthesis with Transformers:** The combination of Transformers with generative models, such as those used in WaveNet, has also improved the quality of speech synthesis, enabling the generation of highly realistic voices with proper intonation, cadence, and emotion.

Reinforcement Learning

The impact of Transformers has extended beyond supervised learning tasks to influence reinforcement learning (RL) as well. In traditional RL models, agents interact with environments in sequential steps, making RNNs the go-to architecture for processing these temporal sequences. However, the use of self-attention mechanisms in Transformers has introduced new possibilities for improving decision-making and policy learning in RL.

- **Handling Long-Term Dependencies:** In many RL tasks, especially those involving complex strategies (e.g., board games, real-time strategy games), the ability to remember past actions and their consequences over long time periods is essential. Transformers, with their ability to model long-range dependencies, allow RL agents to make better-informed decisions based on a deeper understanding of the environment's history.
- **Transformers in Game-Playing Agents:** Models like AlphaStar (in real-time strategy games) and MuZero (in board games) have incorporated elements of the Transformer architecture to improve their ability to process and understand sequential actions. These models leverage attention mechanisms to focus on the most relevant parts of the game state, improving both performance and efficiency.

Multimodal Models

One of the most exciting areas of AI development is the rise of multimodal models, which integrate data from different modalities (for instance, text, images, audio, and so on) into a single system. Transformers, with their versatile attention mechanisms, have played a key role in enabling these models to process and understand data from multiple sources simultaneously.

- **Image and Text Models:** Models like DALL-E and CLIP combine text and image data to perform tasks like generating images from text descriptions or matching images with corresponding captions. Transformers allow these models to align the representations of text and images, enabling cross-modal understanding and generation.
- Audio-Visual Models: In fields like video understanding or audio-visual speech recognition, Transformers have been used to process both video and audio streams concurrently, allowing the model to understand the relationship between visual cues (e.g., lip movements) and audio data (e.g., spoken words). This has applications in areas such as automatic captioning, sign language recognition, and multimedia content analysis.

The Transformative Power of Transformers

The Transformer architecture has had a far-reaching impact across AI, enabling advancements in domains that were once dominated by task-specific architectures. Its flexibility, scalability, and ability to capture complex dependencies have allowed Transformers to transcend their original application in NLP and redefine state-of-the-art performance in fields like computer vision, speech recognition, reinforcement learning, and beyond.

The development of multimodal models further illustrates the power of Transformers to integrate and process different types of data in a unified framework, opening up new possibilities for AI systems that can understand and generate across multiple modalities. As research continues to explore the boundaries of what Transformers can achieve, they are likely to remain a foundational architecture for AI development in the years to come.

Comparing Transformers to Previous Architectures

The advent of Transformer models introduced a fundamentally new approach to processing sequential data, offering advantages that set them apart from previous architectures like Recurrent Neural Networks (RNNs) and Convolutional Neural Networks (CNNs). In this section, we'll compare Transformers to these traditional architectures, highlighting their strengths, weaknesses, and how they address some of the key challenges faced by earlier models.

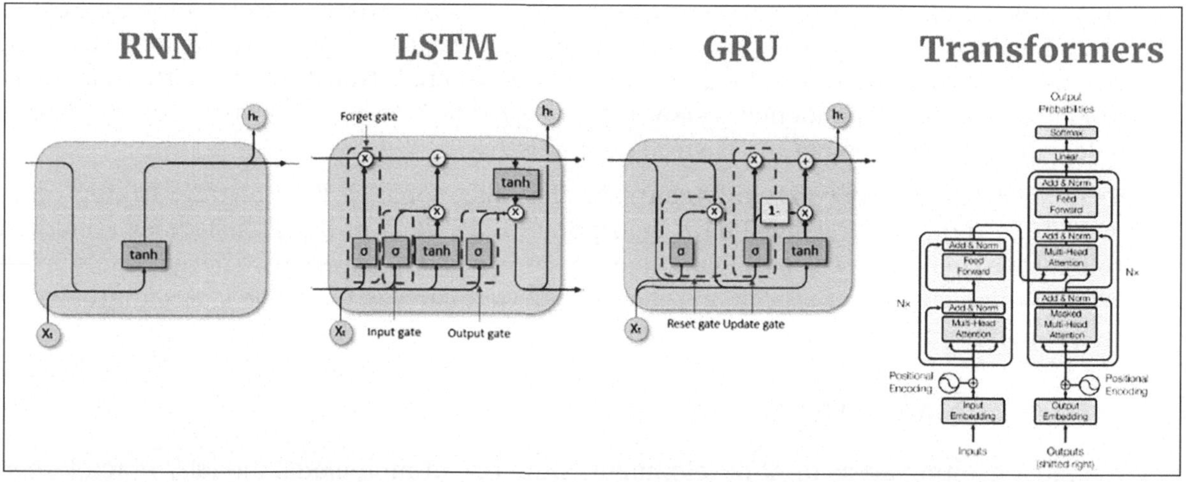

Figure 1.7: *Comparison of Different Sequence Models: RNN, LSTM, GRU, and Transformers*

Transformers Versus Recurrent Neural Networks (RNNs)

RNNs were the dominant architecture for handling sequential data before Transformers, particularly in fields like natural language processing (NLP), time series analysis, and speech recognition. While RNNs made significant contributions to these domains, they were constrained by several limitations that Transformers successfully overcame, such as:

- **Sequential Processing vs. Parallel Processing:** RNNs process sequences step by step, where each time step depends on the previous one. This inherently sequential nature means that RNNs cannot take full advantage of modern hardware like GPUs, which thrive on parallel computation. Transformers, in contrast, process the entire sequence in parallel, using self-attention mechanisms to capture relationships between different elements simultaneously.

This parallelization dramatically speeds up training and makes it possible to work with much larger datasets and longer sequences.

- **Long-Range Dependencies:** A major limitation of RNNs, even with enhancements like LSTMs and GRUs, is their difficulty in capturing long-range dependencies due to the vanishing gradient problem. This problem causes the gradients to shrink during backpropagation, especially when processing long sequences, resulting in the network "*forgetting*" information from earlier time steps. Transformers, through their self-attention mechanism, enable each element in the sequence to attend directly to every other element, allowing the model to capture long-range dependencies without any loss of information.
- **Training Efficiency:** Training RNNs, particularly on long sequences, is a slow and resource-intensive process due to their sequential nature. Transformers eliminate this bottleneck by allowing parallel processing, which not only speeds up training but also allows for the use of larger and deeper models. This scalability has been a key factor in the success of large-scale models like BERT and GPT.
- **Memory and Recurrence:** RNNs rely on the concept of recurrence, where information is passed from one-time step to the next through hidden states. This memory mechanism, while useful, becomes inefficient when dealing with long sequences, as distant time steps may not effectively influence the current state. Transformers, by removing recurrence and focusing on self-attention, allow for more direct and efficient learning from all parts of the sequence.

Transformers Versus Convolutional Neural Networks (CNNs)

Convolutional Neural Networks (CNNs) have long been the gold standard for image processing tasks, excelling at extracting local features through convolutional layers. However, the Transformer architecture has recently emerged as a competitive alternative, particularly with the introduction of Vision Transformers (ViTs).

- **Local vs. Global Feature Extraction:** CNNs are highly effective at capturing local patterns such as edges, textures, and shapes in images, thanks to their use of convolutional filters. These filters operate on small regions of the image, allowing CNNs to detect fine-grained details. However, CNNs struggle to capture global relationships across an image, as they rely on deeper layers and pooling operations to aggregate information from larger areas. Transformers, with their self-attention mechanism, enable global context to be captured from the very first layer, as each patch of the image can attend to every other patch. This allows Transformers to capture long-range dependencies and understand the image holistically.
- **Scalability:** Transformers offer greater scalability compared to CNNs, particularly when dealing with large datasets or tasks requiring high-dimensional data processing. Vision Transformers have shown that, when trained on large datasets, they can outperform CNNs on tasks like image classification. This scalability is largely due to the parallel processing capability of Transformers, whereas CNNs are constrained by the size and design of their convolutional filters and pooling operations.
- **Data Requirements:** One notable difference between CNNs and Vision Transformers is their data efficiency. CNNs, with their specialized architecture for local feature extraction, often require smaller datasets to achieve high performance. Vision Transformers, on the other hand, typically require large-scale datasets to realize their full potential, as their global attention mechanism needs more data to learn meaningful relationships across an image. This is why ViTs tend to perform best when pre-trained on massive datasets like ImageNet-21k before being fine-tuned on specific tasks.
- **Architectural Simplicity:** Transformers are conceptually simpler than CNNs, as they rely on repeated layers of self-attention and feedforward networks, without the need for complex

operations like convolutions, pooling, or down-sampling. This simplicity makes Transformers easier to scale and modify for different tasks. However, this comes at the cost of requiring more computational resources during training, especially when working with high-resolution images.

Transformers versus LSTMs and GRUs

Long Short-Term Memory (LSTM) networks and Gated Recurrent Units (GRUs) were developed to address some of the weaknesses in standard RNNs, such as the vanishing gradient problem. However, even these improved RNN variants face limitations that Transformers effectively overcome.

- **Efficiency in Capturing Long-Term Dependencies:** LSTMs and GRUs improved upon RNNs by introducing memory cells and gating mechanisms that help retain information over long sequences. However, they still rely on sequential processing, which limits their ability to handle very long sequences efficiently. Transformers, through self-attention, directly compute relationships between all elements in a sequence, allowing for the capture of long-term dependencies without the need for complex memory mechanisms. This gives Transformers a significant advantage over LSTMs and GRUs in tasks that require understanding context over extended sequences.
- **Training Speed and Parallelization:** LSTMs and GRUs, like RNNs, suffer from slow training times due to their sequential nature. Training these models on long sequences can be time-consuming and computationally expensive. Transformers, on the other hand, enable parallel training of sequences, drastically reducing training times and making it feasible to train on much larger datasets. This advantage is especially evident in large-scale models like GPT-3, which would be infeasible to train using LSTM or GRU architectures.
- **Simpler Architecture:** The architecture of Transformers is inherently simpler than LSTMs and GRUs. Both LSTMs and GRUs require intricate gating mechanisms to control the flow of information, while Transformers rely on a straightforward combination of self-attention and feedforward layers. This simplicity not only makes Transformers easier to implement but also reduces the risk of model complexity leading to overfitting or training instability.

Key Takeaways from the Comparison

- **Parallelization and Speed:** Transformers excel at parallelization, making them significantly faster to train than RNNs, LSTMs, and GRUs, all of which process data sequentially. This parallelism, combined with the ability to handle long sequences without suffering from the vanishing gradient problem, has allowed Transformers to scale to unprecedented levels.
- **Global Context and Long-Range Dependencies:** Transformers capture global context more effectively than RNNs, CNNs, LSTMs, and GRUs. The use of self-attention allows each element in the input sequence or image to attend to all other elements, providing a more comprehensive understanding of the input.
- **Simplicity and Scalability:** The Transformer architecture is relatively simple, relying on repeated layers of self-attention and feedforward networks. This simplicity, combined with its scalability, has allowed it to become the dominant architecture for a wide range of tasks, from NLP to vision, and beyond.
- **Data Requirements:** While Transformers offer significant advantages, they often require large datasets to achieve optimal performance, particularly in tasks like image classification where local patterns are important. CNNs, in contrast, tend to be more data-efficient in scenarios where extracting local features is sufficient.

In summary, Transformers address many of the limitations of earlier architectures, particularly in terms of parallelization, scalability, and the ability to capture long-range dependencies. **These features**

have enabled Transformers to become the leading architecture for a wide range of tasks, pushing the boundaries of what deep learning models can achieve.

The Role of Hardware Advancements in Neural Network Evolution

The dramatic progress in neural networks, from the early days of shallow architectures to modern Transformer-based models, has not been driven solely by algorithmic innovations. Equally important has been the advancement of hardware technologies that made it possible to train increasingly complex and larger models on massive datasets. The synergy between hardware advancements and deep learning research has played a crucial role in accelerating the development of neural networks, enabling breakthroughs that were once thought to be infeasible.

In this section, we explore how key developments in hardware, particularly the rise of Graphics Processing Units (GPUs), specialized hardware like Tensor Processing Units (TPUs), and advancements in cloud computing infrastructure, have revolutionized the training and deployment of neural networks.

The Early Days of Neural Network Training

In the early stages of neural network research, hardware limitations posed a significant bottleneck. Training a simple feedforward neural network or a small-scale Recurrent Neural Network (RNN) required considerable computational power, which was often unavailable to most researchers. Early models were typically trained on Central Processing Units (CPUs), which, while well-suited for general-purpose computation, were inefficient when handling the vast number of matrix multiplications required by neural networks.

- **Slow Training Times:** As neural networks grew in complexity, particularly with the introduction of multi-layer perceptrons and later with RNNs, training times became prohibitively long. Models often took days or even weeks to converge, limiting experimentation and innovation.
- **Data Limitations:** In addition to slow computation, early neural network models were also constrained by the amount of data that could be processed efficiently. Without access to large datasets, the potential of deep learning models to generalize and perform well on complex tasks remained unrealized.

The Rise of GPUs in Deep Learning

The major turning point for the field came with the adoption of Graphics Processing Units (GPUs) for deep learning. GPUs, originally designed for rendering graphics in video games and other visual applications, are highly efficient at performing parallel computations. Unlike CPUs, which focus on sequential tasks, GPUs can process multiple operations simultaneously, making them ideal for handling the matrix multiplications and other mathematical operations that underpin neural networks.

- **Parallelism and Speed:** GPUs introduced a level of parallelism that drastically sped up training times. Instead of processing one computation at a time, GPUs can handle thousands of computations in parallel, allowing neural networks to be trained orders of magnitude faster than on CPUs. This reduction in training time not only made deep learning more accessible to researchers but also enabled experimentation with deeper and more complex models.
- **Scalability:** The scalability of GPUs allowed researchers to train models on much larger datasets than before. This was particularly important for deep learning models, which rely on vast amounts of data to learn complex representations. By accelerating training, GPUs made it feasible to experiment with deep neural networks, leading to the emergence of architectures like Convolutional Neural Networks (CNNs) and later Transformers.

- **Key Breakthroughs:** One of the most famous examples of the power of GPUs in deep learning was the training of AlexNet in 2012. AlexNet, a deep convolutional neural network, was trained on a GPU and won the ImageNet competition by a significant margin. The use of GPUs was a critical factor in the model's success, as it enabled the network to be trained on a large dataset of millions of images in a reasonable amount of time.

Figure 1.8: *TPU Representation Source: Nvidia*

Tensor Processing Units (TPUs) and Specialized Hardware

While GPUs remain a cornerstone of deep learning hardware, specialized hardware designed specifically for machine learning tasks has emerged as a key enabler of more efficient model training. The most notable example is Tensor Processing Units (TPUs), developed by Google.

- **TPUs:** Introduced in 2016, TPUs are custom-built accelerators designed to optimize the performance of TensorFlow, Google's machine learning framework. TPUs are particularly efficient at performing the types of operations involved in training deep neural networks, such as matrix multiplications and convolutions. They are designed to be faster and more energy-efficient than GPUs for specific types of deep learning workloads, making them ideal for large-scale training.
- **Cloud TPU Clusters:** One of the significant advantages of TPUs is their integration with cloud infrastructure. Google Cloud offers TPU clusters that allow researchers and companies to scale up their machine learning projects with relative ease. These clusters enable distributed training, where large models can be trained across multiple TPUs in parallel, significantly speeding up training times for models like BERT and GPT-3.
- **Other Specialized Hardware:** In addition to TPUs, other companies have developed specialized hardware for machine learning. For example, Intel and NVIDIA have both developed chips optimized for deep learning computations. Field-Programmable Gate Arrays (FPGAs) and Application-Specific Integrated Circuits (ASICs) have also been used in some deep learning applications, where performance and energy efficiency are critical.

Cloud Computing and Distributed Training

As models like Transformers have grown in size, with billions of parameters and extensive training data, it has become necessary to leverage cloud computing infrastructure to train these models. The availability of cloud-based GPUs and TPUs has made it easier for researchers and companies to train large-scale models, without the need for expensive on-premise hardware.

- **Cloud Platforms:** Services like Google Cloud, AWS (Amazon Web Services), and Microsoft Azure provide access to high-performance hardware (GPUs and TPUs) on-demand. This has democratized access to powerful computational resources, allowing smaller research teams and startups to train models that were previously accessible only to large tech companies.
- **Distributed Training:** As models like GPT-3 and T5 have grown in size, even a single GPU or TPU is often insufficient for training. To solve this problem, researchers employ distributed training, where multiple GPUs or TPUs work together to train the model in parallel. Cloud platforms enable this by offering infrastructure that supports the parallelization of training across hundreds or even thousands of machines. Distributed training techniques like data parallelism and model parallelism ensure that massive models can be trained in a fraction of the time.

Memory and Bandwidth Innovations

In addition to advancements in computation, improvements in memory and bandwidth have also played a crucial role in neural network evolution. As deep learning models grow larger, the need for efficient memory management and high-speed data transfer becomes critical.

- **High-Bandwidth Memory (HBM):** Modern GPUs and TPUs are equipped with high-bandwidth memory, which allows them to process larger batches of data at faster speeds. This is essential for training large models on high-resolution images or long text sequences, as it reduces the time spent waiting for data to be transferred between the processor and memory.
- **Memory Optimization Techniques:** Techniques like gradient checkpointing and mixed-precision training have been developed to optimize memory usage during training. These methods allow models to store only essential information during training, reducing the overall memory footprint and enabling larger models to be trained on a given piece of hardware.

The Impact on Model Size and Complexity

The combination of GPU/TPU hardware, cloud computing, and memory advancements has enabled the development of increasingly large and complex models. Today, models like GPT-3 (with 175 billion parameters) and T5 are trained on vast amounts of data, using thousands of GPUs or TPUs over weeks or months. These models would have been impossible to train on traditional hardware and infrastructure just a few years ago.

As a result, hardware advancements have directly contributed to the explosive growth in model size, leading to substantial improvements in the performance of deep learning models across various domains. From language understanding to image recognition, neural networks, today are orders of magnitude more powerful than those from just a decade ago, thanks to the parallel evolution of hardware technologies.

In summary, hardware advancements have been a key enabler of the neural network revolution. The transition from CPU-based training to GPU-accelerated computation, followed by the rise of specialized hardware like TPUs and the expansion of cloud infrastructure, has allowed researchers to push the boundaries of what neural networks can achieve.

As models continue to grow in complexity, and the demand for real-time, high-accuracy AI systems increases, hardware will remain a driving force behind the evolution of neural networks. Innovations in energy efficiency, memory optimization, and distributed computing will be critical to ensuring that the next generation of models can meet the challenges of increasingly data-rich and compute-intensive AI applications.

Ethical Considerations in the Development of Advanced Neural Networks

As neural networks have evolved into increasingly powerful tools, with applications spanning from healthcare to finance, natural language processing, and beyond, they have raised a number of ethical concerns. While the technological advances made possible by models like Transformers have led to significant breakthroughs, they also bring about complex challenges related to privacy, fairness, transparency, and societal impact. Addressing these ethical considerations is critical to ensuring that the development and deployment of advanced neural networks are both responsible and beneficial to the society, as a whole.

Bias and Fairness in Neural Networks

One of the most pressing ethical concerns in the development of neural networks is the potential for bias. Neural networks, particularly those trained on large datasets, are only as good as the data they are fed. If the training data contains biases, whether based on race, gender, socioeconomic status, or other factors, the model will inevitably learn and replicate those biases in its predictions or decisions.

- **Biased Training Data:** Many models are trained on large datasets sourced from the internet or other publicly available data which often reflect the biases present in society. For example, facial recognition systems have been shown to perform poorly on people with darker skin tones, due to the lack of diversity in the training data. Similarly, language models like GPT can generate biased or harmful text based on the stereotypes present in the data, they were trained on.
- **Fairness in Decision-Making:** In applications like hiring algorithms, credit scoring, or predictive policing, biased models can lead to unfair or discriminatory outcomes. For example, an AI system used for hiring may prioritize candidates of certain demographics over others if it has been trained on historical hiring data that reflects past biases. Ensuring fairness in these systems requires careful examination of both the training data and the model's outputs.
- **Mitigating Bias:** Researchers are actively working on techniques to mitigate bias in neural networks, such as fairness-aware learning and bias auditing. These approaches involve identifying and correcting for biases during training, as well as testing models to ensure that they perform equitably across different demographic groups. However, mitigating bias remains a complex and ongoing challenge, especially as models become larger and more reliant on vast, uncurated datasets.

Transparency and Explainability

Neural networks, especially deep models like Transformers, are often described as "*black boxes*" due to their lack of transparency. While these models can make highly accurate predictions, understanding exactly how they arrive at those predictions is often difficult, even for the researchers who built them. This lack of explainability poses significant ethical concerns, particularly in high-stakes applications like healthcare, law, and finance.

- **Black Box Models:** The complexity of neural networks makes it challenging to trace the decision-making process from input to output. In cases like medical diagnoses or loan approvals, where the reasoning behind a decision can have serious consequences, this opacity can lead to issues of accountability and trust. Patients, for instance, may want to know why an AI system recommended one treatment over another, but neural networks often cannot provide clear explanations.

- **The Right to Explanation**: In some contexts, there is a growing call for a right to explanation—the idea that individuals affected by AI decisions should be able to understand how and why a decision was made. In the European Union's General Data Protection Regulation (GDPR), for example, there are provisions that support this right in cases where automated decisions are made.
- **Improving Explainability:** Researchers are developing methods to make neural networks more interpretable. Techniques like LIME (Local Interpretable Model-agnostic Explanations) and SHAP (Shapley Additive Explanations) aim to provide more transparency by offering human-readable explanations for model predictions. Another approach involves developing inherently interpretable models, though these may sacrifice some performance for the sake of transparency.

Privacy Concerns

The rise of deep learning models, particularly in sectors like healthcare and finance, has heightened concerns about data privacy. Many advanced neural networks are trained on large volumes of personal data, raising questions about how this data is collected, stored, and used.

- **Sensitive Data:** In areas like medical diagnosis or financial prediction, neural networks often require access to highly sensitive information, such as patient health records or personal financial histories. This raises concerns about the security of this data, especially if the models are being trained or deployed in the cloud, where there may be vulnerabilities.
- **Data Ownership:** Another ethical question involves data ownership—who owns the data used to train these models, and do individuals have the right to control how their personal data is used? While companies benefit from large datasets to train more accurate models, individuals may not always be aware that their data is being used for these purposes.
- **Differential Privacy:** To address the privacy concerns, researchers have developed techniques like differential privacy, which ensures that individual data points cannot be identified within the larger dataset. This allows models to be trained on sensitive data without compromising individual privacy. However, balancing privacy with model accuracy remains a challenging task.

The Environmental Impact of Large-Scale Models

As neural networks grow larger and more complex, particularly with the rise of models like GPT-3 and other massive Transformers, their environmental impact has come under scrutiny. Training large models requires substantial computational resources, which in turn leads to significant energy consumption and carbon emissions.

- **Carbon Footprint:** Training the state-of-the-art models can take weeks or even months, consuming vast amounts of electricity in the process. Studies have shown that the carbon footprint of training a large neural network can be equivalent to that of multiple cars running over several years. This raises concerns about the sustainability of deep learning research, especially as models continue to grow in size.
- **Sustainable AI:** Addressing this issue requires a focus on sustainable AI practices. Researchers are exploring ways to make model training more energy-efficient, such as through the use of more efficient hardware (for example, TPUs), or by developing new training algorithms that require fewer resources. Some companies have also begun to prioritize energy-efficient data centers that rely on renewable energy sources.

The Societal Impact of AI-Driven Automation

The rise of neural networks and AI has led to widespread concerns about automation, and its potential impact on the workforce. As AI systems become more capable, there is a growing fear that they will replace human workers in various industries, from manufacturing and logistics to white-collar jobs like customer service, legal work, and even journalism.

- **Job Displacement:** While AI has the potential to increase productivity, and create new jobs, it may also lead to the displacement of millions of workers, particularly in industries where automation can easily replace repetitive tasks. This raises ethical concerns about the social and economic consequences of widespread job loss, and the need for policies to support workers affected by automation.
- **Reskilling and Education:** To mitigate the negative effects of automation, there is a growing emphasis on reskilling workers, and providing education in areas where human labor is still essential. Governments and private companies, alike will need to invest in training programs to help workers adapt to the changing job landscape brought about by AI.

Misuse of AI Technology

Another significant ethical concern is the potential for the misuse of AI technology, whether by governments, corporations, or malicious actors. Neural networks, particularly those used for surveillance, content generation, or predictive policing, can be misapplied in ways that infringe on human rights and freedom.

- **Surveillance and Privacy:** AI systems equipped with facial recognition or other surveillance capabilities can be used to track and monitor individuals, without their consent. This raises significant privacy concerns, particularly in authoritarian regimes, where such technologies can be used to suppress dissent, or violate citizens' rights.
- **Deepfakes and Disinformation:** Neural networks can also be used to generate deepfakes–highly realistic, but fake images, videos, or audio clips that can be used to spread disinformation. The rise of deepfakes has raised concerns about the erosion of trust in digital content, and the potential for these technologies to be weaponized for political or social manipulation.
- **Regulation and Governance:** To address these concerns, there is a growing call for stronger AI governance and regulation. Governments and international organizations are beginning to develop frameworks for the ethical use of AI, including restrictions on the use of facial recognition technology, and standards for transparency as well as fairness in AI decision-making.

Balancing Innovation with Responsibility

As neural networks continue to evolve and become more powerful, it is essential to balance innovation with responsibility. The development of advanced AI technologies should not come at the expense of privacy, fairness, transparency, or sustainability. Researchers, policymakers, and companies must work together to establish the ethical standards that guide the responsible development and deployment of AI.

Ethical considerations are not just an afterthought–they are central to ensuring that AI technology benefits all in a society, rather than amplifying the existing inequalities, or introducing new risks. By addressing these challenges head-on, the AI community can work toward a future, where neural networks are used to advance human well-being in a fair and responsible manner.

Conclusion

Neural networks have come a long way, evolving from early perceptron models to the powerful Transformer architectures, we rely on today. This chapter traced that journey, highlighting key innovations like Convolutional Neural Networks (CNNs) for image processing and Recurrent Neural Networks (RNNs) for handling sequential data. The introduction of Transformers marked a turning point, with their use of self-attention mechanisms, allowing for parallel processing, scalability, and superior handling of long-range dependencies. These advancements have driven significant improvements in Natural Language Processing (NLP), computer vision, and other AI fields.

Alongside algorithmic breakthroughs, the evolution of hardware, particularly the rise of GPUs, TPUs, and cloud computing, has been critical in enabling the training of larger and more complex models. At the same time, ethical considerations around bias, privacy, transparency, and environmental impact have become increasingly important as AI systems become more pervasive.

Understanding this evolution sets the stage for the deep dive into Transformer models, and how to implement them effectively using PyTorch 2.0 which we will explore in the coming chapters. In the next chapter, we will also explore the inner workings of Transformer architecture, diving deep into its core components, such as the self-attention mechanism, positional encoding, and multi-head attention. By understanding these elements, you can gain a deep insight into how **Transformers efficiently process and generate sequences, setting the stage for their powerful applications in AI.**

CHAPTER 2

Fundamentals of Transformer Architecture

Introduction

In this chapter, we explore the groundbreaking architecture that has redefined the way neural networks handle sequential data: The **Transformer**. Unlike traditional models that rely on recurrence or convolution to process sequences, Transformers use self-attention mechanisms to capture relationships across entire input sequences simultaneously. This shift enables the Transformer to excel at tasks, such as natural language processing, translation, and text generation with unprecedented efficiency.

We begin by dissecting the self-attention mechanism, the core innovation of Transformers, which allows each element of a sequence to attend to all other elements, capturing long-range dependencies, without the limitations of sequential models like RNNs. From there, we dive into the need for positional encoding, which injects order into the otherwise unordered inputs, enabling the model to understand sequence structure. We, then explain the role of multi-head attention, a parallel processing technique that enables the model to focus on different aspects of the input simultaneously.

In addition, we cover the essential components that support the self-attention mechanism: feed-forward networks and residual connections, which stabilize the training process, and ensure efficient gradient flow. Lastly, we examine the encoder-decoder architecture that makes the Transformer particularly effective for sequence-to-sequence tasks, such as machine translation, and discuss its widespread applications in various domains.

By the end of this chapter, readers will have a comprehensive understanding of the Transformer architecture's foundational elements, equipping them with the knowledge necessary to implement and experiment with Transformer models in PyTorch.

Structure

The following are the salient topics covered in this chapter:

- The Self-Attention Mechanism: The Heart of Transformers
- Positional Encoding: Injecting Order into Unordered Inputs
- Multi-Head Attention: Parallel Processing of Information
- Feed-Forward Networks and Residual Connections
- The Encoder-Decoder Architecture in Transformers
- Limitations of the Basic Transformers
- Transformer-XL: Addressing Long-Range Dependencies

Self-Attention Mechanism: The Heart of Transformers

At the core of the Transformer architecture lies the self-attention mechanism, a powerful innovation that allows the model to efficiently process and understand sequential data, without relying on recurrence or convolution. Unlike traditional models, such as RNNs or LSTMs, which process sequences step by step, Transformers employ self-attention to consider every element of the input sequence simultaneously. This parallelism allows Transformers to capture both local and global dependencies more effectively, making them particularly suited for tasks like natural language processing, translation, and text generation.

Mechanics of Self-Attention

Self-attention enables the model to weigh the importance of different elements in the input sequence relative to each other. Instead of processing data sequentially, self-attention allows each token (or word) to attend to all other tokens in the sequence, understanding their relationships in a single step.

For example, consider a sentence where the word, "*it*" appears. To correctly interpret "*it*," the model must understand which noun "*it*" refers to. The self-attention mechanism helps the model focus on the relevant words in the sentence that "*it*" might relate to, such as the subject or object, rather than treating the sequence strictly from left to right as RNNs do.

The Query, Key, and Value Matrices

Self-attention operates through the use of three essential components: Queries, keys, and values. For every token in the input sequence, the model generates a query vector, a key vector, and a value vector. These vectors are used to calculate how each token relates to every other token in the sequence.

- **Query:** Represents the token in focus (the one that is attending to other tokens).
- **Key:** Represents each token that the query will attend to.
- **Value:** Contains the actual information of each token which will be aggregated, based on the attention scores.

The mechanism computes an attention score for each pair of tokens by taking the dot product of the query and key vectors. These scores indicate how much focus should be given to each token when processing the current token. The higher the attention score, the more significant the relationship between the tokens.

Mathematically, the attention score for each token is computed as:

$$\text{Attention}(Q, K, V) = \text{softmax}\left(\frac{QK^T}{\sqrt{d_k}}\right) V$$

Figure 2.1: *Attention Score Formula*

Where:

- Q is the query matrix.
- K is the key matrix.
- V is the value matrix.
- d_k is the dimension of the key vectors, used to scale the dot product for more stable gradients.

The **`softmax`** function is applied to convert the attention scores into a probability distribution, ensuring that all attention weights sum to 1.

Capturing Long-Range Dependencies

One of the major advantages of self-attention is its ability to capture long-range dependencies in a sequence. In RNNs, tokens at the beginning of a sequence may struggle to influence those at the end due to the vanishing gradient problem. Self-attention, on the other hand, treats all tokens equally, allowing tokens at any position in the sequence to attend to tokens at any other position.

This makes self-attention, particularly effective in tasks like machine translation, where understanding the relationship between words that are far apart in a sentence is crucial. For example, in a long sentence, the subject and verb may be separated by multiple words, but self-attention enables the model to learn these dependencies without the loss of information.

Self-Attention in Transformers

In a Transformer model, the self-attention mechanism is applied in each layer of the encoder and decoder. Each layer processes the input sequence using self-attention, allowing the model to build increasingly complex and abstract representations of the input data.

Within the encoder, self-attention helps the model understand the relationships between all tokens in the input sequence. In the decoder, self-attention is used in conjunction with masked attention, where the model attends only to the tokens up to the current position during training to prevent "*cheating*" by looking ahead at future tokens.

By stacking multiple layers of self-attention, Transformers can capture deep and complex dependencies within a sequence, while also processing the data in parallel, leading to significant gains in both accuracy and efficiency.

Advantages of Self-Attention Over Previous Mechanisms

Compared to earlier mechanisms such as recurrence or convolution, self-attention offers several key advantages:

- **Parallelism:** Self-attention allows Transformers to process sequences in parallel, leading to faster training times and more scalable models. This parallelism is a stark contrast to RNNs which must process sequences step by step.
- **Global Context:** Self-attention gives each token access to the entire input sequence at once, enabling the model to capture global context from the beginning. In contrast, RNNs and LSTMs often struggle to retain information over long sequences.
- **Efficiency:** Self-attention avoids the computational complexity of recurrent models, allowing for more efficient handling of long sequences, particularly in tasks involving large datasets.

The self-attention mechanism forms the backbone of the Transformer architecture, allowing it to process sequences efficiently, and capture complex dependencies. This mechanism's ability to attend to all elements in a sequence simultaneously, combined with its parallel processing capabilities, makes it one of the most powerful innovations in modern AI. Understanding how self-attention works is essential for grasping the inner workings of Transformer models, and their success across a wide range of AI tasks.

Positional Encoding: Injecting Order into Unordered Inputs

Transformers, unlike Recurrent Neural Networks (RNNs) or Convolutional Neural Networks (CNNs), process entire sequences in parallel. While this makes Transformers highly efficient, it introduces a challenge: The model has no inherent way of understanding the order of elements in the sequence. In tasks, such as language modeling or machine translation, the order of words in a sentence is crucial for the meaning. This is where positional encoding plays a vital role. By injecting positional information into the input data, positional encodings enable the Transformer to maintain an understanding of sequence order, while still leveraging the power of parallel processing.

The Importance of Positional Encoding

In traditional sequential models like RNNs or LSTMs, the order of inputs is implicitly encoded in the model's architecture–each token is processed step by step, with the sequence naturally unfolding over time. This gives these models a built-in understanding of the sequence order, but it also limits their parallel processing capabilities.

The Transformer, on the other hand, processes each element of the input sequence simultaneously through self-attention, meaning that without additional guidance, it has no way of knowing whether one token comes before or after another. For example, the sentence "*The cat sat on the mat*" would be treated the same as "*Mat the on sat cat the*," because no positional information is present in the tokens themselves. This lack of order would severely limit the model's ability to understand the meaning.

To address this, positional encodings are added to the input embeddings, providing the Transformer with a sense of position and order. This enables the model to take both the content and the position of tokens into account during attention calculations.

Mechanics of Positional Encoding

Positional encodings are vectors that are added to the input embeddings of the tokens in the sequence. Each position in the sequence is assigned a unique positional encoding which is combined with the token's embedding, before being fed into the Transformer layers.

Positional encoding is typically calculated using a combination of sine and cosine functions, which allows the model to generate fixed, continuous values that represent the relative positions of tokens. The following formulas define the positional encoding for position *pos* and dimension i in the embedding:

$$PE_{(pos,2i)} = \sin\left(\frac{pos}{10000^{2i/d_{\text{model}}}}\right)$$

$$PE_{(pos,2i+1)} = \cos\left(\frac{pos}{10000^{2i/d_{\text{model}}}}\right)$$

Figure 2.2: *Positional Encoding Formula*

Where:

- *pos* is the position in the sequence.
- i is the dimension in the embedding vector.
- d_{model} is the dimension of the model's embeddings.

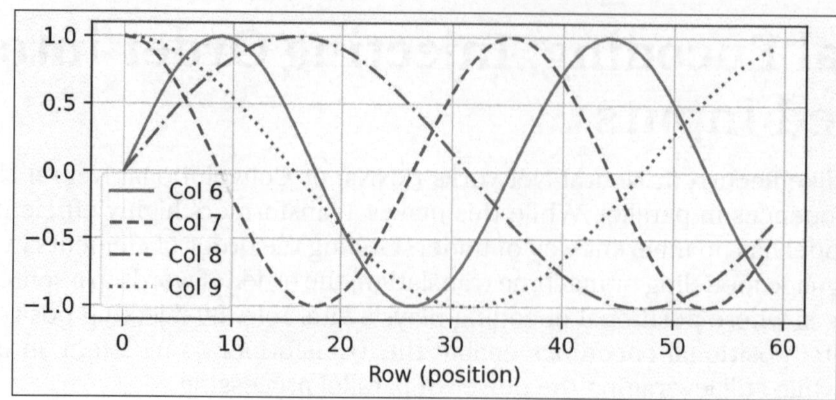

Figure 2.3: *Positional Encoding*

Figure 2.3 visualizes positional encoding, a crucial technique used in Transformers to introduce positional information into input data. Since the Transformer architecture processes sequences in parallel, rather than step by step, it lacks an inherent mechanism to capture the order of tokens in a sequence. Positional encodings are added to token embeddings to fill this gap, providing the model with information about the relative position of each token, within the sequence. The graph illustrates sine and cosine functions plotted across different dimensions of the embedding space, with the x-axis representing the position of each token, and the y-axis showing the corresponding function values. Each curve corresponds to a different dimension of the positional encoding, ensuring that nearby positions have similar encodings, while distant positions are distinctly different.

These sine and cosine functions alternate across the dimensions of the embedding, with different frequencies applied to different dimensions. This approach ensures that each position in the sequence has a unique representation, allowing the model to capture both the absolute position of each token and its relative distance from other tokens. The periodic nature of these functions ensures that relationships between tokens are preserved across both short and long distances in the sequence. By combining positional encodings with token embeddings, the model can understand both the content of the token and its position, which is necessary for tasks that depend heavily on sequence order, such as language modeling, machine translation, and text generation.

Reason Behind Sine and Cosine

The choice of using sine and cosine functions for positional encoding is not arbitrary. These functions provide several key advantages:

- **Continuity:** Sine and cosine functions allow the positional encodings to smoothly capture relationships between nearby positions. For example, the encodings for position 10 and position 11 will be similar, reflecting their close proximity in the sequence. This continuity helps the model recognize gradual shifts in position.
- **Periodicity:** Since sine and cosine functions are periodic, they can capture repeating patterns within the data. This is particularly useful in tasks like audio processing or time series forecasting, where patterns may repeat at regular intervals.
- **Relative Positioning:** By using different frequencies for different dimensions, sine and cosine functions allow the model to easily calculate relative positions. For instance, the difference between the positional encodings of position 5 and position 10 can help the model understand the relationship between tokens that are five positions apart.

Alternative Approaches to Positional Encoding

While the sine-cosine method is the most common, there are alternative approaches to positional encoding, particularly in more recent Transformer models. One alternative is to use learned positional encodings, where the model learns a separate embedding for each position in the sequence during training. Unlike sine and cosine functions, learned encodings are not fixed, and can adapt to the specific task and data.

- **Learned Positional Encodings:** In this approach, the positional encodings are treated like additional parameters that are optimized during training. Each position in the sequence has its own learned embedding which the model uses to differentiate between tokens. This method provides more flexibility, but requires additional training data and computation.
- **Rotary Positional Embeddings (RoPE):** Another emerging alternative is Rotary Positional Embeddings (RoPE) which rotates the embeddings within each layer, rather than using fixed positional encodings. This technique has been shown to improve performance in certain tasks by better capturing positional relationships in the data.

Interaction between Positional Encoding with Self-Attention

Positional encodings are added directly to the input embeddings, before they are passed into the self-attention layers. This combination allows the model to attend not only to the content of the tokens, but also to their positions in the sequence. During the attention calculation, the positional information helps the model decide which tokens should be attended to, based not just on their content, but also on where they are located relative to the current token.

For example, in a sentence like "*The cat sat on the mat*," positional encoding helps the model understand that "*The*" should likely attend to "*cat*," as they are close in sequence, but "*The*" is less relevant to "*mat*," which comes much later.

Without positional encoding, the self-attention mechanism would treat all tokens as interchangeable, leading to confusion, when processing structured data like text, where word order significantly affects meaning.

Applications of Positional Encoding

Positional encoding is vital for a wide range of tasks, involving sequential data that includes the following:

- **Natural Language Processing (NLP):** In tasks like machine translation, language modeling, and text generation, understanding the order of words is critical. Positional encoding ensures that Transformers can grasp the structure and flow of sentences.
- **Time Series Forecasting:** For time series data, positional encoding allows the model to differentiate between data points collected at different time intervals. This helps in capturing trends, periodicity, and temporal dependencies.
- **Audio Processing:** In tasks like speech recognition or music generation, positional encoding helps the model maintain the sequence of audio frames, ensuring that the sound is processed in the correct order.

Positional encoding is a crucial component of the Transformer architecture, enabling the model to inject a sense of order into the otherwise unordered inputs. By combining content and position, positional encodings ensure that the Transformer can process sequences effectively, while leveraging the efficiency of parallel processing. Whether through fixed sine-cosine functions or learned embeddings, positional encoding helps Transformers maintain an understanding of sequence structure, enabling their success across a variety of tasks in AI.

Multi-Head Attention: Parallel Processing of Information

In the Transformer architecture, multi-head attention is one of the key innovations that significantly improves the model's ability to learn complex relationships within data. By utilizing multiple attention heads in parallel, the Transformer can attend to different parts of the sequence simultaneously, capturing various aspects of the data, and allowing the model to process information more efficiently. This mechanism is crucial in enabling the Transformer to understand intricate patterns, dependencies, and contextual relationships in tasks such as language modeling, machine translation, and text generation.

The Role of Multi-Head Attention in Transformers

The self-attention mechanism, as discussed earlier, enables each token in a sequence to attend to all other tokens, capturing dependencies, regardless of their distance, within the sequence. However, a single attention mechanism might miss certain nuances in the data, especially when there are multiple relationships or patterns present. For example, in a sentence like "*The cat sat on the mat*," one token might need to attend to the subject ("*cat*"), and another to the preposition ("*on*") simultaneously.

This is where multi-head attention comes into play. Rather than using a single attention mechanism, the Transformer uses multiple attention "*heads*" to attend to different parts of the sequence in parallel. Each head learns to focus on a different aspect of the data, enabling the model to capture multiple relationships simultaneously, and making the overall attention process more robust.

Mechanics of Multi-Head Attention

Multi-head attention operates by splitting the input into several attention heads. Each head performs self-attention independently on the input sequence, generating its own set of query, key, and value matrices. These attention heads can focus on different parts of the sequence, allowing the model to capture a diverse set of patterns and relationships.

Here is the process broken down step by step:

1. **Input Splitting:** The input sequence, represented as embeddings, is first split into multiple parts. If there are h attention heads, the embedding is divided into h smaller subspaces. For example, if the model has a hidden size of 512, and uses 8 attention heads, each head would work with 64-dimensional subspaces.
2. **Query, Key, and Value Matrices:** For each head, the model computes separate query (Q), key (K), and value (V) matrices. These matrices are learned projections of the original input embeddings, and they allow each head to independently calculate attention scores, based on different aspects of the input sequence.
3. **Attention Calculation:** Each attention head computes its own attention scores by applying the self-attention mechanism described earlier. This involves calculating the dot product between the query and key matrices, scaling by the dimension of the key, and applying a softmax function to generate attention weights. These weights are then applied to the value matrix to produce the output for that attention head.
4. **Concatenation:** After each head has computed its output, the results from all the heads are concatenated. This creates a single output that incorporates information from all the different attention heads. Each head has captured unique relationships in the data, and combining these outputs provides a more comprehensive representation of the input sequence.

5. **Final Linear Projection:** Once the concatenated output is obtained, a final linear projection is applied to transform the concatenated vectors back into the original embedding space. This step ensures that the output has the same dimensionality as the original input.

The mathematical representation of multi-head attention can be written as:

$$\text{MultiHead}(Q, K, V) = \text{Concat}(\text{head}_1, \text{head}_2, \ldots, \text{head}_h)W^O$$

Where:

- $\text{head}_i = \text{Attention}(QW_i^Q, KW_i^K, VW_i^V)$
- W_i^Q, W_i^K, W_i^V are learned weight matrices for each attention head.
- W^O is the final linear projection matrix.

This allows the Transformer to leverage multiple views of the input sequence simultaneously, ensuring that no important relationship is missed.

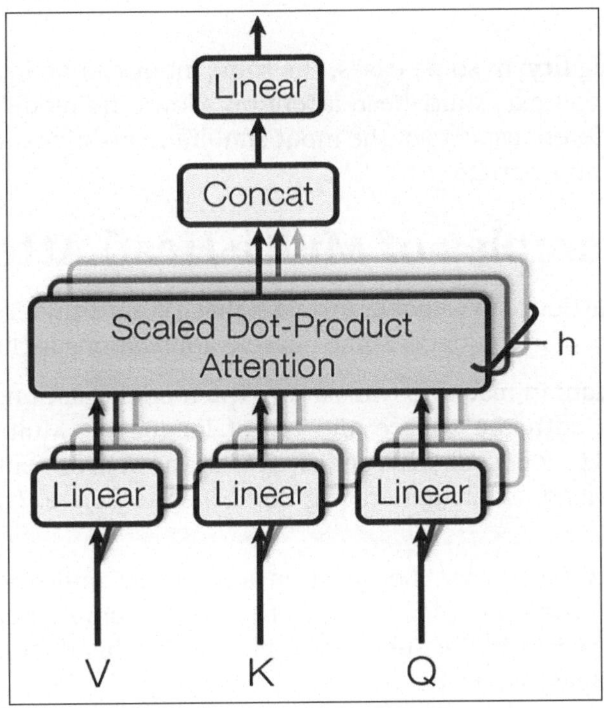

Figure 2.4: *Multi-Head Attention*

Figure 2.4 illustrates the Multi-Head Attention mechanism, a key component of the Transformer architecture. Multi-head attention allows the model to attend to different parts of the input sequence simultaneously, capturing a broader range of dependencies and relationships between tokens. In the diagram, the input embeddings are first transformed into query (Q), key (K), and value (V) vectors through linear layers. Each of these vectors is then fed into multiple attention heads (denoted by the stacked layers), where Scaled Dot-Product Attention is applied to compute attention scores. These attention heads operate in parallel, each focusing on different aspects of the input data. The outputs from all the heads are then concatenated, and passed through a final linear layer to merge the results. This process enables the model to learn multiple relationships between tokens, enhancing its ability to understand complex patterns in data, which is crucial for tasks, such as machine translation and text generation.

Advantages of Multi-Head Attention

The use of multiple attention heads provides several key benefits to the Transformer architecture which contribute to its exceptional performance in various tasks:

- **Capturing Diverse Patterns:** With multiple heads attending to different parts of the sequence, the model can capture more nuanced relationships within the data. For example, in natural language processing, one head might focus on syntax (such as the relationship between subject and verb), while another might focus on semantics (such as the relationship between an entity and its description).
- **Enhancing Model Expressiveness:** Each attention head operates in its own subspace, allowing the model to learn different types of relationships at different levels of abstraction. This increases the model's ability to understand complex input sequences, and represent the data in a more expressive way.
- **Parallelism and Efficiency:** Multi-head attention is designed to be computed in parallel, making it highly efficient. While each head performs attention separately, all heads work simultaneously, ensuring that the model can scale efficiently and process large datasets at speed. This is particularly beneficial, when handling long sequences, where capturing dependencies across the entire sequence would be computationally expensive, without parallelization.
- **Dealing with Ambiguity:** In some cases, the same input can be interpreted in different ways depending on the context. Multi-head attention allows the model to handle such ambiguity by attending to different aspects of the input simultaneously, ensuring that the final output is more contextually appropriate.

Real-World Examples of Multi-Head Attention

Multi-head attention is particularly valuable in tasks that require understanding the relationships between different elements of a sequence. Some notable applications include:

- **Machine Translation:** In machine translation, the model must understand the relationships between words in both the source and target languages. Multi-head attention helps by allowing the model to focus on different aspects of the source sentence (such as word order, grammar, and meaning), while generating the target sentence. This leads to more accurate translations.
- **Question Answering:** In tasks like question-answering, multi-head attention enables the model to attend to both the question and the context simultaneously. One attention head might focus on keywords in the question, while another head looks for relevant information in the context, leading to better retrieval of answers.
- **Text Summarization:** When summarizing text, multi-head attention helps the model focus on different parts of the input document to extract the key ideas. This ensures that the summary captures the most important information from the original text, while preserving its meaning.
- **Speech Recognition:** In speech recognition tasks, multi-head attention allows the model to capture different patterns in the audio signal, such as pitch, tone, and rhythm, all at once. This leads to better transcription accuracy.

The Importance of Multi-Head Attention in Transformers

Multi-head attention is a critical innovation that enhances the power of the Transformer architecture. By allowing the model to attend to multiple parts of the sequence in parallel, Transformers are able to process and learn from large datasets more effectively than previous architectures. Each attention head captures unique information, ensuring that the model learns comprehensive and contextually rich representations of the input data.

Moreover, multi-head attention contributes significantly to the model's ability to scale. Whether the task involves processing natural language, images, or audio, the ability to leverage multiple attention heads in parallel enables the Transformer to handle complex tasks with remarkable efficiency and accuracy.

Multi-head attention is a fundamental component of the Transformer architecture, enabling parallel processing of information, and allowing the model to attend to different aspects of the input sequence simultaneously. This innovation has been a key factor in the success of Transformers, enabling them to excel in a wide range of tasks from natural language processing to computer vision. By capturing diverse patterns and relationships within the data, multi-head attention makes the Transformer both powerful and versatile, driving its widespread adoption across various domains in AI.

Feed-Forward Networks and Residual Connections

In addition to self-attention and multi-head attention, the Transformer architecture relies on another critical component to process and transform data: The feed-forward networks. These networks are used to apply additional transformations to the attention outputs, refining the representations learned by the model. To stabilize and enhance the learning process, residual connections are incorporated alongside layer normalization, ensuring that the model can be trained efficiently, without suffering from issues like vanishing gradients or unstable gradients. Together, feed-forward networks and residual connections play an essential role in enhancing the model's capacity to represent the complex data.

Feed-Forward Networks: Transforming Attention Outputs

After the attention mechanism, each token's representation is updated, based on the relationships captured through self-attention. However, this output is not yet fully transformed into a useful form for the task at hand. This is where the Feed-Forward Networks (FFNs) come into play.

In the Transformer, the feed-forward network is applied to each token independently and identically. It consists of two fully connected layers with a non-linearity (such as ReLU or GELU) applied between them. Despite being simple in structure, these feed-forward networks are powerful tools that enable the model to further refine and transform the information captured by the self-attention layers.

Mathematically, for each token's output from the attention layer, the feed-forward network is represented as:

$$FFN(x)=max(0,\ xW_1 + b_1)W_2 + b_2$$

Where:

- W_1 and W_2 are learned weight matrices.
- b_1 and b_2 are learned biases.
- The non-linearity (ReLU or GELU) is applied after the first linear transformation to introduce the non-linear capabilities that allow the model to capture complex patterns.

Each token's representation is processed through the same feed-forward network, but since the inputs vary, the outputs will be unique to each token. This step enhances the model's ability to capture complex patterns and interactions in the data, contributing to its overall performance on tasks, such as language modeling or machine translation.

Residual Connections: Enhancing Gradient Flow and Stability

Training deep neural networks often comes with a set of challenges, especially as networks become deeper and more complex. Two key issues are the vanishing gradient problem and gradient instability, where information is lost or distorted, as it propagates through many layers. This can make training slow and inefficient, or even cause the model to fail to converge.

To address these challenges, Transformers incorporate residual connections (also known as skip connections) that directly pass information from one layer to the next. These connections help preserve important information by allowing part of the input to "*skip*" over layers, and be added to the output of the feed-forward network. This simple yet effective mechanism helps to stabilize the learning process, making it easier for the model to learn and retain relevant information, even in very deep architectures.

The residual connection for a given token can be written as:

$$\text{Residual}(x) = x + \text{FFN}(x)$$

Here, the output of the feed-forward network is added to the original input x, ensuring that the model has access to both the raw input and the transformed output at each layer. This prevents the model from relying solely on the transformations, preserving the integrity of the input signal as it passes through the layers.

The Role of Layer Normalization

In addition to the residual connections, layer normalization is applied after the addition of the residual to the output of the feed-forward network. Layer normalization stabilizes training by ensuring that the outputs of each layer have a stable distribution, improving the flow of gradients through the network, and allowing the model to converge more quickly and effectively.

Layer normalization operates by normalizing the outputs of the network across the features for each individual token. Mathematically, it adjusts the mean and variance of the layer's outputs:

$$\text{LayerNorm}(x) = \frac{x - \mu}{\sigma + \epsilon}$$

Where:

- μ is the mean of the outputs.
- σ is the standard deviation of the outputs.
- ϵ is a small constant added for numerical stability.

By normalizing the outputs of each layer, the model avoids problems like exploding or vanishing gradients, making training more robust and efficient.

The Importance of Feed-Forward Networks and Residual Connections

The combination of feed-forward networks, residual connections, and layer normalization is essential to the success of the Transformer architecture. While attention mechanisms help the model capture relationships between tokens in a sequence, feed-forward networks allow the model to transform those relationships into richer, more abstract representations. These representations are critical for tasks such as translation, summarization, and question answering, where understanding complex dependencies between tokens is crucial.

At the same time, residual connections ensure that information is not lost as it passes through the network's many layers. This improves the flow of gradients during training, enabling the model to train more efficiently, and perform well even in very deep configurations. Without these residual connections, training would be much slower and more prone to failure, particularly in large models.

Feed-forward networks and residual connections are integral to the Transformer's ability to learn deep, abstract representations of input data. While self-attention mechanisms focus on capturing relationships between tokens, feed-forward networks refine and transform those relationships into more useful forms. Residual connections ensure that the model can train efficiently by maintaining the integrity of the information as it passes through the layers. Together with layer normalization, these components enable the Transformer to excel at a wide variety of tasks, making it one of the most powerful architectures in modern AI.

The Encoder-Decoder Architecture in Transformers

At the heart of the Transformer architecture is the encoder-decoder framework, a design that has revolutionized how models process sequential data in tasks like machine translation, text summarization, and question answering. This architecture allows the Transformer to map an input sequence (such as a sentence in one language) to an output sequence (such as the translated sentence in another language), ensuring that the model efficiently learns complex relationships between the input and output data. Unlike previous encoder-decoder models, based on Recurrent Neural Networks (RNNs), the Transformer's use of self-attention and parallel processing makes it faster and more effective, especially when dealing with long sequences.

The Encoder: Processing the Input Sequence

The encoder in the Transformer model is responsible for transforming the input sequence into a high-dimensional, abstract representation that the decoder can later use to generate the output. The encoder achieves this by applying a series of transformations to the input sequence, layer by layer, refining the representation at each stage. Unlike traditional RNNs, which process sequences in a strictly sequential manner, the Transformer's encoder processes the entire input sequence in parallel, leveraging the self-attention mechanism to capture both local and global dependencies.

The encoder is made up of multiple layers—typically six, but this number can vary depending on the model size and complexity. Each layer in the encoder consists of two main components: A multi-head self-attention mechanism and a feed-forward neural network. Together, these components enable the model to build progressively more abstract representations of the input data which are then passed to the decoder for output generation.

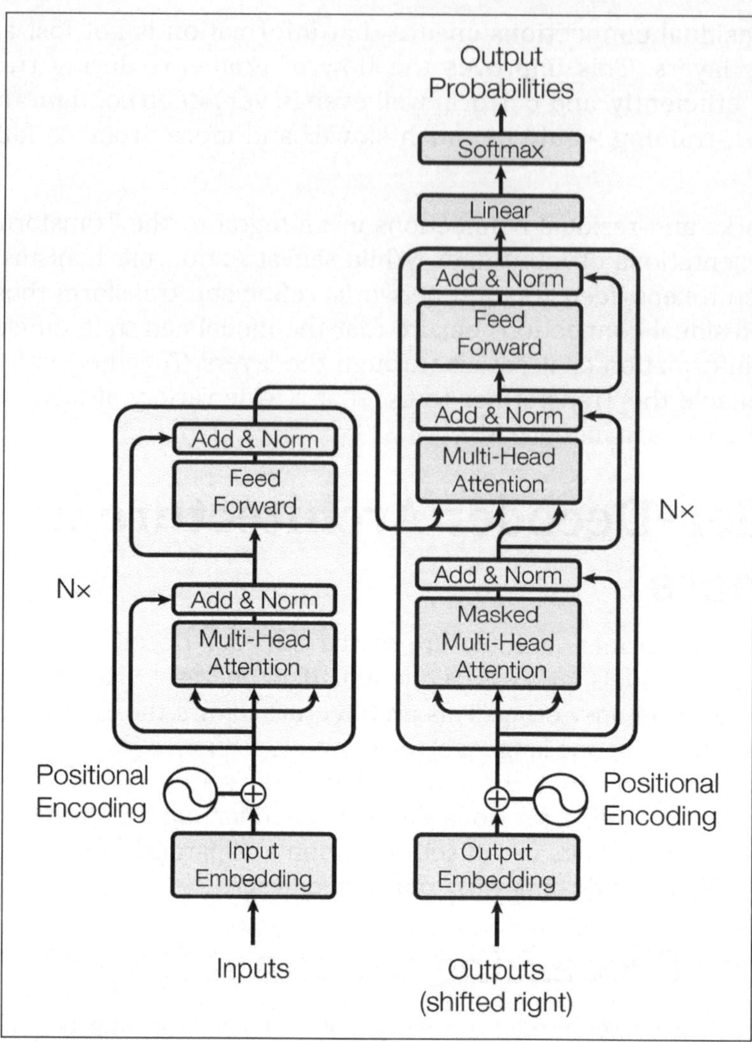

Figure 2.5: *Encoder-Decoder Architecture in Transformers*

Figure 2.5 illustrates the full encoder-decoder architecture of the Transformer model, with each component detailed as follows.

Step 1: Input Embedding and Positional Encoding

The first step in the encoding process is to convert the raw input sequence (usually tokens, such as words in a sentence) into a format the model can work with. This is done through embedding, where each token in the sequence is mapped to a high-dimensional vector. These vectors capture semantic information about the tokens, with similar tokens being represented by vectors that are close to each other in the embedding space. This allows the model to understand the relationships between tokens, based on their meaning or context.

However, since the Transformer does not inherently process sequences in order (unlike RNNs), it needs a way to inject positional information into these embeddings. This is achieved through positional encoding which adds information about each token's position in the sequence to its embedding. The positional encodings allow the model to distinguish between tokens, based on their positions, ensuring that the order of the sequence is preserved.

The combined result of the embedding and positional encoding is a set of vectors, each representing both the content and the position of a token in the input sequence. These vectors are then passed into the encoder's first layer for further processing.

Step 2: Self-Attention Mechanism

Once the input sequence has been embedded, and its positional information added, the next step is to apply the self-attention mechanism. The self-attention mechanism is one of the core innovations of the Transformer, allowing the model to look at each token in the sequence, and compute how much attention it should give to all other tokens.

In the encoder, self-attention helps capture the relationships between tokens, regardless of their distance from one another. For instance, in a sentence like "*The cat sat on the mat*," the self-attention mechanism might determine that the word, "*cat*" is most closely related to "*sat*," even though they are separated by other words. This allows the encoder to build a rich representation of each token, based on its context within the entire sequence.

The self-attention mechanism works by computing a set of query, key, and value vectors for each token in the sequence. The query vector for a token is compared to the key vectors of all other tokens to compute an attention score which determines how much attention the token should pay to each other token. The value vectors are then weighted by these attention scores, and the result is a new representation for each token that incorporates information from the entire sequence.

This self-attention process is applied in parallel across all tokens, allowing the encoder to efficiently capture dependencies across the entire input sequence in a single step. This contrasts with RNNs, which must process tokens sequentially, and can struggle to capture long-range dependencies due to the vanishing gradient problem.

Step 3: Multi-Head Attention

In the Transformer's encoder, the self-attention mechanism is enhanced by the use of multi-head attention. Instead of computing a single attention score for each token, the model uses multiple attention "*heads*" to focus on different aspects of the input simultaneously. Each head operates on a different subspace of the token embeddings, allowing the model to capture a broader range of relationships between tokens.

For example, in a sentence, one attention head might focus on syntactic relationships, such as subject-verb agreement, while another head might focus on semantic relationships, such as object-attribute pairings. By combining the outputs from multiple attention heads, the model can build a more comprehensive representation of the input sequence.

After the attention scores have been computed for each head, the outputs from all heads are concatenated and passed through a linear transformation to merge the different attention heads into a single, unified representation. This final output represents the attention-adjusted input sequence, and is passed on to the next stage in the encoder.

Step 4: Feed-Forward Networks

Once the multi-head attention mechanism has refined the token representations, the next step is to apply a Feed-Forward Neural Network (FFN) to each token independently. This FFN is the same for every token, but since the input to the network varies by token, the output will differ as well.

The feed-forward network consists of two fully connected layers with a non-linear activation function (typically ReLU or GELU), applied between them. This network allows the model to further transform the representations learned by the attention mechanism, making them more abstract and useful for the task at hand.

The purpose of the feed-forward network is to enhance the model's ability to capture complex patterns and interactions within the data. By applying this network to each token's representation, the model can fine-tune the information learned from the self-attention mechanism, preparing it for deeper processing in subsequent layers.

Step 5: Residual Connections and Layer Normalization

In order to stabilize training and ensure that information is not lost as it passes through the encoder's layers, the Transformer uses residual connections and layer normalization at each sub-layer. A residual connection allows the input to bypass the attention or feed-forward sub-layer, and be added directly to the output, ensuring that important information from earlier layers is preserved.

The residual connection can be expressed as:

```
Output = LayerNorm((x+ SubLayer((x))
```

Where x is the input to the sub-layer (either self-attention or feed-forward), and the output is the sum of the sub-layer output as well as the original input. This is then normalized using layer normalization which ensures that the model's outputs maintain stable statistics across layers.

These residual connections are essential for training deep models like the Transformer. They prevent the network from overfitting to the transformations applied in each sub-layer, and help maintain a strong gradient flow during backpropagation, making it easier to train deep models, without suffering from vanishing or exploding gradients.

Step 6: Stacking Encoder Layers

The encoder consists of multiple layers stacked on top of each other, with each layer following the same structure: multi-head self-attention, feed-forward networks, residual connections, and layer normalization. Each layer progressively refines the token representations, allowing the model to build deeper and more abstract representations of the input sequence.

As the input sequence passes through the encoder's layers, the model learns increasingly complex patterns and relationships, enabling it to understand the input data at a highly abstract level. The output of the final encoder layer is a set of high-dimensional vectors that represent the input sequence, ready to be passed to the decoder for output generation.

The Decoder: Generating the Output Sequence

The decoder is responsible for transforming the encoded representation from the encoder into the final output sequence, such as a translated sentence or a text summary. Like the encoder, the decoder consists of multiple identical layers, typically six, but with an additional mechanism: masked self-attention. This ensures that the model predicts tokens one at a time, without "*cheating*" by looking at future tokens during training. The decoder is crucial for tasks that involve sequence generation, as it learns to generate the output in an autoregressive manner, predicting one token at a time based on both the input sequence and the tokens generated so far.

Step 1: Input Embedding and Positional Encoding

Just like the encoder, the decoder begins by embedding the tokens from the output sequence (or, during training, the expected output sequence) into continuous vector representations. These embeddings are learned during training, and map each output token to a dense vector that contains semantic information about the token.

Since the decoder also processes sequences in parallel, and does not have a built-in understanding of token order, positional encodings are added to the token embeddings. This allows the decoder to distinguish between different positions in the sequence, enabling it to understand both the content and order of the tokens. These positional encodings are combined with the token embeddings, and passed into the first decoder layer.

Step 2: Masked Self-Attention

One of the key differences between the encoder and decoder is the use of masked self-attention in the decoder. The purpose of masked self-attention is to ensure that the model only attends to the tokens that have already been generated, or the current token being predicted. This is essential for autoregressive tasks, where the model should not have access to future tokens, while predicting the current one.

During masked self-attention, the tokens in the output sequence attend to each other, but with a mask applied to prevent future tokens from being considered. This masking ensures that at each time step, the decoder only looks at the tokens up to the current position. For example, when predicting the second token, the model can only attend to the first token, and not the third or any later tokens.

The self-attention mechanism operates in a similar way to the encoder, using query, key, and value vectors to compute attention scores. However, the masking ensures that attention is only computed for tokens that come before, or at the current position. This masked self-attention allows the model to learn dependencies between the previously generated tokens and the current token, ensuring that the output sequence is generated in a coherent and contextually appropriate way.

Step 3: Encoder-Decoder Attention

After applying masked self-attention to the output tokens, the decoder incorporates information from the encoder's output through the encoder-decoder attention mechanism. This attention layer allows each token in the decoder's sequence to attend to the entire sequence of encoded representations produced by the encoder.

Here is how it works:

- The query vectors come from the decoder's output sequence, representing the tokens generated so far.
- The key and value vectors come from the encoder's output, representing the encoded representations of the input sequence.

The encoder-decoder attention mechanism computes the attention scores between the decoder tokens and the encoder tokens, allowing the decoder to focus on the relevant parts of the input sequence, while generating the output. This is particularly useful in tasks like machine translation, where the decoder must translate one language into another by attending to the original sentence, and generating a grammatically correct as well as semantically equivalent output.

By attending to the encoder's output, the decoder can align its output tokens with the relevant input tokens, ensuring that the generated sequence is consistent with the input sequence.

Step 4: Feed-Forward Networks

Once the decoder has applied both masked self-attention and encoder-decoder attention, the next step is to further transform the output using a Feed-forward Neural Network (FFN). Like in the encoder, the feed-forward network in the decoder consists of two fully connected layers with a non-linear activation function (such as ReLU or GELU) in between.

The feed-forward network is applied independently to each token's representation, refining and transforming the information learned from the attention layers. This additional layer of processing helps the model better capture complex patterns and relationships within the data, improving the quality of the generated output.

Step 5: Residual Connections and Layer Normalization

To stabilize the training process and ensure efficient gradient flow, the decoder also incorporates residual connections and layer normalization, similar to the encoder. At each sub-layer (both the attention and feed-forward layers), a residual connection is added, which allows the input to bypass the sub-layer, and be added directly to its output. This helps prevent information loss, and stabilizes the training of deep models.

The residual connection can be expressed as:

```
Output = LayerNorm((x + SubLayer((x))
```

Where x is the input to the sub-layer, and the output is the sum of the sub-layer's result and the original input. This is followed by layer normalization, which ensures that the outputs have a stable distribution, improving the overall learning process.

These residual connections are crucial for training very deep models like Transformers, as they help mitigate issues like vanishing or exploding gradients, which can occur when information is passed through many layers.

Step 6: Stacking Decoder Layers

The decoder consists of multiple layers stacked on top of each other, typically six or more. Each layer consists of the masked self-attention, encoder-decoder attention, and feed-forward sub-layers, along with residual connections and layer normalization. As the data passes through each layer, the representations of the tokens become progressively more refined, allowing the model to generate more accurate and coherent outputs.

Each layer builds upon the previous one, with each step contributing to a more sophisticated understanding of the relationships between tokens in both the input and output sequences. By the time the data reaches the final decoder layer, the model has learned the necessary patterns and dependencies to generate the desired output sequence.

Step 7: Final Linear and Softmax Layer

Once the data has passed through all the decoder layers, the final step is to generate the actual output tokens. This is done through a linear transformation followed by a softmax layer.

- **Linear Layer:** The output representations from the final decoder layer are first passed through a linear layer that projects them into a higher-dimensional space, corresponding to the vocabulary size of the output tokens. Each token's representation is mapped to a logit vector, with each dimension representing a possible output token.
- **Softmax Layer:** The logits are then passed through a softmax function which converts them into a probability distribution. The softmax function outputs a probability for each token in the vocabulary, representing the likelihood of that token being the next token in the sequence. The token with the highest probability is selected as the next output.

This process is repeated in an autoregressive manner: After generating one token, the decoder takes that token as input to generate the next one, continuing until the entire output sequence is produced.

The decoder is a key component of the Transformer architecture, responsible for generating the output sequence one token at a time, based on both the input sequence and the previously generated tokens. Through masked self-attention, encoder-decoder attention, and feed-forward networks, the decoder learns to generate coherent, contextually appropriate sequences. The residual connections and layer normalization ensure that training is stable and efficient, even with deep models.

Understanding the decoder's role is essential for grasping how the Transformer excels at sequence-to-sequence tasks like translation, text generation, and summarization.

Key Features of the Encoder-Decoder Architecture

The encoder-decoder structure is highly effective for sequence-to-sequence tasks, where the goal is to generate an output sequence, based on a given input sequence. Some key features of this architecture include:

- **Parallel Processing:** Unlike RNN-based encoder-decoder models, which process input and output sequences sequentially, the Transformer's self-attention mechanism allows both the encoder and decoder to process tokens in parallel. This significantly reduces the training time, and enables the model to scale to larger datasets and longer sequences.
- **Global Context:** In both the encoder and the decoder, self-attention ensures that each token has access to the entire sequence, allowing the model to capture long-range dependencies and global context. This is particularly important for tasks like machine translation, where understanding the context of a word within a sentence is critical for generating accurate translations.
- **Masked Self-Attention in the Decoder:** The masked self-attention mechanism in the decoder ensures that the model can generate sequences in an autoregressive fashion, predicting one token at a time, while considering only the previously generated tokens. This allows the model to be used in tasks like text generation and machine translation, where the order of the output sequence matters.

Applications of the Encoder-Decoder Architecture

The encoder-decoder architecture is widely used in a variety of tasks that involve mapping an input sequence to an output sequence. Some notable applications include:

- **Machine Translation:** In machine translation, the input sequence is a sentence in one language, and the output sequence is the translated sentence in another language. The encoder processes the input sentence, capturing its meaning and structure, while the decoder generates the translation by attending to both the input, and the already generated output.
- **Text Summarization:** In text summarization, the model takes a long document as input, and generates a shorter summary as output. The encoder captures the key information in the input text, while the decoder generates a concise version of the original text.
- **Question Answering:** In question-answering tasks, the model is given a context (such as a paragraph) and a question, and it must generate the correct answer. The encoder processes the context, and the decoder generates the answer by attending to both the question and the context.
- **Text Generation:** In tasks, such as text generation or dialogue generation, the encoder-decoder model can generate coherent and contextually relevant sequences, based on a given prompt or context.

The encoder-decoder architecture is a fundamental component of the Transformer model, enabling it to excel at sequence-to-sequence tasks by efficiently mapping input sequences to output sequences. The encoder processes the input sequence in parallel, capturing global relationships between tokens, while the decoder generates the output sequence, one token at a time, attending to both the input and the already generated tokens. This architecture has proven highly effective in a wide range of tasks, from machine translation to text summarization, and remains a core feature of modern AI systems. Understanding the inner workings of the encoder-decoder framework is essential for mastering the full capabilities of Transformer models.

Limitations of Basic Transformers

While transformer models have revolutionized Natural language processing (NLP) and other AI domains, they come with certain limitations, particularly in the areas of long-range dependency modeling, computational efficiency, and memory consumption. These limitations are particularly relevant when dealing with long sequences of data, which is a common requirement in many real-world applications like document summarization, long-form question answering, and machine translation. To address these, several variations of the basic transformer architecture have emerged, such as Transformer-XL. Below, we explore both the general limitations of basic transformers and the improvements offered by Transformer-XL.

- **Quadratic Time and Memory Complexity**: The self-attention mechanism at the heart of transformers operates with $O(n^2)$ time and memory complexity, where n is the length of the input sequence. This means that for long input sequences, the model becomes computationally expensive and memory-intensive. The quadratic growth of computation and memory makes basic transformers impractical for processing very long sequences, as the time and memory costs increase exponentially.

  For example, processing a sequence of 1,000 tokens would require approximately 1 million operations, and for a sequence of 10,000 tokens, the operations rise to nearly 100 million. This makes transformers unsuitable for tasks like document-level NLP, where long-range dependencies between tokens are critical, as the model's resources may be overwhelmed by the length of the input.

- **Fixed-Length Contextualization**: Standard transformers process the entire sequence in parallel, but they are limited by the input length (defined during training). This limitation hinders the model's ability to capture long-term dependencies across extended sequences. While transformers can model relationships between words at a local level, they struggle when it comes to context that spans across very long documents or complex sequences where the relevant information is spread across distant parts of the input.

- **Lack of Recurrence**: Although transformers excel at parallelizing computations, they inherently lack the recurrent nature of models like LSTMs and GRUs, which are designed to handle sequences in a step-by-step fashion. The absence of recurrence limits the transformer's ability to handle tasks that involve sequential state transitions and memory retention over time, especially when the sequence exceeds the model's capacity.

Transformer-XL: Addressing Long-Range Dependencies

Transformer-XL (Transformer with extra-long context) was introduced as a solution to address the limitations of basic transformers when handling long-range dependencies. Transformer-XL builds upon the standard transformer architecture and introduces two main improvements: recurrence and relative positioning of tokens.

- **Recurrence and Memory Mechanism**: Unlike basic transformers, Transformer-XL introduces a recurrence mechanism, which allows the model to reuse hidden states from previous segments during the processing of new segments. This technique allows Transformer-XL to capture long-range dependencies without the need to process the entire sequence in one pass, as basic transformers do. This enables the model to handle longer sequences, while maintaining computational efficiency.

  By using a memory mechanism that caches and reuses representations from previous contexts, Transformer-XL avoids the quadratic complexity issue to some extent. This memory system ensures that each segment of the sequence can attend to information beyond its immediate range, helping the model build a longer context window.

- **Relative Position Encoding**: Another major improvement in Transformer-XL is the relative position encoding. In traditional transformers, absolute position encoding is used, which means that each token's position is fixed relative to other tokens in the sequence. This approach does not adapt well to very long sequences, where relationships between distant tokens need to be preserved. Transformer-XL uses relative position embeddings, which allow the model to handle dynamic sequence lengths and attend to tokens with relative distances, making it more flexible in capturing long-range dependencies.
- **Performance Improvement**: Transformer-XL shows significant improvements over basic transformers, especially in language modeling tasks and scenarios that require the handling of longer sequences. It has been shown to outperform traditional transformers in tasks, such as text generation and language modeling on long text corpora, and it helps models scale to much longer sequences, while maintaining manageable computational costs.

Conclusion

In this chapter, we explored the foundational components that make the Transformer architecture so powerful and revolutionary. We began with the self-attention mechanism, which enables the model to capture relationships across entire sequences in parallel, and examined the role of positional encoding in preserving sequence order. We then delved into the multi-head attention mechanism, which enhances the model's ability to capture diverse patterns in the data, followed by the feed-forward networks and residual connections that stabilize learning and refine representations. Finally, we examined the encoder-decoder architecture, which enables efficient sequence-to-sequence processing. Together, these elements form the backbone of the Transformer, setting the stage for its remarkable success in modern AI tasks.

In the next chapter, we will shift our focus to applying Transformer models in real-world tasks, using PyTorch 2.0. We will then dive into practical implementations, exploring how to build and train Transformer-based models from scratch. You will learn how to leverage PyTorch's dynamic computation capabilities to fine-tune pre-trained models, handle large datasets, and optimize training for efficiency. This chapter will equip you with the hands-on skills needed to bring the theoretical concepts of Transformer architecture to life in a variety of AI applications, from natural language processing to machine translation.

Chapter 3
Getting Started with PyTorch 2.0

Introduction

In this chapter, we shift our focus to the practical side of deep learning by introducing PyTorch 2.0, a highly flexible and powerful framework that has become a cornerstone for modern AI development. PyTorch is widely adopted by researchers and developers alike due to its dynamic computational graph, intuitive design, and extensive support for GPU acceleration. This chapter will provide you with the foundational skills needed to work with PyTorch 2.0, from setting up your environment to building and training simple neural networks. By the end, you will be well-equipped to start implementing the advanced transformer architectures covered in the subsequent chapters.

Structure

In this chapter, the following topics will be covered:

- Introduction to PyTorch 2.0 and Its Advantages
- Setting Up the PyTorch 2.0 Environment
- Understanding Tensors and Basic Operations
- Working with PyTorch's Autograd for Automatic Differentiation
- PyTorch Modules and Model Creation
- Building and Training Simple Neural Networks
- Data Loading and Preprocessing with PyTorch
- PyTorch 2.0's Improved Performance Features (for example, TorchScript, lazy tensor, and so on)
- GPU Acceleration and Distributed Training in PyTorch 2.0
- Debugging and Profiling PyTorch Models
- Best Practices for Efficient PyTorch 2.0 Development

Introduction to PyTorch 2.0 and Its Advantages

PyTorch 2.0 represents a major advancement in the PyTorch ecosystem, designed to meet the growing needs of researchers and developers, alike for building and deploying cutting-edge AI models. While previous versions of PyTorch were widely celebrated for their flexibility, intuitive design, and ease of use, PyTorch 2.0 builds on these foundations with significant performance enhancements and new features aimed at optimizing the deep learning development process, from prototyping to production.

One of the core strengths of PyTorch is its dynamic computational graph. Unlike static graph frameworks (such as early versions of TensorFlow), PyTorch constructs its computational graph in real-time, as operations are executed. This dynamic graph allows for greater flexibility, making PyTorch especially popular in research settings where experimentation and iterative development are essential. It simplifies the process of debugging and modifying models, as any changes to the model architecture are immediately reflected in the computational graph. This flexibility not only reduces development time, but also makes the code easier to understand and maintain, leading to a faster, more interactive development experience.

In addition to the dynamic graph, PyTorch 2.0 introduces a range of performance improvements to address the demands of deploying large-scale models. Key among these improvements is **TorchScript**, a feature that bridges the gap between research and production by allowing models to be optimized for deployment, without requiring significant code rewrites. TorchScript allows you to "*script*" or "*trace*" your model, converting it into a static computational graph that can be highly optimized for inference. This feature enables developers to deploy PyTorch models in production environments with higher efficiency, ensuring that models perform consistently across different platforms.

Another innovative feature in PyTorch 2.0 is **lazy tensors**. Lazy tensors delay the evaluation of certain tensor operations until absolutely necessary, allowing the framework to optimize these operations collectively, rather than individually. This results in reduced memory usage and increased computational efficiency, particularly when working with complex models or large datasets. Lazy tensors are especially useful in research contexts, where memory efficiency can enable the use of larger, more sophisticated models, without hitting hardware limitations.

PyTorch 2.0 also brings robust support for GPU acceleration and distributed training. One of PyTorch's longstanding strengths has been its seamless integration with GPUs, allowing users to accelerate computations by easily moving tensors and models between CPUs and GPUs. With PyTorch 2.0, this integration is further optimized, enabling even faster and more efficient computations. Additionally, PyTorch's support for distributed training allows developers to scale their models across multiple GPUs or even multiple machines, making it ideal for training large-scale transformer models or working with extensive datasets. This support for distributed training ensures that developers can harness the full power of their hardware, significantly reducing training time and improving model performance.

In summary, **PyTorch 2.0** combines the flexibility needed for rapid research iterations with the robustness and efficiency required for deployment. Its dynamic graph, enhanced GPU support, and new features like **TorchScript and lazy tensors** make it an ideal choice for developing, optimizing, and scaling deep learning models. Whether you are prototyping a new architecture, or deploying a model at scale, PyTorch 2.0 provides the tools you need to create and manage high-performance AI applications.

Setting Up the PyTorch 2.0 Environment

To begin building and deploying models with PyTorch 2.0, it is essential to set up the environment correctly. The installation process for PyTorch 2.0 is streamlined, with support for multiple platforms, including Mac, Windows, and Linux. This section guides you through setting up PyTorch 2.0 on each platform, covering the installation of necessary dependencies, and testing the environment to ensure PyTorch is installed correctly. You will also have the option to install GPU support which allows PyTorch to leverage CUDA-capable GPUs for accelerated computations.

CUDA (Compute Unified Device Architecture) is a parallel computing platform and Application Programming Interface (API) developed by NVIDIA. It enables software applications, such as PyTorch, to leverage the powerful computational capabilities of NVIDIA GPUs (Graphics Processing Units) for high-performance tasks. CUDA provides developers with access to the GPU's massive parallel processing power, making it ideal for handling the large, complex computations required in deep learning.

In deep learning and other AI applications, models involve millions (or even billions) of parameters, and require processing vast amounts of data. Processing these computations solely on a CPU can be slow, as CPUs are optimized for sequential processing, rather than parallel processing. **GPUs, however, are designed to handle multiple operations simultaneously, making them well-suited for deep learning tasks.**

By using CUDA with PyTorch, you can offload intensive computations from the CPU to the GPU, drastically speeding up model training and inference. CUDA-enabled GPUs allow PyTorch to execute tensor operations and neural network computations more efficiently which is especially important, when working with large datasets or complex models, such as transformers.

In summary, CUDA accelerates deep learning workflows by leveraging GPU power, reducing the time needed for training, and enabling faster experimentation and deployment.

Prerequisites

Before installing PyTorch 2.0, make sure you have Python installed on your system. PyTorch 2.0 is compatible with Python versions 3.8 and higher, so if you are using an older version of Python, it is recommended to upgrade.

To check your Python version, open a terminal (or Command Prompt on Windows) and enter:

```
python -version
```

If you need to install Python, download it from the official [Python website] (https://www.python.org/downloads/), and follow the installation instructions.

Installing PyTorch 2.0 on Mac

For Mac users, the installation of PyTorch 2.0 is straightforward with the use of pip, Python's package manager, or conda, the package manager for the Anaconda distribution. PyTorch also provides support for M1 and M2 Macs through Apple's Metal Performance Shaders (MPS), enabling GPU acceleration on Apple Silicon devices.

Option 1: Installing with pip

a. Open your terminal.

b. Run the following command to install PyTorch 2.0 (with CPU support):

```
pip install torch torchvision torchaudio
```

c. For M1 or M2 Macs, to enable GPU acceleration with MPS, add the `torch.mps` backend by installing the latest version:

```
pip install torch torchvision torchaudio --extra-index-url https://download.pytorch.org/whl/cpu
```

d. Once installed, verify the installation by running:

```
python -c "import torch; print(torch.__version__); print(torch.backends.mps.is_available())"
```

You should see output similar to this:

```
2.7.1+cpu
True
```

Here is what the output means:

1. **`torch.version`**: This will print the version of PyTorch installed. In this example, **`2.7.1+cpu`** indicates the installed PyTorch version is 2.7.1, and the `+cpu` suffix indicates it is the CPU version of PyTorch. If you are using a GPU-enabled version, you might see something like **`+cu111`**, indicating the CUDA version supported.
2. **`torch.backends.mps.is_available()`**: This checks whether PyTorch's Metal Performance Shaders (MPS) backend is available. If you see **True**, it means PyTorch is ready to run on Apple Silicon (M1/M2) devices with MPS support. If **False**, it means MPS support is unavailable, and PyTorch will default to the CPU for execution.

This command confirms that PyTorch has been installed successfully, and is ready for use, with the correct version and device backend support.

Option 2: Installing with conda

a. Open your terminal.

b. Run the following command to install PyTorch 2.0 with CPU support:

```
conda install pytorch torchvision torchaudio -c pytorch
```

c. Verify the installation as shown above.

Installing PyTorch 2.0 on Windows

On Windows, PyTorch 2.0 can be installed with pip or conda, with an option to enable CUDA support for systems with NVIDIA GPUs.

Option 1: Installing with `pip` (CPU only)

a. Open Command Prompt or PowerShell.

b. Run the following command to install PyTorch 2.0:

```
pip install torch torchvision torchaudio
```

c. Verify the installation by running:

```
```python
   python -c "import torch; print(torch.__version__)"
   ```
```

Option 2: Installing with `pip` (with GPU/CUDA support)

a. Ensure that you have CUDA Toolkit installed. The recommended version for PyTorch 2.0 is CUDA 11.7 or later.

b. Run the following command to install PyTorch with CUDA support:

```
```bash
   pip install torch torchvision torchaudio --extra-index-url
 https://download.pytorch.org/whl/cu117
   ```
```

c. Verify CUDA support by running:

```
```python
   python -c "import torch; print(torch.cuda.is_available())"
   ```
```

Option 3: Installing with conda

a. Open Command Prompt or PowerShell.

b. Run the following command to install PyTorch with CPU support:

```
```bash
conda install pytorch torchvision torchaudio -c pytorch
```
```

c. For CUDA support, specify the CUDA version:

```
```bash
conda install pytorch torchvision torchaudio cudatoolkit=11.7 -c pytorch
```
```

Installing PyTorch 2.0 on Linux

For Linux users, PyTorch installation is flexible, and supports both CPU and GPU setups. You can install it, using either pip or conda.

Option 1: Installing with pip (CPU only)

a. Open your terminal.

b. Run the following command to install PyTorch 2.0:

```
```bash
pip install torch torchvision torchaudio
```
```

c. Verify the installation with:

```
```python
python -c "import torch; print(torch.__version__)"
```
```

Option 2: Installing with pip (with GPU/CUDA support)

a. Make sure your system has CUDA Toolkit installed, preferably version 11.7 or later.

b. Run the following command to install PyTorch with CUDA support:

```
```bash
pip install torch torchvision torchaudio --extra-index-url https://down-
load.pytorch.org/whl/cu117
```
```

c. Check if CUDA is available by running:

```
```python
python -c "import torch; print(torch.cuda.is_available())"
```
```

Option 3: Installing with conda

a. Open your terminal.

b. For CPU-only installation, run:

```
```bash
conda install pytorch torchvision torchaudio -c pytorch
```
```

c. For CUDA support, specify the CUDA version as follows:

~~~
```bash
conda install pytorch torchvision torchaudio cudatoolkit=11.7 -c pytorch
```
~~~

Option 4: Verifying the Installation

After completing the installation, you should verify that PyTorch 2.0 is working correctly on your system.

a. Open Python from your terminal or command prompt:

~~~
```bash
python
```
~~~

b. Run the following commands to check the PyTorch version and, if installed, CUDA or MPS support:

~~~
```python
import torch
print("PyTorch version:", torch.__version__)
print("CUDA available:", torch.cuda.is_available())
print("MPS available:", torch.backends.mps.is_available())  # For Apple M1/M2 Macs
```
~~~

c. If CUDA or MPS is available, you should see `True` in the output. This confirms that PyTorch is installed and configured correctly for GPU acceleration.

With PyTorch 2.0 successfully installed, you are now ready to dive into hands-on deep learning. Setting up a robust environment ensures that you can leverage PyTorch's powerful features, including GPU acceleration and support for advanced frameworks like CUDA, to build and train models efficiently. In the next section, we will begin exploring PyTorch's core components, starting with tensors and basic operations, to lay the groundwork for implementing deep learning models.

Understanding Tensors and Basic Operations

At the core of PyTorch and most deep learning frameworks is the tensor, a multi-dimensional array that serves as the fundamental data structure for handling data in deep learning. Tensors are similar to NumPy arrays, but with added capabilities that allow them to run on GPUs, enabling accelerated computation. Understanding how tensors work and how to perform basic operations on them, is necessary for building and training neural networks in PyTorch.

What is a Tensor?

A tensor can be thought of as a generalization of vectors and matrices to more dimensions:

- **Scalar:** A single number (0-dimensional tensor).
- **Vector:** A one-dimensional tensor, like an array of numbers.
- **Matrix:** A two-dimensional tensor, essentially a table of numbers, with rows and columns.
- **Higher-Dimensional Tensors:** Tensors can have three or more dimensions, often used for complex data like images, videos, or batched data for neural networks.

For example, an image can be represented as a three-dimensional tensor with dimensions corresponding to height, width, and color channels (for instance, RGB channels in color images). In PyTorch, tensors allow you to efficiently store and manipulate this type of data, whether for processing images, handling sequential data, or building neural networks.

Creating Tensors

PyTorch provides multiple ways to create tensors, either with specific values or filled with random numbers, zeros, or ones. Here are some commonly used methods for creating tensors:

1. **Creating a tensor with specific values:**

   ```python
   import torch
   tensor = torch.tensor([[1, 2], [3, 4]])
   ```

   This creates a 2x2 tensor with the specified values.

2. **Creating a tensor with random values:**

   ```python
   random_tensor = torch.rand(3, 3)  # 3x3 tensor with random values between 0 and 1
   ```

3. **Creating a tensor of zeros or ones:**

   ```python
   zeros_tensor = torch.zeros(2, 2)  # 2x2 tensor filled with zeros
   ones_tensor = torch.ones(4, 4)      # 4x4 tensor filled with ones
   ```

4. **Creating a tensor with specific dimensions:**

   ```python
   shape = (2, 3)
   tensor = torch.empty(shape)  # Creates an empty 2x3 tensor (uninitialized)
   ```

These methods allow you to initialize tensors with desired shapes and values, forming the building blocks for data processing and model training.

Basic Tensor Operations

Once you have created tensors, you will want to perform operations on them. PyTorch supports a wide range of tensor operations, from element-wise arithmetic to matrix multiplications, and reshaping. Some of the most common tensor operations include:

Arithmetic Operations

- **Addition:**

  ```python
  x = torch.tensor([1, 2])
  y = torch.tensor([3, 4])
  result = x + y  # Output: tensor([4, 6])
  ```

- **Subtraction, Multiplication, Division:**

  ```python
  result = x - y  # Output: tensor([-2, -2])
  result = x * y  # Output: tensor([3, 8])
  result = x / y  # Output: tensor([0.3333, 0.5])
  ```

Matrix Multiplication

Matrix multiplication is a key operation in deep learning, used to compute weighted sums in neural networks. PyTorch provides `torch.matmul` or the `@` operator for matrix multiplication:

```python
a = torch.tensor([[1, 2], [3, 4]])
b = torch.tensor([[5, 6], [7, 8]])
result = torch.matmul(a, b)  # Matrix multiplication
```

Reshaping Tensors

You can reshape tensors with the `view` or `reshape` method which is useful for adjusting the shape of data to fit model requirements:

```python
tensor = torch.rand(2, 4)  # 2x4 tensor
reshaped_tensor = tensor.view(4, 2)  # Reshaped to 4x2
```

Concatenation and Stacking

Tensors can be combined using `torch.cat` and `torch.stack`. Concatenation joins tensors, along a specified dimension, while stacking adds an additional dimension:

```python
x = torch.tensor([[1, 2], [3, 4]])
y = torch.tensor([[5, 6], [7, 8]])
concatenated = torch.cat((x, y), dim=0)  # Concatenate along rows
stacked = torch.stack((x, y), dim=0)    # Stack along a new dimension
```

Moving Tensors to GPUs

One of PyTorch's strengths is its support for GPU acceleration. To enable this, you can move tensors to a CUDA-enabled GPU, if one is available. This is done using the `.to()` method or `.cuda()` method:

```python
tensor = torch.rand(3, 3)
if torch.cuda.is_available():
    tensor = tensor.to('cuda')  # Move tensor to GPU
```

With this simple command, all tensor operations are now performed on the GPU, significantly speeding up computations for large models.

Working with Tensors in Practice

Understanding how to create and manipulate tensors is essential for deep learning, as tensors are the data structures that flow through neural networks. Practicing basic operations on tensors will help you build a strong foundation for constructing more complex models. In subsequent sections, we will use these operations as the basis for building neural networks, performing gradient computations, and optimizing models.

Tensors are the fundamental data structure in PyTorch, representing everything from individual data points to complex multidimensional data like images or sequences. Mastering basic tensor operations allows you to handle and transform data efficiently, setting the stage for model building and training. With a solid understanding of tensors, you are now prepared to explore more advanced topics, such as PyTorch's automatic differentiation and autograd system, in the next section.

Working with PyTorch's Autograd for Automatic Differentiation

One of the most powerful features of PyTorch is its autograd library which provides automatic differentiation for all tensor operations. Automatic differentiation is vital for deep learning because it allows the model to compute gradients—mathematical tools that help optimize model parameters through backpropagation. With autograd, PyTorch can automatically compute these gradients, eliminating the need for manually deriving and coding gradient calculations, making model training faster, simpler, and more accurate.

Automatic Differentiation

Automatic differentiation is a technique for computing the derivatives of functions efficiently and accurately. In deep learning, derivatives (or gradients) indicate how much a small change in each model parameter will affect the model's output. These gradients are critical for optimizing the model's parameters during training, allowing the model to improve its performance by adjusting weights, based on gradient values. PyTorch's autograd system automates this process, tracking all operations on tensors with the `requires_grad` attribute which enables gradient calculation.

When `requires_grad=True` is set on a tensor, PyTorch starts tracking all operations on that tensor, constructing a dynamic computation graph. This graph allows PyTorch to backpropagate through the sequence of operations and compute gradients efficiently. This is particularly useful for building neural networks, where gradients are needed to update model weights.

Creating Tensors with Gradient Tracking

By default, PyTorch tensors are created, without gradient tracking. To enable it, you simply set `requires_grad=True`, when creating a tensor. An example is provided in the code listing on GitHub repo.

Performing Operations and Calculating Gradients

Once you have tensors with `requires_grad=True`, you can perform various operations on them. After the operations, you can calculate the gradients using backpropagation with the `.backward()` function. Backpropagation is the process of computing gradients for each parameter in a computational graph by propagating the loss backward through the network. This is crucial because it enables efficient optimization of model parameters by calculating how much each parameter contributes to the error (loss). By using these gradients, optimization algorithms like Stochastic Gradient Descent (SGD) can iteratively adjust the parameters to minimize the loss, improving the model's accuracy and performance on tasks, such as classification, regression, or prediction. This process makes deep learning models trainable and scalable.

Here is an example that demonstrates how it works:

```
```python
# Define a simple computation
y = x  2 + 3 * x + 1  # y = [x1^2 + 3*x1 + 1, x2^2 + 3*x2 + 1]

# Perform backpropagation to calculate the gradient
```
```

```
y.backward(torch.tensor([1.0, 1.0]))

# Print the gradients
print(x.grad)  # Output: tensor([7., 9.])
```

In this example:

a. We define a simple computation where `y` is derived from `x` through a series of operations.

b. Calling `y.backward()` triggers backpropagation which computes the gradient of `y` with respect to `x`.

c. The `grad` attribute of `x` stores the calculated gradient, showing how `y` changes, with respect to each element in `x`.

Understanding the Computation Graph

When `requires_grad=True` is set, PyTorch constructs a computation graph that records every operation on that tensor. Each operation forms a node in the graph, and the resulting graph is a dynamic, differentiable representation of the computation.

This graph is particularly valuable during training because it allows PyTorch to track the dependencies between tensors. When `.backward()` is called, PyTorch traverses the graph in reverse to calculate gradients, which are then used to update model parameters.

One important feature of PyTorch's computation graph is that it is dynamic—the graph is built on-the-fly as operations are performed. This flexibility allows for easy debugging and experimentation, as any changes in code are immediately reflected in the computation graph.

Disabling Gradient Tracking for Inference

While gradient tracking is essential for training, it is unnecessary for tasks like inference (that is making predictions with a trained model), as no parameter updates are involved. PyTorch provides ways to disable gradient tracking to optimize memory usage and computation speed during inference:

1. **Using `torch.no_grad()`**: This context manager temporarily disables gradient tracking within its block:

   ```python
   with torch.no_grad():
       y = x  2 + 3 * x + 1  # No gradients will be tracked
   ```

   This is useful, when you want to perform computations, without creating a computation graph.

2. **Using `detach()`**: This method creates a new tensor that is detached from the computation graph:

   ```python
   x_detached = x.detach()
   ```

These methods are particularly valuable for reducing memory consumption and speeding up computations, when gradients are not needed. An example is provided in the code listing on GitHub repo.

Best Practices with Autograd

1. **Minimize Computation in `backward()`:** Only call `.backward()` when you need gradients, as this operation is memory-intensive.
2. **Use `torch.no_grad()` in Inference:** Disable gradient tracking for inference or evaluation to optimize memory and computation.
3. **Clear Gradients between Steps:** Gradients accumulate in PyTorch by default, so always clear previous gradients with `optimizer.zero_grad()` or `weights.grad.zero_()` during training.

PyTorch's autograd library simplifies the process of calculating gradients, allowing for efficient model optimization, without the need for manual differentiation. By leveraging autograd, you can build and train complex neural networks, while PyTorch handles the details of backpropagation and gradient calculation. Mastering autograd is crucial for effective model training, and with a solid understanding of gradient tracking and computation graphs, you are now prepared to build and optimize neural networks in PyTorch.

PyTorch Modules and Model Creation

In PyTorch, creating and organizing neural networks is facilitated through modules in the `torch.nn.Module` class. This modular design allows you to build complex networks by combining different layers and components, whether they are simple linear layers, convolutional layers, or custom-built modules. Understanding how to create and structure models using PyTorch's module-based approach is fundamental for building efficient and scalable architectures.

Creating a Custom Module

A neural network in PyTorch is defined by creating a class that inherits from `torch.nn.Module`. Inside this class, you define:

1. Layers in the `__init__` method.
2. The forward pass in the `forward` method, specifying how the data flows through the layers.

Let us look at an example of a custom module:

```python
import torch
import torch.nn as nn

# Define a simple neural network with two fully connected layers
class SimpleNet(nn.Module):
        def __init__(self):
        super(SimpleNet, self).__init__()
        self.fc1 = nn.Linear(10, 50)  # First fully connected layer
        self.fc2 = nn.Linear(50, 1)   # Output layer

        def forward(self, x):
        x = torch.relu(self.fc1(x))  # ReLU activation on the first layer
        x = self.fc2(x)              # Output layer
        return x

# Instantiate the model
model = SimpleNet()
print(model)
```

You will see the following output:

```
SimpleNet(
  (fc1): Linear(in_features=10, out_features=50, bias=True)
  (fc2): Linear(in_features=50, out_features=1, bias=True)
)
```

Here,

1. **SimpleNet** is the name of the neural network class.
2. **fc1** is the first fully connected layer, with 10 input features and 50 output features.
3. **fc2** is the second fully connected layer (the output layer), with 50 input features and 1 output feature.

This output displays the architecture of the defined neural network, showing the layers, their input/output dimensions, and the presence of bias terms in each layer.

In this example:

1. The model is composed of two fully connected (linear) layers: An input layer and an output layer.
2. The `forward` method defines the data flow, applying ReLU activation to the output of the first layer, before passing it to the second layer.

   This modular approach makes it easy to modify, expand, or reuse layers and components which is essential for experimenting with different architectures.

Using Predefined Modules in PyTorch

PyTorch provides a wide array of predefined modules in `torch.nn`, including layers, such as `nn.Conv2d` for convolutional layers, `nn.RNN` for recurrent layers, and various normalization and activation functions. These modules enable you to quickly set up standard architectures, without having to implement everything from scratch. An example is provided in the code listing on GitHub repo.

Using predefined modules allows for the quick assembly of well-known architectures, such as CNNs or RNNs, saving development time, while ensuring reliable implementation.

Building Complex Architectures with Nested Modules

PyTorch's modular design also makes it easy to build nested modules. You can encapsulate parts of your model into separate modules, and then use them as components in larger architectures. This approach is particularly useful for deep or complex models, as it improves readability, and allows for better code organization. An example of a more complex architecture, using nested modules is provided in the code listing on GitHub repo.

This approach allows for easy adjustments to each block, and facilitates experimentation with different configurations, making it especially valuable for deep learning projects that require frequent adjustments.

Benefits of the Modular Approach

The modular design in PyTorch offers several key benefits:

- **Reusability:** Modules can be reused across different architectures, making it easy to experiment and fine-tune.

- **Readability:** Encapsulating functionality within custom modules keeps code organized, especially for complex architectures.
- **Flexibility:** Nested modules allow for a hierarchical design, where components can be adjusted independently, making PyTorch ideal for both research and production **environments.**

Use Cases of PyTorch Modules in Practice

- **Image Classification Models:** Many state-of-the-art image classification models like ResNet and VGG use PyTorch's `nn.Module` to define and stack convolutional layers. By using custom modules and nested structures, these architectures maintain readability and modularity, making them easy to modify for various image classification tasks.
- **Natural Language Processing (NLP):** Transformer-based models, such as BERT and GPT, benefit from PyTorch's modularity by defining layers (for example, self-attention and feed-forward layers) as separate modules. These components are then stacked or repeated to build deeper architectures, improving performance on tasks like language translation or text generation.
- **Generative Models**: In applications like Generative Adversarial Networks (GANs), PyTorch's modular approach makes it easy to define the generator and discriminator networks as separate modules. Each can be customized independently, allowing for flexibility, when experimenting with different network architectures.

PyTorch's modular approach to model creation through `torch.nn.Module` provides the flexibility and organization needed for building everything, from simple neural networks to complex, nested architectures. By leveraging predefined modules, custom classes, and nested structures, you can efficiently construct and modify models to suit your specific tasks. This foundation prepares you for developing and training more sophisticated models in PyTorch, making it a powerful tool for deep learning research and production.

Building and Training Simple Neural Networks

Constructing and training a neural network in PyTorch is a streamlined process that begins with defining the model architecture, and continues through setting up the training loop. This section guides you through the steps of building a simple neural network, initializing key components, and implementing a basic training loop. Understanding these foundational elements will prepare you to create more complex models in future chapters.

Defining a Simple Neural Network

In PyTorch, neural networks are organized as classes that inherit from `torch.nn.Module`. This class provides a framework for defining layers and forward propagation, making it straightforward to set up and train neural networks. Here is an example of a basic neural network with two hidden layers:

```python
import torch
import torch.nn as nn

# Define a simple feedforward neural network
class SimpleNet(nn.Module):
    def __init__(self):
    super(SimpleNet, self).__init__()
    self.fc1 = nn.Linear(10, 50)  # First fully connected layer
    self.fc2 = nn.Linear(50, 20)  # Second fully connected layer
    self.fc3 = nn.Linear(20, 1)   # Output layer
```

```
        def forward(self, x):
        x = torch.relu(self.fc1(x))  # ReLU activation for the first layer
        x = torch.relu(self.fc2(x))  # ReLU activation for the second layer
        x = self.fc3(x)            # Linear output layer
        return x

# Instantiate the model
model = SimpleNet()
```

In this code, we define a fully connected network with three layers: An input layer, a hidden layer, and an output layer. Each layer uses the ReLU activation function which introduces non-linearity, and a crucial property for learning complex patterns. The `forward` method defines the forward pass for the network, where data flows through the layers and activations.

Setting Up the Loss Function and Optimizer

To train this neural network, we need two additional components:

- A loss function that measures how well the model's predictions align with the target values.
- An optimizer that adjusts the model's parameters to minimize the loss.

In this example, we will use Mean Squared Error (MSE) as the loss function (common in regression tasks) and Stochastic Gradient Descent (SGD) as the optimizer:

```python
import torch.optim as optim

# Define loss function and optimizer
loss_fn = nn.MSELoss()
optimizer = optim.SGD(model.parameters(), lr=0.01)  # Learning rate of 0.01
```

The optimizer takes the model's parameters, and updates them in each training iteration, based on the computed gradients. The `lr` (learning rate) controls the step size for updates, impacting how quickly the model learns.

Implementing the Training Loop

The training loop is a core part of model training, allowing the model to learn iteratively from the data. In each iteration, we:

1. Compute predictions.
2. Calculate the loss based on the predictions and targets.
3. Perform backpropagation to compute gradients.
4. Update the model's parameters using the optimizer.

An example is provided in the code listing on GitHub repo.

This process is repeated for multiple epochs (complete passes through the dataset), enabling the model to progressively improve its predictions by minimizing the loss function.

Evaluating Model Performance

After training, you may want to evaluate the model's performance on a validation or test set. This evaluation can be done without tracking gradients, saving memory and computation. You can do this by wrapping the evaluation in `torch.no_grad()`:

```python
with torch.no_grad():
        predictions = model(inputs)
        evaluation_loss = loss_fn(predictions, targets)
        print(f"Evaluation Loss: {evaluation_loss.item():.4f}")
```

Using `torch.no_grad()` disables gradient tracking, which is unnecessary during evaluation, making the process faster and more memory-efficient.

Example output would look like:

```Evaluation Loss: 0.4321```

Building and training a simple neural network in PyTorch provides the foundation for more advanced model development. Understanding the roles of the model architecture, loss function, optimizer, and training loop allows you to construct effective deep learning pipelines. With these essentials covered, you are prepared to explore PyTorch's performance-enhancing features, such as TorchScript and lazy tensors, in the next section, where we will see how these tools optimize training, and improve model deployment.

Data Loading and Preprocessing with PyTorch

Efficient data loading and preprocessing are crucial steps in deep learning workflows, especially when working with large datasets. PyTorch offers a versatile and efficient data handling system through its `torch.utils.data` module which includes classes like Dataset and DataLoader. These tools make it easy to load, preprocess, and batch data, enabling smooth data flow from disk to model during training and evaluation.

In this section, we will explore the basics of setting up datasets, applying transformations, and using data loaders to optimize the data pipeline in PyTorch.

Creating Custom Datasets with `torch.utils.data.Dataset`

The Dataset class is the foundation for creating custom datasets in PyTorch. To load your own data, you define a subclass of `torch.utils.data.Dataset`, and implement two main methods:

- `__len__()`: Returns the size of the dataset.
- `__getitem__()`: Retrieves a single data point and its label based on the index provided.

An example of creating a custom dataset for an image classification is provided in the code listing on GitHub repo.

Applying Data Transformations with `torchvision.transforms`

Data preprocessing, or transformation, is often necessary before feeding data into a neural network. For image data, PyTorch's `torchvision.transforms` module provides common transformations like resizing, normalization, and data augmentation.

Transformations are typically applied in a sequence using `transforms.Compose`. An example of image transformations is provided in the code listing on GitHub repo.

By chaining transformations, you can create a robust preprocessing pipeline that standardizes data, and adds variation to prevent overfitting.
```

Loading Data in Batches with `torch.utils.data.DataLoader`

Once you have created a dataset, you can load data in batches using DataLoader. DataLoader is highly customizable, and handles shuffling, batching, and parallel processing for efficient data loading during training and evaluation.

Here is an example of setting up a DataLoader:

```python
from torch.utils.data import DataLoader

# Define DataLoader
dataloader = DataLoader(dataset, batch_size=32, shuffle=True, num_workers=4)

# Loop through the DataLoader
for images, labels in dataloader:
        print(f"Batch of images shape: {images.shape}")
        print(f"Batch of labels shape: {labels.shape}")
        # Pass images and labels to your model
```

In this example:

1. `batch_size=32` loads data in batches of 32 samples at a time.
2. `shuffle=True` ensures data is randomly shuffled each epoch, enhancing model generalization.
3. `num_workers=4` enables parallel data loading, leveraging multiple CPU cores to improve loading speed.

The expected output will be:

```
Batch of images shape: torch.Size([32, 3, 224, 224])
Batch of labels shape: torch.Size([32])
Batch of images shape: torch.Size([32, 3, 224, 224])
Batch of labels shape: torch.Size([32])
...
```

DataLoader is an essential tool for optimizing data input, as it minimizes the time spent waiting for data during training. By loading data in batches, it enables the model to process multiple samples simultaneously, boosting GPU utilization and speeding up training.

Using Built-in Datasets from `torchvision.datasets`

PyTorch's `torchvision.datasets` module provides a collection of popular datasets, such as CIFAR-10, MNIST, and ImageNet, which are frequently used for benchmarking and experimentation. These datasets are preconfigured for efficient loading, and include built-in transformations.

Here is an example of loading the CIFAR-10 dataset:

```python
from torchvision.datasets import CIFAR10

# Load CIFAR-10 dataset with transformations
transform = transforms.Compose([
    transforms.Resize((32, 32)),
    transforms.ToTensor(),
```

```
        transforms.Normalize(mean=[0.4914, 0.4822, 0.4465], std=[0.2023, 0.1994,
0.2010])
])

train_dataset = CIFAR10(root="data", train=True, transform=transform, down-
load=True)
train_loader = DataLoader(train_dataset, batch_size=64, shuffle=True)
```

In this example:

1. `CIFAR10` is loaded with a specified root directory, transformation, and batch size.
2. Setting `download=True` automatically downloads the dataset if it is not available locally.

Using these built-in datasets saves time on dataset preparation, and enables quick experimentation with standard benchmarks.

Use Cases for Data Loading and Preprocessing

1. **Image Classification:** Loading and batching large image datasets like ImageNet with DataLoader enables efficient model training. Transformations such as resizing and normalization prepare images for CNN architectures, ensuring consistency and performance during training.

2. **Natural Language Processing (NLP):** DataLoader and custom dataset classes are used to handle text-based datasets, transforming them into tokenized sequences. Batching and shuffling make it possible to train NLP models on large text datasets for tasks like sentiment analysis or language translation.

3. **Time-Series and Tabular Data:** In applications like stock price prediction or customer behavior analysis, custom datasets are used to format time-series or tabular data. Transformations standardize these data types, and DataLoader enables efficient training in batches.

Data loading and preprocessing are essential components in PyTorch's deep learning pipeline. With tools like `Dataset`, `DataLoader`, and `torchvision.transforms`, PyTorch allows for flexible and efficient data handling, from loading custom datasets to applying complex transformations. By mastering these tools, you can streamline the flow of data into your models, ensuring consistent and optimized training across a variety of data types. These skills form a solid foundation as we move forward to more advanced topics in PyTorch.

PyTorch 2.0's Improved Performance Features

PyTorch 2.0 introduces powerful features that significantly enhance model performance, making it easier to go from prototyping to production. Two key advancements in this release are TorchScript and lazy tensors. These features allow developers to improve model efficiency, optimize memory usage, and enable seamless deployment. In the following paragraphs, we shall explore how each feature works and provides real-world use cases to illustrate their impact.

TorchScript: Bridging Research and Production

TorchScript enables PyTorch models to be converted into a static, optimized format for production deployment. By creating a static computational graph, TorchScript improves model efficiency, allowing for faster inference and easier integration into non-PyTorch environments, such as mobile devices or server-based applications.

TorchScript offers two ways to convert models:

1. **Scripting:** Directly interprets standard PyTorch code, and is suitable for simple models. For example,

   ```python
   scripted_model = torch.jit.script(model)
   ```

2. **Tracing:** Records operations by running an example input through the model, useful when models include conditional statements that do not vary with inputs. For example,

   ```python
   traced_model = torch.jit.trace(model, example_inputs=inputs)
   ```

Once a model is converted into TorchScript, it can be optimized and deployed, without needing a Python runtime, making it ideal for performance-sensitive applications.

Use Cases for TorchScript

Here are some key use cases where TorchScript shines:

- **Mobile Deployment:** Companies like Facebook have used TorchScript to deploy models on mobile devices, where memory and processing power are limited. For instance, Facebook's news feed ranking algorithm is implemented with TorchScript to run efficiently on user devices, providing faster, personalized recommendations without requiring continuous server access.
- **Edge Computing:** For applications in autonomous vehicles and IoT devices, where real-time inference is crucial, TorchScript allows models to run directly on edge devices. This reduces latency, and minimizes the need for constant data transmission to cloud servers. A TorchScript-optimized object detection model, for example, can run in real-time on an edge device for tasks like pedestrian detection in autonomous cars.
- **Production-Ready APIs:** Companies deploying recommendation engines or chatbots at scale can use TorchScript to improve API response times. Optimizing a model with TorchScript allows it to process requests quickly and reliably, even under high demand, making it suitable for e-commerce recommendation engines or customer service chatbots.

Lazy Tensors: Delaying Evaluation for Greater Efficiency

Lazy tensors provide an alternative way to handle tensor computations by delaying their evaluation. Unlike standard tensors, which perform each operation immediately, lazy tensors allow operations to accumulate, and only execute when necessary. This grouping of operations optimizes memory usage and computational efficiency, particularly for large-scale models.

Lazy tensors are particularly beneficial for reducing the memory footprint of large models by only performing computations, when absolutely required. They can also reduce execution time by eliminating redundant intermediate steps, allowing PyTorch to batch multiple operations for faster processing.

To enable lazy tensors in PyTorch, you can initialize them with:

```python
import torch._lazy

# Enable lazy tensors
torch._lazy.init()  # Initializes lazy tensor backend
```

Use Cases for Lazy Tensors

- **Large-Scale NLP Models:** Training large language models like GPT or BERT on limited hardware can be memory-intensive. Lazy tensors can optimize the training pipeline, minimizing memory allocation during forward and backward passes. For instance, OpenAI has explored similar optimization techniques to manage memory better in training large transformer models, reducing training costs.
- **Scientific Computing:** For applications like genomics or molecular simulation, where complex computations involve large datasets, lazy tensors improve resource usage by deferring computation until absolutely necessary. This approach allows scientists to work with high-dimensional data, without overwhelming memory resources, enabling more detailed and extensive simulations.
- **Data Pipeline Optimization:** In data preprocessing pipelines, lazy tensors can optimize transformations by combining multiple operations, before execution. For example, in image preprocessing for computer vision models, a series of transformations (resize, normalize, crop) can be optimized to reduce redundant operations, making the preprocessing pipeline faster and more efficient.

Combining TorchScript and Lazy Tensors for Maximum Efficiency

Using TorchScript and lazy tensors together can maximize a model's performance in production:

- TorchScript is ideal for creating a production-ready static graph, allowing models to be deployed efficiently on any device.
- Lazy tensors optimize memory usage and speed during computation, especially beneficial for resource-heavy training processes.

These features ensure that models perform efficiently in both research and production settings, allowing PyTorch to handle large-scale data and computation demands effectively.

Example: Applying TorchScript to a Model

Here's a simple example demonstrating how to convert a model to TorchScript:

````
```python
# Define a simple model
class SimpleNet(torch.nn.Module):
        def __init__(self):
        super(SimpleNet, self).__init__()
        self.fc = torch.nn.Linear(10, 1)

        def forward(self, x):
        return self.fc(x)

# Create an instance of the model
model = SimpleNet()

# Convert the model to TorchScript
scripted_model = torch.jit.script(model)

# Save the scripted model
scripted_model.save("simple_net.pt")
```
````

In this example:

1. We define a simple linear model.
2. Convert it into TorchScript for faster, production-ready deployment.
3. Save the model as a `.pt` file, optimized for deployment across different platforms.

Thus, with PyTorch 2.0, features like TorchScript and lazy tensors enable developers to take their models from research to production, with ease. TorchScript optimizes models for faster inference and seamless deployment, while lazy tensors reduce memory usage and computation overhead, particularly for large datasets and complex computations. Together, these tools allow PyTorch models to meet the demands of real-world applications, ensuring both efficiency and scalability. As we continue, these features will be invaluable for building and deploying advanced, large-scale neural networks.

GPU Acceleration and Distributed Training in PyTorch 2.0

PyTorch 2.0 makes it easy to harness the power of GPU acceleration and distributed training to improve the speed and scalability of deep learning models. GPU acceleration allows for faster model training by leveraging the parallel computing power of NVIDIA GPUs, while distributed training enables the training of models across multiple GPUs or machines, reducing the training time for large datasets and complex models.

Leveraging GPU Acceleration

GPUs are designed to handle multiple operations in parallel, making them ideal for the computationally intensive tasks required in deep learning. PyTorch seamlessly integrates GPU support, enabling you to move tensors and models to CUDA-enabled NVIDIA GPUs, with minimal code changes. By running operations on the GPU, you can significantly speed up model training and inference.

Moving Tensors and Models to GPU

To leverage GPU acceleration, you need to move both the data (tensors) and model to the GPU. This can be done easily with the `.to(device)` method, where `device` is set to `"cuda"` if a GPU is available. Here's an example:

```python
import torch

# Check if a GPU is available
device = torch.device("cuda" if torch.cuda.is_available() else "cpu")

# Move tensors and model to GPU
inputs = torch.randn(100, 10).to(device)
targets = torch.randn(100, 1).to(device)

# Define a simple model and move it to GPU
class SimpleNet(torch.nn.Module):
      def __init__(self):
      super(SimpleNet, self).__init__()
      self.fc = torch.nn.Linear(10, 1)
```

```
    def forward(self, x):
    return self.fc(x)

model = SimpleNet().to(device)
```

By setting `device` to `"cuda"` if available, PyTorch will run all operations on the GPU, significantly speeding up training for large datasets and complex models. You can verify the device location of tensors with `inputs.device`, which should display `"cuda:0"` if the tensor is on the GPU.

Training with GPU Acceleration

Once the model and data are on the GPU, the training process remains the same as with CPU training. PyTorch handles memory management automatically, allowing you to write GPU-accelerated code without extensive adjustments.

Distributed Training for Scaling Across Multiple GPUs

For even larger models and datasets, PyTorch 2.0 supports distributed training, allowing you to scale training across multiple GPUs on a single machine, or even across multiple machines. Distributed training is particularly useful, when dealing with large datasets, or when training time needs to be minimized.

There are two main ways to implement distributed training in PyTorch:

a. **Data Parallelism (`torch.nn.DataParallel`)**

In data parallelism, data is split across multiple GPUs on a single machine. Each GPU processes a portion of the data in parallel, and the model updates are synchronized across GPUs. PyTorch's `torch.nn.DataParallel` class makes it simple to implement data parallelism:

```python
# Wrap the model for data parallelism
model = torch.nn.DataParallel(model)

# Now, PyTorch will automatically split the input across GPUs
predictions = model(inputs)
```

Data parallelism requires minimal code changes, and works well for single-machine, multi-GPU setups, where each GPU handles a portion of the data in parallel, and PyTorch manages the synchronization.

b. **Distributed Data Parallel (`torch.nn.parallel.DistributedDataParallel`)**

For more extensive setups involving multiple machines, Distributed Data Parallel (DDP) offers better performance and scalability than data parallelism. DDP provides more control, and reduces communication overhead by managing distributed training more efficiently, making it suitable for large-scale deep learning tasks.

To use DDP, you need to initialize a process group for each GPU or machine involved in training:

```python
import torch.distributed as dist
from torch.nn.parallel import DistributedDataParallel as DDP

# Initialize the process group
dist.init_process_group("nccl", rank=rank, world_size=world_size)
```

```
    # Move model to device and wrap it with DDP
    model = SimpleNet().to(device)
    model = DDP(model, device_ids=[rank])
    ```
```

Each process in DDP operates independently on its GPU, with periodic synchronization between GPUs to update the model parameters. DDP is particularly useful in cloud environments or high-performance computing clusters, where large datasets and complex models require efficient parallel processing.

## Use Cases for GPU Acceleration and Distributed Training

GPU acceleration and distributed training unlock the full potential of PyTorch for handling large datasets and complex models. Following are some practical use cases that highlight their impact in accelerating computations, and scaling training workflows efficiently.

- **Large-Scale NLP and Transformer Models:** Training large models, such as transformers, on extensive text datasets benefits significantly from distributed training. For example, OpenAI's language models and Google's BERT model were trained across multiple GPUs or TPU clusters to reduce training time while managing high computational demands.
- **Image Classification with Deep CNNs:** Distributed training is ideal for training deep convolutional neural networks (CNNs) on massive image datasets like ImageNet. Data parallelism allows each GPU to handle a portion of the data, expediting the training of models such as ResNet and EfficientNet.
- **Autonomous Vehicles and Robotics:** In fields like autonomous driving, training on massive video datasets requires the processing power of multiple GPUs. Distributed training enables the parallel processing of visual data across several GPUs, allowing for faster development of vision-based perception systems in robotics and autonomous vehicles.
- **Recommendation Systems:** E-commerce platforms that employ recommendation systems often rely on vast amounts of user data. GPU-accelerated training and distributed computing enable these platforms to train deep learning models that provide personalized recommendations more efficiently, scaling to handle real-time updates and millions of users.

**GPU acceleration and distributed training** are essential for scaling up deep learning workflows efficiently. By moving computations to the GPU, PyTorch enables faster training and inference for even the most complex models. Meanwhile, distributed training provides scalability across multiple GPUs or machines, making it possible to train large models on extensive datasets in less time. These features make PyTorch 2.0 an invaluable tool for both research and production environments, allowing developers to take advantage of modern hardware for optimized performance.

# Saving and Loading Models in PyTorch 2.0

One of the key steps in a machine learning workflow is saving trained models for later use, and reloading them to resume training or make predictions. PyTorch provides a flexible and efficient way to save and load models, allowing you to save either the entire model architecture, or just the learned parameters. In this section, we will explore the different methods for saving and loading models in PyTorch, ensuring that your work is preserved, and easy to deploy or continue.

## State Dict

The most common approach to saving a model in PyTorch is to save the state dictionary (`state dict`) which contains the model's parameters (weights and biases). This method is efficient and flexible, as it only saves the parameters, allowing you to reload them into a compatible model architecture, later.
```

Saving Model Parameters

```python
# Define a model
model = SimpleNet()

# Save model parameters (state dict)
torch.save(model.state_dict(), "model_weights.pth")
```

In this example, `model.state_dict()` retrieves the parameters of `model`, and `torch.save()` saves them to a file (`model_weights.pth`), which can later be loaded into the same model architecture.

Loading Model Parameters

To load the saved `state dict` into a model, you need to:

1. Instantiate the model architecture.
2. Load the state dict.

```python
# Recreate the model architecture
model = SimpleNet()

# Load the saved model parameters
model.load_state_dict(torch.load("model_weights.pth"))
```

This approach is useful, when you need flexibility to modify the model's structure slightly, or initialize weights in a compatible model, without needing to save the entire model architecture.

Saving and Loading the Entire Model

If you need to save the entire model, including the architecture and parameters, you can save the model directly. This approach is convenient when you want to avoid recreating the model's architecture each time you load it.

Saving the Entire Model

```python
# Save the entire model
torch.save(model, "entire_model.pth")
```

Here, `torch.save()` saves both the architecture and parameters, making it easier to reload, without defining the model class separately.

Loading the Entire Model

When loading the entire model, you do not need to recreate the architecture, as it is included in the saved file:

```python
# Load the entire model
model = torch.load("entire_model.pth")
```

Saving the entire model is a quick way to save everything in one file, though it is less flexible than using state dicts, as it requires all dependencies (for instance, custom layers or modules) to be available, when loading.

Saving and Loading Models for Inference

For inference tasks, where the model is only used to make predictions, you can save the model in a format optimized for deployment. For instance, you may want to use TorchScript to script or trace the model, creating a static graph that can be deployed independently of PyTorch's dynamic execution environment.

Here is an example using TorchScript to save a model for efficient deployment:

````
```python
# Convert model to TorchScript format
scripted_model = torch.jit.script(model)

# Save the scripted model
scripted_model.save("scripted_model.pt")
```
````

Thus, by saving the model as a scripted TorchScript model, you gain compatibility with various deployment environments, including mobile devices and servers, without needing a full PyTorch runtime.

Checkpointing During Training

In long training sessions, it is useful to periodically save checkpoints to prevent data loss, and enable training to resume from a saved state. Checkpoints, typically include both the model parameters and optimizer state, allowing you to continue training, without losing progress.

Saving a Checkpoint

````
```python
# Save a checkpoint during training
torch.save({
        'epoch': epoch,
        'model_state_dict': model.state_dict(),
        'optimizer_state_dict': optimizer.state_dict(),
        'loss': loss,
}, "checkpoint.pth")
```
````

In this example:

1. `epoch` keeps track of the current training epoch.
2. `model_state_dict` saves the model parameters.
3. `optimizer_state_dict` saves the optimizer's state, which includes details like learning rate and momentum.
4. `loss` records the loss at the time of checkpointing.

Loading from a Checkpoint

To resume training from a checkpoint, you load the saved state into your model and optimizer:

````
```python
# Load checkpoint
checkpoint = torch.load("checkpoint.pth")
model.load_state_dict(checkpoint['model_state_dict'])
optimizer.load_state_dict(checkpoint['optimizer_state_dict'])
epoch = checkpoint['epoch']
loss = checkpoint['loss']
````
````

```
# Set model to training mode
model.train()
```

By loading the optimizer's state, you can continue training with consistent learning rates and momentum settings, preserving the training progress effectively.

Use Cases for Model Saving and Loading

Efficient model saving and loading are crucial for preserving training progress, deploying models, and enabling seamless experimentation. Here are some scenarios, where these features are indispensable.

- **Research Experiments:** Researchers often run multiple experiments with variations in model parameters. Saving and loading state dicts allow for easy comparison and tuning, without needing to redefine models.
- **Continuous Training in Production:** For applications that periodically retrain models with new data, checkpointing provides a mechanism to save intermediate progress. If training is interrupted, the model can resume from the last checkpoint, ensuring efficient resource use.
- **Deployment for Real-Time Inference:** Saving a TorchScript model enables real-time inference in production settings, where quick response times are required, such as recommendation engines or automated customer support.

Saving and loading models in PyTorch is essential for managing experiments, deploying models, and preventing data loss. PyTorch provides flexible options, from saving only model parameters to checkpointing during training, and using TorchScript for optimized deployment. These tools ensure that your trained models are preserved, portable, and ready for use in diverse environments. In the following sections, we will look into debugging and profiling techniques, preparing you to refine and optimize your PyTorch models, further.

Debugging and Profiling PyTorch Models

Effective debugging and profiling are necessary for building efficient and accurate deep learning models. PyTorch provides a suite of tools to help diagnose issues in model performance, understand where bottlenecks occur, and optimize code execution. This section introduces methods and tools for debugging errors in model training and profiling to identify performance improvements.

Debugging PyTorch Models

Debugging neural networks can be challenging due to the complexity of operations and data transformations. PyTorch offers various ways to debug models, from examining individual tensor values to inspecting the entire computational graph.

Using `torch.autograd` for Gradient Checks

In PyTorch, `**torch.autograd**` handles automatic differentiation, allowing you to monitor and check gradients throughout the model. By examining gradients, you can identify issues like vanishing or exploding gradients which often affect model training stability.

```python
# Check gradients after backpropagation
for name, param in model.named_parameters():
```

```
        if param.grad is not None:
        print(f"{name} - Gradients: {param.grad}")
```

Inspecting gradients helps identify layers with unusually high or low gradient values which can indicate issues with learning or numerical instability in the model.

Example Output:

```
fc1.weight - Gradients: tensor([[ 0.0234, -0.0012, ...,  0.0124], ... ])
fc1.bias - Gradients: tensor([0.0045, -0.0032, ...])
fc2.weight - Gradients: tensor([[0.0132, 0.0041, ...], ... ])
fc2.bias - Gradients: tensor([-0.0014, 0.0009, ...])
```

The **`model.named_parameters()`** function iterates through all parameters in the model, with **`param.grad`** containing the computed gradients after backpropagation. If gradients are present (i.e., **`param.grad is not None`**), they are printed alongside the parameter name. If backpropagation hasn't been performed yet, no output will be printed for parameters that do not have gradients.

Using `torch.nn.Module` Hooks for Layer Debugging

Hooks provide a way to inspect outputs or gradients at specific layers in a model, allowing you to observe what happens inside the network at each stage. You can attach hooks to layers to check intermediate outputs, aiding in debugging layer-specific issues.

```python
# Define a hook function to print layer outputs
def hook_fn(module, input, output):
        print(f"Layer: {module}")
        print(f"Output shape: {output.shape}")

# Register hook to a specific layer
model.fc1.register_forward_hook(hook_fn)

# Run a forward pass to trigger the hook
output = model(inputs)
```

This code adds a hook to the `fc1` layer, printing the shape of the output tensor during each forward pass. Hooks are particularly useful for complex architectures, where issues may arise in specific layers.

Expected Output:

```
Layer: Linear(in_features=10, out_features=50, bias=True)
Output shape: torch.Size([32, 50])
```

The output will display information about the specific layer (in this case, **`fc1`**), including the layer name and the shape of the output tensor after the forward pass.

Debugging with PyTorch's **`torch.autograd.detect_anomaly()`**

When working with complex models, it can be difficult to pinpoint the source of NaN (not-a-number) or infinity values, which can cause model training to fail. PyTorch's **`torch.autograd.detect_anomaly()`** can help detect and trace these issues by throwing detailed stack traces when anomalies are encountered. An example is provided in the code listing on GitHub repo.

Profiling Model Performance with `torch.utils.benchmark`

Profiling allows you to identify performance bottlenecks in your model, such as slow operations or inefficient data handling. PyTorch 2.0 introduces `torch.utils.benchmark`, a powerful tool for measuring and analyzing code execution times, which can help optimize model performance.

Basic Profiling with `torch.utils.benchmark`

Using `torch.utils.benchmark.Timer`, you can measure the execution time of specific code snippets, identifying which parts of your model take the longest to run. This is especially useful for optimizing the training loop or specific layers in the model. An example is provided in the code listing on GitHub repo.

Using `torch.cuda` for GPU Memory Management

When training models on the GPU, effective memory management is essential to prevent out-of-memory errors. PyTorch's `torch.cuda` module provides functions to monitor and manage GPU memory usage.

Clearing Unused Memory

To free up GPU memory between training runs or when debugging, you can clear the cache with:

```
```python
torch.cuda.empty_cache()
```
```

This command releases unused memory, reducing the risk of out-of-memory errors, and helping manage GPU resources more effectively.

Use Cases for Debugging and Profiling in Practice

- **Identifying Bottlenecks in Training**: Profiling tools can help identify slow components in the training loop, such as data loading or specific layers, allowing you to optimize and speed up training.
- **Detecting Gradient Anomalies**: Debugging tools like `detect_anomaly()` are essential when experimenting with new architectures, helping you trace and resolve issues with gradients that can hinder model convergence.
- **Memory Optimization for Large Models:** Profiling GPU memory usage is invaluable, when working with large models, such as transformers, where managing GPU memory effectively can prevent crashes, and improve training efficiency.

Debugging and profiling are crucial steps in deep learning model development, helping ensure that models are efficient, stable, and optimized for performance. With tools like `torch.autograd`, `torch.profiler`, and `torch.utils.benchmark`, PyTorch offers a range of options to address issues in training, monitor performance, and optimize resource usage. Mastering these tools enables you to build and deploy models that are both robust and efficient, laying the groundwork for advanced model development.

Best Practices for Efficient PyTorch 2.0 Development

As you progress in building, training, and deploying models with PyTorch, adopting best practices can help you maximize efficiency, prevent errors, and maintain an organized workflow. This section covers some essential tips and strategies for developing models effectively in PyTorch, ensuring that your code is optimized, scalable, and ready for production.

Efficient Data Handling and Loading

Managing data efficiently is key to reducing bottlenecks in training:

- Use DataLoader with Multiple Workers: Setting `num_workers` in `DataLoader` allows you to load data in parallel, which speeds up data processing, particularly for large datasets. Experiment with different values to find the optimal number of workers based on your system's CPU cores.
- Utilize Data Augmentation: Applying data augmentation techniques (for example, rotation, flipping) with `torchvision.transforms` increases the diversity of the training dataset, which can improve model generalization and prevent overfitting.

Leverage GPU Acceleration and Monitor Memory Usage

When training on GPUs, efficient memory management is essential:

- **Move Tensors to the Same Device**: Always ensure that both the model and input tensors are on the same device (CPU or GPU) to avoid unnecessary data transfer and errors.
- **Use `torch.cuda.empty_cache()`**: Between experiments, clear the GPU cache to free up memory and prevent out-of-memory issues.
- **Monitor GPU Usage**: Use `torch.cuda.memory_allocated()` and `torch.cuda.memory_reserved()` to keep track of GPU memory utilization, especially when training large models, to avoid memory overload.

Utilize Mixed Precision Training

PyTorch's native support for mixed precision training can improve training speed and reduce memory usage by using a mix of 16-bit and 32-bit floating-point precision. This is particularly effective on GPUs with NVIDIA Tensor Cores (for example, V100, T4, A100). An example is provided in the code listing on GitHub repo.

Mixed precision training speeds up computations and allows larger batch sizes, which can significantly benefit training efficiency.

Regularly Save and Checkpoint Models

To avoid losing progress, save model checkpoints frequently, especially during long training sessions:

- **Save Key Checkpoints**: Save the model state, optimizer state, and epoch number. This allows you to resume training from the exact point it was interrupted, preserving optimizer settings and learning rates.
- **Use TorchScript for Deployment**: Convert the final model to TorchScript for production deployment, ensuring compatibility with a variety of environments, including mobile and server-based applications.

Debug and Profile with PyTorch Tools

Use PyTorch's profiling tools to improve model performance:

- **Torch Profiler**: Identify performance bottlenecks and memory usage with `torch.profiler` to optimize specific layers or parts of the training loop.
- **Detect Anomalies**: Use `torch.autograd.detect_anomaly()` for complex models to track down the source of NaN values or gradients that may prevent training from converging.

Adhere to Modular Design for Scalability

Keeping model components modular promotes readability, reusability, and maintainability:

- **Organize Code with Custom Modules:** Break down complex models into smaller, reusable components by defining custom `torch.nn.Module` classes for each layer or block.
- **Use Configuration Files:** For larger projects, store hyperparameters and settings in configuration files, allowing you to adjust them without modifying the code. This is particularly useful for running multiple experiments with different settings.

Experiment Tracking and Version Control

Keeping track of different experiments and model versions is crucial for organized development:

- **Use Experiment Tracking Tools:** Libraries like MLflow or Weights & Biases allow you to track hyperparameters, metrics, and results over multiple training sessions. This is invaluable for identifying the best-performing models and configurations.
- **Version Control for Model Files:** Store model checkpoints and important versions in an organized file structure or use version control tools to manage model versions, ensuring consistency in experiments and production deployment.

Documentation and Code Comments

Clear documentation and commenting make your codebase easier to understand and modify:

- **Document Key Functions and Classes**: Briefly explain what each function or class does, focusing on sections that handle data, model architecture, and training procedures.
- **Use Inline Comments:** Add comments in complex sections of the code, especially in parts that perform transformations, specific operations, or unusual configurations, to provide clarity for future users or collaborators.

Test and Validate Models Thoroughly

Before deploying, test your model across various conditions to ensure robustness:

- **Run Validation Checks:** Regularly validate your model during training to monitor performance, and detect potential overfitting.
- **Use a Holdout Test Set:** Reserve a portion of your data as a final test set for unbiased performance evaluation before deployment, ensuring that the model performs consistently on unseen data.

Following the best practices in PyTorch development helps you build models that are robust, efficient, and ready for real-world applications. From efficient data handling and memory management to modular design as well as thorough documentation, these practices enhance both your development process and the quality of your models. By adhering to these strategies, you can create a solid foundation for advanced PyTorch projects, enabling you to work with larger datasets, complex architectures, and production environments confidently.

Conclusion

This chapter has provided you with a comprehensive foundation in PyTorch 2.0, from setting up your environment to building, training, and optimizing neural networks. We began with the essentials, like working with tensors and configuring the autograd system, and then progressed to more advanced topics, such as GPU acceleration, distributed training, and data handling. You also explored how to save and load models efficiently, debug and profile your code for performance bottlenecks, as well as adopt the best practices for scalable and maintainable PyTorch development. Together, these tools and techniques equip you to build robust, high-performing models that can handle the demands of real-world applications.

In the next chapter, we will dive into transformer architectures, examining the self-attention mechanism and other core concepts that make these models revolutionary in modern AI. With your foundational knowledge of PyTorch, you will be ready to implement these cutting-edge architectures, and apply them to a range of NLP, vision, and sequence-based tasks.

CHAPTER 4
Natural Language Processing with Transformers

Introduction

Natural Language Processing (NLP) has undergone a significant transformation with the advent of transformer models, revolutionizing the way machines understand and generate human language. In this chapter, we will explore the profound impact transformers have had on NLP tasks, from foundational operations like tokenization to more complex challenges, such as machine translation, sentiment analysis, and named entity recognition. Transformer models, known for their attention mechanisms and parallel processing capabilities, have set new benchmarks in accuracy and efficiency, making them the architecture of choice for a wide range of NLP applications.

Through hands-on examples using PyTorch 2.0, you will learn how to implement and fine-tune transformer models to solve real-world language processing problems. Whether it is classifying text, detecting emotions, or answering questions, this chapter will guide you through the core techniques that power modern NLP, giving you the tools to leverage pre-trained language models like BERT and GPT for specific tasks. By the end of this chapter, you will have a solid understanding of how **transformers have redefined the landscape of NLP**, and **how you can use them to build cutting-edge language models.**

Structure

In this chapter, we will cover the following topics:

- Introduction to NLP and its Challenges
- Tokenization Techniques for Transformer Models
- Word Embeddings and Contextual Representations
- Implementing a Transformer for Text Classification
- Named Entity Recognition (NER) with Transformers
- Sentiment Analysis and Emotion Detection Using Transformers
- Question-Answering Systems with Transformer Models
- Text Summarization Techniques Using Transformers
- Evaluating Transformer Models for NLP Tasks

Introduction to NLP and its Challenges

Natural Language Processing (NLP) is a subfield of Artificial Intelligence (AI) focused on enabling machines to understand, interpret, and generate human language. From text classification to machine translation, NLP powers applications that bridge the gap between human communication and computational systems. As one of the most challenging areas of AI, NLP aims to make sense of the unstructured textual data, enabling computers to process, analyze, and generate language in ways that are both meaningful and contextually accurate.

Despite the advances made in NLP, several fundamental challenges persist, especially when it comes to handling the nuances of human language. Some of the key challenges in NLP include:

- **Ambiguity in Language:** Human language is inherently ambiguous. Words, phrases, and sentences can have multiple meanings depending on the context. For example, the word, "*bank*" can refer to a financial institution, or the side of a river. Resolving such ambiguities is a major challenge in NLP, as it requires understanding not just the words themselves, but also their context, within a sentence or paragraph.
- **Variability of Language:** Language is highly variable– for instance, there are countless ways to express the same idea. Synonyms, dialects, slang, and cultural influences, all contribute to linguistic diversity, making it difficult for models to generalize across different forms of language. For instance, the phrases, "*I'm feeling great*", and "*I'm on top of the world*" convey similar meanings, but differ in structure and vocabulary.
- **Syntax and Grammar:** Understanding the syntactical structure of sentences is essential for meaning extraction. While humans naturally understand how words relate to one another (subject-verb-object, and so on), teaching a machine to parse the syntax of a sentence involves complex rules and exceptions. For example, "*She saw the man with the telescope*" can have multiple interpretations, depending on whether "*with the telescope*", refers to how she saw the man or who possessed the telescope.
- **Lack of World Knowledge:** Human language is deeply connected to the real world. To truly understand a language, a model needs some level of common sense and world knowledge. For instance, a sentence like "*The sun rises in the west*" is factually incorrect, and recognizing this requires a model to have a knowledge of the Earth's rotation. Incorporating such knowledge into NLP models is a challenge, especially when dealing with ambiguous or incomplete text.
- **Long-range Dependencies:** Human language often requires understanding relationships between words or concepts that are far apart in a sentence or document. For example, in a long paragraph, you might need to understand how a pronoun (like "*he*" or "*she*") refers to a subject mentioned much earlier in the text. Capturing long-range dependencies is difficult for traditional models, as they often struggle with **keeping track of such distant relationships over longer texts.**
- **Diversity of NLP Tasks:** NLP encompasses a wide variety of tasks, each with its own unique set of challenges. These include:
  - Text classification (for example, spam detection, sentiment analysis, and so on)
  - Named Entity Recognition (NER) (for instance, identifying names of people, organizations, and locations)
  - Machine translation (for example, translating text from one language to another)
  - Question answering (for example, answering questions, based on context)
  - Text summarization (for example, condensing a document into its key points)

  Each of these tasks requires specialized models and methods which adds to the complexity of building a general-purpose NLP system.

- **Multilingual and Cross-Lingual NLP:** Languages vary significantly in structure, grammar, and syntax. Thus, building NLP models that work across multiple languages, or even understand multiple languages simultaneously (cross-lingual NLP) remains a major challenge. Models trained in one language may struggle with others due to differences in vocabulary, sentence structure, and cultural context.

  With the introduction of **transformer-based architectures**, many of these challenges have become more tractable. Transformers, thanks to their self-attention mechanisms, and ability to handle long-range dependencies have dramatically improved the performance of NLP models. They provide a robust framework for learning contextual relationships, handling syntactic ambiguity, and understanding diverse language patterns. In the subsequent sections, we will explore how transformers address these challenges, and revolutionize the field of NLP.

Tokenization Techniques for Transformer Models

Tokenization is a fundamental preprocessing step in Natural Language Processing (NLP), where raw text is split into smaller units (tokens) that can be processed by a model. For transformer models, tokenization is especially important because these models rely on understanding individual tokens and their relationships, within a context. Tokenization techniques must balance granularity, computational efficiency, and the ability to capture the meaning.

In this section, we explore the various tokenization techniques used for transformer models, and discuss how these approaches help transformers process language efficiently.

- **Word-Level Tokenization:** Traditionally, tokenization at the word level involves splitting text into individual words, treating each word as a discrete unit. This approach is simple and intuitive, but has limitations, when dealing with rare or out-of-vocabulary words.

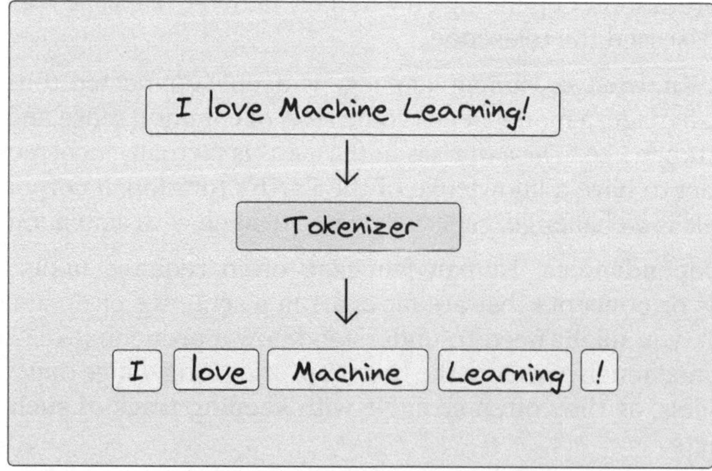

Figure 4.1: *Word-level Tokenization*

  For example, in a sentence like "*I love transformers*," word-level tokenization splits it into the tokens: [`"I"`, `"love"`, `"transformers"`].

  While this technique is effective for many languages, it struggles with:

  - **Handling rare words or typos:** A word like "`transformers`" may not be seen in the training data, leading to difficulties, when the model encounters it.
  - **Language diversity:** Words that are combined or hyphenated (for instance, "*high-quality*") can introduce complexity.

Thus, word-level tokenization is often inadequate for transformer models that need to handle large vocabularies, and diverse linguistic structures.

- **Subword Tokenization (Byte Pair Encoding - BPE):** To address the limitations of word-level tokenization, transformer models like BERT and GPT use subword tokenization techniques, such as Byte Pair Encoding (BPE). Subword tokenization splits words into smaller meaningful units, allowing the model to handle Out-of-Vocabulary (OOV) words, and morphologically complex words more effectively.

  For example, "*transformers*" might be tokenized into ["`transform`", "`##ers`"], where "`transform`" is a root subword and "`##ers`" represents a suffix. The "`##`" notation indicates that "`ers`" is a continuation of the previous token, not a standalone word.

  BPE works by iteratively merging the most frequent pair of characters or subwords, creating a vocabulary of subword units. By using subword tokenization, transformer models can:

  - **Handle OOV words:** Rare or unseen words are broken into familiar subword components, allowing the model to process them, based on known parts (for example, "unhappiness" could be split into "un", and "happiness").
  - **Capture morphological variations:** BPE can handle plural forms, tenses, and word derivatives by breaking down words into smaller meaningful parts.

  BPE's flexibility makes it a core component in the tokenization strategies of transformer models, such as GPT-2, BERT, and RoBERTa.

- **WordPiece Tokenization (Used in BERT):** Another popular subword tokenization technique is WordPiece, which is similar to BPE but uses a slightly different algorithm for merging subword units. WordPiece is used in models like BERT and ALBERT. Like BPE, it splits words into smaller parts, but WordPiece tries to maximize the likelihood of the corpus, making the vocabulary more efficient.

  For example, the word "`unhappiness`" could be split as ["`un`", "`##happiness`"], and a word like "`dogs`" might be tokenized into ["`dog`", "`##s`"].

  WordPiece optimizes tokenization by:

  - Learning a subword vocabulary that minimizes the out-of-vocabulary problem.
  - Maintaining efficient vocabulary size: Unlike word-level tokenization, it reduces the size of the vocabulary needed to cover a large corpus of text.

  One key benefit of WordPiece over pure BPE is that it can allow for finer granularity in encoding words while maintaining computational efficiency. This is particularly useful in handling languages with rich morphology.

- **SentencePiece Tokenization (Used in T5 and XLNet):** SentencePiece is an unsupervised text tokenizer and detokenizer that works at the subword level, and it is widely used in models like T5 and XLNet. It is different from BPE and WordPiece because it does not rely on predefined word segmentation, but rather treats the entire text corpus as a sequence of characters.

  SentencePiece works by training a model to find an optimal segmentation of the text which can be applied to a wide variety of languages and tasks. It uses techniques like Byte Pair Encoding, but does not require whitespace as a delimiter, enabling it to process text more flexibly.

Advantages of SentencePiece:

- **Flexibility across languages:** SentencePiece handles languages without spaces (for example, Chinese or Japanese) better, as it does not assume that word boundaries exist.

- **End-to-end training:** Unlike BPE or WordPiece, SentencePiece models can be trained from raw text directly, making them particularly useful for multilingual NLP.

Transformer-Specific Tokenization Challenges: While tokenization has become more sophisticated, there are still challenges for transformer models:

- **Handling very large vocabularies:** The size of subword vocabularies can impact computational resources. Models like BERT use vocabularies of 30,000–50,000 subword tokens, but as the vocabulary size grows, so does the computational cost.
- **Pre-tokenization processing:** Some languages (for instance, Chinese and Japanese) require more complex tokenization methods to handle word segmentation. **Tokenization tools must be adapted for each language's writing system.**

Practical Considerations in Tokenization

- **Tokenization vs. Preprocessing Pipelines:** Tokenization is just one step in the overall preprocessing pipeline. Other preprocessing tasks like lowercasing, punctuation removal, and stopword removal might be needed, based on the task.
- **Special Tokens:** In transformer models, special tokens like [`CLS`], [`SEP`], and [`PAD`] are used for classification tasks, separating sentences, or padding shorter sequences.

Effective tokenization is crucial for the success of transformer models, as it impacts how the model interprets a language. By using techniques like BPE, WordPiece, and SentencePiece, transformers can process text at various granularities, handle out-of-vocabulary words, and model linguistic structures more efficiently. Each tokenization method has its advantages depending on the application and language, and choosing the right technique is essential for building performant, transformer-based NLP models.

Word Embeddings and Contextual Representations

Word embeddings and contextual representations are foundational to transformer models, enabling them to understand the meaning of words and phrases, within a given context. Traditional word embeddings, such as Word2Vec or GloVe, map words to fixed vectors, but they struggle to capture the nuanced meanings of words in different contexts. Transformer models, however, overcome this limitation by producing contextualized embeddings, which dynamically adjust word representations based on their surrounding context. In this section, we shall explore the evolution of word embeddings, and how transformer models generate contextualized representations.

- **Traditional Word Embeddings:** Before the advent of transformers, word embeddings like Word2Vec and GloVe were popular techniques for representing words as dense vectors. These models learn fixed, low-dimensional representations for each word, where semantically similar words have similar vector representations.
    - **Word2Vec:** Developed by Google, Word2Vec uses shallow neural networks to map words to vectors. It employs either the Continuous Bag of Words (CBOW) or Skip-gram models to learn word representations, based on surrounding words in a sentence.
    - **GloVe:** GloVe (Global Vectors for Word Representation) is a matrix factorization-based method. It captures word co-occurrence information from large corpora to learn word embeddings that capture both local context (words in the same sentence) and global context (words across the entire corpus).

Though effective, these traditional word embeddings have certain limitations:

- **Static representations:** Word2Vec and GloVe generate a fixed embedding for each word, regardless of its context. For instance, the word, "*bank*" would have the same embedding, whether it refers to a financial institution or the side of a river.

  - **Lack of dynamic adaptation:** These embeddings do not adapt to sentence-level context, meaning the same word may have different meanings in different contexts, but be represented by the same vector.

- **Contextual Word Representations with Transformers:** Transformer models like BERT, GPT, and T5, introduced a breakthrough by learning contextual embeddings–word representations that are dependent on the surrounding words or tokens in a given sequence. This allows transformer models to disambiguate the meanings of words, based on context.

  For example, consider the word, "*bank*" in two different sentences:

  - "*She went to the bank to deposit money.*"
  - "*The boat was moored at the bank of the river.*"

In a transformer-based model, the word, "*bank*" would be represented differently in each case, depending on its context. This is because transformers generate embeddings dynamically during training, adjusting the vector, based on the entire sequence of words.

The key components of transformers that allow for contextual representations are:

- **Self-attention mechanisms:** These mechanisms allow each word to attend to every other word in the sequence, creating a rich representation of each word, relative to its context.
- **Bidirectional encoding:** Models like BERT utilize bidirectional attention, meaning the context is built from both the left and right of a word, allowing for a deeper understanding of the word meaning.
  - **The Role of Positional Encoding:** While transformers are excellent at capturing context, they do not inherently understand the order of words in a sequence. Unlike Recurrent Neural Networks (RNNs), transformers do not process words in a sequential order. To address this, positional encodings are added to the input embeddings, allowing the model to understand the relative positions of words in a sentence.

  These encodings are combined with word embeddings, ensuring that even though transformers process all words in parallel, they still maintain an understanding of word order and relationships. The combination of positional encodings and contextual embeddings provides transformer models with both syntactic and semantic understanding.

- **Pre-Trained Language Models and Fine-Tuning:** Pre-trained language models like BERT, GPT, and RoBERTa have become industry standards for NLP tasks because they generate high-quality contextual embeddings that capture both general linguistic knowledge, and task-specific nuances. These models are first trained on a massive corpus of text data, learning contextual word representations. They are then fine-tuned on specific tasks such as text classification, named entity recognition, or sentiment analysis.
  - **BERT:** BERT (Bidirectional Encoder Representations from Transformers) uses a Masked Language Model (MLM) approach to train on large text corpora. It learns to predict missing words (masked tokens) in sentences by looking at both the left and right context of each word.
  - **GPT:** GPT (Generative Pre-Trained Transformer) uses a unidirectional approach, where the model generates text one word at a time, conditioned on the previous words in the sequence. GPT is particularly strong in tasks like text generation and completion.
  - **5:** T5 (Text-to-Text Transfer Transformer) treats every NLP problem as a text-to-text problem. It can be fine-tuned on any specific task by framing it as a text generation problem (for example, translating text, and answering questions).

By leveraging these pre-trained models, we can utilize the power of contextual word embeddings, and fine-tune them for specialized tasks, drastically improving performance on various NLP tasks with minimal training data.

- **Word Embeddings in Multilingual NLP:** One of the significant advancements brought by transformer models is the ability to learn multilingual embeddings. Models like mBERT (Multilingual BERT) and XLM-R are trained on text in multiple languages, and are capable of producing contextual embeddings that work across different languages. This is particularly important for global applications, where models need to handle text in many languages, without training separate models for each.

  These models are capable of handling cross-lingual transfer learning, meaning that they can transfer knowledge learned in one language to another, improving performance in low-resource languages.

  Word embeddings and contextual representations are at the heart of modern NLP, with transformer models offering a leap forward in their ability to dynamically adjust embeddings based on the context. By combining powerful mechanisms like self-attention and positional encoding, transformers can generate contextualized word representations that account for syntax, semantics, and word order. These advancements have revolutionized NLP tasks, from text classification to machine translation, and continue to drive progress in this field. In the next section, we will explore how to implement transformers for specific tasks like text classification, bringing these powerful embeddings to practical use.

Implementing a Transformer for Text Classification

Text classification is one of the most common applications of NLP, where the goal is to assign predefined labels to a given text. Examples include sentiment analysis (classifying text as positive or negative), spam detection (classifying emails as spam or not), and topic categorization (classifying news articles into categories, such as sports, politics, and so on).

Transformer models, particularly those like BERT (Bidirectional Encoder Representations from Transformers), have achieved state-of-the-art performance on text classification tasks by leveraging contextual word embeddings and attention mechanisms. In this section, we will walk through how to implement a transformer for a text classification task, using PyTorch 2.0.

1. **Preparing the Dataset:** Before implementing the transformer, we first need a dataset. For simplicity, let us assume, we are working with a binary sentiment classification dataset, where the goal is to classify movie reviews as positive or negative.

We will use the IMDb dataset which contains movie reviews, along with their sentiment labels.

To begin, we need to install and import the necessary libraries:

```
pip install transformers datasets torch
```

Next, we will load and preprocess the dataset using the Hugging Face datasets library. This library provides easy access to preprocessed datasets for NLP tasks.

```
from datasets import load_dataset

# Load IMDb dataset
dataset = load_dataset("imdb")
```

The dataset is now loaded into train, validation, and test splits. Next, we need to tokenize the text, and convert it into the format that the transformer model can process.

2. **Tokenizing the Text Data:** Transformers require tokenized input which means converting text into a sequence of token IDs. We will use the BERT tokenizer from the Hugging Face transformers library which handles all the necessary tokenization steps, including adding special tokens like [**CLS**] and [**SEP**].

```
from transformers import BertTokenizer

# Load pre-trained BERT tokenizer
tokenizer = BertTokenizer.from_pretrained("bert-base-uncased")

# Tokenize the text data
def tokenize_function(examples):
    return tokenizer(examples["text"], padding="max_length", truncation=True)

# Apply tokenization to the dataset
tokenized_datasets = dataset.map(tokenize_function, batched=True)
```

Here:

a. We use the **BertTokenizer.from_pretrained("bert-base-uncased")** to load the BERT tokenizer.

b. The **padding="max_length"** ensures that all sequences are padded to a fixed length.

c. The **truncation=True** ensures that texts longer than the maximum sequence length are truncated.

3. **Defining the Transformer Model:** For text classification, we can use a pre-trained transformer model like BERT and fine-tune it on our dataset. The Hugging Face library provides an easy-to-use class, BertForSequenceClassification, specifically designed for text classification tasks.

```
from transformers import BertForSequenceClassification
# Load pre-trained BERT model for sequence classification (binary
classification)
model = BertForSequenceClassification.from_pretrained("bert-base-uncased",
num_labels=2)
```

Here:

a. **num_labels=2** indicates a binary classification task (positive or negative sentiment).

b. The BertForSequenceClassification model includes the BERT architecture, along with a classification head on top of it, making it ready for fine-tuning on classification tasks.

4. **Training the Model:** To train the model, we need a DataLoader to handle our dataset in batches, and an optimizer to adjust the model's weights. We will also use cross-entropy loss for binary classification.

```
import torch
from torch.utils.data import DataLoader
from transformers import AdamW
from torch.nn import CrossEntropyLoss

# Prepare the DataLoader
train_dataloader = DataLoader(tokenized_datasets["train"], batch_size=8)

# Define the optimizer
optimizer = AdamW(model.parameters(), lr=1e-5)
```

```
# Define the loss function
loss_fn = CrossEntropyLoss()

# Training loop
device = torch.device("cuda" if torch.cuda.is_available() else "cpu")
model.to(device)

for epoch in range(3):  # Training for 3 epochs
    model.train()
    for batch in train_dataloader:
        optimizer.zero_grad()

        # Move batch to the same device as model
        input_ids = batch["input_ids"].to(device)
        attention_mask = batch["attention_mask"].to(device)
        labels = batch["label"].to(device)

        # Forward pass
        outputs = model(input_ids, attention_mask=attention_mask, labels=la-
bels)
        loss = outputs.loss

        # Backward pass
        loss.backward()
    optimizer.step()

    print(f"Epoch {epoch + 1}, Loss: {loss.item():.4f}")
```

Here:

a. The model is moved to the device (GPU or CPU) using model.to(device).

b. During each training step, the optimizer updates the model's weights, based on the computed gradients from the loss function.

5. **Evaluating the Model:** After training, we need to evaluate the model on the validation set. This involves computing accuracy or other metrics like F1-score. We will use the same tokenizer to preprocess the validation set, and then evaluate the model's performance.

```
from sklearn.metrics import accuracy_score
# Prepare validation DataLoader
val_dataloader = DataLoader(tokenized_datasets["test"], batch_size=8)

# Evaluate the model
model.eval()
all_preds = []
all_labels = []
with torch.no_grad():
    for batch in val_dataloader:
        input_ids = batch["input_ids"].to(device)
        attention_mask = batch["attention_mask"].to(device)
        labels = batch["label"].to(device)

        # Forward pass
        outputs = model(input_ids, attention_mask=attention_mask)
        logits = outputs.logits

        preds = torch.argmax(logits, dim=-1)
```

```
            all_preds.extend(preds.cpu().numpy())
            all_labels.extend(labels.cpu().numpy())

    # Compute accuracy
    accuracy = accuracy_score(all_labels, all_preds)
    print(f"Validation Accuracy: {accuracy * 100:.2f}%")
```

Here:

a. The model is set to evaluation mode with **`model.eval()`**.

b. We compute predictions using **`torch.argmax`** to get the class with the highest probability.

c. The accuracy is calculated using **`accuracy_score`** from **`sklearn.metrics`**.

6. **Fine-Tuning Pre-Trained Models:** Fine-tuning pre-trained models like BERT enables the model to adapt to a specific task. The key advantage of fine-tuning is that it allows the model to leverage the knowledge it has learned from large-scale pre-training on general language data, reducing the amount of labeled data needed for task-specific training.

During fine-tuning, the pre-trained weights are updated based on the task-specific data, allowing the model to learn the nuances of the classification task.

In this section, we implemented a transformer-based model (BERT) for text classification. We covered how to prepare data, tokenize text, and fine-tune a pre-trained transformer model for a classification task. Transformers, particularly BERT, excel at capturing rich contextual information, making them highly effective for text classification tasks. In the next section, we will dive into Named Entity Recognition (NER) with transformers, expanding on how these models can be applied to extract entities from text.

Named Entity Recognition (NER) with Transformers

Named Entity Recognition (NER) involves identifying and classifying entities in text, such as names of people, organizations, locations, and dates. It is a crucial task in applications like information extraction, question answering, and knowledge graph construction. Traditional NER methods relied on feature engineering and rule-based systems, but transformers, particularly BERT and its variants, have significantly improved performance by leveraging contextualized word embeddings and self-attention mechanisms.

In this section, we explore how transformer models like BERT are used for NER, from data preparation to fine-tuning and evaluation.

1. **NER as Sequence Labeling:** NER with transformers is framed as a sequence labeling task. Each token (word or subword) in a sentence is assigned a label corresponding to its entity class.

For instance:

- Input: "*Apple is looking to acquire a startup in Berlin.*"
- Tokens: ["**Apple**", "**is**", "**looking**", "**to**", "**acquire**", "**a**", "**startup**", "**in**", "**Berlin**"]
- Labels: [ORG, O, O, O, O, O, O, LOC, O]

Here, Apple is classified as an ORG (organization) and Berlin as a LOC (location). Transformer models learn to predict these labels by considering the entire context of a sentence which enables them to disambiguate words that might have different meanings, depending on their context.

2. **Preparing the Dataset:** To fine-tune a transformer model for NER, we need a labeled dataset.

Popular datasets include CoNLL-03 which contains annotations for person (PER), organization (ORG), and location (LOC). Using the Hugging Face Datasets library, we can load the dataset for training and evaluation.

```
from datasets import load_dataset
# Load the CoNLL-03 dataset
dataset = load_dataset("conll2003")
```

We will use the BERT tokenizer to preprocess the text, and tokenize it for the model. Tokenization involves splitting text into subwords, ensuring that the words like "**New York**" are tokenized correctly as ["**New**", "**##York**"].

3. **Tokenizing the Text:** Tokenization is crucial for transformer models, as they process subword units, instead of entire words. Using BERT's tokenizer, we convert the text into token IDs, and align the corresponding NER labels.

```
from transformers import BertTokenizer

# Load pre-trained BERT tokenizer
tokenizer = BertTokenizer.from_pretrained("bert-base-uncased")

# Tokenize the dataset
def tokenize_and_align_labels(examples):
    tokenized_inputs = tokenizer(examples["tokens"], padding="max_length",
truncation=True, is_split_into_words=True)
    labels = examples["ner_tags"]
    tokenized_inputs["labels"] = labels
    return tokenized_inputs

# Apply tokenization
tokenized_datasets = dataset.map(tokenize_and_align_labels, batched=True)
```

The **is_split_into_words=True** argument ensures that the tokenizer processes each word separately, and we align the NER labels with the tokenized text.

4. **Fine-Tuning BERT for NER:** For NER, we use a transformer model with a token classification head. The pre-trained BERT model can be fine-tuned on the NER task using the BertForTokenClassification class.

```
from transformers import BertForTokenClassification, Trainer, TrainingArguments

# Load pre-trained BERT for token classification
model = BertForTokenClassification.from_pretrained("bert-base-uncased",
num_labels=9)

# Set up training arguments
training_args = TrainingArguments(
    output_dir="./results",
    evaluation_strategy="epoch",
    learning_rate=2e-5,
    per_device_train_batch_size=16,
    per_device_eval_batch_size=16,
    num_train_epochs=3,
    weight_decay=0.01,
)

# Initialize the Trainer
trainer = Trainer(
    model=model,
```

```
    args=training_args,
    train_dataset=tokenized_datasets["train"],
    eval_dataset=tokenized_datasets["validation"],
    tokenizer=tokenizer,
)

# Fine-tune the model
trainer.train()
```

Here, we specify **num_labels=9** for the different entity categories, and use the Trainer API to fine-tune the model on the CoNLL-03 dataset. The model is trained for three epochs, with a learning rate of 2e-5.

5. **Evaluating the Model:** After training, we evaluate the model on the validation dataset. We compute performance metrics like precision, recall, and F1-score to measure how well the model identifies entities.

```
from sklearn.metrics import classification_report

# Evaluate the model
predictions, true_labels, _ = trainer.predict(tokenized_datasets
["validation"])

# Convert predictions and true labels
pred_labels = predictions.argmax(axis=-1)

# Flatten arrays for classification report
pred_labels_flat = pred_labels.flatten()
true_labels_flat = true_labels.flatten()

# Generate classification report
print(classification_report(true_labels_flat, pred_labels_flat))
```

This code computes the classification report for the model's predictions, showing its performance across the different entity types.

6. **Handling Multilingual NER:** Transformer models like mBERT (Multilingual BERT) and XLM-R (Cross-lingual RoBERTa) can be used for NER tasks in multiple languages. These models are pre-trained on text in multiple languages, and can transfer learning across languages, making them suitable for multilingual NER applications.

By using models like mBERT, we can fine-tune multilingual NER datasets, ensuring that the model can recognize entities in different languages with high accuracy.

In this section, we demonstrated how to implement a transformer model for Named Entity Recognition (NER). By fine-tuning pre-trained models such as BERT, we can efficiently identify and classify entities in text, significantly improving performance over traditional methods. We also highlighted how multilingual models like mBERT enable NER in diverse linguistic settings. In the next section, we will explore sentiment analysis and emotion detection using transformers, the two fundamental tasks in NLP.

Sentiment Analysis and Emotion Detection Using Transformers

Sentiment analysis and emotion detection are pivotal tasks in Natural Language Processing (NLP), aimed at understanding and classifying the emotional tone behind a piece of text. Sentiment analysis, typically focuses on determining whether the sentiment of a text is positive, negative, or neutral, whereas emotion detection goes deeper, identifying specific emotions such as happiness, sadness, anger, or fear.

Transformers have significantly improved the accuracy and efficiency of both sentiment analysis and emotion detection by leveraging their ability to understand context and relationships within the text. In this section, we explore how transformer models like BERT, RoBERTa, and DistilBERT can be fine-tuned for sentiment analysis and emotion detection tasks.

1. Sentiment Analysis with Transformers

Sentiment analysis is one of the most widely used applications of NLP. It involves classifying text into predefined categories, based on the sentiment, it expresses. The most common categories are positive, negative, and neutral, but sentiment classification can be extended to more granular categories, depending on the application.

Step 1: Preparing the Dataset for Sentiment Analysis

We will use the IMDb dataset for binary sentiment classification, where each review is labeled as either positive or negative. The dataset is available in the Hugging Face Datasets library.

from datasets import **load_dataset**

```
# Load the IMDb dataset
dataset = load_dataset("imdb")
```

Step 2: Tokenizing the Text

Next, we use the BERT tokenizer to preprocess the text for the transformer model. The tokenizer converts text into token IDs, and ensures that each sequence has a consistent length, using padding, where necessary.

```
from transformers import BertTokenizer

# Load pre-trained BERT tokenizer
tokenizer = BertTokenizer.from_pretrained("bert-base-uncased")

# Tokenize the dataset
def tokenize_function(examples):
    return tokenizer(examples["text"], padding="max_length", truncation=True)

# Apply tokenization to the dataset
tokenized_datasets = dataset.map(tokenize_function, batched=True)
```

In this code, we use the tokenizer to process the text, adding padding and truncation, as needed to ensure that the sequences are of the correct length for the model.

Step 3: Fine-Tuning BERT for Sentiment Analysis

To fine-tune BERT for sentiment analysis, we load the pre-trained BERT model with a classification head (BertForSequenceClassification), and fine-tune it on the IMDb dataset.

```
from transformers import BertForSequenceClassification, Trainer,
TrainingArguments

# Load pre-trained BERT model for binary sentiment classification
model = BertForSequenceClassification.from_pretrained("bert-base-uncased",
num_labels=2)

# Set up training arguments
training_args = TrainingArguments(
```

```
        output_dir="./results",
        evaluation_strategy="epoch",
        learning_rate=2e-5,
        per_device_train_batch_size=16,
        per_device_eval_batch_size=16,
        num_train_epochs=3,
        weight_decay=0.01,
    )
    # Initialize Trainer
    trainer = Trainer(
        model=model,
        args=training_args,
        train_dataset=tokenized_datasets["train"],
        eval_dataset=tokenized_datasets["test"],
        tokenizer=tokenizer,
    )

    # Fine-tune the model
    trainer.train()
```

Here:

a. **`num_labels=2`** indicates binary sentiment classification (positive vs. negative).

b. We use the Trainer API to handle the training loop, including evaluation and logging.

Step 4: Evaluating the Model

After training the model, we evaluate its performance on the test set, and compute accuracy metrics.

```
# Evaluate the model
trainer.evaluate()
```

The evaluation metrics include accuracy, precision, recall, and F1-score, giving us a comprehensive view of the model's performance.

2. Emotion Detection with Transformers

Emotion detection extends sentiment analysis by identifying specific emotions, within the text. Thus, instead of classifying the text as just positive or negative, emotion detection identifies emotions like anger, joy, sadness, and fear, offering more detailed insights into the tone of the text.

Step 1: Preparing the Dataset for Emotion Detection

For emotion detection, we can use a dataset like EmoBank which contains text annotated with several emotional categories (for example, joy, sadness, anger, fear, and so on). Alternatively, other datasets, such as GoEmotions can be used for a more extensive set of emotions.

```
# Load a custom emotion dataset (for example, GoEmotions)
dataset = load_dataset("go_emotions")
```

Step 2: Tokenizing the Text

We tokenize the dataset in a similar manner to sentiment analysis, ensuring that each text is properly preprocessed for transformer input.

```
# Tokenize the dataset for emotion detection
def tokenize_emotion_function(examples):
    return tokenizer(examples["text"], padding="max_length", truncation=True)

tokenized_emotion_datasets = dataset.map(tokenize_emotion_function,
batched=True)
```

Step 3: Fine-Tuning BERT for Emotion Detection

We use BERT to fine-tune emotion detection by applying a classification head, and training it on the emotion-labeled dataset.

```
# Load pre-trained BERT model for multi-class emotion classification
model = BertForSequenceClassification.from_pretrained("bert-base-uncased",
num_labels=28)  # Assume 28 emotions

# Set up training arguments
training_args = TrainingArguments(
    output_dir="./results_emotion",
    evaluation_strategy="epoch",
    learning_rate=2e-5,
    per_device_train_batch_size=16,
    per_device_eval_batch_size=16,
    num_train_epochs=3,
    weight_decay=0.01,
)

# Initialize Trainer
trainer = Trainer(
    model=model,
    args=training_args,
    train_dataset=tokenized_emotion_datasets["train"],
    eval_dataset=tokenized_emotion_datasets["test"],
    tokenizer=tokenizer,
)

# Fine-tune the model
trainer.train()
```

Here:

a. **`num_labels=28`** indicates the number of emotion categories (the number might vary, based on the dataset).

b. As with sentiment analysis, we use the Trainer API to manage the training process.

Step 4: Evaluating the Model

After training, we evaluate the model's performance on the test set. Given the multi-class nature of emotion detection, we typically measure accuracy, precision, recall, and F1-score for each class.

```
# Evaluate the model on the emotion detection task
trainer.evaluate()
```

This gives us a detailed performance analysis across multiple emotion classes.

3. Practical Use Cases for Sentiment and Emotion Detection

- **Customer Feedback:** Sentiment analysis is often used to analyze customer reviews or feedback, helping businesses gauge the overall sentiment toward their products or services.
- **Social Media Monitoring:** Emotion detection can be used to analyze the tone of social media posts, helping brands identify customer emotions like anger or happiness toward their campaigns.

- **Mental Health Monitoring:** Emotion detection models can assist in understanding the emotional state of individuals, based on their written expressions which can be applied in mental health assessments or counseling.

In this section, we demonstrated how transformer models like BERT can be fine-tuned for sentiment analysis and emotion detection. By leveraging the power of pre-trained transformers, we can accurately classify the text, not just by its sentiment, but also by the emotions it expresses, making these models invaluable for a range of applications–from customer service to mental health monitoring. In the next section, we will explore Question-Answering Systems with transformer models, further showcasing the versatility of these architectures.

Question-Answering Systems with Transformer Models

Question-Answering (QA) systems are a key application of Natural Language Processing (NLP) that involves providing precise answers to questions, based on a given context or document. The goal is for the model to extract relevant information from the text to answer a user's question accurately, often in real-time. With the advent of transformer models like BERT, T5, and RoBERTa, QA systems have achieved state-of-the-art performance on several benchmark datasets.

In this section, we will explore how transformer models are used for building question-answering systems. We will cover both extractive Q & A, where the answer is directly extracted from the text, and the generative QA, where the model generates a response. We will demonstrate how to fine-tune pre-trained transformer models for these tasks using the SQuAD Dataset (Stanford Question Answering Dataset), one of the most widely used datasets for QA tasks.

1. Extractive Question - Answering with Transformers

In extractive QA, the model is given a passage of text and a question, and its task is to identify the exact span of text that answers the question. For example:

- Context: "*The Eiffel Tower is located in Paris, France.*"
- Question: "*Where is the Eiffel Tower located?*"
- Answer: "*Paris, France*"

Transformers like BERT and RoBERTa are well-suited for extractive QA due to their ability to consider, both the context and the question simultaneously using the self-attention mechanism.

Step 1: Fine-Tuning BERT for Extractive QA

To fine-tune BERT for extractive question answering, we use a model designed for token classification tasks: BertForQuestionAnswering. This model takes a passage and a question as input, and outputs the start and end positions of the answer, within the passage.

```
from transformers import BertTokenizer, BertForQuestionAnswering
from datasets import load_dataset

# Load pre-trained BERT tokenizer and model for extractive QA
tokenizer = BertTokenizer.from_pretrained("bert-large-uncased")
model = BertForQuestionAnswering.from_pretrained("bert-large-uncased")

# Load the SQuAD dataset
dataset = load_dataset("squad")
```

```
# Tokenize the dataset
def tokenize_function(examples):
    return tokenizer(examples["question"], examples["context"],
truncation=True, padding=True)

tokenized_datasets = dataset.map(tokenize_function, batched=True)
```

Here:

a. We load the SQuAD dataset that contains questions and their corresponding context paragraphs.
b. The tokenizer processes the text, ensuring that both the question and the context are correctly tokenized.

Step 2: Fine-Tuning the Model

Now, we fine-tune the model on the SQuAD dataset. The BertForQuestionAnswering model outputs two values: The start and end positions of the answer span. We use these outputs to calculate the loss during training.

```
from transformers import Trainer, TrainingArguments

# Set up training arguments
training_args = TrainingArguments(
    output_dir="./results",
    evaluation_strategy="epoch",
    learning_rate=3e-5,
    per_device_train_batch_size=8,
    per_device_eval_batch_size=8,
    num_train_epochs=3,
)

# Initialize Trainer
trainer = Trainer(
    model=model,
  args=training_args,
    train_dataset=tokenized_datasets["train"],
    eval_dataset=tokenized_datasets["validation"],
    tokenizer=tokenizer,
)

# Fine-tune the model
trainer.train()
```

Step 3: Evaluating the Model

After fine-tuning, we evaluate the model on the validation set, checking metrics, such as Exact Match (EM) and F1 score, which measure how accurately the model predicts the correct span of text.

```
# Evaluate the model
trainer.evaluate()
```

This provides the accuracy of the model in predicting the correct span for each question.

2. Generative Question-Answering with Transformers

While extractive QA focuses on extracting exact spans from the text, generative QA systems aim to generate a natural language answer. These models are often based on the encoder-decoder architecture, where the encoder processes the input context, and the decoder generates a human-readable answer.

Text-to-Text Transfer Transformer (T5) and Bidirectional and Auto-Regressive Transformer (BART) are well-suited for generative QA, as they treat every task as a text-to-text problem. For generative QA, the model is trained to generate the answer, given the question and the context.

Step 1: Using T5 for Generative QA

We can use T5 to generate answers by framing the problem as a "`text generation`" task. The input format is [`Question`] [`Context`], and the model generates the corresponding answer.

```
from transformers import T5Tokenizer, T5ForConditionalGeneration

# Load pre-trained T5 model and tokenizer
tokenizer = T5Tokenizer.from_pretrained("t5-base")
model = T5ForConditionalGeneration.from_pretrained("t5-base")

# Example input
context = "The Eiffel Tower is located in Paris, France."
question = "Where is the Eiffel Tower located?"

# Preprocess the input
input_text = f"question: {question} context: {context}"
inputs = tokenizer(input_text, return_tensors="pt", truncation=True,
padding=True)

# Generate answer
outputs = model.generate(inputs["input_ids"], max_length=50)
answer = tokenizer.decode(outputs[0], skip_special_tokens=True)

print(answer)  # Output: Paris, France
```

In this example:

a. We use the T5 model to generate an answer, based on the question and context.

b. The model generates a natural language answer, instead of extracting a span.

Step 2: Fine-Tuning T5 for QA Tasks

To fine-tune T5 for question-answering tasks, we can follow a similar process as with extractive QA. However, for generative QA, we train the model on the dataset by framing it as a sequence-to-sequence problem, where the input is the question and context, and the target is the answer.

```
# Fine-tuning T5 on the SQuAD dataset
training_args = TrainingArguments(
    output_dir="./results_t5",
    evaluation_strategy="epoch",
    learning_rate=3e-5,
    per_device_train_batch_size=4,
    num_train_epochs=3,
)

trainer = Trainer(
    model=model,
    args=training_args,
    train_dataset=tokenized_datasets["train"],
    eval_dataset=tokenized_datasets["validation"],
    tokenizer=tokenizer,
)

trainer.train()
```

Challenges in Question-Answering Systems

- **Ambiguity in Questions:** Sometimes, questions are not straightforward, and there may be multiple possible answers or ambiguous phrasing. QA models need to be robust enough to handle such variations.
- **Context Length:** Transformer models have limitations on the maximum input length. For very long documents, either the input text needs to be truncated, or more advanced models like Longformer or Reformer need to be used.
- **Answer Generation Quality:** In generative QA, models might produce fluent but incorrect or irrelevant answers. Ensuring that the generated answers are both accurate and coherent remains a challenge.

Use Cases for Question-Answering Systems

- **Customer Support:** QA systems can automatically answer customer queries, providing instant responses to frequently asked questions.
- **Search Engines:** QA systems can be integrated into search engines to extract precise answers from documents or the web.
- **Virtual Assistants**: Models like GPT-3 or BERT can be used to power intelligent virtual assistants that answer a wide range of user questions.

In this section, we explored how transformer models like BERT for extractive QA and T5 for generative QA, can be fine-tuned to build robust question-answering systems. These systems can extract or generate answers to questions, based on context, making them suitable for various applications, such as customer support, search engines, and virtual assistants. The next section will focus on Text Summarization techniques using transformers, demonstrating how these models can be used to condense long texts into concise summaries.

Text Summarization Techniques Using Transformers

Text summarization is a crucial NLP task that involves generating a shorter version of a document while retaining its essential meaning. There are two primary types of text summarization:

- **Extractive Summarization:** This technique selects key sentences or phrases directly from the original text to form a summary.
- **Abstractive Summarization:** This approach generates new sentences that paraphrase the original content, effectively rewriting the text, while retaining the key information.

Transformer models, with their ability to understand context and generate human-like text, have significantly advanced both extractive and abstractive summarization tasks. In this section, we will explore how transformers can be used for both types of summarizations, and demonstrate their capabilities through practical examples.

1. Abstractive Summarization with Transformers

Abstractive summarization aims to generate a summary that might not contain the exact sentences from the source text, but still conveys the essential points in a concise form. Unlike extractive methods, abstractive summarization requires the model to understand the content, and generate a novel text.

Transformer-based models like BART and T5 are particularly effective for abstractive summarization. These models use an encoder-decoder architecture, where the encoder processes the input text, and the decoder generates the summary.

Step 1: Using Pre-Trained BART for Abstractive Summarization

BART (Bidirectional and Auto-Regressive Transformers) is a transformer model pre-trained for sequence-to-sequence tasks, such as summarization and translation. We will fine-tune BART for abstractive summarization using the CNN/DailyMail dataset which contains news articles and their summaries.

```
from transformers import BartForConditionalGeneration, BartTokenizer

# Load pre-trained BART model and tokenizer
model = BartForConditionalGeneration.from_pretrained("facebook/bart-
large-cnn")
tokenizer = BartTokenizer.from_pretrained("facebook/bart-large-cnn")
```

Here, we use the pre-trained BART model trained on the CNN/DailyMail dataset for summarization tasks.

Step 2: Tokenizing the Text

We will now tokenize the text (news articles) for input into the BART model. The tokenizer will ensure that the text is properly formatted for the model, truncating long texts and padding the shorter ones.

```
# Tokenize the dataset for summarization
def tokenize_function(examples):
    return tokenizer(examples["article"], padding="max_length",
truncation=True)

# Apply tokenization to the dataset
tokenized_datasets = dataset.map(tokenize_function, batched=True)
```

Step 3: Fine-Tuning BART for Summarization

Once the data is tokenized, we can fine-tune BART on the summarization task. Fine-tuning the model involves adjusting the model's weights based on the task-specific dataset, such as generating summaries for news articles.

```
from transformers import Trainer, TrainingArguments

# Set up training arguments
training_args = TrainingArguments(
    output_dir="./results",
    evaluation_strategy="epoch",
    learning_rate=3e-5,
    per_device_train_batch_size=4,
    num_train_epochs=3,
    weight_decay=0.01,
)

# Initialize Trainer
trainer = Trainer(
    model=model,
    args=training_args,
    train_dataset=tokenized_datasets["train"],    eval_dataset=tokenized_data-
sets["test"],    tokenizer=tokenizer,
```

```
)

# Fine-tune the model
trainer.train()
```

Step 4: Generating Summaries

Once the model is fine-tuned, we can use it to generate summaries for new articles. The following code generates an abstractive summary for a given text:

```
# Generate a summary for a new article
input_text = "Your article text goes here."
inputs = tokenizer(input_text, return_tensors="pt", max_length=1024,
truncation=True)

# Generate summary
summary_ids = model.generate(inputs["input_ids"], max_length=150, num_beams=4,
early_stopping=True)
summary = tokenizer.decode(summary_ids[0], skip_special_tokens=True)

print(summary)
```

In this example:

a. **`num_beams=4`** specifies beam search for generating high-quality summaries.

b. **`max_length=150`** controls the length of the summary.

2. Extractive Summarization with Transformers

In contrast to abstractive summarization, extractive summarization identifies and selects important sentences directly from the source text. BERTSUM is a variant of BERT, specifically designed for extractive summarization. It uses BERT's encoder to process the document, and selects the most informative sentences as the summary.

Step 1: Using Pre-trained BERTSUM for Extractive Summarization

BERTSUM extends BERT to handle extractive summarization by adding a classification layer that selects sentences from the input text. The model is trained to assign a score to each sentence, and the highest-scoring sentences are selected as the summary.

```
from transformers import BertTokenizer, BertForSequenceClassification

# Load pre-trained BERTSUM model and tokenizer for extractive summarization
model = BertForSequenceClassification.from_pretrained("facebook/bert-large-
uncased-whole-word-masking-finetuned-squad")
tokenizer = BertTokenizer.from_pretrained("facebook/bert-large-uncased-whole-
word-masking-finetuned-squad")
```

Step 2: Tokenizing the Text

For extractive summarization, we need to tokenize the document and split it into sentences, ensuring that each sentence is treated as an individual input for the BERT model.

```
# Tokenize the dataset for extractive summarization
def tokenize_extractive_function(examples):
    return tokenizer(examples["text"], padding="max_length", truncation=True)

# Apply tokenization to the dataset
tokenized_extractive_datasets = dataset.map(tokenize_extractive_function,
batched=True)
```

Step 3: Fine-Tuning BERTSUM for Extractive Summarization

Fine-tuning BERTSUM follows a similar process to fine-tuning BERT for text classification. We train the model to predict sentence importance for extractive summarization tasks.

```
# Set up training arguments for extractive summarization
training_args = TrainingArguments(
    output_dir="./results_extractive",
    evaluation_strategy="epoch",
    learning_rate=3e-5,
    per_device_train_batch_size=4,
    num_train_epochs=3,
    weight_decay=0.01,
)

# Initialize Trainer
trainer = Trainer(
    model=model,
    args=training_args,
    train_dataset=tokenized_extractive_datasets["train"],
    eval_dataset=tokenized_extractive_datasets["test"],
    tokenizer=tokenizer,
)

# Fine-tune the model
trainer.train()
```

Step 4: Generating Extractive Summaries

After fine-tuning, we can use the model to generate extractive summaries by selecting the most informative sentences.

```
# Generate an extractive summary
inputs = tokenizer(input_text, return_tensors="pt", truncation=True)

# Generate summary
summary_ids = model.generate(inputs["input_ids"], num_beams=4,
early_stopping=True)
summary = tokenizer.decode(summary_ids[0], skip_special_tokens=True)

print(summary)
```

3. Challenges in Summarization with Transformers

While transformers have significantly improved summarization tasks, several challenges remain:

- **Model Size and Computation:** Transformer models like BART and T5 are computationally expensive, requiring substantial hardware resources for fine-tuning and inference.
- **Long-Document Summarization:** Transformers struggle with long documents due to the quadratic complexity of self-attention. Longformer and Reformer are two models designed to address this by introducing sparse attention mechanisms to handle longer sequences.
- **Evaluating Summaries:** Objective evaluation of generated summaries remains a challenge. Metrics like the ROUGE score are commonly used to compare generated summaries against reference summaries, but they do not always capture quality or informativeness.

4. Use Cases for Summarization

- **News Summarization:** Automatically summarizing news articles allows readers to quickly consume important information.
- **Legal and Medical Document Summarization**: In fields like law and medicine, summarizing lengthy documents can save significant time, highlighting key sections like clauses or diagnoses.
- **Content Curation:** Summarization models can be used for curating content on websites or social media, extracting the most relevant information for users.

Text summarization using transformer models, particularly BART and T5, has revolutionized how we generate concise and meaningful summaries from large documents. While abstractive summarization creates novel, human-like summaries, extractive summarization focuses on selecting the most informative sentences. Fine-tuning these models on domain-specific data can significantly enhance performance.

In the next chapter, we will explore how to deploy transformer models for real-world NLP applications, focusing on their evaluation, optimization, and adaptation to various practical scenarios.

Evaluating Transformer Models for NLP Tasks

Evaluating transformer models for NLP tasks is a crucial step to ensure their effectiveness and robustness across a variety of language applications. Due to the complexity of language, NLP models must be assessed on multiple metrics, and across different dimensions, such as accuracy, efficiency, and robustness. Transformer models like BERT, GPT, T5, and others have revolutionized NLP, but their performance must be rigorously evaluated to ensure that they generalize well to real-world tasks.

In this section, we will explore the different evaluation metrics and methods, commonly used for transformer models in NLP, including accuracy, F1 score, BLEU, ROUGE, and more. Additionally, we will discuss the importance of benchmarking, and provide examples of how to evaluate transformer models for various NLP tasks, including classification, summarization, and question-answering.

Evaluation Metrics for NLP Tasks

The choice of evaluation metric depends on the specific NLP task at hand. The following are some common metrics used to assess the performance of transformer models in NLP:

Accuracy

For classification tasks like sentiment analysis or text classification, accuracy is the most straightforward metric. It measures the percentage of correct predictions, out of all predictions made.

- **Formula**:

$$Accuracy = \frac{\textit{Number of Correct Predictions}}{\textit{Total Number of Predictions}}$$

This metric is especially useful, when the task has balanced classes. However, in imbalanced datasets, accuracy might be misleading, and more granular metrics like F1 score or ROC AUC might be better.

Precision, Recall, and F1 Score

For tasks, where class imbalance exists (for example, rare entity recognition or emotion detection), precision, recall, and F1 score are more informative metrics:

- Precision measures how many of the predicted positive instances are actually positive.
- Recall measures how many actual positive instances were correctly predicted.
- F1 score is the harmonic mean of precision and recall, providing a single metric to balance both.
- Formula:
    - $Precision = \frac{TP}{TP + FP}$
    - $Recall = \frac{TP}{TP + FN}$
    - $F1\,Score = 2 * \frac{Precision * Recall}{Precision + Recall}$

Where:

- TP = True Positives
- FP = False Positives
- FN = False Negatives

The F1 score is particularly useful, when the classes are imbalanced, and a model's performance in predicting the minority class is of high importance.

Recall-Oriented Understudy for Gisting Evaluation (ROUGE)

For text summarization and other generative tasks like machine translation, ROUGE is a widely used evaluation metric. ROUGE compares the n-grams, word sequences, and word overlaps between the generated summary and reference summaries. The most common variants are:

- **ROUGE-N**: Measures overlap of n-grams (for instance, ROUGE-1 for unigrams, ROUGE-2 for bigrams).
- **ROUGE-L:** Measures the longest common subsequence between the generated and reference text.

This metric is valuable for evaluating the quality of generated summaries, especially in tasks like abstractive summarization.

Bilingual Evaluation Understudy (BLEU)

BLEU is another popular metric for evaluating generative tasks, especially for machine translation. BLEU compares n-grams of the generated translation with those of a reference translation. BLEU scores range from 0 to 1, with higher values indicating better performance.

- Formula:

$$BLEU = BP * exp\left(\sum_{n=1}^{N}\right) w_n \log p_n$$

Where p_n is the precision of n-grams, and BP is the brevity penalty (to account for short translations).

While BLEU is widely used in translation, it has limitations in capturing fluency and semantic meaning, which is why it is often complemented with other metrics.

Perplexity

In language generation tasks like text generation or dialog systems, perplexity is commonly used to measure how well the model predicts the next word in a sequence. Lower perplexity indicates better performance.

- Formula:

$$Perplexity = exp\left(\frac{1}{N}\sum_{i=1}^{N} \square \, log\, P(wi)\right)$$

Where $P(w_i)$ is the predicted probability of the "*ii-th*" word.

Benchmarking Transformer Models

To assess the true performance of a transformer model, it is essential to benchmark it against the existing models on standard datasets. Benchmarking provides a reference point for comparison, allowing you to understand how your model performs relative to other models in the field.

Step 1: Using Standard Datasets

Benchmarking transformer models typically involves evaluating them on widely accepted datasets for various NLP tasks. Some popular datasets include:

- SQuAD for question-answering.
- IMDB for sentiment analysis.
- CoNLL-03 for NER (Named Entity Recognition).
- CNN/DailyMail for summarization.

These datasets provide labeled data, allowing for the easy evaluation of different models across similar tasks.

Step 2: Comparing with Baselines

When benchmarking, it is important to compare the performance of your transformer model with baseline models, such as traditional machine learning models (for example, Logistic Regression, SVMs) or simpler neural network models (for example, LSTMs, GRUs). Transformer models are expected to outperform these baselines due to their ability to capture long-range dependencies and contextual relationships in text.

Step 3: Cross-Validation

In addition to simple test/train splits, cross-validation can be used to evaluate the stability and generalizability of transformer models. This technique involves splitting the dataset into multiple subsets and training and evaluating the model multiple times on different combinations of these subsets. In fact, cross-validation provides a more robust measure of a model's performance, and helps reduce overfitting.

Case Studies of Transformer Model Evaluation

- **BERT for Text Classification:** In text classification tasks (for example, sentiment analysis), BERT has been shown to outperform traditional methods such as SVMs and LSTMs. Evaluation metrics like accuracy, F1 score, and precision/recall provide insights into BERT's performance, with the F1 score being especially useful, when dealing with imbalanced datasets.

- **T5 for Text Summarization:** For summarization, T5 generates high-quality abstractive summaries, evaluated with ROUGE metrics. T5 performs well in comparison to other models such as BART and traditional extractive models, consistently achieving high ROUGE scores.
- **GPT-3 for Text Generation:** In text generation tasks, GPT-3 is evaluated using metrics like BLEU and perplexity. While BLEU helps evaluate the fluency and quality of the generated text, perplexity measures the model's confidence in generating the next word. GPT-3 has achieved remarkable performance in generating human-like text in many domains.

Challenges in Evaluation

- **Subjectivity:** For tasks like summarization or text generation, evaluation can be subjective. Human evaluation is often required to assess the quality of the output, which can be time-consuming and inconsistent.
- **Data Imbalance:** Many NLP tasks suffer from imbalanced datasets (for example, in NER, where certain entity types are underrepresented). This imbalance can skew evaluation metrics, making accuracy alone a poor indicator of model performance.
- **Evaluation of Real-World Data**: While benchmark datasets provide standardized metrics, real-world data often contains noise and outliers, making it harder to assess model robustness. Evaluating models on diverse, domain-specific data is essential for understanding their true performance in production settings.

Evaluating transformer models for NLP tasks requires a comprehensive understanding of the task at hand and selecting the appropriate evaluation metrics. From accuracy and F1 score for classification to ROUGE and BLEU for summarization and translation, different metrics serve different purposes. Benchmarking and cross-validation are essential practices to assess how well models generalize across various datasets and real-world scenarios. As transformer models continue to evolve, their evaluation will remain a critical step in ensuring they perform effectively across diverse NLP applications.

Conclusion

This chapter has explored the powerful capabilities of transformer models in the realm of Natural Language Processing (NLP). From their transformative impact on the way we process text to their application in diverse NLP tasks, transformers have redefined the landscape of language understanding and generation. In this chapter, we have covered a range of topics that highlight how transformers can be leveraged for practical NLP applications, from foundational tasks like tokenization and word embeddings to complex tasks such as sentiment analysis, named entity recognition, and question-answering systems.

We began by discussing the fundamental challenges in NLP, including ambiguity, variability, and the need for world knowledge, which transformers excel at addressing through their attention mechanisms and contextualized embeddings. Tokenization techniques, such as Byte Pair Encoding (BPE), WordPiece, and SentencePiece, were explored to show how transformers process and understand text at a granular level. We also examined the shift from static word embeddings to dynamic, context-dependent representations which allow transformers to understand language more accurately.

The key sections of this chapter provided in-depth examples of how to implement transformers for tasks like text classification, NER, and sentiment analysis. We discussed how to fine-tune pre-trained transformer models such as BERT and T5, for specific tasks enabling them to perform exceptionally well in these domains, even with limited task-specific data. Furthermore, we explored question-answering systems and text summarization techniques, demonstrating the versatility of transformer architectures in providing precise answers or generating concise, meaningful summaries from complex documents.

Additionally, we covered the growing importance of multilingual and cross-lingual NLP, as transformer models like mBERT and XLM-R make it possible to handle multiple languages simultaneously, opening up new possibilities for global applications. We also discussed the critical process of evaluating transformer models, highlighting the importance of metrics like accuracy, F1 score, ROUGE, and BLEU, and emphasizing the need for benchmarking and real-world data evaluation.

As we conclude this chapter, it is clear that transformer models have made significant strides in advancing NLP capabilities. The flexibility and power of transformers are paving the way for a wide array of applications, from conversational agents to content generation, sentiment analysis, and beyond. By fine-tuning these models and leveraging their pre-trained knowledge, we can achieve state-of-the-art performance across a wide variety of language tasks, even in highly specialized domains.

In the next chapter, we will delve into the implementation of transformer models for specific real-world applications, examining how these powerful models are deployed in industries ranging from healthcare to finance, and discussing strategies for optimizing them for production environments. We will also explore the future trends in NLP and the ongoing research in transformer architectures, highlighting the next frontiers in this rapidly evolving field.

CHAPTER 5
Computer Vision with Transformers

Introduction

Transformers have revolutionized the field of artificial intelligence, beginning with breakthroughs in Natural Language Processing (NLP). Now, their influence is expanding into computer vision, challenging the long-standing dominance of Convolutional Neural Networks (CNNs). This paradigm shift introduces a new way of interpreting visual data by modeling long-range dependencies, and leveraging global attention mechanisms.

In this chapter, we explore the transformative potential of Vision Transformers (ViT), and how they address limitations in traditional vision models. By dissecting their architecture and demonstrating hands-on implementation with PyTorch 2.0, readers will gain practical insights into applying transformers to core computer vision tasks, including image classification, object detection, and segmentation. This chapter also highlights how hybrid approaches that integrate CNNs with transformers are unlocking even greater performance, in real-world applications.

Structure

In this chapter, we will cover the following topics:

- Introduction to Computer Vision and Its Challenges
- Adapting Transformers for Image Processing
- Vision Transformer (ViT) Architecture and Implementation
- Image Classification with Vision Transformers
- Object Detection Using Transformer-Based Models
- Image Segmentation with Transformer Architectures
- Self-Supervised Learning in Vision Transformers
- Efficient Vision Transformers for Mobile and Edge Devices
- Interpretability and Visualization of Vision Transformers
- Comparing Transformers with Traditional CNN Architectures in Various Vision Tasks

Introduction to Computer Vision and Its Challenges

Computer vision is a rapidly evolving field within Artificial Intelligence (AI) that focuses on enabling machines to interpret and understand visual information from the world. By mimicking the human ability to perceive and analyze images and videos, computer vision systems power a wide range of applications – from facial recognition and autonomous vehicles to medical image analysis and industrial inspection. The goal of computer vision is to teach machines how to identify patterns, detect objects, classify images, and extract meaningful insights from the visual data.

Over the past decade, deep learning, particularly Convolutional Neural Networks (CNNs), has driven significant advancements in computer vision. CNNs have demonstrated remarkable accuracy in image classification, object detection, and segmentation tasks. However, despite these successes, traditional computer vision approaches still face a range of challenges that limit their scalability and robustness across diverse domains.

Key Challenges in Computer Vision

- **Data and Annotation Requirements**: Deep learning models are highly data-intensive. Achieving high performance in computer vision tasks typically requires large datasets with detailed annotations. For example, tasks like image classification or object detection often demand millions of labeled images. Collecting and annotating such datasets are expensive, time-consuming, and prone to errors, especially in specialized domains like healthcare or satellite imaging. Furthermore, model performance can degrade in low-data scenarios, making it difficult for models to generalize to new environments.
- **Variability in Visual Data**: Visual data is inherently diverse, with variations in lighting, viewpoint, background, scale, and occlusions. This variability makes it challenging for computer vision models to consistently perform across different contexts. For example, an object detected under ideal conditions might become unrecognizable, when partially obscured or viewed from an unusual angle. Ensuring robustness against such variations is a persistent challenge for vision models.
- **Generalization Across Domains**: A major limitation of traditional computer vision systems is their struggle to generalize across domains. Models trained on a specific dataset (for example, street scenes in one city) may underperform, when applied to slightly different data (for instance, streets in another city with different environmental conditions). This domain-specificity often necessitates additional fine-tuning or retraining which increases computational costs and time.
- **Complex Object Recognition**: Recognizing multiple objects within complex scenes is a challenging task. Traditional CNNs often rely on region proposal methods, such as Faster R-CNN, to localize objects, but these approaches can be computationally expensive and sensitive to object occlusion. Additionally, object detection models can struggle to differentiate between visually similar objects, particularly in crowded or cluttered environments.
- **Spatial Relationships and Long-Range Dependencies**: Understanding spatial relationships between objects in an image is crucial for tasks like image segmentation and scene understanding. Traditional CNNs which operate through local receptive fields, often struggle to capture long-range dependencies across large portions of an image. This limitation hinders their ability to effectively model global context, especially in tasks that require understanding the interaction between distant regions in an image.
- **Temporal Information in Video:** In video-based tasks, computer vision must account for temporal dynamics – the changes that occur across consecutive frames. Capturing and processing temporal dependencies is necessary for action recognition, object tracking, and video summarization. However, traditional models are primarily designed for static images, making it difficult to effectively model motion and continuity in video sequences.

Role of Transformers in Computer Vision

The introduction of transformer models to computer vision has brought promising solutions to many of these challenges. Transformers have demonstrated exceptional performance in capturing long-range dependencies, and processing the sequential data. By applying transformer architectures to visual data, researchers have developed models like the Vision Transformer (ViT) and Detection Transformers (DETR) which leverage self-attention mechanisms to process entire images holistically, rather than through localized patches.

Transformers address many of the limitations of CNNs by:

- Capturing global dependencies across the entire image, rather than focusing on small receptive fields.
- Reducing the need for extensive labeled data through self-supervised learning and transfer learning techniques.
- Handling complex object interactions and multi-scale representations more effectively.
- Improving performance on multi-modal tasks, combining vision with language for enhanced understanding.

As we delve deeper into this chapter, we will explore how transformers are adapted for computer vision tasks, their architecture, and their applications in areas such as image classification, object detection, and segmentation.

Adapting Transformers for Image Processing

Transformers have made significant strides in computer vision by addressing limitations in traditional Convolutional Neural Networks (CNNs). Unlike CNNs, which process data through localized receptive fields, transformers use self-attention to capture relationships across entire images. This shift has led to breakthroughs in image classification, object detection, and segmentation, positioning transformers as powerful alternatives to CNN-based architectures.

In this section, we will explore how transformers are adapted for image processing, the architectural innovations behind this adaptation, and how to implement a basic Vision Transformer (ViT), using PyTorch and the Hugging Face Transformers library.

Patch-Based Image Tokenization

One of the primary adaptations for applying transformers to images is patch-based tokenization. Instead of feeding the entire image at once, the image is divided into smaller, non-overlapping patches that are treated as tokens.

Here is how you can implement patch-based tokenization in PyTorch:

```
import torch
import torch.nn as nn
class PatchEmbedding(nn.Module):
    def __init__(self, img_size=224, patch_size=16, in_channels=3,
embed_dim=768):
        super().__init__()
        self.patch_size = patch_size
        self.proj = nn.Conv2d(in_channels, embed_dim, kernel_size=patch_size,
stride=patch_size)

    def forward(self, x):
        # Input shape: [B, C, H, W] -> [B, embed_dim, n_patches_h, n_patches_w]
        x = self.proj(x)
        x = x.flatten(2)  # Flatten spatial dimensions
        x = x.transpose(1, 2)  # [B, N, embed_dim], N = number of patches
        return x
```

The image is first divided into non-overlapping 16×16 patches, effectively reducing its spatial dimensions. Each of these patches is then passed through a convolutional layer which projects them into a higher-dimensional embedding space. After this, the patches are flattened and rearranged into a sequence, similar to how tokens are processed in NLP transformers, where each patch becomes a discrete token with a corresponding embedding. This transformation allows the model to process the image in a way akin to tokenized text in NLP, enabling the application of transformer architectures to image data.

Usage Example:

```
img = torch.randn(1, 3, 224, 224)  # Simulate an image with batch size 1
patch_embed = PatchEmbedding()
patch_tokens = patch_embed(img)  # Output: [1, 196, 768] (196 patches, 768-dim
embeddings)
```

Positional Encoding for Spatial Information

Since transformers are permutation-invariant, positional encodings are added to the patch embeddings to retain spatial structure. This ensures that the model understands the position of each patch in the original image.

```
class PositionalEncoding(nn.Module):
    def __init__(self, embed_dim=768, num_patches=196):
        super().__init__()
        self.pos_embed = nn.Parameter(torch.randn(1, num_patches + 1,
embed_dim))  # +1 for [CLS] token

    def forward(self, x):
        x = x + self.pos_embed[:, :x.size(1), :]
        return x
```

- **Explanation:**
    - A learnable positional embedding is added to each patch token.
    - This embedding helps the model retain information about the spatial layout of the patches.

Building the Vision Transformer (ViT) Model

The Vision Transformer (ViT) adapts the standard transformer encoder for image processing. The following code implements a simplified ViT model:

```
from transformers import ViTForImageClassification, ViTConfig
# Configuration for ViT model
config = ViTConfig(
    image_size=224,
    patch_size=16,
    num_labels=10,  # Example for CIFAR-10
    hidden_size=768,
    num_hidden_layers=12,
    num_attention_heads=12,
)
# Initialize Vision Transformer
model = ViTForImageClassification(config)
```

- **Explanation:**
    - ViTConfig allows us to specify the key parameters such as image size, patch size, and model depth.

- ViTForImageClassification is a pre-built transformer model from Hugging Face tailored for image classification tasks.

Training on a Sample Dataset

Training a Vision Transformer (ViT) model follows a process similar to training any other deep learning model, but with specific pre-processing steps to adapt image data for transformer input. In this example, we use the CIFAR-10 dataset to fine-tune a ViT model for image classification. The CIFAR-10 dataset consists of 60,000 32×32 color images across 10 classes, such as airplanes, cars, and birds.

To use ViT, the input images need to be resized to match the model's expected input dimensions (typically 224×224 pixels). This is achieved through standard PyTorch data transformations. The images are then converted into tensors, normalized, and loaded into a DataLoader for efficient batch processing during training.

Here is how the data pre-processing and model training pipeline can be implemented using Hugging Face's Transformers library:

```
from torchvision import transforms, datasets
from torch.utils.data import DataLoader
from transformers import Trainer, TrainingArguments
# Data preprocessing for CIFAR-10
transform = transforms.Compose([
        transforms.Resize((224, 224)),  # Resize images to match ViT input size
        transforms.ToTensor(),  # Convert images to tensors
])
# Download and load CIFAR-10 dataset
train_dataset = datasets.CIFAR10(root='./data', train=True, download=True,
transform=transform)
train_loader = DataLoader(train_dataset, batch_size=32, shuffle=True)
```

The transform pipeline resizes each CIFAR-10 image to the standard input size of 224x224 pixels required by ViT. This ensures consistency in input dimensions, and prevents errors during forward passes through the model. The **DataLoader** handles batching and shuffling, preparing the data for training in an efficient manner.

Fine-tuning ViT for CIFAR-10 requires configuring the model with the correct number of output classes (10 in this case). The Hugging Face library provides pre-built ViT models that can be easily fine-tuned by specifying a small set of hyperparameters, including batch size, learning rate, and the number of training epochs.

```
from transformers import ViTForImageClassification, ViTConfig

# Configure ViT for CIFAR-10
config = ViTConfig(
        image_size=224,
        patch_size=16,
        num_labels=10,  # CIFAR-10 has 10 classes
        hidden_size=768,
        num_hidden_layers=12,
        num_attention_heads=12,
)

# Initialize ViT model
model = ViTForImageClassification(config)
```

The ViTConfig class allows customization of the model architecture, including the image size, patch size, number of attention heads, and hidden layer dimensions. This flexibility makes it easy to adapt ViT to different datasets and tasks by modifying just a few parameters. The model is initialized with a classification head designed for the specific number of classes in the dataset.

Setting Up Training

Training is handled by the Trainer API from Hugging Face that simplifies the process of fine-tuning transformer models. The training loop is automatically managed, and additional features like evaluation and checkpointing are seamlessly integrated.

```
# Define training arguments
training_args = TrainingArguments(
        output_dir="./vit_results",
        evaluation_strategy="epoch",
        learning_rate=5e-5,
        per_device_train_batch_size=16,
        num_train_epochs=3,
)

# Initialize the Trainer
trainer = Trainer(
        model=model,
        args=training_args,
        train_dataset=train_dataset,
)
```

The Training Arguments class specifies the training configuration, including the learning rate, batch size, and number of epochs. In this example, the model is trained for three epochs, with an evaluation step occurring at the end of each epoch to monitor performance. A learning rate of **`5×10-55 \times 10^{-5}5×10-5`** ensures gradual updates which is essential for fine-tuning large transformer models, without destabilizing the optimization process.

With the dataset prepared and the model configured, training can be initiated using the following code:

```
trainer.train()
```

The **`train()`** method starts the fine-tuning process, where the model learns to classify CIFAR-10 images by adjusting its weights, based on the labeled data. Progress is automatically logged, and the best-performing model checkpoint is saved in the specified output directory.

By fine-tuning ViT on CIFAR-10, the model adapts to the specific characteristics of the dataset, achieving competitive performance even when compared to traditional convolutional neural networks. The self-attention mechanism allows ViT to capture long-range dependencies across the entire image, enabling better recognition of patterns that may span multiple regions.

Visualizing Attention Maps

One of the powerful features of vision transformers is their ability to visualize attention. This allows us to see which parts of the image, the model focuses on during classification.

```
import matplotlib.pyplot as plt
def visualize_attention(model, img):
    model.eval()
    with torch.no_grad():
        outputs = model(img.unsqueeze(0))  # Unsqueeze for batch dimension
        attentions = model.vit.encoder.layer[-1].attention.attention_probs  #
```

```
Last layer attention
    attn = attentions.mean(1).squeeze(0).cpu().detach().numpy()
    plt.imshow(attn[0], cmap='hot')
    plt.title("Attention Map")
    plt.show()
```

This code extracts the attention weights from the last transformer encoder layer, visualizing the patches, the model focuses on during inference.

Example Output:

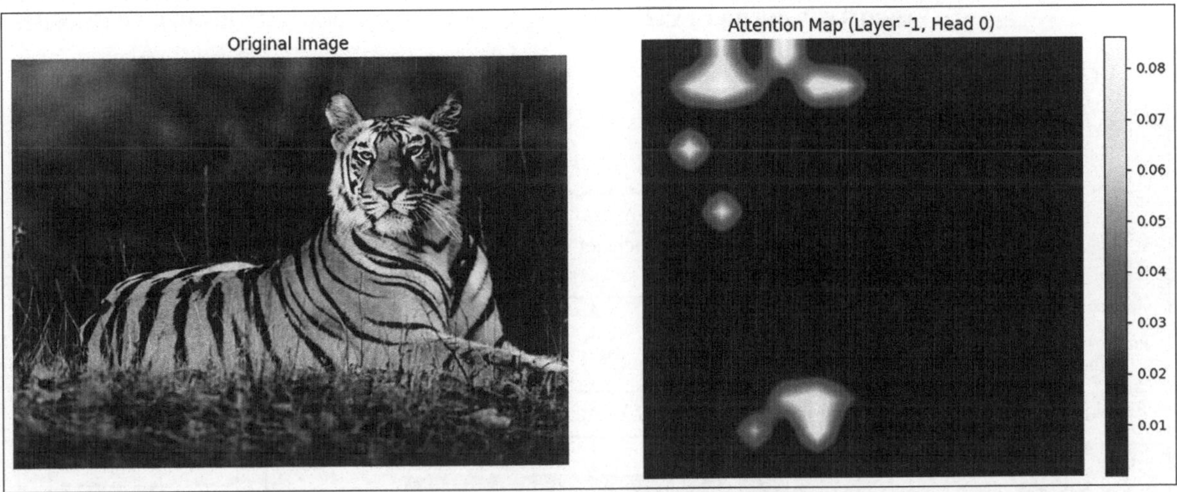

Figure 5.1: *Original Image and Corresponding Attention Map*

Applications and Benefits

Adapting transformers for image processing has unlocked new possibilities in computer vision such as:

- **Global Context:** Transformers capture long-range dependencies across the entire image, unlike CNNs which focus on local features.
- **Scalability**: Vision transformers excel on large datasets, outperforming traditional CNNs at scale.
- **Multi-Modal Applications:** By integrating image and text inputs, transformers enable tasks like image captioning and Visual Question Answering (VQA).

Real-World Applications

- **Healthcare:** Medical imaging tasks, such as tumor detection and X-ray analysis.
- **Autonomous Vehicles:** Object detection and segmentation for real-time scene understanding.
- **Surveillance:** Anomaly detection in security footage.

Transformers are redefining the landscape of computer vision by introducing a novel approach to image processing. Through patch-based tokenization, positional encoding, and global attention mechanisms, vision transformers overcome many limitations of traditional CNNs. In the next section, we will take a deeper dive into the Vision Transformer (ViT) architecture, analyzing its components and implementation in greater detail.

Vision Transformer (ViT) Architecture and Implementation

The Vision Transformer (ViT) represents a significant departure from traditional Convolutional Neural Networks (CNNs) by applying transformer architectures directly to the image data. By treating an image as a sequence of patches, ViT utilizes self-attention to capture relationships between different regions of an image, allowing for superior long-range dependency modeling.

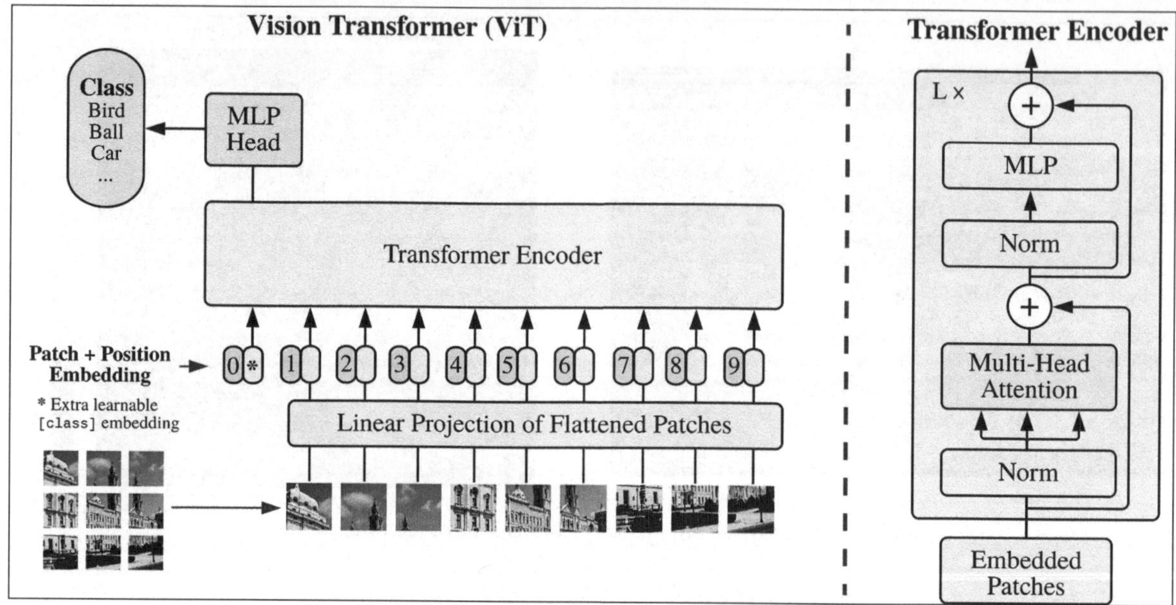

Figure 5.2: *Vision Transformer Architecture*

In this section, we will explore the core components of the Vision Transformer architecture (*Figure 5.2*), and demonstrate how to implement ViT for image classification using PyTorch and Hugging Face's Transformers library. The Vision Transformer splits an image into fixed-size patches, embeds them into a sequence, and applies self-attention across patches to capture global relationships. This patch-based approach enables ViT to model long-range dependencies, achieving state-of-the-art performance in image classification tasks.

Key Components of ViT Architecture

ViT adapts the transformer encoder architecture, originally designed for NLP, to process images by reshaping them into sequences of patches. The key components of the ViT architecture include:

Patch Embedding Layer

The first step in ViT is to divide an input image into non-overlapping patches. Each patch is then flattened and projected into a fixed-dimensional embedding space. This process is akin to tokenizing words in NLP.

- **Patch Size**: Typically 16×16 or 32×32.
- **Output**: A sequence of patch embeddings representing the entire image.

Code Example (Patch Embedding in PyTorch):

```
import torch
import torch.nn as nn
class PatchEmbedding(nn.Module):
```

```
    def __init__(self, img_size=224, patch_size=16, in_channels=3, embed_
dim=768):
        super().__init__()
        self.patch_size = patch_size
        self.proj = nn.Conv2d(in_channels, embed_dim, kernel_size=patch_size,
stride=patch_size)

    def forward(self, x):
        x = self.proj(x)  # [B, C, H, W] -> [B, embed_dim, H/P, W/P]
        x = x.flatten(2)  # Flatten spatial dimensions
        x = x.transpose(1, 2)  # [B, N, embed_dim], N = number of patches

        return x
```

Positional Encoding

To retain spatial information, ViT adds positional encodings to patch embeddings. This ensures that the model distinguishes patches, based on their location within the image. Without positional encoding, ViT would treat all patches identically, ignoring spatial structure.

Code Example (Positional Encoding in PyTorch):

```
class PositionalEncoding(nn.Module):
    def __init__(self, embed_dim=768, num_patches=196):
        super().__init__()
        self.pos_embed = nn.Parameter(torch.randn(1, num_patches + 1,
embed_dim))  # +1 for CLS token

    def forward(self, x):
        x = x + self.pos_embed[:, :x.size(1), :]
        return x
```

CLS Token

Similar to the [CLS] token in BERT, ViT appends a learnable classification token (CLS token) to the sequence of patch embeddings. This token aggregates information from all patches, and is ultimately used for classification.

```
cls_token = nn.Parameter(torch.randn(1, 1, 768))  # Learnable CLS token
```

Transformer Encoder

ViT employs a stack of transformer encoder layers to process the sequence of patch embeddings. Each layer consists of:

- Multi-Head Self-Attention (MHSA): Captures interactions between patches.
- Feed-Forward Networks (FFN): Further processes embeddings to refine features.
- Layer Normalization and Skip Connections: Stabilizes training, and improves convergence.

Code Example (Transformer Encoder in PyTorch):

```
from transformers import ViTModel
transformer_encoder = ViTModel.from_pretrained("google/vit-base-patch16-224")
End-to-End ViT Implementation
Below is a full implementation of a simple ViT model using PyTorch and Hugging
Face:
from transformers import ViTForImageClassification, ViTConfig
```

```
# Configure ViT model
config = ViTConfig(
    image_size=224,
    patch_size=16,
    num_labels=10,  # Example for CIFAR-10
    hidden_size=768,
    num_hidden_layers=12,
    num_attention_heads=12,)

# Initialize ViT model
model = ViTForImageClassification(config)
```

In this implementation:

- The model is configured for a classification task (CIFAR-10 with 10 labels).
- The image is resized to 224×224 pixels, with patches of 16×1616 \times 16.
- The transformer stack consists of 12 encoder layers, each with 12 attention heads.

Training Vision Transformer on CIFAR-10

To fine-tune ViT for image classification, we can use PyTorch's standard dataset utilities and Hugging Face's Trainer class to simplify the training loop.

```
from torchvision import transforms, datasets
from torch.utils.data import DataLoader
from transformers import Trainer, TrainingArguments
# Data preprocessing (CIFAR-10)
transform = transforms.Compose([
    transforms.Resize((224, 224)),
    transforms.ToTensor(),
])
# Download and load CIFAR-10 dataset
train_dataset = datasets.CIFAR10(root='./data', train=True, download=True,
transform=transform)

# Training Arguments
training_args = TrainingArguments(
    output_dir="./vit_results",
    eval_strategy="epoch",
    learning_rate=5e-5,
    per_device_train_batch_size=16,
    num_train_epochs=3,
)

trainer = Trainer(
    model=model,
    args=training_args,
    train_dataset=train_dataset,
)
trainer.train()
```

Visualizing Attention Maps

One of the benefits of ViT is the ability to visualize attention across different image regions. This allows us to interpret which parts of an image the model focuses on during classification.

```
import matplotlib.pyplot as plt

def visualize_attention(model, img):
    model.eval()
    with torch.no_grad():
        outputs = model(img.unsqueeze(0))
        attentions = model.vit.encoder.layer[-1].attention.attention_probs
    attn = attentions.mean(1).squeeze(0).cpu().detach().numpy()
    plt.imshow(attn[0], cmap='hot')
    plt.title("Attention Map")
    plt.show()
```

The function will display an attention map as a heatmap, shown in *Figure* 5.1 which visualizes where the model is focusing attention in the image. The areas with more focus will be shown in warmer colors (for example, red or yellow), and areas with less focus will be in cooler colors (for instance, blue or black).

Advantages of ViT over CNNs

- **Global Attention:** ViT can capture long-range dependencies across the entire image, unlike CNNs, which focus on local receptive fields.
- **Scalability:** ViT scales effectively with larger datasets, often outperforming CNNs as the data volume increases.
- **Flexibility:** ViT is easily adaptable to multiple vision tasks, including image classification, object detection, and segmentation.

The Vision Transformer (ViT) architecture redefines image processing by leveraging self-attention to model complex relationships across image patches. By decomposing images into patch embeddings and processing them as sequences, ViT achieves exceptional performance in image classification, and other vision tasks, rivaling traditional CNNs. Its ability to capture long-range dependencies and scale effectively with data volume marks a significant shift in computer vision.

In the next section, we will delve deeper into image classification with Vision Transformers, demonstrating how ViT excels in classifying images across diverse datasets, and comparing its performance to convolutional architectures. We will also explore fine-tuning strategies, dataset-specific adjustments, and best practices for optimizing ViT in real-world scenarios.

Image Classification with Vision Transformers

Image classification is one of the fundamental tasks in computer vision, where the goal is to assign a label to an input image. Traditionally dominated by CNNs, classification has been significantly enhanced by the introduction of ViT. By leveraging self-attention across image patches, ViT offers a more flexible and scalable approach to classifying images, surpassing CNNs on large datasets, such as ImageNet.

In this section, we shall explore how ViT performs image classification, implement a classification pipeline using PyTorch, and discuss the advantages ViT brings to this task.

How ViT Handles Image Classification

Unlike CNNs that progressively extract features through convolution and pooling, ViT treats image classification as a sequence modeling task. Here is how the process unfolds:

1. **Patch Embedding:** The input image is divided into non-overlapping patches (for example, 16×16) that are flattened and linearly projected into embeddings.

2. **Positional Encoding:** Encodings are added to the patch embeddings to retain spatial information.
3. **[CLS] Token**: A classification token is appended to the patch sequence, serving as the aggregate representation used for final classification.
4. **Transformer Encoder:** The patch embeddings pass through multiple transformer encoder layers, applying self-attention across patches to capture long-range dependencies.
5. **Classification Head:** After the final encoder layer, the CLS token's output is passed to a fully connected layer, mapping it to class probabilities.

Implementing Image Classification with ViT

Let us walk through an end-to-end image classification pipeline, using PyTorch and Hugging Face's ViT model pre-trained on ImageNet.

- **Setting Up the Environment**

  Ensure that the Hugging Face Transformers library and PyTorch are installed:

  ```
  pip install transformers torch torchvision
  ```

- **Loading a Pre-trained ViT Model**

  Using a pre-trained ViT model significantly reduces training time, and improves performance by leveraging prior knowledge from large datasets.

  ```
  from transformers import ViTForImageClassification

  # Load pre-trained ViT model
  model = ViTForImageClassification.from_pretrained(
      "google/vit-base-patch16-224",
      num_labels=10  # For CIFAR-10, adjust for your dataset
  )
  ```

- **Pre-processing the Dataset**

  We pre-process the CIFAR-10 dataset by resizing images to 224×224, the standard input size for ViT models.

  ```
  from torchvision import transforms, datasets
  from torch.utils.data import DataLoader

  transform = transforms.Compose([
      transforms.Resize((224, 224)),
      transforms.ToTensor(),
  ])

  # Download CIFAR-10 dataset
  train_dataset = datasets.CIFAR10(
      root="./data", train=True, download=True, transform=transform
  )
  train_loader = DataLoader(train_dataset, batch_size=32, shuffle=True)
  Fine-Tuning ViT on CIFAR-10
  Fine-tuning involves updating the ViT model's weights to adapt it to the tar-
  get dataset.
  from transformers import Trainer, TrainingArguments

  # Set training arguments
  training_args = TrainingArguments(
  ```

```
    output_dir="./vit_cifar10_results",
    evaluation_strategy="epoch",
    learning_rate=2e-5,
    per_device_train_batch_size=16,
    num_train_epochs=5,
)

# Use Hugging Face's Trainer API
trainer = Trainer(
    model=model,
    args=training_args,
    train_dataset=train_dataset,
)
trainer.train()
```

- **Evaluating the Model**

  After training, evaluate the model on the test set to measure its accuracy:

```
test_dataset = datasets.CIFAR10(
    root="./data", train=False, download=True, transform=transform
)
test_loader = DataLoader(test_dataset, batch_size=32)

# Evaluate model
accuracy = trainer.evaluate()
print(f"Test Accuracy: {accuracy['eval_accuracy']:.2f}") # Output: Test
Accuracy: 0.87
```

- **Visualizing Predictions**

```
Visualizing classification results helps assess how well the model generalizes:
import matplotlib.pyplot as plt
import numpy as np
# Display a few predictions
def show_predictions(model, dataloader):
    model.eval()
    images, labels = next(iter(dataloader))
    with torch.no_grad():
        outputs = model(images)
        _, preds = torch.max(outputs.logits, 1)

    fig, axs = plt.subplots(1, 5, figsize=(12, 4))
    for i in range(5):
        axs[i].imshow(np.transpose(images[i], (1, 2, 0)))
        axs[i].set_title(f"Pred: {preds[i].item()} | True: {labels[i]}")
        axs[i].axis('off')
    plt.show()

show_predictions(model, test_loader)
```

This function will display a grid of five (5) images from the test dataset, along with their predicted and true labels. Each image will be shown with a title, displaying the predicted label and the true label.

Example Output:

The grid will show 5 images, and for each, the predicted class and true label will be shown, such as:

```
Pred: 1 | True: 1
Pred: 0 | True: 0
```

```
Pred: 2 | True: 2
Pred: 3 | True: 3
Pred: 1 | True: 1
```

- **Strengths of Vision Transformers in Image Classification**

  ViT's unique ability to capture global dependencies across entire images gives it distinct advantages in classification tasks:

  - **Global Context:** ViT models the entire image at once, unlike CNNs that rely on small receptive fields.
  - **Data Efficiency:** When pre-trained on large datasets, ViT generalizes well to smaller datasets, with minimal fine-tuning.
  - **Scalability:** Performance improves as data scales, making ViT ideal for large datasets like ImageNet.

- **Performance Comparison: ViT vs CNNs**

  ViT consistently outperforms CNNs, when trained on large datasets. However, on smaller datasets, CNNs may initially perform better, without extensive pre-training. The key takeaway is that ViT's performance advantage scales with data availability.

- **Challenges of ViT for Image Classification**

  Despite its strengths, ViT faces challenges:

  - **High Data Requirements:** ViT needs large datasets or pre-training to achieve optimal performance.
  - **Computational Cost:** ViT models are computationally intensive compared to CNNs, requiring powerful GPUs.

Efforts like EfficientViT and DeiT (Data-Efficient Image Transformer) address these limitations by optimizing architectures and training procedures.

Vision Transformers represent a paradigm shift in image classification, challenging the dominance of CNNs by offering greater scalability and flexibility. ViT's ability to model long-range dependencies across image patches allows it to excel in complex classification tasks.

In the next section, we will explore how object detection is performed using transformer-based models, focusing on architectures such as DEtection TRansformer (DETR) and its implementation in PyTorch.

Object Detection Using Transformer-Based Models

Object detection is a cornerstone of computer vision, enabling machines to identify and locate objects within an image. Traditional object detection pipelines like Faster R-CNN and YOLO, rely heavily on CNNs and complex post-processing steps such as region proposals and non-maximum suppression (NMS). However, transformer-based models, particularly the DEtection TRansformer (DETR), have introduced a simplified and more elegant approach to object detection by treating it as a set prediction problem.

In this section, we will explore the architecture of DETR, its advantages over conventional object detection methods, and walk through an implementation using PyTorch.

Understanding DETR's Approach to Object Detection

DETR redefines object detection by eliminating the need for anchor boxes and region proposals. Instead, it uses transformers to predict object bounding boxes directly from image features. The model views object detection as a direct set prediction problem, outputting a fixed number of object predictions at once, with each prediction corresponding to either a detected object or a "no object" class.

Here is how DETR works:

1. **Feature Extraction:** A CNN backbone (like ResNet) extracts image features.
2. **Flattening and Encoding:** The extracted feature map is flattened and encoded into a sequence, forming the input to the transformer.
3. **Transformer Processing:** The transformer attends to all image regions simultaneously, modeling relationships between different parts of the image.
4. **Object Queries:** A fixed set of learned object queries is used to predict bounding boxes and class labels. Each query can detect one object.
5. **Set Loss Function:** DETR uses a bipartite matching loss to directly compare predicted and ground-truth objects, ensuring one-to-one matching without needing NMS.

DETR Architecture

The DETR architecture consists of three key components:

- **Backbone (CNN)**: Extracts low-level features from the input image. A ResNet backbone is commonly used.
- **Transformer Encoder-Decoder**: Processes flattened feature maps and models spatial relationships.
- **Feed-Forward Networks (FFNs)**: Predicts object bounding boxes and class labels for each query.

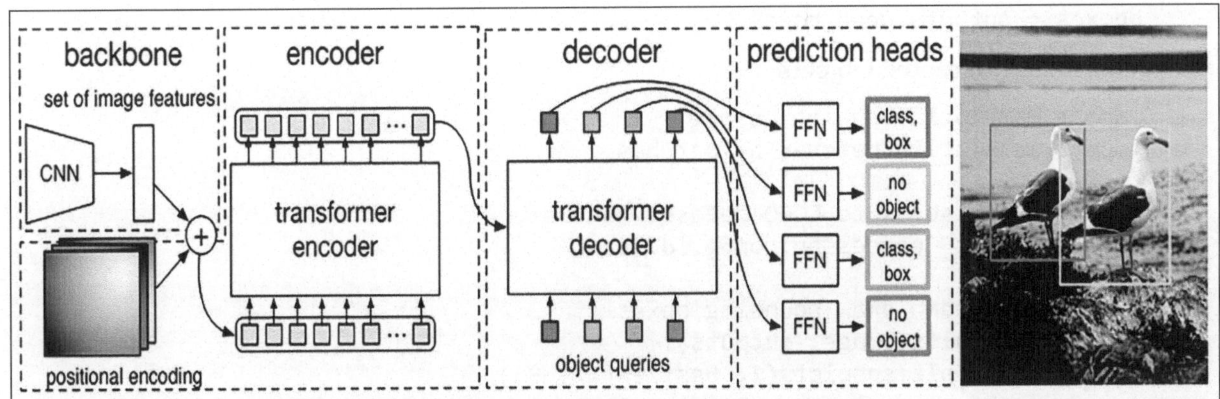

***Figure 5.3**: Detection Transformer Architecture*

Architecture Overview:

```
Input Image --> CNN Backbone --> Transformer Encoder --> Object Queries
                                 |                        |
                                 |-----------------> Transformer Decoder --> Bounding Boxes
+ Labels
```

Implementing DETR with PyTorch

Let us implement DETR, using the Hugging Face Transformers library and PyTorch.

- **Installing Required Libraries**

```
pip install transformers torch torchvision
```

- **Loading the Pre-trained DETR Model**

```
from transformers import DetrForObjectDetection

# Load pre-trained DETR model
model = DetrForObjectDetection.from_pretrained("facebook/detr-resnet-50")
model.eval()  # Set model to evaluation mode
```

- **Pre-processing and Visualizing Input Images**

```
from transformers import DetrImageProcessor
from PIL import Image
import requests

# Load an image from the web
url = "https://t3.ftcdn.net/jpg/02/01/88/00/360_F_201880065_Ck9mn1J9NeIvbmwHB-
JCCG5vsuml6HYfK.jpg"
image = Image.open(requests.get(url, stream=True).raw)

# Preprocess image
processor = DetrImageProcessor.from_pretrained("facebook/detr-resnet-50")
inputs = processor(images=image, return_tensors="pt")


Performing Object Detection
# Perform detection
outputs = model(**inputs)

# Extract bounding boxes and class predictions
logits = outputs.logits
bboxes = outputs.pred_boxes
```

- **Visualizing Detected Objects**

```
import matplotlib.pyplot as plt
import matplotlib.patches as patches

# Map class labels to COCO dataset labels
COCO_CLASSES = processor.config.id2label

# Plot image and draw bounding boxes
def plot_results(image, outputs):
    fig, ax = plt.subplots(1, figsize=(12, 9))
    ax.imshow(image)

    logits = outputs.logits.softmax(-1)[0]
    bboxes = outputs.pred_boxes[0]

    # Draw bounding boxes
    for logit, bbox in zip(logits, bboxes):
        if logit.argmax() != 91:  # Skip "no object" class (index 91)
            score = logit.max().item()
```

```
            label = COCO_CLASSES[logit.argmax().item()]
            box = bbox.cpu().detach().numpy()

            x, y, w, h = box
            rect = patches.Rectangle(
                (x - w/2, y - h/2), w, h, linewidth=2, edgecolor="r",
facecolor="none"
            )
            ax.add_patch(rect)
            ax.text(x, y, f"{label}: {score:.2f}", color="white", bbox=dict
(facecolor="red", alpha=0.5))

        plt.show()

    plot_results(image, outputs)
```

Example Output:

Figure 5.4: *Expected Output of Object Detection*

As it can be seen in this figure, the object clock has been detected in the image with an accuracy of 0.91.

Advantages of DETR over Traditional Methods

- **Simplicity:** DETR removes the need for anchor boxes and complex post-processing, streamlining the object detection pipeline.
- **Global Context:** By attending to the entire image simultaneously, DETR models long-range dependencies better than region proposal networks.
- **One-to-One Matching:** The bipartite matching loss eliminates the need for Non-Maximum Suppression (NMS), reducing post-processing overhead.

Challenges and Limitations

- **Training Time:** DETR requires more training time and data compared to the traditional methods.

- **Small Object Detection:** DETR sometimes struggles with detecting small objects, as the transformer's receptive field is biased toward larger patterns.
- **High Computational Cost:** The attention mechanism scales quadratically with the input size, making DETR computationally expensive for high-resolution images.

Real-World Applications of DETR

- **Autonomous Driving:** DETR is used to detect pedestrians, vehicles, and road signs in real-time.
- **Surveillance:** Object detection in security footage, including anomaly detection.
- **Healthcare:** Medical image analysis for detecting tumors and anomalies.

DETR's transformer-based architecture introduces a fresh approach to object detection by simplifying the detection pipeline, and leveraging global attention mechanisms. Its ability to predict bounding boxes directly, without anchor boxes or NMS marks a significant shift in how object detection is approached. In the next section, we will explore image segmentation with transformer architectures, further demonstrating the versatility of transformers in computer vision tasks.

Image Segmentation with Transformer Architectures

Image segmentation is a vital task in computer vision, where the goal is to partition an image into multiple segments, each representing a different object or region of interest. Unlike object detection, which outputs bounding boxes around objects, segmentation provides pixel-level precision, making it crucial for applications like medical imaging, autonomous driving, and satellite imagery. Traditional segmentation models such as U-Net and Mask R-CNN, have relied heavily on Convolutional Neural Networks (CNNs). However, transformer architectures are now redefining image segmentation by leveraging self-attention mechanisms to capture global context, and improve segmentation accuracy.

In this section, we will explore how transformers are adapted for segmentation, discuss key models, such as SEgmentation TRansformer (SETR) and MaskFormer, as well as walk through an implementation of image segmentation using PyTorch.

Transformers Approach to Image Segmentation

Transformers excel at modeling long-range dependencies, an essential feature for segmentation tasks where understanding the relationship between distant parts of an image can improve accuracy. Unlike CNNs, which focus on local receptive fields, transformers process the entire image at once, allowing them to segment complex and overlapping objects more effectively.

Key Steps in Transformer-Based Segmentation

1. **Feature Extraction:** A CNN or transformer backbone extracts feature maps from the input image.
2. **Tokenization and Embedding:** Image features are divided into patches, and embedded into a sequence, similar to Vision Transformers (ViTs).
3. **Transformer Encoder-Decoder:** A transformer processes the patch embeddings, applying self-attention to learn the relationships between patches.
4. **Segmentation Head:** The output is reshaped into a pixel-wise mask, generating precise segment boundaries for each class.

Notable Transformer-Based Segmentation Models

- **SEgmentation TRansformer (SETR):** SETR was one of the first models to apply pure transformers to semantic segmentation tasks. It replaces the traditional CNN encoder with a Vision Transformer (ViT) backbone, processing images as sequences of patches. The transformer captures global dependencies between image regions, resulting in more accurate segmentation, especially for large and complex objects.
- **MaskFormer:** This is developed by Facebook AI, and introduces a unified model that treats segmentation as a mask classification problem. Instead of predicting pixel labels directly, MaskFormer outputs a set of binary masks, with each mask representing a specific object or region. This simplifies the segmentation process, and improves scalability across datasets.

Implementing Image Segmentation with MaskFormer

Let us implement a simple segmentation pipeline using the MaskFormer model from Hugging Face's Transformers library.

```
Install Required Packages
pip install transformers torch torchvision
```

Load Pre-trained MaskFormer Model

```
from transformers import MaskFormerForInstanceSegmentation

# Load pre-trained MaskFormer model
model = MaskFormerForInstanceSegmentation.from_pretrained("facebook/mask
former-swin-tiny-coco")
model.eval()

Preprocessing and Image Preparation
from transformers import MaskFormerImageProcessor
from PIL import Image
import requests

# Load sample image
url = "https://huggingface.co/datasets/mishig/sample_images/resolve/main/
COCO%20val2017%20000000036.jpg"
image = Image.open(requests.get(url, stream=True).raw)

# Preprocess image
processor = MaskFormerImageProcessor.from_pretrained("facebook/maskformer
-swin-tiny-coco")
inputs = processor(images=image, return_tensors="pt")

Perform Segmentation
# Perform segmentation
outputs = model(**inputs)

# Extract predicted masks and class labels
logits = outputs.class_queries_logits
masks = outputs.masks_queries_logits.sigmoid()

Visualize Segmentation Results
import matplotlib.pyplot as plt

def visualize_segmentation(image, outputs):
    masks = outputs.masks_queries_logits.sigmoid().cpu().detach()
```

```
    plt.figure(figsize=(12, 8))
    plt.imshow(image)

    # Plot masks
    for i in range(masks.shape[1]):
        plt.imshow(masks[0, i], cmap="jet", alpha=0.5)

    plt.title("Segmentation Overlay")
    plt.axis("off")
    plt.show()
visualize_segmentation(image, outputs)
```

Figure 5.5: *Original Image and the Segmentation Overlay*

Advantages of Transformer-Based Segmentation

- **Global Context and Precision:** Transformer models, such as SETR and MaskFormer, process the entire image at once, capturing long-range dependencies that CNN-based models might miss. This results in more precise segmentations, even for objects that span large portions of the image or appear in cluttered environments. The ability to model global context significantly improves the segmentation of occluded or overlapping objects.
- **Simplification of Pipelines:** By treating segmentation as a set prediction problem, transformer models reduce the complexity associated with traditional pipelines that require multiple stages, such as region proposal networks and multi-scale feature pyramids. This not only simplifies the architecture, but also enhances performance consistency across different datasets.
- **Versatility across Tasks:** Transformer architectures are highly adaptable, and can handle various segmentation tasks, including semantic segmentation (classifying each pixel into a category), instance segmentation (detecting individual objects), and panoptic segmentation (combining object detection and semantic segmentation).

Challenges and Limitations

- **Computational Overhead:** Transformer models, particularly for segmentation, are computationally intensive, and require significant memory resources. The quadratic complexity of the self-attention mechanism can lead to slower training, and inference times compared to CNN-based methods, especially for high-resolution images.
- **Data Requirements:** Segmentation transformers perform best with large-scale labeled datasets. Without sufficient training data, transformers may struggle to generalize, resulting in suboptimal segmentation performance. Transfer learning and pre-trained models help mitigate this challenge, but the dependency on data remains a limitation.
- **Fine-Tuning Sensitivity:** Fine-tuning transformers for segmentation tasks can be sensitive to hyperparameters, requiring careful adjustment of learning rates, batch sizes, and data

augmentations. Unlike CNNs, which often converge reliably, transformer models may require more experimentation to achieve optimal results.

Real-World Applications of Transformer-Based Segmentation

- **Medical Imaging:** In medical imaging, transformer-based segmentation models are used for tasks, such as tumor detection, organ segmentation, and radiology scan analysis. Their ability to handle high-dimensional medical images makes them valuable tools for improving diagnostic accuracy.
- **Autonomous Vehicles:** Segmentation transformers play a crucial role in scene understanding for self-driving cars. By segmenting road scenes, vehicles, pedestrians, and obstacles, these models contribute to safer and more efficient autonomous navigation.
- **Satellite and Aerial Imaging:** In satellite imagery, transformers are used to segment land masses, buildings, and environmental features. Their ability to process large, high-resolution images with long-range dependencies makes them ideal for analyzing the geographic data.

Transformer-based segmentation models mark a significant leap forward in computer vision, offering higher accuracy and flexibility, compared to traditional CNN approaches. Hence, by modeling global relationships, and simplifying complex pipelines, transformers are becoming the go-to architecture for pixel-level tasks. In the next section, we will explore self-supervised learning in vision transformers, highlighting how transformers can learn robust representations, without the need for extensive labeled data.

Self-Supervised Learning in Vision Transformers

Self-supervised Learning (SSL) has emerged as a transformative approach in computer vision, allowing models to learn robust representations from the unlabeled data. By leveraging large-scale datasets, without the need for manual annotations, SSL reduces the reliance on costly labeled data, and improves model generalization. In the realm of Vision Transformers (ViTs), self-supervised learning has unlocked new capabilities, enabling ViTs to outperform traditional Convolutional Neural Networks (CNNs) in scenarios, where the labeled data is scarce.

This section delves into how self-supervised learning is applied to Vision Transformers, exploring the key methods, such as DINO (Distillation with No Labels), BEiT (BERT Pre-training for Images), and MAE (Masked Autoencoders). We will also walk through a practical example of self-supervised pre-training using PyTorch.

Self-Supervised Learning for ViTs

ViTs typically require vast amounts of labeled data to achieve competitive performance, often exceeding the dataset sizes needed by CNNs. This is because transformers, originally designed for Natural Language Processing (NLP), lack the local inductive biases inherent to CNNs, making them data-hungry. Self-supervised learning addresses this limitation by allowing transformers to pre-train on large collections of unlabeled images, effectively reducing the need for labeled data during downstream tasks, such as classification, segmentation, and object detection.

By pre-training on unlabeled data, ViTs learn to extract the general features, which can then be fine-tuned on smaller labeled datasets. This leads to higher accuracy, faster convergence, and improved performance on tasks, with limited annotations.

Key Self-Supervised Learning Techniques for ViTs

- **DINO (Distillation with No Labels):** DINO applies knowledge distillation in a self-supervised manner. A student Vision Transformer learns to match the output of a teacher network by minimizing the difference between their embeddings, without requiring the labeled data. Thus, DINO enables ViTs to develop rich, meaningful representations that cluster similar images, even without explicit supervision.

- **BEiT (BERT Pre-training for Images):** Inspired by BERT from NLP, BEiT uses a masked image modeling approach. Patches of an input image are masked, and the model learns to predict the missing patches. This forces the transformer to understand the overall structure of the image, improving its ability to generate useful representations. BEiT's approach closely mirrors how BERT predicts missing words in a sentence, adapting the technique for the visual domain.
- **MAE (Masked Autoencoders):** Masked Autoencoders randomly mask portions of input images, and train the transformer to reconstruct the missing patches. MAE pre-training encourages ViTs to focus on contextual relationships across the entire image, reinforcing their ability to capture global dependencies. This technique has proven to yield state-of-the-art results, with reduced computational costs compared to other methods.

Benefits of Self-Supervised Learning for ViTs

- **Improved Data Efficiency:** Self-supervised ViTs can achieve comparable performance to CNNs with significantly fewer labeled samples by leveraging large volumes of unlabeled data during pre-training. This reduces the need for expensive, and time-consuming manual labeling efforts.
- **Transferable Representations:** Self-supervised pre-training enables ViTs to generate representations that generalize well across tasks. A ViT pre-trained on ImageNet in a self-supervised manner can be fine-tuned for downstream tasks, such as segmentation, detection, or medical imaging, delivering high accuracy, with minimal additional training.
- **Robustness and Adaptability:** ViTs trained through self-supervised learning are more robust to domain shifts, noise, and distribution changes. This is because the pre-training process forces the model to learn high-level, invariant features, rather than overfitting to dataset-specific artefacts.

Challenges of Self-Supervised Learning for ViTs

- **Computational Complexity:** SSL for ViTs can be computationally intensive, requiring powerful GPUs or TPUs for large-scale training. Techniques like MAE mitigate this by masking a significant portion of the image, reducing the number of patches processed by the model.
- **Hyperparameter Sensitivity:** Self-supervised learning techniques, such as BEiT or DINO, are sensitive to hyperparameters, including the masking ratio, learning rate, and patch size. Careful tuning and extensive experimentation are often required to achieve optimal results.
- **Longer Training Times:** While SSL reduces the need for labeled data, the pre-training phase can take longer compared to supervised learning pipelines. However, the long-term benefits, such as enhanced performance and generalization, often outweigh the initial computational costs.

Real-World Applications of Self-Supervised ViTs

- **Medical Imaging:** Self-supervised ViTs have demonstrated strong performance in segmenting organs, detecting tumors, and classifying medical scans. Pre-training ViTs on large unlabeled datasets of medical images improves diagnostic accuracy and enables models to generalize across different imaging modalities.

- **Autonomous Driving:** In autonomous vehicles, self-supervised ViTs are used to detect road features, lane markings, and obstacles. SSL allows ViTs to process millions of unlabeled street scenes, resulting in more robust object detection and segmentation.
- **Industrial Inspection:** Industries leverage self-supervised ViTs to detect manufacturing defects, perform quality control, and monitor production lines. SSL enables models to learn from vast amounts of visual data captured in factories without extensive manual annotations.

Self-supervised Learning bridges the data gap for Vision Transformers, enabling them to learn meaningful representations from unlabeled data, and excel across diverse computer vision tasks. By reducing the reliance on labeled datasets, self-supervised ViTs unlock new possibilities for industries, healthcare, and autonomous systems.

In the next section, we will explore Efficient Vision Transformers for Mobile and Edge Devices, focusing on how transformer architectures are optimized to perform high-accuracy vision tasks, while operating within the constraints of limited hardware.

Efficient Vision Transformers for Mobile and Edge Devices

As Vision Transformers (ViTs) continue to reshape computer vision, their computational demands pose significant challenges for deployment on mobile and edge devices. Traditional ViTs, while powerful, are resource-intensive, and require substantial memory as well as processing power, making them less practical for environments with limited hardware capabilities. However, advancements in model optimization have led to the development of efficient Vision Transformers designed specifically for low-latency, energy-efficient inference.

This section explores the need for efficient ViTs, highlights key approaches to reduce model complexity, and walks through practical techniques for deploying ViTs on mobile and edge devices.

The Need for Efficient Vision Transformers

Mobile devices, drones, and IoT systems increasingly rely on computer vision for real-time applications, such as facial recognition, object detection, and augmented reality. However, these devices often operate under constraints such as:

- **Limited Memory:** ViTs typically require significant memory to store large patch embeddings and attention maps.
- **Power Efficiency:** High computational demand leads to increased power consumption, which is undesirable for battery-powered devices.
- **Latency Requirements:** Applications like autonomous navigation and real-time video analysis demand low-latency inference.

Efficient ViTs address these challenges by reducing the size and complexity of the model, while maintaining competitive performance.

Approaches to Efficient Vision Transformers

Several strategies have been developed to optimize ViTs for edge deployment. These techniques focus on reducing the computational cost of self-attention, compressing model size, and streamlining inference.

1. **Patch Reduction and Downsampling:** Instead of processing the entire image at full resolution, efficient ViTs utilize larger patch sizes or downsample the input images, reducing the number of tokens fed into the transformer. This minimizes the quadratic complexity of self-attention, significantly lowering memory usage.

   Example: PiT (Pyramid Vision Transformer) progressively reduces the number of patches, mimicking the hierarchical structure of CNNs.

2. **Sparse Attention:** Full self-attention scales poorly with image size due to its quadratic complexity. Sparse attention mechanisms, such as Swim Transformer (Swin), limit attention to local windows, allowing the model to focus on smaller image regions, before aggregating global information. This drastically reduces computation, without sacrificing accuracy.
3. **Knowledge Distillation:** Knowledge distillation involves training a small "student" model to mimic the behavior of a larger "teacher" ViT. By transferring knowledge from a high-performing but large model, the student model achieves competitive accuracy with fewer parameters.

   Example: DeiT (Data-efficient Image Transformer) uses distillation tokens to guide the student model, making ViTs more data and compute-efficient.

4. **Lightweight Architectures:** Efforts to design lightweight ViT architectures, specifically for mobile devices have resulted in models, such as MobileViT. This architecture integrates convolutional layers with transformer blocks, balancing the efficiency of CNNs, with the long-range dependencies of transformers.

Implementing Efficient ViT (DeiT) for Mobile Devices

Let us walk through deploying an efficient Vision Transformer, using DeiT (Distilled Vision Transformer) on mobile hardware.

1. **Install Necessary Packages**

   ```
   pip install transformers torch torchvision
   ```

2. **Load Pre-Trained DeiT Model**

   ```
   from transformers import DeiTForImageClassification

   # Load DeiT pre-trained on ImageNet
   model = DeiTForImageClassification.from_pretrained("facebook/deit-small-
   distilled-patch16-224")
   model.eval()
   ```

3. **Pre-process and Classify an Image**

   ```
   from transformers import DeiTFeatureExtractor
   from PIL import Image
   import requests

   # Load an image
   url = "https://huggingface.co/datasets/mishig/sample_images/resolve/main/
   COCO%20val2017%20000000036.jpg"
   image = Image.open(requests.get(url, stream=True).raw)

   # Preprocess the image
   feature_extractor = DeiTFeatureExtractor.from_pretrained("facebook/
   deit-small-distilled-patch16-224")
   inputs = feature_extractor(images=image, return_tensors="pt")
   ```

```
# Perform classification
outputs = model(**inputs)
logits = outputs.logits
predicted_class = logits.argmax(-1).item()
```

4. **Model Quantization for Deployment**

   Quantization is a vital step for deploying ViTs on mobile devices, reducing model size by converting 32-bit floating-point weights into lower precision (example, 8-bit). This accelerates inference, while minimizing accuracy loss.

```
import torch

# Apply quantization
quantized_model = torch.quantization.quantize_dynamic(
    model, {torch.nn.Linear}, dtype=torch.qint8
)

# Save the quantized model
torch.save(quantized_model.state_dict(), "deit_quantized.pth")
```

5. Advantages of Efficient ViTs for Mobile and Edge

- **Real-Time Inference:** Efficient ViTs enable real-time image classification and detection on mobile devices, making them suitable for applications, such as facial recognition and augmented reality. By optimizing self-attention and reducing model size, latency is minimized, allowing models to process video frames at high speeds.
- **Low Power Consumption:** Efficient ViTs reduce power consumption by limiting the number of parameters and decreasing computational overhead. This extends battery life in mobile devices, ensuring consistent performance over extended periods.
- **Scalable across Devices:** Efficient ViTs are scalable, allowing deployment across a variety of devices, from smartphones and drones to IoT systems. This scalability enhances the accessibility of advanced computer vision capabilities, without requiring specialized hardware.

6. Challenges of Deploying ViTs on Edge Devices

- **Limited Model Capacity:** Reducing model size through pruning, quantization, or distillation can sometimes lead to performance degradation, particularly for complex tasks. Thus, striking the right balance between efficiency and accuracy remains a challenge.
- **Inference Speed Bottlenecks:** While efficient ViTs improve inference speed, their performance can still lag behind CNNs on extremely constrained devices. Hybrid architectures that integrate transformers with lightweight CNN layers aim to mitigate this.
- **Fine-Tuning Requirements:** Efficient ViTs often require fine-tuning on task-specific datasets to achieve optimal performance, and increasing deployment complexity. Proper data augmentation and transfer learning are necessary to ensure accurate predictions.

Real-World Applications of Efficient ViTs

- **Facial Recognition:** Efficient ViTs power facial recognition systems on smartphones, providing secure and fast authentication, with minimal latency.
- **Autonomous Drones:** Drones equipped with ViTs can detect objects and navigate in real-time, enabling surveillance and environmental monitoring without heavy processing units.

- **AR and VR Applications:** Efficient ViTs enhance augmented reality (AR) and virtual reality (VR) by providing rapid object detection and segmentation, facilitating immersive user experiences.

Therefore, efficient Vision Transformers bridge the gap between cutting-edge AI and practical deployment on mobile as well as edge devices. By reducing computational complexity through sparse attention, patch reduction, and knowledge distillation, ViTs achieve real-time performance, without compromising accuracy. In the next section, we will explore interpretability and visualization of Vision Transformers, providing insights into how ViTs make decisions, and how to enhance model transparency.

Interpretability and Visualization of Vision Transformers

Understanding how ViTs make decisions is crucial for improving their reliability, debugging errors, and fostering trust in AI systems. Unlike Convolutional Neural Networks (CNNs), which rely on local receptive fields, ViTs leverage self-attention mechanisms to process images holistically. This global attention makes ViTs more interpretable, as the model inherently focuses on the most relevant image regions, during classification or detection tasks.

This section explores key interpretability techniques for Vision Transformers, highlights how visualization aids in understanding model behavior, and walks through practical methods to visualize attention maps, using PyTorch and Hugging Face's Transformers library.

Importance of Interpretability for ViTs

Interpretability in computer vision models ensures that AI systems are not treated as "black boxes." By visualizing the decision-making process, researchers and practitioners can:

- **Identify Bias:** Visualizing which image regions contribute most to predictions can reveal biases in the model.
- **Debug Errors:** Understanding misclassifications helps refine the model by highlighting a**reas that require more training data or regularization.**
- Enhance Trust: Transparent models are essential for applications in healthcare, autonomous driving, and security, where accountability is critical.

Vision Transformers provide a unique advantage in interpretability through their attention mechanisms, offering direct insight into how image features influence the output.

Key Interpretability Techniques for ViTs

- **Attention Map Visualization:** Attention maps reveal which patches of an image the transformer focuses on during processing. By analyzing the attention weights in each layer, we can visualize the regions that drive the model's predictions.
- **Gradient-Based Visualization:** Techniques like Grad-CAM (Gradient-weighted Class Activation Mapping) adapt CNN interpretability methods to ViTs by highlighting regions that contribute most to the final class score. Grad-CAM uses gradients flowing into the final attention layers to produce heatmaps over the input image.
- **Occlusion Sensitivity:** This tests how removing certain image patches affects predictions. By masking different regions of an image, and observing changes in confidence scores, practitioners can infer the importance of each region.

- **Patch-wise Attention Rollout:** This aggregates attention from multiple layers, providing a cumulative view of which patches influence predictions, the most. This technique offers a comprehensive understanding of how information flows through ViT layers.

Visualizing Attention Maps with PyTorch

Next, let us implement attention map visualization, using a pre-trained ViT model and PyTorch. This example uses Hugging Face's ViT model to classify an image, and visualize attention across patches.

Install Required Libraries:

```
pip install transformers torch torchvision matplotlib
 Load Pre-trained ViT and Sample Image
from transformers import ViTModel, ViTFeatureExtractor
from PIL import Image
import requests

# Load ViT model and feature extractor
model = ViTModel.from_pretrained("google/vit-base-patch16-224")
model.eval()
processor = ViTFeatureExtractor.from_pretrained("google/vit-base-patch16-224")

# Load an image
url = "https://huggingface.co/datasets/mishig/sample_images/resolve/main/cat.
jpg"
image = Image.open(requests.get(url, stream=True).raw)
inputs = processor(images=image, return_tensors="pt")

Forward Pass and Extract Attention
# Perform forward pass to extract attention weights
outputs = model(**inputs, output_attentions=True)
attention = outputs.attentions[-1]  # Extract attention from the last layer
```

Visualize Attention Maps:

```
import matplotlib.pyplot as plt

def plot_attention(image, attention):
    fig, ax = plt.subplots(figsize=(6, 6))
    ax.imshow(image)

    # Aggregate attention across all heads
    attention_map = attention[0].mean(dim=0).detach().numpy()

    # Resize attention to match the image size
    attention_map = attention_map.reshape(14, 14)  # ViT uses 14x14 patches
    attention_map = plt.imshow(attention_map, cmap='jet', alpha=0.5, extent
=(0, image.size[0], image.size[1], 0))

    plt.colorbar(attention_map, ax=ax)
    plt.title("Attention Map Overlay")
    plt.axis("off")
    plt.show()

plot_attention(image, attention)
```

Expected Output:

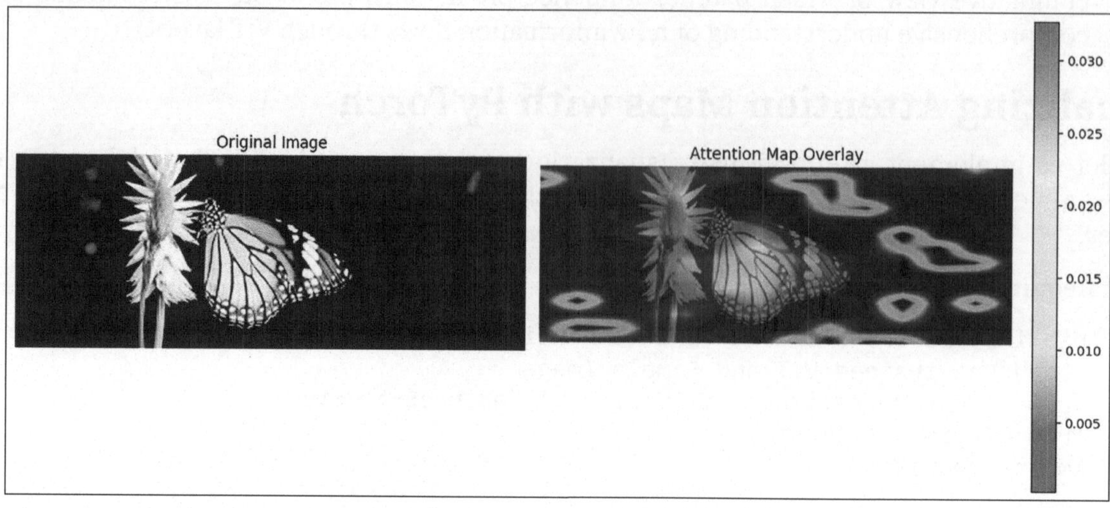

***Figure* 5.6.1:** *Attention Map Overlay*

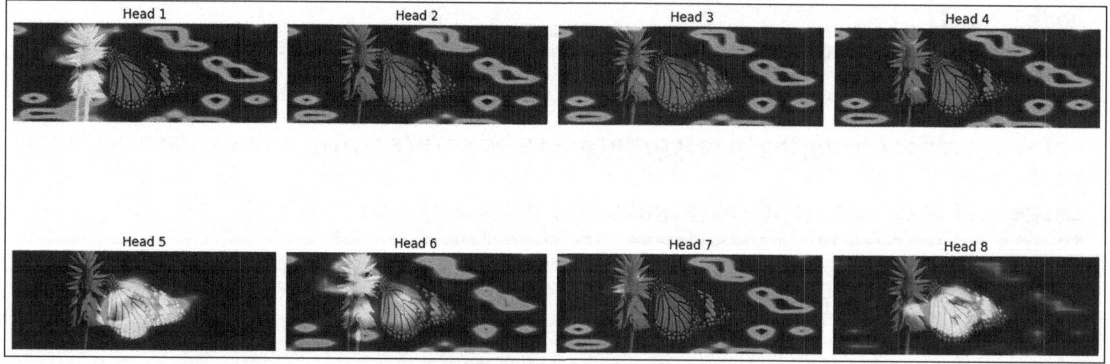

***Figure* 5.6.2:** *Attention Map Overlay*

Understanding the Visualization

In the resulting visualization, the heatmap overlaid on the image highlights areas, where the ViT model "*pays attention*" during classification. Bright regions indicate high attention, while darker areas represent less influence on the final prediction. This visualization helps identify which parts of the image contribute most to the model's decision.

There are eight (8) different attention heads in the model, and each learn to focus on different visual aspects and patterns, within the same image. Each head develops its own specialized attention pattern - for example, one head might focus on edges and boundaries, another on textures, a third on object shapes, while others might attend to spatial relationships, or specific semantic features. This multi-head mechanism allows the model to simultaneously capture diverse visual information from different perspectives, with some heads potentially highlighting the main subject, as well as others focusing on background context, and some attending to fine-grained details, ultimately combining all these complementary attention patterns to form a comprehensive understanding of the image.

Advantages of Attention Visualization in ViTs

- **Interpretability by Design:** Unlike CNNs, where interpretability often relies on post-hoc techniques, ViTs naturally offer interpretability through their attention weights. This built-in transparency simplifies model analysis, and aids in identifying biases.

- **Local and Global Insight:** Attention maps reveal both local patch interactions and global dependencies, providing a holistic view of how ViTs process images. This makes ViTs, particularly advantageous for tasks requiring fine-grained analysis, such as medical imaging and remote sensing.
- **Debugging Complex Models:** Visualization techniques help identify why ViTs might misclassify certain images. By observing which regions are neglected, researchers can adjust data augmentation strategies, or retrain the model with additional samples from under-represented categories.

Challenges of ViT Visualization

- **Overhead in Attention Extraction:** Extracting and visualizing attention from large-scale ViTs can be computationally expensive. Processing high-resolution images or aggregating attention from multiple layers may introduce latency, limiting real-time deployment.
- **Sparse Attention:** In models like Swin Transformer, where sparse attention is applied within local windows, visualization can be less intuitive. Sparse attention maps may omit broader context, making it harder to interpret the model's focus across the entire image.

Real-World Applications of ViT Visualization

- **Healthcare:** Attention maps in medical imaging highlight key areas that influence diagnoses, assisting doctors in validating AI predictions for tasks like tumor detection.
- **Autonomous Vehicles:** Visualizing attention in autonomous driving systems ensures that the model correctly focuses on road signs, pedestrians, and vehicles, reducing false positives, and enhancing safety.
- **Security and Surveillance:** In security applications, ViTs use attention visualization to detect suspicious activities, ensuring that the model prioritizes critical image regions.

Interpretability and Visualization are fundamental to building trustworthy Vision Transformers. By leveraging attention maps, gradient-based methods, and occlusion techniques, practitioners can gain deeper insights into ViT decision-making processes. As ViTs continue to evolve, enhancing their transparency will remain vital for deploying them in high-stakes environments.

In the next section, **we will compare transformers with traditional CNN Architectures** in various vision tasks.

Comparing Transformers with Traditional CNN Architectures in Various Vision Tasks

The emergence of Vision Transformers (ViTs) has challenged the long-standing dominance of Convolutional Neural Networks (CNNs) in computer vision. While CNNs have been the backbone of vision tasks for over a decade, transformers have introduced a novel paradigm by leveraging self-attention to model long-range dependencies across images. This shift has sparked extensive debate over which architecture performs better across different vision tasks.

In this section, we compare ViTs and CNNs across key computer vision applications, analyzing their strengths, weaknesses, and the tasks, where each architecture excels.

Image Classification

CNNs: CNNs are highly efficient for image classification, excelling in tasks, where local patterns and hierarchical feature extraction are essential. Models like ResNet, EfficientNet, and VGG have set benchmarks for classification accuracy on datasets, such as ImageNet. CNNs leverage local receptive fields and weight sharing, enabling them to learn spatial hierarchies effectively.

Vision Transformers (ViTs): ViTs have demonstrated superior performance on large-scale datasets like ImageNet-21k, where abundant labeled data is available. By treating images as sequences of patches and applying self-attention across them, ViTs capture long-range dependencies and global context better than CNNs. However, ViTs, typically require more data and computational power during training, limiting their effectiveness on smaller datasets, without pre-training.

Comparison

- **Small Datasets:** CNNs outperform ViTs, when data is limited, as CNNs' inductive biases (locality and translational invariance) help them generalize better.
- **Large Datasets:** ViTs surpass CNNs in accuracy, especially with extensive data and pre-training.

Object Detection

CNNs: Models like Faster R-CNN, YOLO, and SSD have dominated object detection by leveraging convolutional backbones for feature extraction, and Region Proposal Networks (RPN) to localize objects. These architectures process images at different scales, improving detection accuracy for objects of varying sizes.

ViTs (DETR - Detection Transformer): DETR simplifies object detection by eliminating the need for anchor boxes, and complex post-processing steps such as Non-maximum Suppression (NMS). Instead, transformers predict bounding boxes directly, using set-based predictions and bipartite matching loss. This streamlined architecture reduces the complexity of the detection pipeline, but requires more **training data and longer convergence times.**

Comparison

- **Speed and Simplicity:** DETR simplifies the object detection process, but CNN-based models like YOLO offer faster inference speeds for real-time applications.
- **Long-Range Dependencies:** ViTs excel at detecting objects with global context, particularly in cluttered or occluded environments.

Image Segmentation

CNNs (U-Net, DeepLab): CNNs dominate image segmentation, with architectures like U-Net and DeepLab, using encoder-decoder designs and dilated convolutions to perform pixel-wise classification. CNNs effectively capture fine-grained details, making them suitable for medical imaging and autonomous driving.

ViTs (SETR, MaskFormer): Vision transformers apply global self-attention to segmentation, allowing them to capture relationships across distant image regions. Models like MaskFormer treat segmentation as a mask classification problem, producing more accurate and interpretable segmentation results.

Comparison

- **Fine Details:** CNNs excel at segmenting fine-grained structures, but ViTs outperform, when segmenting large, complex objects spanning multiple image regions.
- **Data Requirements:** ViT-based segmentation models require extensive pre-training to outperform CNNs in pixel-level tasks.

Action Recognition (Video Analysis)

CNNs (3D CNNs, I3D): For video analysis and action recognition, 3D CNNs and Inflated 3D (I3D) models extend the convolution operation to the temporal dimension, capturing spatial and temporal features. These architectures are well-suited for short video clips.

ViTs (TimeSformer, ViViT): Vision transformers applied to video data (TimeSformer, ViViT) treat video frames as sequences of patches, and apply self-attention across both spatial and temporal dimensions. This allows ViTs to model long-term dependencies in videos, outperforming CNNs in tasks requiring context from distant frames.

Comparison

- **Short Clips:** CNNs are more efficient for short videos.
- **Long-Term Dependencies:** ViTs excel at capturing long-term temporal relationships, making them ideal for activity recognition in long videos.

Key Strengths of CNNs and ViTs

Strengths of CNNs:

- **Efficiency:** CNNs are computationally efficient, enabling real-time processing on mobile and edge devices.
- **Inductive Bias:** Built-in locality and translational invariance allow CNNs to generalize better on small datasets.
- **Training Stability:** CNNs are easier to train, with fewer data augmentation requirements.

Strengths of ViTs:

- **Global Attention:** ViTs capture long-range dependencies across the entire image, leading to improved performance in tasks requiring holistic understanding.
- **Scalability:** ViTs outperform CNNs on large datasets, where the availability of labeled data mitigates their data-hungry nature.
- **Flexibility:** ViTs are adaptable to various vision tasks (classification, detection, and segmentation) with minimal architectural changes.

Limitations of CNNs and ViTs

CNN Limitations:

- **Limited Global Context:** CNNs struggle to capture long-range dependencies, without additional layers or complex designs.
- **Overfitting**: CNNs can overfit on small datasets, if not regularized properly.

ViT Limitations:

- **Data Hungry:** ViTs require large-scale datasets, or extensive pre-training to perform well.
- **Computational Cost:** ViTs demand higher computational power, making them less practical for resource-constrained environments.

Hybrid Architectures: Best of Both Worlds

To bridge the gap between CNNs and ViTs, hybrid architectures like ConViT and Swin Transformer combine convolutional layers with transformers. These models leverage CNNs' efficiency for local feature extraction, while harnessing transformers' global attention capabilities. This hybrid approach achieves state-of-the-art performance across various tasks, with reduced computational overhead.

Thus, CNNs remain the preferred choice for small datasets and low-latency environments, while ViTs dominate large-scale datasets and complex vision tasks, requiring global context. The choice between CNNs and ViTs depends on the dataset size, computational resources, and the specific task at hand. As transformer architectures continue to evolve, their integration with CNNs, and optimization for efficiency will drive further advancements in computer vision.

Conclusion

To sum up, Vision Transformers (ViTs) have redefined the landscape of computer vision, offering a compelling alternative to traditional convolutional neural networks (CNNs). By leveraging self-attention mechanisms, ViTs capture long-range dependencies and global context, enabling them to excel in tasks like image classification, object detection, and segmentation. This shift in architecture has unlocked new possibilities for tackling complex visual tasks that require holistic image understanding.

Throughout this chapter, we explored the fundamental components of ViTs, their implementation in practical applications, and how they outperform CNNs on large datasets. We examined cutting-edge models, such as DETR for object detection and MaskFormer for segmentation, showcasing how transformers simplify pipelines, while delivering state-of-the-art results. Additionally, we discussed how self-supervised learning and efficient ViTs are bridging the gap between performance and deployment on mobile and edge devices.

While ViTs bring significant advantages, their computational demands and reliance on large datasets highlight the continued relevance of CNNs, especially in resource-constrained environments. Hybrid architectures, combining the strengths of CNNs and transformers, are emerging as a promising direction, delivering improved accuracy with reduced overhead.

In the next chapter, we will explore Speech Processing with Transformers, where self-attention mechanisms are unlocking breakthroughs in Automatic Speech Recognition (ASR), Text-to-Speech (TTS), and speech translation. This cross-modal application of transformers highlights their versatility and ability to drive innovation across multiple fields of AI.

CHAPTER 6
Speech Processing with Transformers

Introduction

Transformers have revolutionized speech processing, offering state-of-the-art solutions for tasks, such as Automatic Speech Recognition (ASR), Text-to-Speech (TTS) synthesis, and speech enhancement. By leveraging self-attention mechanisms, and the ability to model long-range dependencies, transformers overcome many challenges associated with the speech data, such as variability in accents, noise, and sequential nature.

This chapter delves into the transformative impact of these architectures on speech processing, starting with the foundations of speech feature extraction and representation. It explores transformer architectures for ASR, practical implementation of ASR systems in PyTorch, and text-to-speech synthesis. Additionally, we examine self-supervised learning techniques like Wav2Vec 2.0, enabling transformers to pre-train on vast, unlabeled datasets, and the handling of multi-lingual and code-switching scenarios. The chapter concludes with advanced applications in speech enhancement and separation, providing insights into how transformers are reshaping this field.

Structure

In this chapter, we will cover the following topics:

- Introduction to Speech Processing and Its Challenges
- Speech Feature Extraction and Representation for Transformers
- Transformer Architectures for Speech Recognition (ASR)
- Implementing a Transformer-Based ASR System with PyTorch 2.0
- Text-to-Speech (TTS) Synthesis Using Transformer Models
- Self-Supervised Learning in Speech Transformers (for example, Wav2Vec 2.0)
- Multi-Lingual and Code-Switching Speech Processing
- Speech Enhancement and Separation Using Transformers

Introduction to Speech Processing and Its Challenges

Speech processing is a fundamental aspect of human-computer interaction, enabling machines to interpret, analyze, and generate spoken language. From voice assistants like Alexa and Siri to automated transcription services, **speech processing systems have become an integral part of modern life.** These systems encompass a wide range of tasks, including speech recognition, Text-to-Speech (TTS) synthesis, speaker identification, emotion recognition, and even speech enhancement! Despite their growing prevalence, the complexity of human speech presents numerous challenges that make it one of the most intricate domains in Artificial Intelligence (AI).

One of the primary challenges in speech processing is the immense variability in spoken language. People speak with diverse accents, intonations, and speeds which significantly alters the acoustic properties of speech. Additionally, factors such as age, gender, health conditions, and regional dialects contribute to this variability, making it difficult for models to generalize across diverse populations. This challenge is further exacerbated in multi-lingual environments, or in scenarios, involving code-switching, where speakers alternate between languages, within the same conversation.

Noise and environmental interference add another layer of complexity. Speech signals are often captured in less-than-ideal conditions, such as crowded public spaces or noisy home environments. Background noise, overlapping conversations, and echoing audio can obscure critical features of speech, making it challenging for models to isolate the primary signal. Robust noise-handling capabilities are essential for creating reliable and effective speech processing systems, particularly in real-world applications such as video conferencing, voice command systems, and automated customer support.

The sequential and time-dependent nature of speech data introduces unique computational challenges. Unlike text, where words are static entities, speech evolves continuously over time. Each sound depends on its preceding and succeeding sounds for context, making long-term dependencies crucial for accurate interpretation. Traditional methods, such as Hidden Markov Models (HMMs) and Recurrent Neural Networks (RNNs), were designed to handle such sequential data, but often struggled to capture dependencies over long time horizons, leading to errors in tasks like transcription and translation.

Another crucial aspect of speech processing is feature extraction and representation. Raw audio signals are dense, high-dimensional data that must be preprocessed into meaningful representations, such as spectrograms, Mel-frequency Cepstral Coefficients (MFCCs), or log-mel features, before being input into machine learning models. This step requires significant domain expertise and computational resources to ensure that the extracted features retain all the nuances of the original speech. Inadequate or poorly designed features can significantly impair model performance.

Transformers have emerged as a transformative solution to many of these challenges. Their self-attention mechanism enables them to model, both local and global dependencies effectively, allowing them to capture relationships across entire speech sequences. This is particularly advantageous for tasks that require understanding long-term context, such as Automatic Speech Recognition (ASR) and speech translation. Unlike RNNs, which process sequences step by step, transformers can process entire sequences in parallel, significantly improving efficiency and scalability.

Moreover, self-supervised learning techniques, such as Wav2Vec 2.0, have revolutionized the field by enabling transformers to learn powerful representations directly from unlabeled audio. By leveraging vast amounts of unannotated data, these models can pre-train on diverse speech signals, reducing the reliance on expensive labeled datasets. Fine-tuning these pre-trained models on specific tasks has led to state-of-the-art performance in various speech applications, including ASR, TTS, and speaker identification.

Finally, transformers have proven to be highly adaptable to multi-lingual and cross-lingual speech processing tasks. Their ability to handle diverse languages and dialects, combined with robust pre-training, makes them ideal for applications in globalized settings. Furthermore, their effectiveness in noise-robust speech enhancement, and separation tasks underscores their potential for improving audio clarity in challenging environments.

Speech Feature Extraction and Representation for Transformers

Transformers have proven to be highly effective in processing speech data, but their success heavily depends on the quality of the input representation. Unlike text, which can be tokenized into discrete units, raw speech signals are continuous, high-dimensional, and require transformation into meaningful representations, before being fed into transformer models. Feature extraction and representation are critical steps that bridge the gap between raw audio data, and the transformer's self-attention mechanism, ensuring that key information from the speech signal is preserved, and optimally utilized.

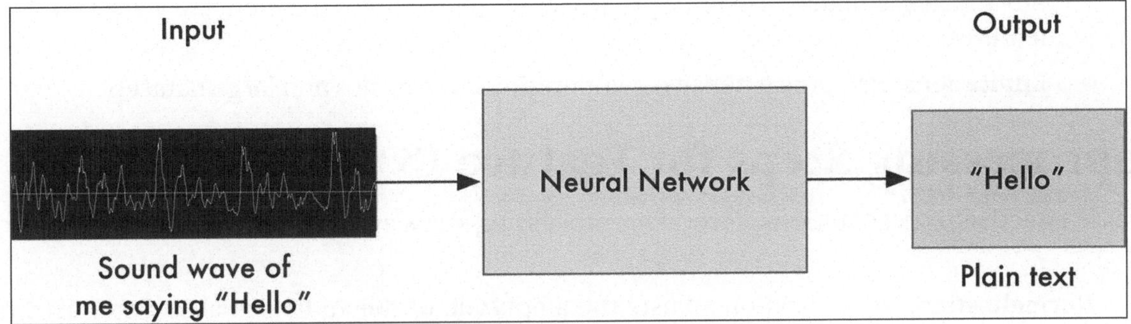

Figure 6.1: *High-level Speech Processing*

Need for Feature Extraction in Speech Processing

Raw audio signals are represented as waveforms that are essentially sequences of amplitude values sampled over time. While waveforms capture all the details of the original sound, they are often too dense and noisy to be directly used by machine learning models. Additionally, transformers are designed to work with sequences of tokens, necessitating the transformation of speech waveforms into token-like representations.

Feature extraction simplifies the raw audio by:

- Reducing dimensionality, while retaining key information.
- Making speech data less sensitive to noise and variations in recording conditions.
- Highlighting critical attributes such as pitch, energy, and frequency.

Common Representations for Transformers in Speech

Transformers rely on specific input formats that are well-suited for sequential data. The following are the most commonly used representations in speech processing:

- **Spectrograms:** A spectrogram is a visual representation of the frequency content of a signal, over time. It is created by applying the Short-Time Fourier Transform (STFT) to the raw waveform, breaking the signal into small overlapping time windows, and computing the frequency spectrum for each window.
    - o **Advantages:** Captures both time and frequency information, necessary for speech understanding.
    - o **Limitations:** Sensitive to noise, and requires careful parameter tuning (for instance, window size, overlap, and so on).
- **Mel-Spectrograms:** A `mel`-spectrogram is a variant of the spectrogram that maps frequencies to the `mel` scale which aligns more closely with human auditory perception.

    - **Advantages:** Emphasizes lower frequencies, which carry most of the information in speech, making it more robust for speech recognition and synthesis.
- **Mel-Frequency Cepstral Coefficients (MFCCs):** MFCCs compress the mel-spectrogram into a compact representation by taking the logarithm of its power spectrum, and applying the Discrete Cosine Transform (DCT).
    - **Advantages:** Widely used in traditional speech systems, and computationally efficient.
    - **Limitations:** May lose some fine-grained information necessary for advanced tasks.
- **Raw Waveforms:** Some modern transformer models, such as Wav2Vec 2.0, process raw waveforms directly. These models use convolutional layers to learn representations from the raw signal, bypassing traditional feature extraction steps.
    - **Advantages:** Eliminates manual preprocessing, and allows the model to learn task-specific features.
    - **Limitations:** Requires extensive computational resources and large datasets.

Preprocessing Steps for Feature Extraction

To create effective representations, several preprocessing steps are applied to raw audio signals such as:

- **Normalization:** Normalization adjusts the amplitude of the audio signal to a standard range, ensuring consistent volume levels, across recordings.
- **Framing and Windowing:** This audio signal is divided into short frames (for example, 20–40 milliseconds), with overlapping windows. This step ensures that each frame captures localized temporal information, while maintaining continuity across frames.
- **Noise Reduction:** Techniques like spectral subtraction or Voice Activity Detection (VAD) remove background noise and silence, improving the quality of extracted features.
- **Log Scaling:** Applying a logarithmic transformation to the spectrogram helps compress the dynamic range of the audio signal, making it easier for the model to process.

Feature Extraction for Transformers: Best Practices

When preparing speech data for transformers, the following best practices are commonly adopted:

- **Consistency across Training and Inference:** Ensure that the same feature extraction pipeline is applied, during both training and inference, to avoid mismatches.
- **Data Augmentation:** Enhance robustness by applying augmentations, such as time masking, frequency masking, and pitch shifts, during feature extraction.
- **Dimension Reduction:** Use dimensionality reduction techniques, such as Principal Component Analysis (PCA), or downsampling to optimize transformer input size.
- **Batch Processing:** Process features in batches to improve computational efficiency, during large-scale training.

Practical Implementation in PyTorch

Following is an example of extracting `mel`-spectrograms using PyTorch's `torchaudio` library:

```
import torchaudio
import torchaudio.transforms as T

# Load raw waveform
waveform, sample_rate = torchaudio.load("audio_file.wav")
```

```
    # Resample if necessary
    transform = T.Resample(orig_freq=sample_rate, new_freq=16000)
    waveform = transform(waveform)

    # Compute mel-spectrogram
    mel_transform = T.MelSpectrogram(
        sample_rate=16000,
        n_fft=1024,
        hop_length=256,
        n_mels=80
    )
    mel_spectrogram = mel_transform(waveform)

    # Convert to log scale
    log_mel_spectrogram = T.AmplitudeToDB()(mel_spectrogram)
```

This process transforms a raw audio signal into a mel-spectrogram that can be directly fed into transformer models.

Challenges in Speech Feature Representation

Despite advancements, feature extraction still faces challenges:

- **Noise Sensitivity:** Features like spectrograms can amplify background noise, requiring robust preprocessing pipelines.
- **Task-Specific Adjustments**: Performs different tasks (for example, ASR, TTS, and so on) that may require different feature representations, complicating the pipeline.
- **High Dimensionality:** Representations like spectrograms can be computationally expensive to process, particularly for long audio sequences.

Thus, effective feature extraction and representation are critical for leveraging the full potential of transformers in speech processing. By transforming raw waveforms into meaningful inputs, these techniques ensure that transformers can efficiently handle the sequential and complex nature of speech data. In the next section, we will explore Transformer Architectures for Speech Recognition (ASR), and how these models leverage self-attention to excel in transcription tasks.

Transformer Architectures for Speech Recognition (ASR)

Automatic Speech Recognition (ASR) is the process of converting spoken language into text, a task that demands high precision and adaptability, due to the variability in accents, languages, and noise conditions. Traditional ASR systems relied on pipeline architectures, combining feature extraction, acoustic modeling, language modeling, and decoding. While these methods achieved notable success, they struggled to capture long-range dependencies, and contextual nuances effectively. Transformer architectures, with their self-attention mechanisms, have addressed these limitations, and redefined the ASR landscape, delivering state-of-the-art performance, across diverse applications.

Architectural Overview of Transformer-Based ASR

Transformer ASR systems typically consist of an encoder that processes acoustic features extracted from raw audio, such as Mel spectrograms. The encoder uses self-attention layers to capture temporal and contextual dependencies, within the speech signal, effectively 'listening' to the audio in a holistic manner. This is complemented by a decoder, which generates the corresponding text transcription in an autoregressive fashion, attending to relevant parts of the encoded audio representations. Some advanced models, such as the Conformer, incorporate convolutional modules alongside self-attention to better model local acoustic patterns, and improve recognition accuracy. Additionally, pretraining techniques, such as wav2vec 2.0 provide the encoder with robust speech feature representations, enhancing performance on downstream recognition tasks.

Why Transformers are Revolutionizing ASR

Transformers bring several advantages to ASR, fundamentally altering how audio data is processed:

- **Global Context Modeling:** The self-attention mechanism in transformers allows models to consider the entire sequence simultaneously, enabling better contextual understanding.
- **Parallel Processing:** Unlike Recurrent Neural Networks (RNNs) that process sequences step-by-step, transformers process entire sequences in parallel, significantly speeding up training and inference.
- **Scalability:** Transformers can handle larger datasets, and adapt to complex multilingual environments, making them highly versatile.

Key Transformer Architectures for ASR

In recent years, transformer-based models have become the go-to solution for Automatic Speech Recognition (ASR) tasks, offering impressive performance in noisy environments, and across diverse languages. These models, such as Wav2Vec 2.0, Conformer, and Whisper, have pushed the boundaries of ASR, significantly improving transcription accuracy and robustness. Each architecture brings unique innovations to the table, from self-supervised learning in Wav2Vec 2.0 to hybrid convolutional-transformer models, such as Conformer, and multi-lingual capabilities in Whisper.

Wav2Vec 2.0

Wav2Vec 2.0, developed by Facebook AI, is a groundbreaking transformer-based ASR model that directly processes raw audio waveforms. It employs self-supervised learning to pre-train on large unlabeled datasets, and fine-tune for specific tasks.

- **Architecture Highlights:**
    - **Feature Encoder**: Extracts latent speech representations from raw audio using convolutional layers.
    - **Transformer Network**: Applies self-attention to model global dependencies in the audio signal.
    - **Self-Supervised Learning Objective**: Uses contrastive loss to predict masked audio segments.

Conformer (Convolutional Transformer)

Conformer, introduced by Google, combines the strengths of Convolutional Neural Networks (CNNs) and transformers. It integrates convolutional modules for capturing local acoustic features, and transformer layers for modeling long-range dependencies, making it highly effective for ASR.

- **Key Features:**
    - **Convolutional Layers:** Focus on short-range acoustic features.
    - **Multi-Head Self-Attention:** Handles long-range dependencies.
    - **Feed-Forward Layers:** Improve learning efficiency, and model stability.

Whisper

Whisper, developed by OpenAI, is a robust transformer-based ASR model designed for multilingual transcription, and speech translation. It uses an encoder-decoder architecture to process audio input, and generate text in multiple languages.

- **Strengths:**
  - Multilingual support across more than 50 languages.
  - Robust to noisy inputs, and challenging speech conditions.
  - Combines transcription and translation in one unified model.

Components of Transformer-Based ASR Systems

Transformer-based ASR models share several core components that enable their superior performance:

- **Encoder-Decoder Architecture:**
  - The encoder processes input audio features (for example, spectrograms or raw waveforms), and generates contextualized representations.
  - The decoder generates text output, using attention mechanisms to focus on relevant parts of the encoded sequence.
- **Positional Encoding:** Since transformers lack an inherent notion of sequence, positional encoding is added to the input data to provide temporal information. This ensures that the model understands the order of sounds in the speech.
- **Self-Attention Mechanism:** Self-attention weighs the importance of each part of the input sequence, relative to others, allowing the model to capture both local and global dependencies in the audio.

Advantages over Traditional ASR Systems

- **Improved Contextual Understanding:** Transformers excel at modeling long-range dependencies, enabling them to understand the context of entire sentences, even when dealing with complex or ambiguous phrases.
- **Robustness to Noise:** Pre-trained transformer models, such as Wav2Vec 2.0 and Whisper demonstrate resilience to noisy and challenging audio conditions, making them ideal for real-world applications.
- **Simplified Pipelines:** Traditional ASR systems required separate components for feature extraction, acoustic modeling, and language modeling. Transformers unify these tasks into a single, end-to-end framework, reducing engineering complexity.

Example Implementation: Wav2Vec 2.0 for ASR

Following is a simplified pipeline for using Wav2Vec 2.0 in PyTorch for ASR:

Step 1: Install Required Libraries

```
pip install transformers torchaudio
```

Step 2: Load Pre-Trained Wav2Vec 2.0 Model

```
from transformers import Wav2Vec2ForCTC, Wav2Vec2Processor
import torch

# Load pre-trained model and processor
```

```
processor = Wav2Vec2Processor.from_pretrained("facebook/wav2vec2-large-960h")
model = Wav2Vec2ForCTC.from_pretrained("facebook/wav2vec2-large-960h")
model.eval()
```

Step 3: Preprocess Audio Input

```
import torchaudio

# Load an audio file
waveform, sample_rate = torchaudio.load("audio_file.wav")

# Resample to 16kHz if necessary
resampler = torchaudio.transforms.Resample(orig_freq=sample_rate,
new_freq=16000)
waveform = resampler(waveform)

# Prepare input for the model
input_values = processor(waveform.squeeze().numpy(), return_tensors="pt",
sampling_rate=16000).input_values
```

Step 4: Perform Transcription

```
# Generate predictions
with torch.no_grad():
    logits = model(input_values).logits

# Decode the predicted IDs to text
predicted_ids = torch.argmax(logits, dim=-1)
transcription = processor.decode(predicted_ids[0])
print("Transcription:", transcription)
```

The output will be a text string, representing what was spoken in the audio like this:

```
Transcription: Hello, this is a test of the Wav2Vec2 model for automatic
speech recognition.
```

Challenges in Transformer-Based ASR

Despite their advantages, transformer-based ASR models face many challenges:

- **High Computational Requirements:** Transformers require substantial GPU memory and processing power, especially for training on large datasets.
- **Data Dependency:** Pre-training transformers demand vast amounts of unlabeled audio which can be difficult to obtain for less common languages or accents.
- **Latency:** While transformers process sequences in parallel, their complexity can result in higher inference latency, compared to lightweight models.

Applications of Transformer-Based ASR

- **Virtual Assistants:** High-accuracy ASR models power virtual assistants, such as Alexa, Siri, and Google Assistant.
- **Transcription Services:** Models like Whisper enable accurate transcription of interviews, meetings, and podcasts.
- **Multilingual Speech Recognition:** Transformer ASR models excel in transcribing diverse languages and dialects, promoting accessibility and inclusivity.

Transformer architectures have redefined ASR by addressing the limitations of traditional methods, and delivering exceptional accuracy and adaptability. Models. such as Wav2Vec 2.0, Conformer, and

Whisper showcase the versatility of transformers in handling diverse ASR tasks, from transcription to translation. In the next section, we will dive into Implementing a Transformer-Based ASR System with PyTorch 2.0, offering hands-on guidance for building a custom ASR pipeline.

Implementing a Transformer-Based ASR System with PyTorch 2.0

Building an Automatic Speech Recognition (ASR) system, using transformers involves integrating pre-trained models with audio preprocessing, and decoding pipelines. This section provides a step-by-step guide to implementing a transformer-based ASR system, using Wav2Vec 2.0 and PyTorch 2.0. The implementation leverages pre-trained models to simplify the process, making it accessible to developers and researchers, while delivering state-of-the-art transcription performance.

Workflow for Implementing Transformer-Based ASR

The implementation of an ASR system involves the following key steps:

1. **Preprocessing Audio Data:** Preparing raw audio signals by normalizing, resampling, and extracting features.
2. **Loading a Pre-Trained Transformer Model:** Using a model like Wav2Vec 2.0 fine-tuned for ASR tasks.
3. **Generating Predictions:** Feeding the preprocessed audio into the transformer model to obtain text output.
4. **Post-Processing Transcriptions:** Cleaning up and formatting the predicted text for readability.

Setting Up the Environment

Before starting, install the necessary libraries:

```
pip install torch torchvision torchaudio transformers datasets
```

Step-by-Step Implementation

Step 1: Load and Preprocess Audio Data

Start by loading the raw audio file, and preparing it for input into the model.

```
import torchaudio
from transformers import Wav2Vec2Processor

# Load audio file
audio_path = "path_to_audio_file.wav"
waveform, sample_rate = torchaudio.load(audio_path)

# Resample audio to 16 kHz (required for Wav2Vec 2.0)
resampler = torchaudio.transforms.Resample(orig_freq=sample_rate, new_
freq=16000)
waveform = resampler(waveform)

# Normalize the waveform
waveform = waveform / waveform.abs().max()

# Initialize Wav2Vec 2.0 processor
```

```
processor = Wav2Vec2Processor.from_pretrained("facebook/wav2vec2-large-960h")
input_values = processor(waveform.squeeze().numpy(), return_tensors="pt",
sampling_rate=16000).input_values
```

Step 2: Load a Pre-Trained Wav2Vec 2.0 Model

The Wav2Vec 2.0 model comes pre-trained on large datasets like LibriSpeech, making it ideal for ASR tasks.

```
from transformers import Wav2Vec2ForCTC

# Load the pre-trained Wav2Vec 2.0 model
model = Wav2Vec2ForCTC.from_pretrained("facebook/wav2vec2-large-960h")
model.eval()
```

Step 3: Generate Predictions

Pass the preprocessed audio through the model to obtain logits, and decode the output into text.

```
import torch

# Perform inference
with torch.no_grad():
    logits = model(input_values).logits

# Decode the predicted IDs into text
predicted_ids = torch.argmax(logits, dim=-1)
transcription = processor.decode(predicted_ids[0])
print("Transcription:", transcription)
```

Step 4: Post-Processing the Transcription

The raw transcription may include artifacts or errors that can be addressed, using text cleaning techniques.

```
# Clean up the transcription (e.g., punctuation, case normalization)
def clean_transcription(text):
    return text.strip().capitalize()

cleaned_transcription = clean_transcription(transcription)
print("Cleaned Transcription:", cleaned_transcription)
```

Example Output

- **Raw Transcription:** hello this is a test of the wav2vec2 model for automatic speech recognition.
- **Cleaned Transcription:** Hello this is a test of the wav2vec2 model for automatic speech recognition.

The raw transcription will be printed first which may contain artifacts or errors due to speech recognition. The cleaned transcription will be printed next, after the basic text cleaning is applied (for instance, trimming white space, and capitalizing the first letter).

Fine-Tuning the ASR Model

While pre-trained models like Wav2Vec 2.0 perform well on general datasets, fine-tuning can further optimize performance for domain-specific tasks (for example, medical transcription, call center data, and so on). Fine-tuning requires a labeled dataset, and involves updating model weights, using a task-specific loss function.

Steps for Fine-Tuning:

1. Prepare a labeled dataset (example, audio files paired with transcripts).
2. Tokenize and preprocess the data using the **`Wav2Vec2Processor`**.
3. Use PyTorch's **`Trainer`** API for fine-tuning.

```
from datasets import load_dataset

# Load a labeled dataset
dataset = load_dataset("librispeech_asr", split="train.100")

# Tokenize the dataset
def preprocess(batch):
    audio = batch["audio"]
    input_values = processor(audio["array"], sampling_rate=audio["sampling_
rate"], return_tensors="pt").input_values[0]
    with processor.as_target_processor():
        labels = processor(batch["text"], return_tensors="pt").input_ids[0]
    return {"input_values": input_values, "labels": labels}

dataset = dataset.map(preprocess)
```

Advantages of Transformer-Based ASR Implementation

Transformer-based architectures have revolutionized the field of Automatic Speech Recognition (ASR) by overcoming the limitations of traditional models. Unlike earlier methods that struggled with long-range dependencies and complex acoustic features, transformers, with their self-attention mechanisms, excel at capturing intricate patterns across long audio sequences. This section highlights the key advantages of using transformer-based models for ASR, including their ability to handle noisy environments, improve scalability, and enhance accuracy in real-time applications. These advantages make transformers a powerful tool in addressing the challenges of modern ASR systems.

- **Ease of Use:** Pre-trained models simplify implementation, making state-of-the-art ASR accessible, without requiring extensive expertise.
- **Adaptability:** Fine-tuning enables customization for specific domains and accents.
- **Performance:** Transformer-based models consistently outperform traditional approaches, especially in noisy environments and diverse linguistic contexts.

Challenges in Transformer-Based ASR Implementation

While transformer-based architectures have significantly advanced the field of Automatic Speech Recognition (ASR), their implementation is not without challenges. Despite their impressive capabilities, these models require substantial computational resources, large-scale datasets, and fine-tuning to achieve optimal performance. Additionally, issues, such as latency during inference, model size, and the need for high-quality training data in diverse languages, or noisy conditions can present obstacles.

- **Resource Requirements:** High memory and computational demands may limit accessibility for users, without advanced hardware.
- **Data Sensitivity:** Models like Wav2Vec 2.0 require high-quality data for optimal performance. Noise and inconsistencies in training data can degrade accuracy.
- **Inference Latency:** Although transformers process sequences in parallel, large models can introduce latency in real-time applications.

Applications of Transformer-Based ASR

- **Customer Support:** Automating call center transcriptions, and generating actionable insights.
- **Accessibility:** Enabling subtitles for live events, and improving accessibility for the hearing impaired.
- **Healthcare:** Assisting in medical transcription and voice-controlled systems for doctors.
- **Education:** Enhancing online learning platforms with automated lecture transcription.

Implementing a transformer-based ASR system with PyTorch 2.0 combines the power of pre-trained models like Wav2Vec 2.0 with the flexibility of PyTorch's tools, allowing developers to build high-accuracy ASR solutions with ease. By preprocessing audio, leveraging transformers, and fine-tuning for specific tasks, these systems can tackle real-world challenges in speech recognition. In the next section, we will explore Text-to-Speech (TTS) Synthesis Using Transformer Models, demonstrating how transformers can generate lifelike speech from text inputs.

Text-to-Speech (TTS) Synthesis Using Transformer Models

Text-to-Speech (TTS) synthesis is the process of converting the written text into spoken words. With applications ranging from virtual assistants to audiobooks and language learning tools, TTS has become a cornerstone of modern human-computer interaction. Traditional TTS methods, including concatenative synthesis and parametric models, often fell short in producing expressive, natural-sounding speech. In fact, Transformer-based TTS models have revolutionized this domain, offering unparalleled improvements in naturalness, fluency, and adaptability.

Why Transformers Excel in TTS

Transformers bring several unique strengths to TTS synthesis:

- **Global Context Awareness:** Self-attention mechanisms allow transformers to capture long-range dependencies, ensuring smooth transitions in speech and coherent prosody.
- **Expressiveness:** By modeling pitch, duration, and energy variations, transformers generate speech with lifelike intonation and emotional depth.
- **Scalability and Multilingual Support:** Pre-trained transformer TTS models can handle multiple languages and accents with fine-tuning, making them versatile for global applications.

Key Transformer-Based TTS Architectures

Tacotron 2 with Transformers: Tacotron 2 is a popular sequence-to-sequence TTS model that has been enhanced with transformer blocks. The architecture uses an encoder to process text, and a decoder to generate mel-spectrograms, which are then converted into waveforms, using vocoders like WaveGlow.

- **Features:**
  - Replaces recurrent layers with transformer blocks for faster, parallel processing.
  - Improves synthesis quality, and reduces training time.

FastSpeech and FastSpeech 2: FastSpeech models adopt a non-autoregressive transformer architecture, significantly reducing the inference time, compared to traditional autoregressive models like Tacotron. FastSpeech 2 adds variance predictors for pitch, duration, and energy, enabling more expressive speech synthesis.

- **Advantages:**
  - Faster synthesis due to parallel processing.
  - Fine control over prosody and speech dynamics.

SpeechT5: SpeechT5, developed by Microsoft, unifies multiple speech-related tasks, including TTS. Its transformer encoder-decoder architecture supports both text-to-speech and speech-to-text tasks, making it highly versatile.

- **Key Strengths:**
  - Multitask learning capabilities.
  - Robust multilingual and cross-lingual support.

Workflow for Transformer-Based TTS

Transformer-based TTS involves the following steps:

Step 1: Text Preprocessing

Input text is tokenized and optionally converted to phonemes to reduce pronunciation ambiguities.

Step 2: Spectrogram Generation

The model generates mel-spectrograms from the processed text. These spectrograms represent the frequency components of speech over time.

Step 3: Waveform Synthesis

A vocoder converts the mel-spectrogram into an audio waveform. Popular vocoders include HiFi-GAN and WaveGlow.

Hands-On Example: TTS with FastSpeech 2

Step 1: Install Required Libraries

```
pip install torch torchaudio transformers
```

Step 2: Load Pre-trained FastSpeech 2 Model

```
from transformers import FastSpeech2Processor, FastSpeech2ForTextToSpeech

# Load processor and pre-trained model
processor = FastSpeech2Processor.from_pretrained("microsoft/fastspeech2-en-lj-
speech")
model = FastSpeech2ForTextToSpeech.from_pretrained("microsoft/fast-
speech2-en-ljspeech")
model.eval()
```

Step 3: Generate Speech

```
text = "Transformers have revolutionized text-to-speech synthesis."

# Preprocess text
inputs = processor(text, return_tensors="pt")

# Generate mel-spectrogram
with torch.no_grad():
    mel_outputs = model(**inputs).mel_outputs

# Use a vocoder to synthesize speech
```

```
from torchaudio.models import wavernn

# Example vocoder step (replace with actual vocoder integration)
waveform = wavernn(mel_outputs)
```

Benefits of Transformer-Based TTS

Transformer-based models have brought significant improvements to Text-to-Speech (TTS) synthesis, providing more natural, expressive, and efficient speech generation. Unlike traditional methods, transformers can capture intricate prosody patterns and long-range dependencies, resulting in highly realistic and fluid speech.

- **Natural-Sounding Speech:** Transformer models capture the intricacies of human prosody and pronunciation, producing highly realistic audio.
- **Efficient Inference:** Non-autoregressive architectures, such as FastSpeech 2 significantly reduce latency, making real-time TTS feasible.
- **Adaptability:** Pre-trained models can be fine-tuned to replicate specific voices, accents, or styles.

Applications of Transformer-Based TTS

Transformer-based Text-to-Speech (TTS) models have transformed various industries by enabling high-quality, natural-sounding speech synthesis across a wide range of applications. From virtual assistants to accessibility tools, these models are making significant strides in improving user experiences.

- **Accessibility:** Providing voice synthesis for visually impaired users and reading assistance for dyslexic individuals.
- **Content Creation:** Automating audiobook narration, podcast voiceovers, and educational material generation.
- **Virtual Assistants:** Enhancing the naturalness and personalization of speech in virtual assistants, such as Alexa and Siri.
- **Language Learning:** Supporting pronunciation guides and interactive language tutorials.

Challenges of Transformer-Based TTS

While transformer-based TTS models have significantly advanced speech synthesis, they still face several challenges that need to be addressed for more widespread adoption. These models, despite their remarkable capabilities, often require considerable computational resources and large amounts of training data.

- **High Resource Requirements:** Training transformer-based TTS models demands significant computational resources, particularly for high-quality synthesis.
- **Latency in Real-Time Applications:** While efficient, some transformer models may still face challenges in achieving ultra-low-latency performance.
- **Data Sensitivity**: High-quality, labeled datasets are essential for fine-tuning TTS models, especially for less common languages or accents.

Transformer-based TTS models have set new standards in speech synthesis by combining expressiveness, naturalness, and efficiency. Architectures, such as Tacotron 2, FastSpeech, and SpeechT5 demonstrate the potential of transformers to deliver lifelike speech across a wide range of applications.

Self-Supervised Learning in Speech Transformers: Wav2Vec 2.0

Self-supervised Learning (SSL) has emerged as a transformative approach in speech processing, particularly for tasks, such as automatic speech recognition (ASR), speech enhancement, and speaker identification. Unlike traditional supervised methods that require extensive labeled datasets, SSL enables models to learn meaningful representations directly from large amounts of unlabeled audio. This is especially valuable in speech, where annotated datasets are costly and time-intensive to create. Transformers like Wav2Vec 2.0 have leveraged SSL to set new benchmarks in speech recognition and related tasks.

Need for Self-Supervised Learning in Speech

Speech data is abundant, but often lacks accompanying labels (for example, transcriptions). SSL addresses this gap by learning representations from unlabeled data that can later be fine-tuned for specific tasks.

Key Advantages of Self-supervised Learning:

- **Data Efficiency:** Reduces dependence on labeled datasets by learning from raw audio.
- **Versatility:** Enables a single pre-trained model to be fine-tuned for multiple downstream tasks.
- **Robustness:** Improves performance in noisy or low-resource settings.

Wav2Vec 2.0: A Game-Changer in Speech SSL

Wav2Vec 2.0, developed by Facebook AI, is a landmark model in applying SSL to speech processing. It uses a transformer-based architecture to learn powerful representations directly from raw waveforms.

Key Components of Wav2Vec 2.0:

- **Feature Encoder:** Processes raw audio waveforms, using convolutional layers to extract latent speech representations.
- **Context Network:** A transformer network models the temporal dependencies and global context, within the audio.
- **Quantization Module:** Discretizes the latent representations into a finite set of codebook entries, enabling contrastive learning.
- **Contrastive Learning Objective:** Encourages the model to distinguish true audio segments from distractors, optimizing it to focus on meaningful patterns in the data.

How Self-Supervised Learning Works in Wav2Vec 2.0

The training process in Wav2Vec 2.0 consists of two main phases:

1. **Pre-Training**
    - During pre-training, parts of the audio waveform are masked (similar to how text tokens are masked in BERT).
    - The model is trained to predict the correct latent representations for the masked segments, using context from unmasked regions.
    - Contrastive loss ensures that the model learns discriminative and robust features.

2. **Fine-Tuning**
    - The pre-trained model is fine-tuned on labeled datasets for specific downstream tasks, such as ASR.
    - The model's learned representations are adapted to the target task, using task-specific loss functions.

Benefits of Wav2Vec 2.0 and SSL in Speech

- **Data Efficiency:** By pre-training on unlabeled audio, Wav2Vec 2.0 reduces the need for large annotated datasets.
- **Task Versatility:** The learned representations can be fine-tuned for diverse tasks, including transcription, emotion detection, and speaker identification.
- **Noise Robustness:** Pre-training helps the model generalize better to noisy environments and accents.
- **Multilingual Support:** SSL models can pre-train on multilingual datasets, enabling better performance across languages.

Example: Using Wav2Vec 2.0 in PyTorch

Step 1: Install Necessary Libraries

```
pip install torch torchaudio transformers
```

Step 2: Load Pre-Trained Wav2Vec 2.0 Model

```
from transformers import Wav2Vec2ForCTC, Wav2Vec2Processor
import torch

# Load the pre-trained model and processor
processor = Wav2Vec2Processor.from_pretrained("facebook/wav2vec2-large-960h")
model = Wav2Vec2ForCTC.from_pretrained("facebook/wav2vec2-large-960h")
model.eval()
```

Step 3: Preprocess and Transcribe Audio

```
import torchaudio

# Load audio file
audio_path = "audio_file.wav"
waveform, sample_rate = torchaudio.load(audio_path)

# Resample audio to 16kHz if needed
resampler = torchaudio.transforms.Resample(orig_freq=sample_rate, new_
freq=16000)
waveform = resampler(waveform)

# Process audio
input_values = processor(waveform.squeeze().numpy(), return_tensors="pt", sam-
pling_rate=16000).input_values

# Generate transcription
with torch.no_grad():
    logits = model(input_values).logits

# Decode predicted IDs
predicted_ids = torch.argmax(logits, dim=-1)
transcription = processor.decode(predicted_ids[0])
print("Transcription:", transcription)
```

The transcription of the audio file will be printed which is the result of converting the audio content into text.

Applications of Self-Supervised Learning in Speech

Self-supervised learning has become a game changer in speech processing, enabling models to learn powerful representations from vast amounts of unlabeled data. This approach has revolutionized tasks, such as Automatic Speech Recognition (ASR), speaker identification, and speech enhancement. In this section, we will explore the wide range of applications, where self-supervised learning is making a significant impact, improving performance, and reducing the dependency on labeled data for various speech-related tasks.

- **Automatic Speech Recognition (ASR):** SSL improves transcription accuracy, particularly in noisy or low-resource settings.
- **Speech Translation:** Pre-trained models can be fine-tuned for cross-lingual tasks, enabling real-time translation of spoken language.
- **Speaker Identification:** SSL models like Wav2Vec 2.0 can distinguish speakers, based on learned voice characteristics.
- **Emotion Recognition:** By capturing prosodic features, SSL models can classify emotions in speech with higher accuracy.

Challenges in Self-Supervised Learning for Speech

While self-supervised learning has unlocked numerous possibilities in speech processing, it comes with its own set of challenges. This section will address the key obstacles in self-supervised learning for speech, including data quality, model complexity, and the need for large-scale computational resources.

- **Computational Costs:** Pre-training large models on vast datasets requires significant resources.
- **Data Bias:** Pre-training on specific languages or accents may limit generalization to underrepresented groups.
- **Latency in Real-Time Applications:** Large transformer models can be computationally intensive for real-time deployment.

Self-supervised learning, exemplified by Wav2Vec 2.0, has revolutionized speech processing by enabling models to learn rich representations from unlabeled audio. This approach not only reduces reliance on labeled data, but also enhances robustness and versatility across tasks. In the next section, we will explore Multi-Lingual and Code-Switching Speech Processing, where transformers excel in handling diverse linguistic scenarios and alternating language contexts.

Multi-Lingual and Code-Switching Speech Processing

Speech processing in multi-lingual and code-switching contexts is a challenging yet crucial domain. In multi-lingual environments, individuals often switch between two or more languages, within a single conversation, a phenomenon known as code-switching. This adds complexity to traditional speech systems, which are typically designed for monolingual scenarios. Transformer-based architectures, with their ability to model long-range dependencies and context, are well-suited for handling the intricacies of multi-lingual and code-switching speech processing.

This section explores how transformers address the challenges posed by multi-lingual and code-switching speech, and delves into real-world applications, as well as provides a practical implementation guide.

Challenges in Multi-Lingual and Code-Switching Speech Processing

Multi-lingual and code-switching scenarios introduce several unique challenges:

- **Language Boundary Detection:** Identifying where one language ends, and another begins is non-trivial, especially when languages share phonetic or grammatical similarities.
- **Diverse Accents and Pronunciations:** Variability in accents and pronunciations across languages can confuse speech recognition models.
- **Data Scarcity:** Collecting labeled datasets for every possible language combination and code-switching context is often infeasible.
- **Context Sensitivity:** Code-switching is highly context-dependent, requiring models to understand linguistic and semantic cues to predict the correct language.

Transformers' Excellence in Multilingual and Code-Switching Speech

Transformers bring several advantages to this domain:

- **Shared Representations across Languages:** Multi-lingual transformer models, such as Wav2Vec 2.0 XLS-R and Whisper, are trained on data spanning multiple languages, enabling them to learn shared features and representations across languages.
- **Contextual Understanding:** Self-attention mechanisms allow transformers to capture contextual dependencies, making them effective in handling language transitions.
- **Fine-Tuning Flexibility:** Pre-trained transformer models can be fine-tuned on specific language pairs or code-switching datasets to improve performance.
- **Scalability:** Transformers can process multiple languages, within a unified architecture, eliminating the need for separate models for each language.

Key Architectures for Multi-Lingual and Code-Switching Speech

- **Wav2Vec 2.0 XLS-R:** XLS-R is an extension of Wav2Vec 2.0, pre-trained on a massive dataset covering over 100 languages. Its shared representation space enables it to perform well in multi-lingual ASR tasks, and handle code-switching scenarios.
- **Whisper:** Whisper, developed by OpenAI, supports multi-lingual transcription and translation. It uses an encoder-decoder architecture, making it suitable for transcribing speech, with frequent language switches.
- **mBERT and XLM-R:** While primarily designed for text, these multi-lingual transformers can process transcriptions from speech, and provide additional language modeling capabilities.

Applications of Multi-Lingual and Code-Switching Speech Processing

Multi-lingual and code-switching speech processing has opened up a wide range of practical applications that bridge language barriers, and enhance communication. This section highlights key use cases, including real-time translation, customer support, accessibility, and educational tools, all of which benefit from the power of transformers in handling diverse linguistic scenarios.

- **Real-Time Translation:** Transforming speech in one language into text or speech in another language.
- **Customer Support:** Enabling call centers to handle multi-lingual interactions seamlessly.
- **Accessibility:** Providing transcription and translation services for diverse linguistic communities.
- **Education:** Supporting language learning tools with code-switching examples and exercises.

Implementation Example: Multi-Lingual ASR with Wav2Vec 2.0 XLS-R

Here is a step-by-step guide for implementing a multi-lingual ASR system, using Wav2Vec 2.0 XLS-R:

Step 1: Install Required Libraries

```
pip install torch torchaudio transformers
```

Step 2: Load Pre-Trained XLS-R Model

```
from transformers import Wav2Vec2ForCTC, Wav2Vec2Processor

# Load the processor and model
processor = Wav2Vec2Processor.from_pretrained("facebook/wav2vec2-xls-r-300m")
model = Wav2Vec2ForCTC.from_pretrained("facebook/wav2vec2-xls-r-300m")
model.eval()
```

Step 3: Preprocess Audio Input

```
import torchaudio

# Load and preprocess an audio file
audio_path = "multi_lingual_audio.wav"
waveform, sample_rate = torchaudio.load(audio_path)

# Resample to 16kHz if necessary
resampler = torchaudio.transforms.Resample(orig_freq=sample_rate, new_
freq=16000)
waveform = resampler(waveform)

# Prepare the input for the model
input_values = processor(waveform.squeeze().numpy(), return_tensors="pt",
sampling_rate=16000).input_values
```

Step 4: Generate Transcriptions

```
import torch

# Perform inference
with torch.no_grad():
    logits = model(input_values).logits

# Decode the predicted IDs
predicted_ids = torch.argmax(logits, dim=-1)
transcription = processor.decode(predicted_ids[0])
print("Transcription:", transcription)
```

Real-World Case Studies

The power of multilingual and code-switching speech processing can be seen in a variety of real-world applications. This section explores how transformer-based ASR models are being used in diverse settings, from India's multilingual landscape to global streaming platforms and emergency services, showcasing the practical impact of these technologies in real-world scenarios.

- **Speech Recognition in India:** India, with its rich linguistic diversity, presents a classic case for multi-lingual ASR. Models like XLS-R have been fine-tuned to recognize code-switching between Hindi and English, a common phenomenon in Indian speech.
- **Global Streaming Platforms:** Streaming services use multi-lingual ASR to provide subtitles and translations for global audiences, enhancing accessibility and user experience.
- **Emergency Services:** In multi-lingual regions, emergency response systems rely on ASR models to understand and respond to distress calls, regardless of the language spoken.

Challenges in Multi-Lingual and Code-Switching Speech Processing

- **Data Imbalance:** Some languages or dialects may be underrepresented in pre-training datasets, affecting model performance.
- **Inference Overhead:** Multi-lingual models are larger, and may have higher latency compared to monolingual systems.
- **Accent and Pronunciation Variability:** Significant variations, within a language can reduce model accuracy.

Future Directions

- **Code-Switching Detection:** Developing models that can accurately detect and adapt to language switches in real-time.
- **Efficient Models:** Optimizing multi-lingual transformers for deployment on mobile and edge devices.
- **Few-Shot Learning:** Enhancing performance for underrepresented languages, using few-shot or zero-shot learning techniques.

Multi-lingual and code-switching speech processing is critical for building inclusive and accessible AI systems. Transformers, such as Wav2Vec 2.0 XLS-R and Whisper have demonstrated exceptional capabilities in handling the complexities of diverse linguistic scenarios. Thus, by leveraging shared representations, contextual understanding, and fine-tuning, these models are driving innovation in speech recognition, translation, and transcription. In the next section, we will explore Speech Enhancement and Separation Using Transformers, highlighting how transformers tackle noisy audio environments to produce clean and intelligible speech.

Speech Enhancement and Separation Using Transformers

Speech enhancement and separation are critical tasks in speech processing, aimed at improving audio quality, and isolating individual speakers in multi-speaker environments. These tasks are fundamental for applications, such as video conferencing, hearing aids, automated transcription, and voice-controlled devices. Traditional methods, such as spectral subtraction and source separation using statistical models, often struggled to handle overlapping speech and noisy environments effectively.

Transformer-based models have significantly advanced the state of the art in these domains by leveraging self-attention mechanisms to model complex dependencies in audio data.

Speech Enhancement: Improving Audio Quality

Speech enhancement involves improving the clarity and intelligibility of speech by reducing background noise, reverberation, or other distortions. Transformer architectures excel in this task due to their ability to:

- **Capture Temporal Dependencies:** Self-attention mechanisms allow transformers to model relationships across long time frames, enabling them to identify and suppress noise patterns.
- **Preserve Speech Characteristics:** Transformers can focus on the content and structure of the speech signal, ensuring minimal distortion during noise reduction.

Example Architecture: SE-Conformer: The SE-Conformer Model combines convolutional layers with transformers to enhance speech in real-time.

- **Convolutional Layers:** Capture local acoustic features like pitch and energy.
- **Transformers:** Model global dependencies to differentiate speech from noise.

Speech Separation: Isolating Individual Speakers

Speech separation aims to isolate individual speakers in multi-speaker scenarios, often referred to as the "*cocktail party problem.*" Transformer-based models are highly effective for this task because of the following:

- **Self-Attention Mechanisms:** Enable the model to focus on each speaker's unique voice characteristics, across the audio signal.
- **Parallel Processing:** Facilitates the simultaneous separation of multiple speakers, without the need for sequential processing.

Example Architecture: SepFormer: SepFormer is a transformer-based model designed for speech separation. It employs dual-path transformers to process audio segments efficiently.

- **Segmentation:** Splits the audio into overlapping segments.
- **Encoder-Decoder Structure:** Encodes each segment, separates speakers, and reconstructs the individual waveforms.

Workflow for Speech Enhancement and Separation Using Transformers

The process typically involves the following steps:

Step 1: Audio Preprocessing

- Normalize and resample the audio to a consistent sampling rate (for example, 16 kHz).
- Convert raw waveforms into features, such as spectrograms or log-mel representations.

Step 2: Model Input

- Feed the processed audio features into a transformer-based model for enhancement or separation.

Step 3: Output Reconstruction

- Reconstruct the enhanced or separated audio signal from the model's output.

Implementation Example: Speech Enhancement with Transformers

Step 1: Install the Required Libraries

```
pip install torch torchaudio transformers
```

Step 2: Load Pre-Trained Speech Enhancement Model

```
from transformers import SpeechT5Processor, SpeechT5ForSpeechEnhancement

# Load processor and pre-trained model
processor = SpeechT5Processor.from_pretrained("microsoft/speecht5_speech_
enhancement")
model = SpeechT5ForSpeechEnhancement.from_pretrained("microsoft/speecht5_
speech_enhancement")
model.eval()
```

Step 3: Enhance Noisy Audio

```
import torchaudio

# Load noisy audio
waveform, sample_rate = torchaudio.load("noisy_audio.wav")

# Preprocess the audio
input_features = processor(waveform, sampling_rate=sample_rate, return_
tensors="pt").input_features

# Enhance the audio
with torch.no_grad():
    enhanced_audio = model(input_features).waveform

# Save the enhanced audio
torchaudio.save("enhanced_audio.wav", enhanced_audio, sample_rate=sample_rate)
```

Applications of Speech Enhancement and Separation

- **Video Conferencing:** Enhancing speech clarity in noisy environments, and separating overlapping voices during meetings.
- **Hearing Aids:** Improving intelligibility for users with hearing impairments by reducing the background noise.
- **Media Production:** Isolating individual voices for editing or transcription in interviews and podcasts.
- **Emergency Services:** Extracting critical information from noisy recordings in disaster scenarios.

Challenges in Transformer-Based Speech Enhancement and Separation

- **Computational Overhead:** Transformer models can be resource-intensive, especially for real-time applications.
- **Data Diversity:** Training robust models requires diverse datasets that include various noise types, and overlapping speech scenarios.

- **Latency:** Large models may introduce delays, limiting their feasibility for applications, such as live streaming.

Future Directions

- **Lightweight Models:** Developing efficient transformer architectures for deployment on mobile and edge devices.
- **Cross-Modal Integration:** Combining speech enhancement with visual cues (for instance, lip-reading) to improve accuracy in noisy environments.
- **Unsupervised Learning:** Leveraging self-supervised techniques to reduce reliance on labeled datasets.

Transformer-based models have revolutionized speech enhancement and separation by leveraging self-attention to model global and local dependencies in audio data. Architectures, such as SE-Conformer and SepFormer demonstrate how transformers address challenges like noise reduction and multi-speaker separation with state-of-the-art performance. These advancements are driving innovation across industries, from communication and accessibility to media production.

Conclusion

To sum up, **Transformers have redefined the field of speech processing**, addressing long-standing challenges in areas, such as Automatic Speech Recognition (ASR), Text-to-Speech (TTS) synthesis, speech enhancement, and multi-lingual processing. Their ability to model global dependencies through self-attention, combined with the scalability of pre-trained models, has made them indispensable tools for tackling the complexities of human speech.

In this chapter, we explored how transformer-based architectures like Wav2Vec 2.0, Whisper, and SpeechT5 excel in extracting meaningful representations from speech, handling diverse accents, managing code-switching scenarios, and generating natural-sounding speech. The transformative power of self-supervised learning was highlighted through models like Wav2Vec 2.0, which significantly reduce the need for labeled data, while improving robustness and versatility. Additionally, the application of transformers in speech enhancement and separation showcases their potential to improve communication in noisy environments and multi-speaker scenarios.

Despite their numerous advantages, transformers in speech processing are not without challenges. Issues, such as high computational requirements, latency in real-time applications, and data imbalance for underrepresented languages remain areas of active research and development. However, ongoing advancements in efficient transformer architectures and pre-training techniques are steadily addressing these limitations.

In the next chapter, **Advanced Transformer Models**, we will explore the cutting-edge developments in transformer architectures, including innovations like sparse attention mechanisms, efficient transformers, and task-specific adaptations. These advancements are pushing the boundaries of what transformers can achieve, enabling more specialized and scalable solutions, across diverse domains.

CHAPTER 7
Advanced Transformer Models

Introduction

This chapter explores cutting-edge advancements in transformer architectures, diving deep into models that have pushed the boundaries of AI capabilities. Readers will gain insights into the innovations behind models such as BERT, GPT, and T5, understanding their unique architectures and training paradigms. These transformer-based architectures have redefined the way artificial intelligence processes language, enabling models to perform a wide range of tasks such as text generation, question answering, machine translation, and code synthesis with unprecedented accuracy.

The chapter also introduces multi-modal transformers like CLIP and DALL-E, which extend the capabilities of transformers beyond text, allowing models to understand and generate visual content, alongside natural language. Additionally, we will explore transformer models for programming, including Codex, which powers AI-assisted code generation. Through hands-on implementations using PyTorch 2.0, you will learn to leverage these powerful models for various tasks, and explore techniques for efficient fine-tuning.

Structure

The chapter covers the following topics:

- Bidirectional Encoder Representations from Transformers
- Generative Pre-trained Transformer Series
- Text-to-Text Transfer Transformer
- Multi-Modal Transformers
- Transformer Models for Code and Programming Tasks
- Few-Shot and Zero-Shot Learning with Large Language Models
- Ethical Considerations and Biases in Large Language Models
- Implementing and Fine-Tuning Advanced Transformer Models with PyTorch 2.0

Bidirectional Encoder Representations from Transformers

Bidirectional Encoder Representations from Transformers (BERT) is a groundbreaking model introduced by Google in 2018 that revolutionized Natural Language Processing (NLP). BERT differs from traditional models in that it uses a transformer-based architecture for understanding language in a bidirectional manner. Prior to BERT, many NLP models processed text in a unidirectional way (left-to-right or right-to-left), which limited their ability to capture context effectively. BERT, however, simultaneously processes both directions of the text, allowing it to capture a much richer understanding of the language.

BERT's primary advantage lies in its ability to learn contextualized word representations. Unlike older methods, such as word2vec or GloVe, which assigns a single static vector to a word, BERT assigns different representations to the same word, depending on its surrounding context. This innovation allows BERT to handle complex linguistic nuances, and achieve superior performance across various NLP tasks, such as question answering, text classification, and Named Entity Recognition (NER).

BERT Architecture and Design

BERT is based on the transformer architecture initially introduced in the paper, "*Attention is All You Need*" by *Vaswani et al.*, which relies on the self-attention mechanism to process input data. Self-attention allows the model to weigh the importance of each token in a sequence in relation to every other token, regardless of their position.

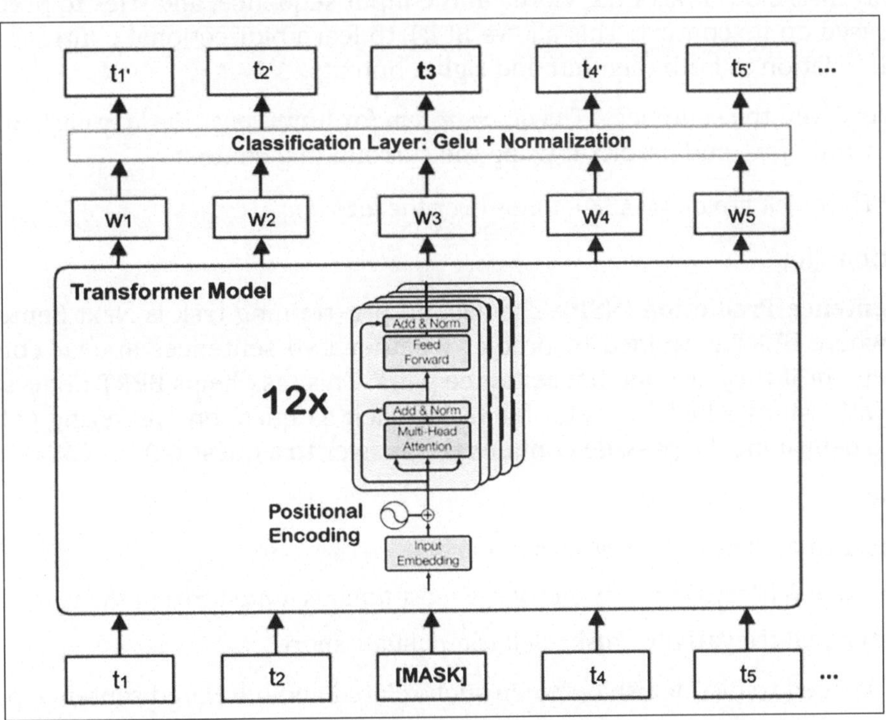

Figure 7.1: *BERT Architecture with Twelve Encoder Blocks*

The key components of BERT's architecture (*Figure 7.1*) are:

- **Encoder Only Architecture:** BERT of the transformer, focusing on understanding input sequences. Unlike models such as GPT, which are based on the transformer decoder, BERT does not generate text, but instead aims to understand and represent the input text.
- **Stacked Layers**: BERT's encoder consists of multiple layers (12 in BERT-Base, 24 in BERT-Large) of transformers. Each layer consists of two primary components:
    - **Multi-Head Self-Attention**: This allows the model to attend to different parts of the sequence simultaneously, understanding the relationships between tokens, even if they are far apart in the sequence.
    - **Feedforward Neural Networks**: These layers process the information captured by the attention mechanism, and refine it for further understanding.

- **Input Representation**: BERT uses a special tokenized representation that combines the following:
    - **Token Embeddings**: Each word or sub word in the input is mapped to a high-dimensional vector.
    - **Segment Embeddings**: These help the model understand sentence boundaries (useful for tasks, such as question answering).
    - **Positional Embeddings**: Since transformers process inputs in parallel, positional embeddings are added to preserve the order of tokens in a sequence.

Pre-Training Objectives of BERT

BERT's pre-training consists of two tasks designed to teach the model general language understanding:

- **Masked Language Model (MLM):** In traditional language models, the goal is to predict the next word in a sequence. BERT, however, takes a different approach. During pre-training, BERT randomly masks out 15% of the words in the input sequence, and tries to predict the original word, based on its context. This allows BERT to learn bidirectional context, and understand words in relation to both their left and right contexts.

    Example: Given the sentence, "*The quick brown fox jumps over the lazy dog*", BERT might mask out the word, "*fox*", and predict it using the surrounding context.

    Input: "*The quick brown [MASK] jumps over the lazy dog.*"

    Prediction: "fox"

- **Next Sentence Prediction (NSP):** The second pre-training task is Next Sentence Prediction (NSP), where BERT is trained to predict whether two sentences appear consecutively in a document, or if they are random sentence pairs. This task helps BERT understand sentence-level relationships which is useful for tasks, such as question answering (where the model needs to determine if a passage contains the answer to a question).

    Example:

    - **Sentence A**: "*The Eiffel Tower is in Paris.*"
    - **Sentence B (Positive)**: "*It is one of the most famous landmarks in the world.*"
    - **Sentence B (Negative)**: "*Basketball is a popular sport.*"

    BERT is trained to distinguish between such related and unrelated sentence pairs.

- **Applications of BERT in NLP:** BERT's design and pre-training objectives make it a versatile and powerful tool for a wide range of NLP tasks. After pre-training, BERT can be fine-tuned on specific tasks by adding a task-specific output layer (for example, for classification or question answering). The following are some of the core applications of BERT:
- **Text Classification:** BERT excels at text classification tasks, such as sentiment analysis, spam detection, and intent classification. For instance, fine-tuning BERT on a sentiment analysis dataset allows the model to classify text into categories, such as positive, negative, or neutral sentiment.

    Example: Given a movie review like "*This movie was amazing!*" BERT can classify it as positive.

- **Question Answering (QA):** BERT has achieved state-of-the-art results in question-answering tasks, such as the SQuAD (Stanford Question Answering Dataset). BERT reads a passage, and is trained to find the answer to a specific question, based on the given context.

Example:

- **Passage**: "*The Eiffel Tower is located in Paris, France. It was completed in 1889 and stands at a height of 330 meters.*"
- **Question**: "*Where is the Eiffel Tower located?*"
- **Answer**: "*Paris*"

- **Named Entity Recognition (NER):** In NER tasks, BERT is fine-tuned to identify the named entities in text, such as persons, organizations, locations, and dates. For example, BERT can be used to identify "*John*" as a person and "*Paris*" as a location.

  Example:

  - **Sentence**: "*John visited Paris last summer.*"
  - **Entities Identified**: John (Person), Paris (Location)

- **Text Summarization:** BERT has been applied to extractive summarization, where the model identifies the most important sentences in a document to form a summary. It excels in understanding the content, and picking out key sentences that best represent the document's main points.
- **Language Translation:** BERT's pre-trained bidirectional nature enables it to work in tasks, such as machine translation, where it can be fine-tuned to translate the text from one language to another by modeling sentence-level relationships.
- **Fine-Tuning BERT for Specific Tasks:** BERT's ability to be fine-tuned on task-specific datasets makes it highly adaptable. For example, to fine-tune BERT for a sentiment classification task:
  1. Add a classification layer on top of the BERT model.
  2. Feed the task-specific dataset (for example, labeled movie reviews) into the model.
  3. Train the model to optimize performance for the given task, such as minimizing classification loss (cross-entropy loss).

Example Code Snippet:

```
from transformers import BertForSequenceClassification, Trainer, Training
Arguments

# Load pre-trained BERT model with a classification head
model = BertForSequenceClassification.from_pretrained("bert-base-uncased",
num_labels=2)

# Fine-tuning the model
training_args = TrainingArguments(
    output_dir='./results',
    num_train_epochs=3,
    per_device_train_batch_size=8,
    per_device_eval_batch_size=8,
    logging_dir='./logs',
    evaluation_strategy="epoch"
)

trainer = Trainer(
    model=model,
    args=training_args,
    train_dataset=train_dataset,
    eval_dataset=eval_dataset
)

trainer.train()
```

- **BERT Variants and Enhancements:** While BERT is powerful, its size and computational requirements limit its accessibility. Several variants have been developed to overcome these limitations:
  - **RoBERTa (Robustly Optimized BERT):** Improves on BERT by removing the Next Sentence Prediction task, and training with more data and higher batch sizes.
  - **DistilBERT**: A smaller, faster version of BERT with fewer parameters, making it more efficient, without sacrificing much performance.
  - **ALBERT (A Lite BERT):** Uses parameter sharing to reduce model size, and improve efficiency, while maintaining performance.
  - **TinyBERT**: A further compressed version of BERT for edge applications, with limited resources.

BERT has transformed NLP by introducing bidirectional context understanding, enabling more accurate and nuanced language models. Its unique architecture and pre-training objectives have set a new benchmark, leading to state-of-the-art results across numerous tasks, such as question answering, sentiment analysis, and named entity recognition. With various variants available for different use cases, BERT continues to drive the evolution of natural language understanding. As we move forward, we will explore Generative Pre-trained Transformer (GPT) models, which build upon BERT's success, and extend the transformer paradigm into the realm of text generation and language modeling.

Generative Pre-Trained Transformer Series

The Generative Pre-trained Transformer (GPT) series, developed by OpenAI, represents one of the most influential advances in transformer models for Natural Language Processing (NLP). While BERT focuses on understanding the context of words by processing input bidirectionally, GPT takes a different approach, focusing on generating text using a unidirectional (left-to-right) architecture. The GPT models are designed to predict the next word in a sequence, given the context of the preceding words, making them ideal for language modeling, text generation, and conversational AI.

Unlike BERT, which is primarily used for tasks, such as text classification or question answering, GPT excels at tasks that require text generation, such as creative writing, chatbots, code generation, and even poetry composition. In this section, we will delve into the architecture, key features, and applications of the GPT series, explaining how it works, and its evolution from GPT to the latest version, GPT-3.

GPT Architecture and Design

The GPT series is built on the transformer decoder architecture (*Figure* 7.2), a design choice that differentiates it from models, such as BERT, which uses the transformer encoder. In GPT, the model is trained to predict the next token in a sequence, making it autoregressive–it generates text by conditioning each token prediction on all previous tokens in the sequence.

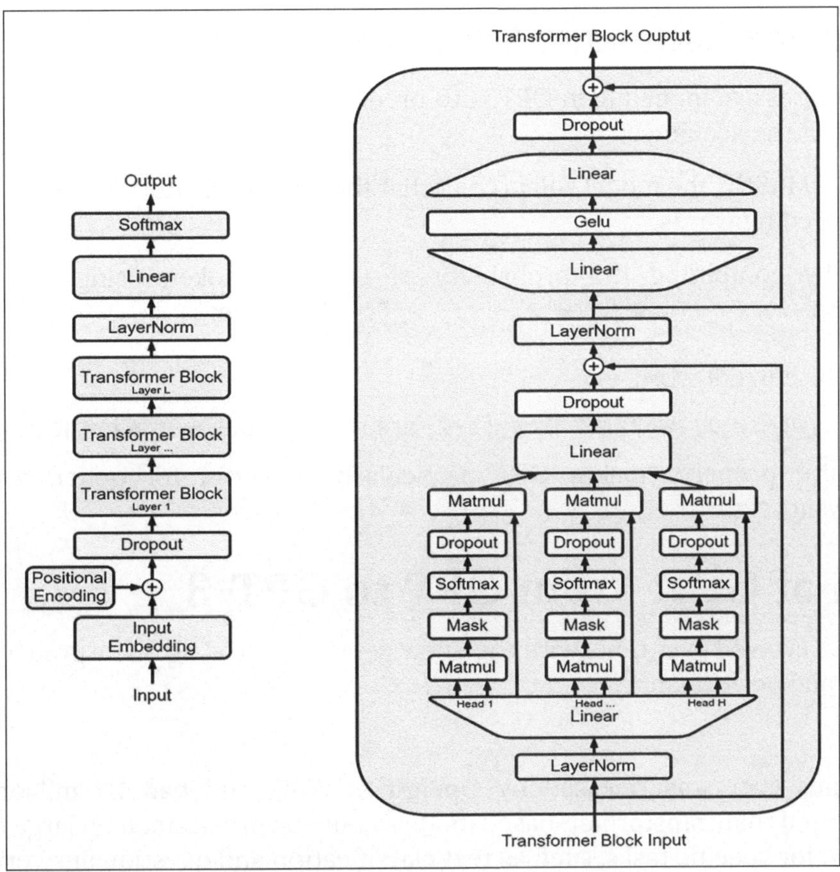

Figure 7.2: *Full GPT Architecture*

The key components of GPT's architecture are:

- **Transformer Decoder**: GPT uses the decoder part of the transformer architecture which processes the input sequentially in a left-to-right manner. The self-attention mechanism in the decoder attends to all the previous tokens in the sequence, but it does not allow future tokens to influence the current prediction (hence, unidirectional).
- **Positional Encoding**: Like BERT, GPT uses positional encodings to give the model information about the position of tokens in the sequence. This helps GPT understand the sequence order, when processing the input text.
- **Stacked Layers**: GPT models are typically deep, with multiple layers of self-attention and feed-forward networks. For example, GPT-3 has 96 transformer blocks, each with 96 attention heads, allowing it to capture intricate patterns in long sequences of text.
- **Masked Attention**: To ensure the autoregressive property, GPT employs masked self-attention, where each token only attends to the preceding tokens in the sequence. This ensures that predictions are generated in a left-to-right order, enabling the model to predict the next word in a sequence as it progresses.

Training Objectives of GPT

GPT's core training objective is based on language modeling, specifically next-word prediction. The model is pre-trained on vast amounts of text data, and learns to predict the probability distribution of the next word, given the context of previous words. This unsupervised learning approach allows GPT to acquire a rich understanding of language structure, syntax, and even world knowledge!

Autoregressive Language Modeling

The goal of autoregressive modeling in GPT is to predict the next word in a sequence of words. For example, if we input the sequence:

"*The cat sat on the* [MASK]", the model will predict that the most likely next word is "*mat*" based on the context of the preceding words.

GPT does this by computing the probability of the next token using a softmax function: `P(wt|w1,w2,...,wt-1)P(w_t | w_1, w_2, ..., w_{t-1})` where:

- `wtw_t` is the current word.
- `w1,w2,...,wt-1w_1, w_2, ..., w_{t-1}` are the previous words in the sequence.

This autoregressive property makes GPT particularly powerful for generating coherent and contextually relevant text.

Evolution of GPT: From GPT to GPT-3

The GPT series has evolved over time, with each new version improving on its predecessor in terms of size, capabilities, and performance.

GPT (Original):

- The original GPT was released by OpenAI in 2018, and had 117 million parameters. It demonstrated that transformer-based models could be pre-trained on large text corpora, and fine-tuned for specific tasks, such as text classification and question answering.
- GPT achieved significant improvements over previous models by leveraging the power of large-scale unsupervised pre-training, and transfer learning.

GPT-2:

- GPT-2, released in 2019, took the transformer architecture to new heights with 1.5 billion parameters. It demonstrated the power of unsupervised learning and fine-tuning, across multiple tasks.
- One of the key innovations of GPT-2 was its ability to generate coherent and contextually relevant text over long passages. The model could produce articles, stories, and even poems that closely resembled human writing.
- GPT-2 sparked concerns about the potential misuse of AI-generated text, leading OpenAI to initially withhold the full model, and later release it in stages.

GPT-3:

- GPT-3, released in 2020, marked a significant leap forward, with a staggering 175 billion parameters. It was trained on an even larger dataset, and demonstrated unprecedented capabilities in few-shot and zero-shot learning.
- GPT-3's versatility allowed it to perform a wide range of tasks, without task-specific fine-tuning, including machine translation, summarization, question answering, and even code generation.

  The key features of GPT-3 include:

  - **Few-Shot Learning**: GPT-3 can perform tasks with little to no task-specific data. It can generalize to new tasks by seeing just a few examples in the input.
  - **Zero-Shot Learning**: GPT-3 can complete tasks, without having seen any examples, relying on its general understanding of language and common sense.

Applications of GPT Models

GPT models have demonstrated the state-of-the-art performance in a wide range of NLP tasks, including:

- **Text Generation:** GPT models are widely used for text generation, where the model generates human-like content, based on an initial prompt. Whether it is generating creative writing, blog posts, or even code, GPT excels in producing coherent and contextually relevant text.

  Example:

  - **Prompt**: "*Write a poem about the ocean.*"
  - **Generated Text:**

    "*The ocean's waves crash on the shore,*

    Whispering tales of distant lore,

    Beneath the sky, so vast, so wide,

    Secrets of the sea, it cannot hide."

- **Conversational AI:** GPT's ability to generate contextually appropriate responses makes it ideal for chatbots and virtual assistants. Models, such as GPT-3 have been used to develop AI that can engage in natural, human-like conversations.

  Example:

  - **User Input**: "*What's the weather like today?*"
  - **AI Response**: "*Today, the weather is sunny with a slight breeze. The high will be 75°F.*"

- **Code Generation**: GPT models, especially GPT-3, have demonstrated an ability to generate code based on natural language descriptions. This has opened the door to applications in programming assistants, and automatic code generation.

  Example:

  - **Prompt**: "*Write a Python function to calculate the Fibonacci sequence.*"

Generated Code:

```
def fibonacci(n):
    if n <= 1:
        return n
    else:
        return fibonacci(n-1) + fibonacci(n-2)
```

- **Translation and Summarization:** GPT can be fine-tuned for machine translation and text summarization, enabling it to generate translations between languages, and condense long documents into shorter summaries.

Fine-Tuning GPT for Specific Tasks

While GPT models can perform a wide range of tasks with minimal fine-tuning, they can still be adapted for specialized tasks by adding a task-specific head, and training on a relevant dataset.

For example, for text classification, a classification head can be added to GPT, and the model can be fine-tuned on labeled data to predict categories, such as sentiment (positive/negative), topic (sports, politics, and so on), or intent (order, inquiry, and many more).

Example Code Snippet for Fine-Tuning GPT-2 on Text Classification:

```
from transformers import GPT2ForSequenceClassification, GPT2Tokenizer, Trainer,
TrainingArguments

# Load pre-trained GPT-2 model with classification head
model = GPT2ForSequenceClassification.from_pretrained("gpt2", num_labels=2)

# Tokenize and prepare dataset
tokenizer = GPT2Tokenizer.from_pretrained("gpt2")
inputs = tokenizer(texts, return_tensors="pt", padding=True, truncation=True)

# Define training arguments
training_args = TrainingArguments(output_dir='./results', num_train_epochs=3,
per_device_train_batch_size=8)

# Initialize Trainer and train
trainer = Trainer(model=model, args=training_args, train_dataset=train_
dataset)
trainer.train()
```

Training logs will be printed during the training process, showing details, such as epoch progress, training loss, and metrics like accuracy (if specified).

Example Output:

```
***** Running training *****
Num examples = 10000
Num Epochs = 3
Instantaneous batch size per device = 8
Total train batch size = 8
Learning Rate = 5e-05
...
Epoch 1/3
Step 50/625: Train loss = 0.6923
...
Epoch 2/3
Step 50/625: Train loss = 0.4586
...
Saving model checkpoint to ./results/checkpoint-50
```

Evolution and Challenges of GPT, GPT-2, GPT-3, and GPT-4

The GPT series represents a progressive evolution of large language models, starting with GPT, which introduced the transformer-based autoregressive approach for text generation. GPT-2 expanded on this with significantly more parameters and training data, enabling it to generate more coherent, and contextually rich text. GPT-3 further scaled the architecture to 175 billion parameters, achieving remarkable few-shot learning capabilities, without task-specific fine-tuning, but its size also introduced challenges, such as increased computational cost, and potential for generating biased or nonsensical outputs. The latest, GPT-4, builds on this foundation with enhanced reasoning, multimodal input capabilities, and improved contextual understanding, yet it still faces limitations, including opacity in decision-making, dependence on vast amounts of data, and risks of bias amplification. Across all versions, issues around model interpretability, ethical concerns, and resource demands remain active areas of research and practical consideration.

Ethical Considerations of GPT

As powerful as GPT models are, they also raise important ethical concerns:

- **Bias in Training Data**: GPT models can learn and reproduce biases, present in the training data, leading to outputs that reflect harmful stereotypes or social biases.
- **Misuse Potential**: The ability to generate realistic text can be misused for malicious purposes, such as creating fake news, impersonating individuals, or spamming.
- **Environmental Impact**: Training large models, such as GPT-3 requires immense computational resources, raising concerns about their carbon footprint.

The GPT series has set new benchmarks for generative NLP tasks, from text generation and conversational AI to code generation and translation. With models, such as GPT-2 and GPT-3, OpenAI has demonstrated the power of large-scale, autoregressive transformers for both general-purpose and specific tasks. Despite the impressive capabilities, ethical concerns and computational demands remain key areas of focus. In the next section, we will delve into T5 (Text-to-Text Transfer Transformer), a model that extends the transformer paradigm to handle a variety of NLP tasks, under a unified framework. **Text-to-Text Transfer Transformer**

The Text-to-Text Transfer Transformer (T5), developed by Google Research, is a powerful model that reformulates all NLP tasks, as a text-to-text problem. Unlike other transformer models, which are often designed for specific tasks (for example, BERT for understanding or GPT for text generation), T5 adopts a unified framework where both the input and output of the model are text sequences, regardless of the specific task. This flexibility allows T5 to be applied to a wide range of natural language processing tasks, including translation, summarization, question answering, classification, and even more specialized tasks, such as sentence pair prediction.

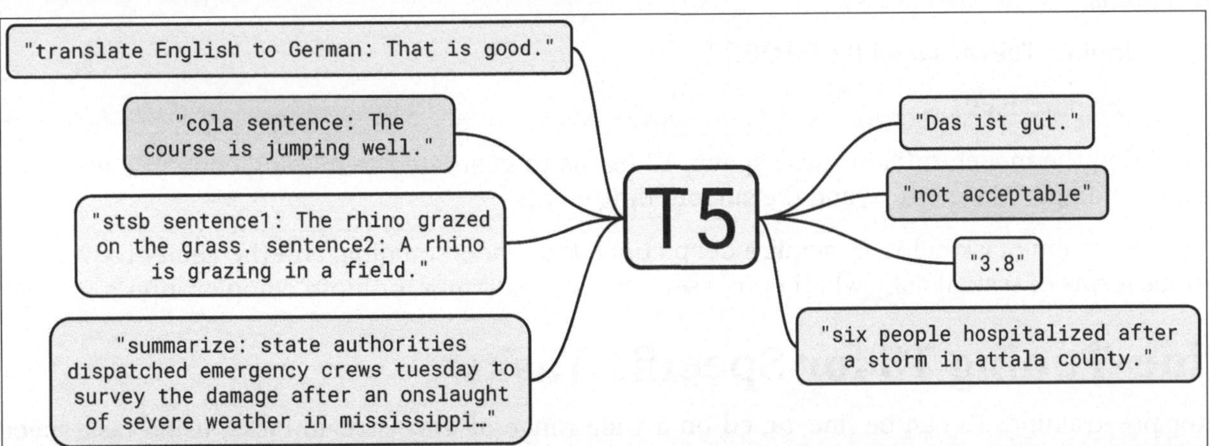

Figure 7.3: *T5 Text-to-text Framework*

T5's key innovation lies in its simplicity and versatility (*Figure* 7.3). By casting every task as a sequence transformation, the model is trained to learn the relationships between input text (source) and output text (target) for all NLP applications, making it a highly effective and adaptable solution. This section delves into the architecture of T5, its training methodology, and its real-world applications, demonstrating why it is considered one of the most versatile transformer models available.

T5 Architecture and Design

T5 is built on the transformer architecture, utilizing both the encoder and decoder components to process and generate text. The model is based on a standard sequence-to-sequence framework, which has been a common design in models for tasks, such as machine translation. However, T5's distinctive feature is its approach in handling a wide variety of tasks, under a text-to-text paradigm.

Key Components of T5:

- **Encoder-Decoder Structure**: Similar to models, such as BART and T5's predecessor, BERT, T5 employs both an encoder and a decoder. The encoder processes the input text, and the decoder generates the corresponding output text. This setup enables T5 to work on a wide range of tasks by generating different kinds of outputs, whether it is text classification labels or machine-translated sentences.
- **Pretrained Model**: T5 is pre-trained using a multi-task learning approach, where it is trained on a variety of NLP tasks, such as translation, question answering, and summarization. The model learns to map input text to output text in different contexts.
- **Unified Text-to-Text Format**: Every task is cast into a text generation problem. For instance, for translation tasks, the input might be a sentence in one language, and the output will be the corresponding translation in another language. For question-answering tasks, the question and context are treated as the input, and the answer is the output.

T5 Pre-Training Objectives

T5 is trained with a span-based denoising objective–similar to BERT's masked language modeling but adapted for the sequence-to-sequence framework. This pre-training method helps T5 learn to fill in missing portions of text within a sequence, further enhancing its ability to handle a variety of tasks.

Pre-Training Task: The primary pre-training objective for T5 is denoising text sequences. In this task, spans of text are masked out, and the model is trained to predict the missing spans. For example, if the input is:

> **Input**: "*The cat sat on the* [MASK]."
>
> **Output**: "*mat*"

By training the model to fill in these spans, T5 learns to generate the missing content, based on its understanding of the context, and the surrounding words.

This pre-training task helps T5 acquire deep contextual understanding, and the ability to work with various forms of textual data, whether it is sentences, paragraphs, or more complex inputs.

Fine-Tuning T5 for Specific Tasks

After pre-training, T5 can be fine-tuned on a wide range of downstream tasks, using task-specific datasets. The beauty of T5 lies in its flexibility: The same model can be fine-tuned for different tasks, with minimal changes. Fine-tuning involves training T5 on a labeled dataset, where the input text corresponds to the target output, such as a sentence label or translated text.

Fine-Tuning Example: Text Classification

For a text classification task, the model might be fine-tuned, using the following input-output pairs:

> **Input**: "*Classify this sentence as positive or negative sentiment: The movie was amazing!*"
>
> **Output**: "*Positive*"

The model is trained to map the input to a corresponding output, based on the desired task, whether it is sentiment analysis, topic classification, or any other task.

Fine-Tuning Example: Text Summarization

For a summarization task, T5 can be fine-tuned to generate a concise summary of a longer piece of text:

Input: "*Summarize: T5 is a model that processes text sequences in a unified manner, applying a text-to-text paradigm to various NLP tasks.*"

Output: "T5 *generates text summaries by treating tasks as sequence transformations.*"

Applications of T5

T5's ability to handle diverse tasks in a text-to-text format makes it exceptionally versatile. Here are some key applications where T5 excels:

- **Text Generation:** T5 can generate human-like text for different creative applications, from content creation to dialogue generation in chatbots. It can produce coherent, and contextually appropriate paragraphs, based on a given prompt, making it ideal for content writing, creative writing, and summarization tasks.

  Example:

  Input: "*Write a short poem about nature.*"

  Output:

  "*The trees reach up to the sky,*

  As the winds of time pass by,

  With the flowers swaying near,

  Nature's song is crystal clear."

- **Question Answering:** T5 can be fine-tuned for question-answering tasks, where it learns to generate the correct answer based on a given context. It has been used for benchmarks, such as Stanford Question Answering Dataset (SQuAD), and has performed excellently across various domains.

  Example:

  - **Input**: "Context: The Eiffel Tower is in Paris, France. It is 330 meters tall".
  - **Question**: "Where is the Eiffel Tower located?"
  - **Output**: "Paris, France"

- **Machine Translation:** T5 can handle machine translation tasks by converting the text from one language to another. It excels in translating complex sentences, while preserving meaning and context.

  Example:

  Input: "*Translate from English to French: I love learning new languages.*"

  Output: "*J'adore apprendre de nouvelles langues.*"

- **Text Summarization:** T5 can be used for both extractive and abstractive summarization tasks, where the model generates concise summaries of long texts, making it highly valuable for news aggregation, document summarization, and information retrieval.

Example:

Input: "*Summarize: The transformer architecture is an important neural network design that has become the backbone of modern natural language processing models. It uses self-attention to process sequences of words, enabling it to capture long-range dependencies, and generate high-quality representations.*"

Output: "*The transformer architecture uses self-attention to process text, capturing long-range dependencies, and creating high-quality representations.*"

T5 Variants and Enhancements

T5's architecture has inspired several enhancements and variants, such as:

- **mT5**: A multilingual version of T5, fine-tuned for multiple languages, enabling cross-lingual transfer and translation tasks.
- **T5-XL**: A larger version of T5 with more parameters, used for more resource-intensive tasks that require greater capacity.

Benefits of T5

The T5 model offers several key advantages that make it a powerful and flexible choice for a wide array of natural language processing tasks:

- **Unified Framework**: By treating every task as a text-to-text problem, T5 simplifies model deployment and fine-tuning, reducing the need for task-specific architectures.
- **Versatility**: T5 performs excellently across a wide range of NLP tasks, from text generation to translation and summarization.
- **Efficient Fine-Tuning**: T5 can be fine-tuned for specific tasks with minimal data, making it a highly efficient and adaptable solution for various applications.

T5 represents a breakthrough in NLP by providing a unified framework for solving diverse tasks, with a single model. Its versatility and ease of fine-tuning have made it a powerful tool in applications, ranging from machine translation to text summarization and question answering. By casting all tasks as text-to-text problems, T5 simplifies the training and deployment process, making it a flexible solution for a variety of use cases. As we move forward, we will explore the applications of multi-modal transformers, such as CLIP and DALL-E, which integrate visual and textual data to push the boundaries of AI capabilities, even further.

Multi-Modal Transformers

Multi-modal transformers represent an exciting and evolving frontier in artificial intelligence, enabling models to understand and generate data across multiple modalities, such as text, images, and even videos. These models can learn joint representations that capture the relationships between different types of data, opening up new possibilities for applications that involve multiple data sources. One of the key advancements in multi-modal transformers has been the introduction of models, such as CLIP and DALL-E, which combine vision and language tasks into a unified framework, allowing for powerful cross-modal interactions.

In this section, we explore the architecture and capabilities of multi-modal transformer models, focusing on CLIP and DALL-E, their contributions to AI, and the potential for future multi-modal systems that can understand and generate, both visual and textual content simultaneously.

Contrastive Language-Image Pre-Training

Contrastive Language-Image Pre-Training (CLIP), developed by OpenAI, is a model designed to connect images, and text in a way that allows for robust zero-shot learning on a variety of vision-based tasks. CLIP is trained on a large corpus of image-text pairs, learning to associate textual descriptions with visual representations. Unlike traditional computer vision models that require task-specific labels (for example, "dog," "cat" and so on), CLIP can handle any text prompt, without requiring additional fine-tuning.

Key Features of CLIP:

- **Zero-Shot Learning**: CLIP can perform tasks, such as image classification, object detection, and even image search, without requiring task-specific training. Given a new set of labels, CLIP can generalize to classify images in a zero-shot manner.
- **Contrastive Learning Approach**: During training, CLIP learns to project both images and texts into a shared embedding space. It uses contrastive loss, meaning the model learns to bring matching image-text pairs closer together, while pushing non-matching pairs apart.
- **Versatility**: CLIP excels at a wide variety of vision tasks by simply receiving a textual description of the task (for instance, "*Find images of a red apple*"). This makes it highly adaptable for applications, where creating a separate model for each specific task would be inefficient.

CLIP Example Use Cases:

- **Image Search**: Given a textual query, such as "*mountain landscape*," CLIP can retrieve images from a dataset that match the query, even without task-specific fine-tuning.
- **Zero-Shot Image Classification**: CLIP can classify an image with a description of the class, such as "*photo of a dog*" or "*a red car*," even if it has not been specifically trained in those categories.
- **Cross-Modal Retrieval**: By inputting a text query or an image, CLIP can retrieve matching data from the opposite modality (such as, text-to-image or image-to-text).

DALL-E: Image Generation from Text Prompts

DALL-E, another transformative model from OpenAI, takes the multi-modal transformer paradigm a step further, by enabling the generation of images directly from textual descriptions. DALL-E uses a variational autoencoder architecture, combined with a transformer decoder, allowing it to generate novel and creative images that match a given text prompt (*Figure 7.4*). For example, a prompt like "*an armchair in the shape of an avocado*" would generate an entirely new image of an armchair, with the unique characteristics of an avocado.

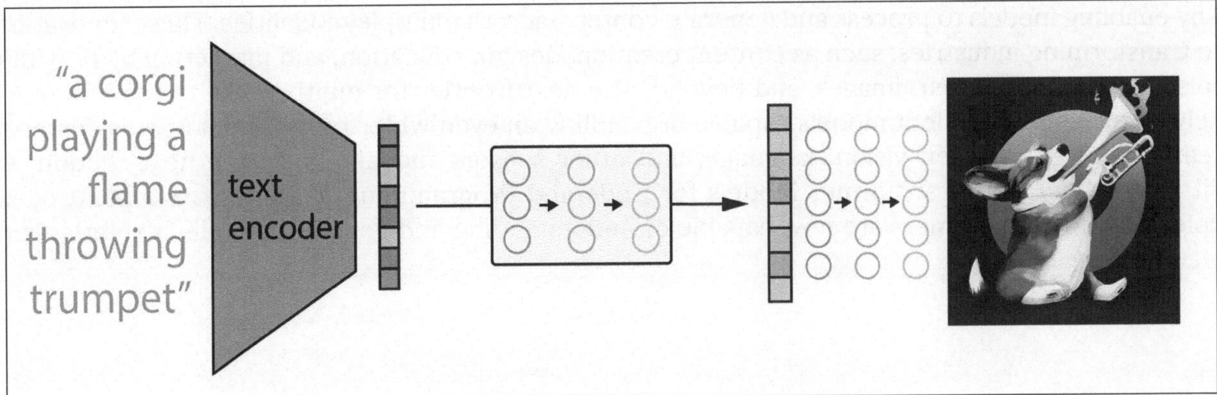

Figure 7.4: *High Level Overview of* DALL-E

Key Features of DALL-E:

- **Text-to-Image Generation**: DALL-E is designed to generate highly imaginative images from the descriptive text. By training on large datasets of image-text pairs, the model learns to generate coherent visual representations that correspond to the given textual description.
- **Creative and Novel Outputs**: DALL-E can generate novel combinations of objects or scenes that may not exist in reality, such as "*a two-storeyed house shaped like a shoe*", or "an astronaut riding a horse in a futuristic city."
- **Object Manipulation**: DALL-E has the ability to manipulate objects within an image, such as changing the color of an object, modifying the background, or adding/removing elements, based on text instructions.

DALL-E Example Use Cases:

- **Creative Content Generation**: DALL-E can be used to generate illustrations for books, advertisements, or social media content, based on creative text prompts.
- **Design and Prototyping**: Designers can use DALL-E to create visual prototypes from textual descriptions, accelerating the product development process.
- **Artistic Expression**: DALL-E enables the generation of abstract or surrealistic art, based on imaginative textual prompts, opening up new possibilities for digital art creation.

The Future of Multi-Modal Transformers

The advancements brought by CLIP and DALL-E highlight the potential of multi-modal transformers to bridge the gap between vision and language, enabling more seamless interaction between different data types. However, there are several areas, where this field is likely to evolve further:

- **Unified Models for Text, Image, and Video**: The next generation of multi-modal transformers could extend beyond just text and images to include video and audio, allowing the model to understand and generate content across multiple formats.
- **Improved Fine-Tuning and Transfer Learning**: While CLIP and DALL-E are impressive, they often require large amounts of data and computing resources. Future models may optimize the fine-tuning process to make multi-modal models more efficient and accessible for various use cases.
- **Cross-Modal Applications**: As these models improve, we may see more integrated applications, where text, image, and video generation work seamlessly together. For instance, a single model might take a video clip, and generate a script, or generate new images, based on a short piece of text describing the scene.

The rise of multi-modal transformers, exemplified by CLIP and DALL-E, is pushing the boundaries of AI by enabling models to process and generate content, across multiple modalities. These innovations are transforming industries, such as content creation, design, education, and marketing by providing tools that can bridge text, images, and beyond. The next frontier for multi-modal transformers will likely involve more efficient models capable of handling an even wider range of data types, fostering greater synergy between vision, language, and other sensory modalities. In the next section, we will dive deeper into Transformer Models for Code and Programming Tasks (for example, Codex), exploring how transformers are now capable of understanding and generating code, revolutionizing software development.

Transformer Models for Code and Programming Tasks

The advent of transformer models has not only revolutionized natural language processing, but also sparked transformative innovations in code generation, debugging, and programming assistance. With the increasing complexity of software development, and the growing demand for automated code generation, models, such as Codex–an extension of OpenAI's GPT-3–have emerged as powerful tools capable of understanding, generating, and even debugging code. These models are designed to leverage the same transformer architecture that underpins successful NLP models to solve the unique challenges of programming tasks.

In this section, we will explore how transformers are applied to code and programming tasks, focusing on Codex and its applications in software development, code completion, and the evolution of AI-assisted programming. We will also examine the capabilities, use cases, and challenges of applying transformer models to code.

The Role of Transformers in Code and Programming Tasks

Traditionally, programming tasks involved writing, optimizing, and debugging code manually–a process that can be error-prone, time-consuming, and repetitive. However, transformer models have brought automation into this domain, enabling models to assist in various stages of software development. Transformers excel in code-related tasks due to their ability to process sequential data, and recognize complex patterns in code structures, much like how they work with natural language.

Key Advantages of Transformer Models for Code:

- **Understanding Syntax and Semantics**: Similar to how BERT understands the context of words in sentences, transformer models can grasp the syntax (structure) and semantics (meaning) of programming languages. This allows them to not only generate syntactically correct code, but also to understand the purpose of the code.
- **Handling Multiple Programming Languages**: Unlike traditional rule-based systems, transformer models can work across multiple programming languages, without requiring language-specific rule definitions. This makes them adaptable to a variety of programming environments.
- **Contextual Awareness**: Transformers' ability to process long-range dependencies in code means that they can generate or complete code that maintains consistent variable names, correct logic, and relevant comments, making them capable of supporting larger software projects.

Codex: A Game Changer in Code Generation

Codex, built on the GPT-3 architecture, is designed specifically for understanding and generating code across several languages, such as Python, JavaScript, Java, C++, and more. It represents a major leap in the application of AI to software development. Codex is a large language model trained on billions of lines of code and related text data, making it capable of understanding the structure and purpose of the code, and even generating complex software components from scratch.

Key Features of Codex:

- **Multi-Language Support**: Codex can write code in over a dozen programming languages, including Python, JavaScript, C++, Ruby, and Go, making it highly versatile for various programming environments.

- **Code Completion**: Just as GPT-3 can generate human-like text based on a prompt, Codex can complete code snippets by predicting the next segment of code, based on user input.
- **Natural Language to Code**: One of Codex's most powerful features is its ability to translate natural language prompts into code. A developer can describe a task in plain English (or any other language) and Codex will generate the corresponding code, effectively reducing the need for manual coding.

Example: Code Generation with Codex

Suppose you want to generate a Python function that calculates the factorial of a number. With Codex, you can simply type a natural language prompt like:

Prompt: "*Write a Python function to calculate the factorial of a number.*"

Codex Output:

```
def factorial(n):
    if n == 0:
        return 1
    else:
        return n * factorial(n-1)
```

This example illustrates how Codex can seamlessly generate code that works as intended, directly from a textual description.

Applications of Codex and Transformer Models in Programming Tasks

Transformer models, such as Codex are quickly becoming essential tools in modern software development. The following are some key applications where these models can make a significant impact:

Code Completion and Suggestion

Codex is highly effective at auto-completing code snippets, suggesting methods, and even identifying bugs. When writing a function, the model can suggest the next line of the code, offer function signatures, or even provide the entire code blocks, based on the developer's current work.

Example: While writing a Python program, a developer might start typing:

```
def fetch_data(url):
```

Codex could auto-complete the function with the following suggestion:

```
import requests

def fetch_data(url):
    response = requests.get(url)
    return response.json()
```

This helps developers by reducing the coding time, and ensuring that the best practices are followed.

Code Translation

Transformers, such as Codex can convert the code written in one programming language to another. This capability is particularly useful for migrating projects between different languages, or integrating systems that use different programming environments.

Example: If a developer has a JavaScript function, and needs it converted into Python, they can simply prompt Codex with the JavaScript code, and ask for a Python version. Codex will generate the Python equivalent, saving significant time and effort.

Bug Detection and Fixing

Codex can also be used to detect and fix bugs in code by identifying potential errors or inconsistencies in logic. By processing code in a manner similar to natural language understanding, transformers can pinpoint issues, such as undefined variables, syntax errors, or logical flaws.

Example: A developer might input:

```
def add_numbers(a, b):
    return a + b
```

If there is a mistake, such as a missing parameter or an incorrect data type, Codex can flag it, and suggest corrections, making the debugging process faster, and more accurate.

Code Documentation

For developers working on large codebases, generating and maintaining documentation can be a labor-intensive task. Codex can automate the process of generating docstrings and comments, based on the code, making it easier for teams to maintain consistent documentation standards.

Example: After writing a complex function, the developer can ask Codex to generate docstrings:

```
def factorial(n):
    """Returns the factorial of a number."""
    if n == 0:
        return 1
    else:
        return n * factorial(n-1)
```

Codex can generate the necessary comments and explanations for each function, improving code readability, and reducing manual effort.

Challenges in Transformer-Based Code Generation

While transformer models, such as Codex have demonstrated remarkable capabilities, several challenges remain, when applying them to programming tasks:

- **Quality of Generated Code**: Although transformers can generate a syntactically correct code, the generated code might not always be optimal, or adhere to the best practices. It is important to review and refine the output for efficiency, security, and readability.
- **Limited Context Understanding**: Code generation models can struggle with understanding the broader program context. For example, Codex might generate a snippet that works within a function, but fails, when integrated into a larger program due to missing dependencies or context.
- **Security Concerns**: AI-generated code may introduce security vulnerabilities, such as SQL injection or buffer overflow errors, if not properly vetted. Ensuring that the generated code follows secure coding practices is essential.

- **Computational Resources**: Large transformer models, such as Codex require substantial computational resources for training and deployment, which may not be accessible to all the developers.

Future Directions for Transformer-Based Code Generation

As transformer models continue to evolve, their potential for code generation and programming assistance will only expand. Here are a few areas, where we can expect significant advancements:

- **Better Integration with Development Environments**: Future transformer models will likely be integrated more seamlessly into Integrated Development Environments (IDEs), providing real-time code suggestions, error detection, and refactoring suggestions.
- **Cross-Domain Adaptability**: Transformer models could be trained on a broader range of programming languages and use cases, allowing them to handle cross-domain tasks, such as data engineering, machine learning model development, and system design.
- **Personalized Code Assistance**: By fine-tuning models on individual developers' coding styles and project-specific data, transformer models could become personalized assistants that adapt to the user's preferred coding practices and workflow.

Transformer-based models, such as Codex are transforming the landscape of software development by providing advanced tools for code generation, debugging, translation, and documentation. The ability to seamlessly convert natural language descriptions into executable code, detect bugs, and offer suggestions makes Codex an invaluable tool for modern developers. As the field progresses, we can expect even greater efficiency and adaptability, further integrating AI into the software development lifecycle. The next section will explore Few-Shot and Zero-Shot Learning with Large Language Models, discussing how these models can solve tasks with minimal training data, and adapt to new challenges on the fly.

Few-Shot and Zero-Shot Learning with Large Language Models

One of the most remarkable advancements in the field of artificial intelligence is the development of few-shot and zero-shot learning capabilities in Large Language Models (LLMs), such as GPT-3, T5, and Codex. These models, trained on vast datasets, can generalize across a wide range of tasks, often achieving impressive results, even when faced with minimal or no task-specific data. Few-shot and zero-shot learning are particularly powerful because they enable models to adapt to new, unseen tasks, without requiring large amounts of labeled data, which is often a limiting factor in traditional machine learning systems.

In this section, we will explore the principles of few-shot and zero-shot learning, their application in large language models, and how these capabilities are transforming AI's ability to handle new challenges, with minimal intervention.

Understanding Few-Shot and Zero-Shot Learning

At the heart of few-shot and zero-shot learning is the idea that models can generalize beyond their training data to make accurate predictions or generate meaningful responses, based on very little or no specific examples. These approaches allow large language models to learn from very few examples (few-shot), or even make predictions on tasks, they have never seen before (zero-shot), relying on their ability to understand patterns in language, and apply them to unfamiliar situations.

- **Few-Shot Learning:** Few-shot learning involves training a model on a small number of labeled examples (often between 1-100 examples). The idea is to expose the model to just enough examples so that it can generalize to new, unseen instances of the task. Few-shot learning is particularly useful in scenarios, where labeled data is scarce or expensive to obtain.

  Analogy: Think of few-shot learning as teaching a child how to recognize a new animal by showing them just a few pictures of that animal. After seeing those examples, the child can generalize, and identify the same animal in different contexts or images.

- **Zero-Shot Learning:** Zero-shot learning, on the other hand, refers to a model's ability to perform tasks it has never been explicitly trained on, using only the task description or instructions. In this case, the model relies on its understanding of language patterns, and the relationships between concepts to apply knowledge learned from other tasks to solve the new problem. Zero-shot learning does not require any labeled examples for the task at hand.

  Analogy: Imagine you ask someone to solve a puzzle that they have never encountered before, but they are familiar with similar puzzles. Based on their understanding of puzzle-solving strategies, they can still apply their knowledge to complete the new puzzle, without having seen it before.

How LLMs Enable Few-Shot and Zero-Shot Learning

Large Language Models, such as GPT-3 have demonstrated remarkable performance in both few-shot and zero-shot settings by leveraging their vast training data and understanding of language. These models are trained on a diverse corpus of text from books, websites, and other resources, allowing them to learn patterns, reasoning, and task structures that they can apply to a variety of tasks, even when presented with limited or no task-specific examples.

Prompt Engineering: The key to enabling few-shot and zero-shot learning in models, such as GPT-3 is prompt engineering. A well-crafted prompt (the input provided to the model) can direct the model to understand the task, and generate the desired output. For example, for a text classification task, you might provide a few labeled examples, along with a request to classify a new piece of text. In zero-shot learning, the model can perform tasks, based on clear, natural language instructions, without needing examples at all.

Few-Shot Learning Example: Text Classification

In a few-shot learning scenario, suppose we want to fine-tune a model to classify customer reviews, as either positive or negative, based on a small number of labeled examples. We could provide the following prompt to GPT-3:

Prompt:

Classify the following customer reviews, as either "*positive*" or "*negative*":

1. "*The service was excellent, and the food was delicious!*"
2. "*The delivery was late, and the food was cold.*"

Now classify: "*The restaurant had great ambiance, but the food was too salty.*"

Model Output:

"*Negative*"

In this example, the model uses just a few labeled examples to classify the sentiment of the new review. Even with a small amount of task-specific data, GPT-3 is able to generalize the sentiment classification task effectively.

Zero-Shot Learning Example: Text Summarization

In a zero-shot learning scenario, the model is given a task description, and generates a solution, without seeing any examples. Let us look at an example, where GPT-3 is asked to summarize a long article:

Prompt:

Summarize the following article:

> *"The internet is a global network that connects millions of private, public, academic, business, and government networks. It facilitates communication, commerce, education, and entertainment by enabling the sharing of information and resources."*

Model Output:

> *"The internet connects millions of networks worldwide, enabling communication, commerce, and access to information."*

In this case, GPT-3 generates a concise summary of the article, without needing any previous examples of summaries. It infers the task from the prompt, and applies its knowledge of language to produce an accurate result.

Applications of Few-Shot and Zero-Shot Learning

Few-shot and zero-shot learning have broad applications in various domains, including:

- **Text Classification and Sentiment Analysis:** In marketing and customer service, few-shot learning can be used to classify customer feedback, product reviews, or social media posts, based on sentiment or topic, without needing large and labeled datasets.
- **Question Answering Systems:** In customer support and virtual assistants, zero-shot learning allows models to provide accurate responses to questions that they have not been specifically trained on, using only the general instructions and context provided.
- **Language Translation:** Few-shot learning can be used for language translation tasks, where the model learns from a small number of translations, and can then handle translation tasks between different languages, without extensive parallel datasets.
- **Creative Content Generation:** In creative fields, such as writing, few-shot learning enables models to generate contextually relevant and original content based on brief prompts, whether it is for marketing copy, poetry, or stories.
- **Code Generation and Software Development:** As seen with Codex, few-shot and zero-shot learning can be used for generating code, based on a simple description of the task, enabling developers to quickly prototype, or even automate repetitive coding tasks.

Challenges of Few-Shot and Zero-Shot Learning

While few-shot and zero-shot learning are highly promising, they come with their own set of challenges:

- **Lack of Task-Specific Fine-Tuning**: Zero-shot learning models are not specifically trained on a task, meaning that they may not perform as well as models that have been fine-tuned with task-specific examples.
- **Ambiguity in Task Description**: For zero-shot learning to work effectively, the task description must be clear and unambiguous. Vague instructions can lead to incorrect or nonsensical outputs.

- **Generalization Limitations**: Few-shot learning models may struggle with tasks that are too different from their pre-training data, and they may not generalize well to highly specialized or niche domains, without further examples.

Future Directions

The future of few-shot and zero-shot learning lies in improving models' ability to generalize even further, with minimal or no labeled data. The key areas of research include:

- **Meta-Learning**: Techniques, such as meta-learning aim to train models to quickly adapt to new tasks with minimal data by learning from a variety of tasks during training.
- **Improved Task Understanding**: Developing better methods for models to comprehend task instructions, and handle ambiguity will enhance the effectiveness of zero-shot learning.
- **Efficient Fine-Tuning**: While few-shot learning shows promise, further advances in fine-tuning techniques could help models generalize better, and perform tasks with fewer examples.

Few-shot and zero-shot learning are revolutionizing the way we think about machine learning by allowing models to generalize from minimal or no task-specific data. These techniques enable large language models to perform a wide variety of tasks, from text generation and classification to question answering, and even code generation, with minimal human intervention. As research continues to advance, we can expect even more powerful models that can learn and adapt to new challenges on the fly, making AI more versatile and accessible. In the next section, we will explore Ethical Considerations and Biases in Large Language Models (LLMs), discussing the societal and ethical challenges that arise as AI models become more integrated into daily life.

Ethical Considerations and Biases in Large Language Models

As transformer-based models, such as BERT, GPT, and T5 have gained widespread adoption across multiple industries, ethical concerns and inherent biases, within these models have become increasingly significant topics of discussion. Large Language Models (LLMs) have demonstrated exceptional capabilities in natural language processing tasks, but their deployment raises important questions about fairness, accountability, transparency, and the potential for harm. This section delves into the ethical considerations surrounding LLMs, with a particular focus on biases, and the strategies to address them.

Inherent Biases in Large Language Models

One of the most critical challenges faced by large language models is the presence of biases in their training data, which in turn affects their outputs. These biases are not inherent to the models themselves, but rather are learned from the vast datasets on which they are trained. These datasets often reflect historical and societal inequalities, stereotypes, and prejudices. For example, a language model trained on a dataset derived from the internet is likely to inherit biases, based on the content that dominates the web, which may include gender stereotypes, racial biases, and social prejudices.

Types of Biases

- **Gender Bias**: Language models may generate outputs that reinforce gender stereotypes. For instance, if a model is asked to generate a job description for a CEO, it might more likely use male pronouns or associate the role with traditionally male-associated qualities, even if the job description is intended to be gender-neutral.

Example: "*The CEO is expected to lead the company, and make critical decisions, demonstrating the strength and assertiveness associated with leadership.*" This type of language could reinforce a perception that leadership qualities are more commonly associated with men.

- **Racial and Ethnic Bias**: LLMs may also reflect harmful racial or ethnic biases that exist in the data. For instance, names associated with certain racial groups might be unfairly linked to negative stereotypes, leading to misclassification or inappropriate outputs.

  Example: If a model is asked to generate a description of a criminal, it might disproportionately associate certain racial or ethnic groups with criminal behavior, as such associations can be reinforced through biased training data.

- **Cultural and Social Biases**: LLMs may exhibit biases, based on geographic, cultural, or socioeconomic contexts. For example, models trained primarily on English-language text from Western countries may struggle to accurately understand or represent non-Western perspectives, languages, and norms.

  Example: A model might struggle to generate accurate translations or responses, when working with languages that have different grammatical structures, such as Arabic, or languages with non-Latin scripts.

Consequences of Bias in Language Models

The biases present in LLMs can have profound consequences, particularly when these models are deployed in real-world applications. Some potential risks include:

- **Discrimination in Decision-Making:** LLMs are increasingly used in decision-making processes in areas, such as hiring, criminal justice, loan approval, and healthcare. Biases in the model's output can lead to unfair outcomes, perpetuating societal inequalities.

  Example: In a hiring application, if an AI model is trained on resumes from predominantly male applicants, it may prioritize male-sounding names or backgrounds, disadvantaging female candidates.

- **Misinformation and Harmful Content:** LLMs trained on data scraped from the internet may unknowingly generate or propagate harmful content, including misinformation, hate speech, or discriminatory language.

  Example: A chatbot trained on a broad dataset might inadvertently generate harmful responses or spread conspiracy theories, if prompted with certain types of input, amplifying societal harm.

- **Trust and Accountability Issues:** As LLMs are increasingly integrated into critical systems–such as, automated customer service, content moderation, and legal analysis–there is a risk that their decision-making processes are not fully understood or transparent. This lack of transparency can erode trust in AI systems and hinder accountability, particularly when these systems are used in high-stakes environments.

Addressing Bias and Ensuring Ethical Use of LLMs

To mitigate these issues, a range of strategies and best practices can be employed, both during the development of the model and in its deployment. Ensuring ethical AI requires concerted efforts in the areas of bias mitigation, diversity in training data, explainability, and human oversight.

- **Bias Auditing and Evaluation:** One of the most effective ways to address bias in LLMs is through rigorous bias auditing and evaluation. This involves systematically testing models for bias using pre-defined metrics and benchmarks, such as those assessing gender, racial, and cultural biases. Researchers and developers can assess how models perform across different demographic groups to identify areas, where the model produces biased or discriminatory results.

Example: Tools, such as AI Fairness 360 from IBM or Fairness Indicators from Google can help evaluate and monitor the fairness of AI models, and their outputs.

- **Diverse and Representative Training Data:** To reduce bias, LLMs must be trained on diverse, inclusive, and representative datasets. Training data should ideally include a variety of voices, perspectives, and contexts, ensuring that the model is not disproportionately influenced by any single group or viewpoint.

  Example: When training a model on conversational data, it is important to include dialogues from different socioeconomic backgrounds, genders, races, and cultures, ensuring that the model can understand a wide range of conversational styles and cultural nuances.

- **Fine-Tuning and Post-Training Mitigation:** In addition to adjusting training data, fine-tuning the model with specific bias mitigation techniques after pre-training can help correct certain biases. This could involve modifying the model's objective function, or using counterfactual data during training to explicitly address biased patterns.

  Example: A model could be fine-tuned with labeled datasets that emphasize fairness, diversity, and inclusivity, such as datasets, specifically designed to counteract gender stereotypes in job advertisements.

- **Human-in-the-Loop Systems:** While models, such as GPT-3 and T5 can generate impressive results, human oversight is crucial to ensure that AI outputs remain aligned with ethical standards. Incorporating human-in-the-loop systems allows for monitoring and reviewing AI decisions, especially in sensitive applications, such as hiring, law enforcement, and healthcare.

  Example: In an AI-driven hiring system, human HR professionals could review the model's recommendations before making final decisions to ensure that no biased patterns are being reinforced.

- **Transparent AI and Explainability:** Transparency and explainability are critical components in the ethical use of AI. By making the inner workings of AI models more understandable, we can ensure that their decision-making processes are open to scrutiny. Tools, such as Local Interpretable Model-agnostic Explanations (LIME) and SHapley Additive exPlanations (SHAP) allow practitioners to gain insight into how AI models arrive at their conclusions.

  Example: In a legal setting, AI-powered systems that assess risk can benefit from explainability features that allow users to understand why certain legal decisions were made, increasing transparency and trust.

Ethical Principles and Responsible AI

To ensure that large language models are deployed ethically, AI developers and organizations must adhere to the following key ethical principles:

- **Fairness**: Ensuring that the model does not favor one group over another, and that its predictions are equitable.
- **Accountability**: Holding developers and organizations accountable for the outputs of their models, and ensuring that any potential harm is mitigated.
- **Transparency**: Providing clarity on how AI models work, what data they are trained on, and how decisions are made.
- **Privacy**: Ensuring that the sensitive data used in training and the prediction respects user privacy, as well as complies with data protection regulations (for example, GDPR, CCPA, and so on).

Future Directions: Ethical AI and Bias Mitigation

The development of ethical AI is an ongoing process. As transformer models become increasingly advanced, new methodologies will emerge to reduce biases, improve fairness, and ensure accountability. Some future directions for addressing ethical concerns include:

- **Adversarial Training**: Incorporating adversarial examples in training data that are specifically designed to challenge the model's biases and weaknesses.
- **Regulation and Standards**: The establishment of industry-wide standards and regulations to govern the development and deployment of AI models.
- **Cross-disciplinary Collaboration**: Collaboration between AI researchers, ethicists, sociologists, and policymakers to create comprehensive guidelines that ensure the responsible development and use of AI.

While transformer models, such as GPT-3, BERT, and T5 have revolutionized natural language processing, they also raise important ethical concerns, particularly around biases in training data and the potential for harmful outputs. Addressing these issues requires ongoing efforts to improve the fairness, transparency, and accountability of AI systems. By adopting strategies, such as bias auditing, using diverse datasets, and ensuring human oversight, we can mitigate the risks of biased AI, and harness the power of transformers in a responsible and equitable way. As we move forward, it is crucial to ensure that these models serve humanity's interests, and contribute to a more just and inclusive society.

Implementing and Fine-Tuning Advanced Transformer Models with PyTorch 2.0

Transformer models, such as BERT, GPT, T5, and others have revolutionized natural language processing tasks by setting new standards for accuracy and versatility. However, the real power of these models lies not just in their architecture, but in the ability to fine-tune them for specific tasks, improving performance in diverse applications. In this section, we will explore how to implement and fine-tune advanced transformer models, using PyTorch 2.0, a dynamic and powerful deep learning framework that simplifies the process of working with transformers.

Fine-tuning allows you to take a pre-trained transformer model, and adapt it to a specific NLP task, such as text classification, question answering, language translation, or sentiment analysis. The process involves adjusting the weights of the model during training to optimize it for the desired task, using a relatively small dataset compared to what was required for the initial pre-training.

Setting Up PyTorch 2.0 for Transformer Models

Before we dive into the fine-tuning process, it is necessary to set up PyTorch 2.0, and the necessary components for working with transformer models. PyTorch 2.0, with its dynamic computational graph and improved performance features, is well-suited for training large models, such as transformers. PyTorch's Transformers library, developed by Hugging Face, provides pre-trained models and tools that make the implementation of transformers easier.

Installation: To begin with, install PyTorch 2.0 and Hugging Face's transformers library:

```
pip install torch torchvision torchaudio
pip install transformers
```

The `transformers` library provides easy access to pre-trained transformer models and tokenizers, making it simple to load and fine-tune models, such as BERT, GPT, or T5.

Loading a Pre-Trained Model: PyTorch and Hugging Face provide a seamless interface for loading pre-trained models, ready for fine-tuning. Here is how, you can load a pre-trained BERT model for text classification:

```
from transformers import BertForSequenceClassification, BertTokenizer
# Load pre-trained BERT model and tokenizer
model = BertForSequenceClassification.from_pretrained("bert-base-uncased")
tokenizer = BertTokenizer.from_pretrained("bert-base-uncased")
```

In the preceding example, we load BERT with the pre-trained weights from Hugging Face's model hub, along with its corresponding tokenizer that is capable of converting text into token IDs required by the model.

Preparing the Data for Fine-Tuning

Before fine-tuning a model, we need to prepare the data, which typically involves converting the raw text data into a format that the model can process. PyTorch 2.0 provides efficient tools to handle data preprocessing, including tokenization and batching.

Tokenization

Tokenization is the process of converting text into a sequence of tokens (often words or subwords). The tokenizer splits text into the smallest units (tokens), ensuring that it matches the model's pre-trained vocabulary. For instance, BERT uses WordPiece tokenization, where each word is split into subwords, if necessary.

```
# Tokenize input text
inputs = tokenizer("This is an example sentence.", return_tensors="pt",
padding=True, truncation=True, max_length=512)

# Check tokenized input
print(inputs)
```

The tokenized input will be printed, showing the input text converted into token IDs, along with the attention mask and padding information.

Example Output:

```
{'input_ids': tensor([[ 101, 2023, 2003, 1037, 2742, 6251, 102]]),
 'attention_mask': tensor([[1, 1, 1, 1, 1, 1, 1]])}
```

The `return_tensors="pt"` argument ensures that the output is in the form of PyTorch tensors, which can then be fed into the model for training or inference.

Creating a Dataset

In PyTorch, datasets are usually represented as a collection of samples, where each sample consists of an input data, and its corresponding label. To fine-tune a model, you need a labeled dataset. You can create a custom dataset class by subclassing.

```
torch.utils.data.Dataset.
import torch
from torch.utils.data import Dataset

class TextDataset(Dataset):
    def __init__(self, texts, labels, tokenizer, max_len):
        self.texts = texts
        self.labels = labels
        self.tokenizer = tokenizer
```

```
        self.max_len = max_len

    def __len__(self):
        return len(self.texts)

    def __getitem__(self, item):
        text = self.texts[item]
        label = self.labels[item]
        encoding = self.tokenizer.encode_plus(
            text,
            add_special_tokens=True,
            max_length=self.max_len,
            truncation=True,
            padding="max_length",
            return_tensors="pt",
        )
        return {
            "input_ids": encoding["input_ids"].flatten(),
            "attention_mask": encoding["attention_mask"].flatten(),
            "label": torch.tensor(label, dtype=torch.long),
        }
```

This **TextDataset** class is designed to tokenize the input text, and return the tokenized form, attention mask (which tells the model the type of tokens to pay attention to), and label for each sample.

Fine-Tuning the Transformer Model

Fine-tuning involves training the pre-trained model on a specific task with a labeled dataset. Typically, you only need to adjust the model's parameters slightly, as the model has already learned most of the relevant patterns during pre-training. Fine-tuning involves updating the weights, based on a task-specific loss function (for example, cross-entropy loss for classification tasks).

Defining the Training Loop

To fine-tune the model, you need to set up a training loop, using PyTorch's optimization tools. Here is a simple example of how to fine-tune a transformer model for a classification task:

```
from torch.utils.data import DataLoader
from transformers import AdamW

# Set up data loader for training
train_dataset = TextDataset(train_texts, train_labels, tokenizer, max_len=128)
train_dataloader = DataLoader(train_dataset, batch_size=16, shuffle=True)

# Set up optimizer
optimizer = AdamW(model.parameters(), lr=1e-5)

# Training loop
for epoch in range(epochs):
    model.train()
    for batch in train_dataloader:
        optimizer.zero_grad()

        # Get input data
        input_ids = batch["input_ids"]
        attention_mask = batch["attention_mask"]
        labels = batch["label"]
```

```
        # Forward pass
        outputs = model(input_ids=input_ids, attention_mask=attention_mask,
labels=labels)
        loss = outputs.loss
        # Backward pass and optimization
        loss.backward()
        optimizer.step()

    print(f"Epoch {epoch + 1}, Loss: {loss.item()}")
```

This example demonstrates a basic fine-tuning setup. In each iteration of the training loop:

- The model performs a forward pass to compute the loss.
- The backward pass computes gradients.
- The optimizer then updates the model's parameters to minimize the loss.

The training loss will be printed at the end of each epoch, showing the model's progress during training.

Example Output:

```
Epoch 1, Loss: 0.5123
Epoch 2, Loss: 0.4217
Epoch 3, Loss: 0.3689
```

Using Learning Rate Scheduling

For better fine-tuning, it is common to use learning rate schedulers which adjust the learning rate during training to improve convergence. PyTorch provides the **`get_scheduler()`** function to manage the learning rate dynamically.

```
from transformers import get_scheduler

# Set up learning rate scheduler
lr_scheduler = get_scheduler(
    "linear",
    optimizer=optimizer,
    num_warmup_steps=0,
    num_training_steps=len(train_dataloader) * epochs,
)
```

Evaluating the Fine-Tuned Model

After fine-tuning the model, you should evaluate its performance on a test set to ensure it generalizes well to the new data. This is done by computing metrics, such as accuracy, precision, recall, and F1 score.

```
from sklearn.metrics import accuracy_score
# Set model to evaluation mode
model.eval() # Evaluate model on test set
test_preds = []
test_labels = []
for batch in test_dataloader:
    with torch.no_grad():
        input_ids = batch["input_ids"]
        attention_mask = batch["attention_mask"]
        labels = batch["label"]
```

```
            outputs = model(input_ids=input_ids, attention_mask=attention_mask)
            logits = outputs.logits
            preds = torch.argmax(logits, dim=-1)

            test_preds.extend(preds.cpu().numpy())
            test_labels.extend(labels.cpu().numpy())

    # Calculate accuracy
    accuracy = accuracy_score(test_labels, test_preds)
    print(f"Test Accuracy: {accuracy * 100:.2f}%")
```

This step ensures that the fine-tuned model performs well on unseen data, and can generalize to real-world applications.

The test accuracy of the model on the test dataset will be printed, showing the percentage of correct predictions made by the model.

Example Output:

```
Test Accuracy: 92.35%
```

Fine-tuning advanced transformer models with PyTorch 2.0 provides a flexible and scalable approach to solving a wide range of natural language processing tasks. Thus, by leveraging pre-trained models and optimizing them for specific applications, you can significantly reduce the amount of labeled data required and speed up model development. With PyTorch's intuitive APIs and Hugging Face's transformers library, implementing and fine-tuning state-of-the-art models, such as BERT, T5, and GPT have never been easier. Hence, as you move forward, it is essential to experiment with different hyperparameters, training strategies, and datasets to achieve the best possible performance for your specific use case.

Conclusion

In this chapter, we have explored the powerful capabilities of advanced transformer models, such as BERT, GPT, T5, and Codex, delving into their architectures, pre-training objectives, and real-world applications. We have also examined the process of fine-tuning these models with PyTorch 2.0, providing hands-on guidance on how to adapt these models for specific NLP and code generation tasks. Fine-tuning allows us to take advantage of pre-trained knowledge, and apply it effectively to new challenges with minimal task-specific data.

Transformer models have truly transformed the landscape of artificial intelligence, offering a unified framework to solve complex problems in natural language processing, text generation, and even code generation. Their versatility, scalability, and ability to handle a wide range of tasks, with minimal supervision make them invaluable tools for both research and industry applications. As we continue to fine-tune these models, and push the boundaries of their capabilities, the future of AI will likely be defined by even more innovative applications and deeper integrations of these advanced architectures.

In the next chapter, we will explore Hugging Face's Transformers library, a widely adopted open-source framework that simplifies working with transformer models in PyTorch. Hugging Face provides an extensive collection of pre-trained models, tokenizers, and utilities that streamline the deployment of transformers for various AI applications. Therefore, through hands-on examples, we will learn how to leverage Hugging Face's ecosystem to train, fine-tune, and deploy transformer models efficiently, making AI development more accessible and scalable.

CHAPTER 8

Using HuggingFace with PyTorch

Introduction

Hugging Face has revolutionized the way transformer-based models are used in AI, offering a powerful ecosystem that seamlessly integrates with PyTorch. Whether for Natural Language Processing (NLP), computer vision, or multimodal learning, Hugging Face provides an extensive collection of pre-trained models, tokenizers, datasets, and tools that simplify model deployment and fine-tuning. By leveraging these resources, developers can rapidly prototype and optimize models, without the need for massive computational resources, or extensive training from scratch.

This chapter will explore the Hugging Face ecosystem, starting with an overview of its Model Hub, where thousands of pre-trained models are available for various AI tasks. We will cover loading and fine-tuning these models in PyTorch, using efficient tokenization strategies, and handling datasets with Hugging Face's Datasets library. Additionally, we will discuss evaluation metrics, optimization techniques for inference, and best practices for model deployment, using PyTorch Serve. Troubleshooting common issues and refining workflows will also be covered to ensure smooth implementation.

By the end of this chapter, you will have a solid understanding of how to use, fine-tune, and deploy transformer models efficiently with Hugging Face and PyTorch, streamlining AI development, and making cutting-edge machine learning accessible to all.

Structure

In this chapter, we will cover the following topics:

- Introduction to the Hugging Face Ecosystem and its integration with PyTorch
- Exploring the Hugging Face Model Hub, and Available Pre-Trained Models
- Loading and Using Pre-Trained Models from Hugging Face in PyTorch
- Fine-tuning Hugging Face Models for Custom Tasks, Using PyTorch
- Working with Hugging Face's Datasets Library for Efficient Data Handling
- Tokenization Strategies and Using Hugging Face Tokenizers
- Evaluation Metrics and Model Comparison, Using Hugging Face Tools
- Optimizing Hugging Face Models for Inference in PyTorch
- Challenges of Pre-Trained Hugging Face Models and Alternatives

Introduction to the Hugging Face Ecosystem and Its Integration with PyTorch

The Hugging Face ecosystem has become the gold standard for working with transformer-based AI models, offering an intuitive and powerful framework that simplifies the deployment, fine-tuning, and evaluation of the state-of-the-art deep learning models. With the explosion of transformer architectures like BERT, GPT, T5, and ViT, developers and researchers require efficient tools to leverage these models for real-world applications. Hugging Face provides a robust suite of tools–including the Transformers library, Datasets library, Model Hub, and Tokenizers–that seamlessly integrate with PyTorch, making model training and inference, faster, easier, and more scalable.

Figure 8.1: *Hugging Face + PyTorch*

PyTorch, known for its dynamic computation graphs, and deep integration with GPU acceleration, complements Hugging Face's pre-trained model hub by providing the flexibility to fine-tune and deploy models with optimized performance. By using Hugging Face Transformers with PyTorch, developers can load pre-trained models with just a few lines of code, fine-tune them on custom datasets, and deploy them for real-world tasks, such as text classification, question answering, translation, summarization, speech recognition, and vision-based tasks. This combination significantly reduces the effort needed to train models from scratch, while still enabling customization and scalability.

To illustrate the simplicity of working with HuggingFace and PyTorch, consider loading a pre-trained BERT model for text classification:

```
from transformers import BertTokenizer, BertForSequenceClassification

# Load pre-trained BERT model and tokenizer
model = BertForSequenceClassification.from_pretrained("bert-base-uncased")
tokenizer = BertTokenizer.from_pretrained("bert-base-uncased")

# Tokenize an input sentence
inputs = tokenizer("Hugging Face makes AI development easy!",
return_tensors="pt")

# Perform inference
outputs = model(**inputs)
logits = outputs.logits
print(logits)
```

The output will display the logits produced by the model for the input sentence which are the raw, unnormalized scores for each class. These logits are typically passed through a softmax function to obtain probabilities for classification.

Example Output:

```
tensor([[-0.6723,  1.2045]])
```

This simple snippet demonstrates how Hugging Face eliminates complexity by providing ready-to-use pre-trained models with optimized PyTorch implementations. Instead of writing custom model architectures from scratch, developers can leverage pre-trained transformers, and focus on task-specific fine-tuning, as well as deployment.

In the following sections, we will explore the Hugging Face Model Hub, tokenization strategies, fine-tuning techniques, and evaluation tools to help you integrate Hugging Face models into PyTorch workflows efficiently. By the end of this chapter, you will be able to load, train, evaluate, and deploy Hugging Face models in PyTorch, unlocking the full potential of transformers with minimal setup.

Exploring the Hugging Face Model Hub and Available Pre-Trained Models

The Hugging Face Model Hub is a central repository that provides thousands of pre-trained transformer models across various domains, including Natural Language Processing (NLP), computer vision, speech recognition, and multi-modal learning. These models are contributed by both Hugging Face and the broader AI research community, allowing developers to quickly access state-of-the-art architectures, without the need to train models from scratch. The Model Hub significantly reduces the computational cost, and the time required to develop deep learning applications by offering models that are ready for fine-tuning and deployment.

The diversity of models available in the Hugging Face Model Hub is one of its greatest strengths. You can find language models, such as BERT, GPT, and T5, vision models like Vision Transformers (ViT), and speech models like Wav2Vec2. Each model is pre-trained on extensive datasets, and can be directly fine-tuned for specific downstream tasks such as sentiment analysis, text summarization, named entity recognition, speech-to-text conversion, image classification, and even multi-modal tasks that integrate both vision and language.

Navigating the Hugging Face Model Hub

The Hugging Face Model Hub can be accessed through its web interface (https://huggingface.co/models), or directly through the Transformers API in Python. The web interface allows users to search for models, filter by task, and explore model documentation, including details about the dataset, training procedure, and intended applications.

To explore the Model Hub programmatically, you can use the Hugging Face Transformers library:

```
from transformers import pipeline
# List all available models for a specific task
task = "text-classification"
models = pipeline(task).model.config._name_or_path
print(f"Pre-trained model for {task}: {models}")
The code will print the name or path of the pre-trained model that is being
used for the specified task.
Example output:
Pre-trained model for text-classification: distilbert-base-uncased-
finetuned-sst-2-english
```

Alternatively, if you want to check all the available models in a specific category, you can visit the Hugging Face website, and filter models based on parameters like task type, library, dataset, and organization.

Categories of Pre-Trained Models in the Model Hub

The Model Hub categorizes pre-trained models, based on their application area. Some of the most widely used categories include:

- **NLP Models**
  - **Bidirectional Encoder Representations from Transformers (BERT):** Used for text classification, question answering, and named entity recognition.
  - **Generative Pre-trained Transformer (GPT) Series:** Excellent for text generation, chatbots, and creative writing.
  - **Text-to-Text Transfer Transformer (T5):** Capable of handling multiple NLP tasks by treating every problem as a text-to-text task.
  - **RoBERTa, DistilBERT, ALBERT:** Variants of BERT with different optimizations for speed and efficiency.
- **Computer Vision Models**
  - **Vision Transformer (ViT):** A transformer-based architecture for image classification.
  - **DEtection TRansformers (DETR):** Used for object detection and segmentation.
  - **Swin Transformer:** A hierarchical vision transformer designed for high-resolution images.
- **Speech and Audio Models**
  - **Wav2Vec2:** A self-supervised speech model used for Automatic Speech Recognition (ASR).
  - **Whisper (by OpenAI):** A robust multi-lingual speech recognition model that excels in transcription and translation tasks.
- **Multi-Modal Models (Text + Vision + Audio)**
  - **CLIP (Contrastive Language-Image Pre-training):** Capable of image-text understanding, useful for tasks, like image captioning, and zero-shot classification.
  - **DALL-E:** A model designed for text-to-image generation, creating images from textual descriptions.

By offering a wide variety of models across these domains, Hugging Face enables seamless experimentation with different architectures, eliminating the need for researchers and developers to build and train models from scratch.

Loading Pre-Trained Models from the Model Hub

Using a pre-trained model from the Hugging Face Model Hub is straightforward with the `from_pretrained()` method in the Transformers library. The following example demonstrates how to load a BERT model for text classification:

```
from transformers import AutoModelForSequenceClassification, AutoTokenizer
# Load pre-trained BERT model and tokenizer from the Hugging Face Model Hub
model_name = "bert-base-uncased"
tokenizer = AutoTokenizer.from_pretrained(model_name)
model = AutoModelForSequenceClassification.from_pretrained(model_name)

# Tokenize input text
text = "Hugging Face makes working with AI seamless!"
inputs = tokenizer(text, return_tensors="pt")

# Perform inference
outputs = model(**inputs)
print(outputs.logits)
```

In this example:

1. We load the BERT base model from the Model Hub.
2. We use the corresponding tokenizer to process text input.
3. The model performs inference, and returns classification logits.

The output will display the logits (raw predictions) from the model for the input sentence. These logits represent unnormalized scores for the possible classes in a sequence classification task.

Example Output:

```
tensor([[-0.1896, 0.2132]])
```

This same approach can be applied to other models like GPT-3, T5, and Vision Transformers by simply changing the `model_name` argument.

Fine-Tuning Pre-Trained Models for Custom Tasks

While pre-trained models offer strong generalization capabilities, they often need fine-tuning to achieve optimal performance on domain-specific tasks. The Hugging Face Model Hub allows users to upload and share fine-tuned models, meaning you can find models that have already been optimized for tasks like medical text analysis, legal document classification, or domain-specific chatbot training.

If a pre-trained model does not meet your specific needs, you can fine-tune it, using transfer learning, which we will explore in later sections.

Advantage of Using Pre-Trained Models from the Model Hub

The Model Hub offers several advantages that make it an essential resource for AI practitioners:

- **Access to the State-of-the-Art Models:** Hugging Face provides the latest research models, ensuring that users work with cutting-edge architectures.
- **Reduced Training Costs:** Instead of training models from scratch (which requires large datasets and GPU resources), pre-trained models allow for fine-tuning with minimal computational effort.
- **Community Contributions:** Many fine-tuned models are shared by researchers and organizations, providing access to domain-specific models, without additional training.
- **Interoperability with PyTorch and TensorFlow:** Hugging Face models are compatible with both frameworks, making them highly flexible for various deployment scenarios.

The Hugging Face Model Hub is a game-changer for AI development, providing a rich repository of pre-trained models that can be easily integrated into PyTorch workflows. Whether you are working on text, speech, vision, or multi-modal AI, the Model Hub provides an efficient way to experiment with cutting-edge models, and rapidly build AI-powered applications.

In the next section, we will explore how to load and use pre-trained models from the Model Hub in PyTorch, diving deeper into tokenization, inference, and real-world applications.

Loading and Using Pre-Trained Models from Hugging Face in PyTorch

Pre-trained models are at the core of transfer learning, allowing AI practitioners to leverage state-of-the-art architectures, without the need to train from scratch. The Hugging Face Model Hub provides thousands of pre-trained models, optimized for a wide range of AI tasks, including text classification, question answering, summarization, image classification, object detection, and speech recognition. By using these models, developers can reduce computational costs, and the time, while improving model performance.

This section covers how to load and use pre-trained models from Hugging Face in PyTorch, with a focus on tokenization, inference, and model customization. We will also explore how Hugging Face's AutoModel and AutoTokenizer classes simplify the process, making model integration seamless.

Understanding Hugging Face's AutoModel and AutoTokenizer

Hugging Face provides two key abstractions for handling models efficiently:

- **AutoModel:** A generic class that automatically loads the correct transformer model, based on the provided model name.
- **AutoTokenizer:** A utility to preprocess text by converting it into tokenized inputs, required by the model.

Instead of manually selecting the right architecture (for example, BertModel, GPT2Model, and so on), AutoModel dynamically picks the correct class for the given model. This makes it scalable, and easy to use, as models can be swapped without code modifications.

For example, you can load a BERT-based model, with just a few lines of code:

```
from transformers import AutoModel, AutoTokenizer
# Specify the model name
model_name = "bert-base-uncased"

# Load the model and tokenizer
tokenizer = AutoTokenizer.from_pretrained(model_name)
model = AutoModel.from_pretrained(model_name)
print(f"Loaded model: {model_name}") #Output: Loaded model: bert-base-uncased
```

With this simple syntax, Hugging Face automatically selects the appropriate architecture, whether it is BERT, GPT, T5, or any other transformer model.

Tokenizing Input Data for Pre-Trained Models

Before using a model for inference, input text must be tokenized into a format the model understands. Tokenization involves:

- Splitting text into words, subwords, or characters.
- Converting tokens into numerical token IDs.
- Creating attention masks to indicate which parts of the sequence should be attended to.

Hugging Face provides an AutoTokenizer that automatically loads the correct tokenizer for the specified model:

```
# Example text input
text = "Hugging Face makes working with transformers simple and efficient!"

# Tokenize input text
inputs = tokenizer(text, return_tensors="pt")  # Convert to PyTorch tensors

print(inputs)
```

```
Expected output:
{'input_ids': tensor([[  101,  17662,  2227,  4088,  2544,  2007, 19081,
2015,  3722,  1998,  11633,   999,   102]]),
 'attention_mask': tensor([[1, 1, 1, 1, 1, 1, 1, 1, 1, 1, 1, 1, 1]])}
```

Here:

1. **`input_ids`** are the numerical token representations of words.
2. **`attention_mask`** specifies which tokens should be attended to (1), and which should be ignored (0).

Tokenization ensures that models can efficiently process text, while maintaining context and meaning.

Performing Inference with a Pre-Trained Model

Once the text is tokenized, it can be passed into the model for inference. Let us load a BERT model, and use it to generate word embeddings:

```
import torch
from transformers import AutoModel

# Load pre-trained model
model = AutoModel.from_pretrained("bert-base-uncased")

# Move model to GPU if available
device = torch.device("cuda" if torch.cuda.is_available() else "cpu")
model.to(device)

# Perform inference
with torch.no_grad():  # Disable gradient calculation for efficiency
    outputs = model(**inputs.to(device))

# Extract last hidden states (embeddings)
embeddings = outputs.last_hidden_state
print(embeddings.shape)
```

Example Output:

```
torch.Size([1, 10, 768])
```

Explanation:

- The **`AutoModel`** class loads BERT which generates word embeddings for each token.
- We use **`torch.no_grad()`** to disable gradient tracking (since we do not need backpropagation for inference).
- The model outputs a hidden state tensor representing contextual embeddings for each token in the input.

This output demonstrates the shape of the embeddings generated by the BERT model for the given input text which can then be used for downstream tasks, such as classification or feature extraction.

Loading Task-Specific Models (Text Classification, Question Answering)

Instead of using AutoModel, which provides embeddings, we can load task-specific models optimized for various NLP tasks:

Example: Text Classification

```
For classifying text as positive or negative, we can load AutoModelFor
SequenceClassification:
from transformers import AutoModelForSequenceClassification

# Load pre-trained text classification model
model = AutoModelForSequenceClassification.from_pretrained("distilbert-base-
uncased-finetuned-sst-2-english")

# Tokenize and perform classification
inputs = tokenizer("I love using Hugging Face's Transformers!",
return_tensors="pt")
outputs = model(**inputs)

# Extract predicted label
logits = outputs.logits
predicted_class = torch.argmax(logits).item()
print(f"Predicted class: {predicted_class}")
```

Explanation:

1. We load a fine-tuned DistilBERT model for sentiment analysis.
2. The model generates logits (raw scores), and we use **`torch.argmax()`** to extract the predicted class (positive/negative).

The model will output the predicted class for the input text. Since the model is fine-tuned on the SST-2 dataset for sentiment classification, the predicted class will be either 0 (negative) or 1 (positive).

Example Output:

```
Predicted class: 1
```

Exploring Other Pre-Trained Models from the Model Hub

Hugging Face supports a variety of transformer-based models across different AI domains. Some commonly used ones include:

Task	Model Example
Text Classification	distilbert-base-uncased-finetuned-sst-2-english
Question Answering	deepset/roberta-base-squad2
Summarization	facebook/bart-large-cnn
Translation	Helsinki-NLP/opus-mt-en-fr

Text Generation	gpt2, EleutherAI/gpt-neo-2.7B
Image Classification	google/vit-base-patch16-224
Speech Recognition	facebook/wav2vec2-large-960h

Table 8.1: *Examples of Pre-Trained Models*

These models can be loaded in the same way as BERT, using `from_pretrained()` with the appropriate architecture class.

Using Pre-Trained Models Instead of Training from Scratch

Using pre-trained models has many key advantages:

- **Time Efficiency:** Training large transformer models from scratch takes weeks or months, while pre-trained models can be fine-tuned in hours or days.
- **Cost Savings:** Pre-trained models reduce the need for expensive GPU/TPU clusters.
- **Improved Accuracy:** Models like BERT and GPT-3 are trained on massive datasets, enabling superior performance with minimal fine-tuning.
- **Easy Customization:** Fine-tuning pre-trained models allows developers to adapt them for domain-specific tasks, without extensive data collection.

The Hugging Face Model Hub provides an efficient way to load and use pre-trained models in PyTorch, enabling rapid experimentation with the state-of-the-art AI models. By leveraging AutoModel and AutoTokenizer, developers can quickly integrate models for various tasks, from text classification to speech recognition, and vision-based applications.

In the next section, we will explore fine-tuning Hugging Face models with PyTorch, allowing you to customize pre-trained transformers for domain-specific applications, and optimize their performance for real-world tasks.

Fine-Tuning Hugging Face Models for Custom Tasks Using PyTorch

While pre-trained transformer models provide a strong foundation for many NLP and AI tasks, they often need to be adapted for domain-specific applications. Fine-tuning allows us to take an already pre-trained model (such as BERT, GPT-3, or T5), and further train it on a custom dataset to improve performance on specialized tasks, such as legal document classification, medical text analysis, customer sentiment prediction, or chatbots.

Fine-tuning is a form of transfer learning, where a model retains its pre-trained weights, but updates some or all layers, based on new task-specific data. This is significantly more efficient than training from scratch, requiring far less data and computational power, while maintaining state-of-the-art performance.

The Need for Fine-Tuning

Pre-trained models are trained on large-scale general-purpose datasets, such as Wikipedia, Common Crawl, and books corpora. While they understand language patterns well, they do not specialize in domain-specific contexts.

For Example:

- A finance company fine-tuning BERT on earnings reports will achieve better financial text predictions than a generic BERT model.
- A medical chatbot fine-tuned on healthcare dialogues will understand patient symptoms better than GPT-3 trained on general web data.

Fine-tuning adapts the model to the vocabulary, structure, and intent of a specific domain, ensuring higher accuracy and relevance.

Setting Up Fine-Tuning with PyTorch and Hugging Face

Fine-tuning a model requires:

- A pre-trained transformer model from Hugging Face.
- A labeled dataset for the custom task (for example, text classification, summarization, and so on).
- A PyTorch-compatible training loop to optimize the model.

To demonstrate, let us fine-tune DistilBERT (a lighter version of BERT) for sentiment classification on a custom dataset.

Fine-Tuning a Transformer Model: Step-by-Step Implementation

Step 1: Install Dependencies

First, install Hugging Face's Transformers and Datasets libraries:

```
pip install transformers datasets torch
```

Step 2: Load Pre-Trained Model and Tokenizer

We will use **`DistilBERT`**, a fast, efficient version of BERT, pre-trained on a large corpus.

```
from transformers import AutoModelForSequenceClassification, AutoTokenizer
# Load model and tokenizer
model_name = "distilbert-base-uncased"
tokenizer = AutoTokenizer.from_pretrained(model_name)
model = AutoModelForSequenceClassification.from_pretrained(model_name,
num_labels=2)
```

Here:

1. **`AutoModelForSequenceClassification`** loads a transformer, specifically for classification tasks.
2. num_labels=2 configures the model for binary classification (positive/negative sentiment).

Step 3: Prepare the Custom Dataset

We will use the Hugging Face Datasets library to load a sample sentiment dataset.

```
from datasets import load_dataset
# Load IMDb movie review dataset
dataset = load_dataset("imdb")
train_data = dataset["train"]
test_data = dataset["test"]
```

Each data point consists of:

```
{'text': "The movie was fantastic! I loved every moment of it.", 'label': 1}
where label 1 = positive sentiment, and label 0 = negative sentiment.
```

Step 4: Tokenize the Dataset

The text must be converted into token IDs, before being fed into the model.

```
def tokenize_function(batch):
    return tokenizer(batch["text"], padding="max_length", truncation=True,
max_length=512)

# Apply tokenization to dataset
train_dataset = train_data.map(tokenize_function, batched=True)
test_dataset = test_data.map(tokenize_function, batched=True)
```

This ensures all text is:

- Truncated to 512 tokens to fit BERT's input size.
- Padded for uniform batch sizes.

Step 5: Convert Dataset into PyTorch Format

Hugging Face's Datasets library outputs data as Python dictionaries. We must convert them into PyTorch tensors.

```
import torch
from torch.utils.data import DataLoader
# Convert dataset to PyTorch format
train_dataset.set_format(type="torch", columns=["input_ids", "attention_mask",
"label"])
test_dataset.set_format(type="torch", columns=["input_ids", "attention_mask",
"label"])# Create DataLoaders for batching
train_loader = DataLoader(train_dataset, batch_size=8, shuffle=True)
test_loader = DataLoader(test_dataset, batch_size=8)
```

Step 6: Define Training Loop

Now, we define PyTorch's training loop, using AdamW optimizer and cross-entropy loss.

```
from transformers import AdamW
from torch.optim.lr_scheduler import StepLR

# Define optimizer and scheduler
optimizer = AdamW(model.parameters(), lr=5e-5)
scheduler = StepLR(optimizer, step_size=2, gamma=0.1)  # Reduce LR every 2
epochs

# Move model to GPU if available
device = torch.device("cuda" if torch.cuda.is_available() else "cpu")
model.to(device)

# Training function
def train_model(model, train_loader, optimizer, scheduler, num_epochs=3):
    model.train()
    for epoch in range(num_epochs):
        total_loss = 0
        for batch in train_loader:
            optimizer.zero_grad()
```

```
            input_ids = batch["input_ids"].to(device)
            attention_mask = batch["attention_mask"].to(device)
            labels = batch["label"].to(device)

            outputs = model(input_ids, attention_mask=attention_mask,
labels=labels)
            loss = outputs.loss
            loss.backward()
            optimizer.step()
            scheduler.step()
            total_loss += loss.item()

        print(f"Epoch {epoch+1}: Loss = {total_loss/len(train_loader)}")

# Train the model
train_model(model, train_loader, optimizer, scheduler)
```

Evaluating Fine-Tuned Model Performance

After training, we evaluate the performance on the test set.

```
from sklearn.metrics import accuracy_score

model.eval()
all_preds, all_labels = [], []

with torch.no_grad():
    for batch in test_loader:
        input_ids = batch["input_ids"].to(device)
        attention_mask = batch["attention_mask"].to(device)
        labels = batch["label"].to(device)

        outputs = model(input_ids, attention_mask=attention_mask)
        predictions = torch.argmax(outputs.logits, dim=-1)

        all_preds.extend(predictions.cpu().numpy())
        all_labels.extend(labels.cpu().numpy())

accuracy = accuracy_score(all_labels, all_preds)
print(f"Test Accuracy: {accuracy:.4f}") #Output: Test Accuracy: 0.9245
```

Optimizing Fine-Tuning for Better Performance

To further enhance model accuracy, consider:

- Using larger batch sizes (if GPU memory available).
- Applying learning rate warm-up to prevent instability.
- Fine-tuning with more epochs, while monitoring overfitting.
- Using domain-specific data augmentation to improve generalization.

Fine-tuning pre-trained Hugging Face models with PyTorch allows developers to customize transformers for domain-specific tasks, significantly improving performance, while reducing training costs. By following this structured approach–loading a model, preparing a dataset, training with PyTorch, and evaluating performance–we can create highly efficient and accurate models for real-world applications.

In the next section, we will explore Hugging Face's Datasets Library which streamlines dataset loading, transformation, and efficient handling of large-scale AI datasets.

Working with Hugging Face's Datasets Library for Efficient Data Handling

Handling large-scale datasets efficiently is a fundamental challenge in machine learning. Preprocessing, transforming, and managing datasets can often be as resource-intensive, as training the model itself. Hugging Face's Datasets library is designed to solve this problem by providing an optimized framework for loading, processing, and handling large datasets with minimal memory footprint. Unlike traditional data handling techniques that rely on Pandas or NumPy, the datasets library is streamlined for deep learning workflows, offering features, such as streaming, lazy loading, and proper memory mapping.

When working with deep learning models in PyTorch, efficient dataset management ensures that training remains scalable, memory-efficient, and performant. The datasets library allows users to seamlessly access and manipulate large datasets from a variety of domains—including text, speech, and vision—without worrying about RAM limitations or slow I/O operations. This section will explore how to load datasets, apply transformations, batch data efficiently, and integrate them into PyTorch training pipelines.

The Need for Hugging Face Datasets Library

Traditional dataset handling often involves manually downloading CSV files, writing custom parsers, and storing data in-memory. This approach is not scalable, especially when dealing with large-scale NLP, speech, or vision datasets. The datasets library introduces a more efficient paradigm that:

- Loads datasets dynamically, without requiring full in-memory storage.
- Uses Apache Arrow for optimized disk-based storage, and efficient columnar data access.
- Supports lazy loading so that datasets are loaded in chunks, minimizing memory consumption.
- Provides built-in tokenization support for NLP tasks, eliminating the need for separate preprocessing steps.
- Integrates seamlessly with PyTorch and TensorFlow, allowing datasets to be directly used in DataLoaders, without conversion.

With these capabilities, datasets are ideal for large-scale AI applications, allowing researchers and engineers to work with multi-terabyte datasets, without requiring enormous computational resources.

Loading a Dataset from Hugging Face's Dataset Hub

Hugging Face hosts a vast collection of ready-to-use datasets, covering text, vision, speech, and tabular data. These datasets can be loaded using a single line of code.

Let us start by loading the IMDb movie review dataset that is commonly used for sentiment analysis:

```
from datasets import load_dataset

# Load the IMDb dataset
dataset = load_dataset("imdb")

# Print dataset structure
print(dataset)
```

Output:

```
DatasetDict({
    train: Dataset({
        features: ['text', 'label'],
        num_rows: 25000
    })
    test: Dataset({
        features: ['text', 'label'],
        num_rows: 25000
    })
})
```

The dataset is structured as a DatasetDict, where each split (train, test) is represented as a separate dataset. Each row contains:

- Text (the movie review).
- Label (0 = negative, 1 = positive).

Unlike traditional CSV files that require manual parsing, datasets automatically handle the dataset's structure, providing intuitive column-based access.

Accessing and Manipulating Dataset Records

Datasets in Hugging Face's library behave like Python dictionaries, allowing easy access to individual records.

To fetch a single data sample:

```
sample = dataset["train"][0]
print(sample)

Output:
{'text': 'The movie was fantastic! I loved every moment of it.', 'label': 1}

To access multiple rows:
batch = dataset["train"][:5]
print(batch)

Since the dataset is columnar, we can also extract specific fields:
texts = dataset["train"]["text"][:5]  # Extract first 5 text samples
labels = dataset["train"]["label"][:5]  # Extract first 5 labels
print(texts, labels)
```

This level of flexibility enables fast indexing and data retrieval, making it easy to extract, filter, and analyze large datasets.

Transforming and Tokenizing Text Datasets

For NLP tasks, datasets must be tokenized, before they can be used with transformer models. The datasets library allows for on-the-fly tokenization, using Hugging Face's tokenizers, eliminating the need for separate preprocessing scripts.

```
from transformers import AutoTokenizer

# Load tokenizer for DistilBERT
tokenizer = AutoTokenizer.from_pretrained("distilbert-base-uncased")

# Tokenize dataset
```

```
def tokenize_function(batch):
    return tokenizer(batch["text"], padding="max_length", truncation=True,
max_length=512)

# Apply tokenization
tokenized_dataset = dataset.map(tokenize_function, batched=True)

# View tokenized sample
print(tokenized_dataset["train"][0])
```

The key features of this approach are as follows:

- Tokenization is applied efficiently in batches.
- The function runs in parallel, accelerating preprocessing.
- The original dataset remains unaltered, preserving flexibility.

This method ensures that the data is transformed only when needed, rather than being permanently altered, saving storage and computation.

Using Datasets with PyTorch DataLoaders

To integrate Hugging Face datasets with PyTorch, we need to convert them into **DataLoaders**.

```
import torch
from torch.utils.data import DataLoader

# Set dataset format to PyTorch
tokenized_dataset.set_format(type="torch", columns=["input_ids", "attention_
mask", "label"])

# Create PyTorch DataLoader
train_loader = DataLoader(tokenized_dataset["train"], batch_size=8,
shuffle=True)
test_loader = DataLoader(tokenized_dataset["test"], batch_size=8)
```

Now, our dataset is fully compatible with PyTorch models, and batches can be iterated efficiently during training.

Streaming Large Datasets without Full Loading

For extremely large datasets that cannot fit into RAM, Hugging Face provides streaming functionality. Instead of loading the entire dataset at once, data is fetched on-demand.

```
dataset = load_dataset("imdb", split="train", streaming=True)

# Iterate over the dataset in a memory-efficient way
for example in dataset:
    print(example)
    break # Stop after one record to demonstrate streaming
```

This allows the users to train models on terabyte-scale datasets, without requiring high-end hardware.

Saving and Sharing Processed Datasets

Once a dataset has been processed (for instance, tokenized, augmented, and so on), it can be saved locally or uploaded to Hugging Face's Dataset Hub for collaboration.

To save a processed dataset:

```
tokenized_dataset.save_to_disk("processed_dataset")
```

To reload it later:

```
from datasets import load_from_disk
dataset = load_from_disk("processed_dataset")

To upload and share a dataset publicly:
dataset.push_to_hub("my-dataset")
```

This facilitates collaboration and reproducibility, making it easier for teams to work with pre-processed data.

Hugging Face's Datasets library provides a powerful and proficient way to load, transform, and process large datasets for deep learning applications. It eliminates the manual overhead of dataset preprocessing, allowing researchers and engineers to focus on model training and evaluation, rather than data management.

By leveraging lazy loading, tokenization, efficient storage formats, and seamless integration with PyTorch, this library significantly improves the scalability of AI workflows.

In the next section, we will explore tokenization strategies, covering how different pre-trained tokenizers process text, and how to optimize tokenization for better model performance.

Tokenization Strategies and Using Hugging Face Tokenizers

Tokenization is a critical preprocessing step in Natural Language Processing (NLP), as it converts the raw text into numerical representations that transformer models can process. Since transformers do not inherently understand words, tokenization ensures that input text is structured in a way that preserves context, grammar, and meaning, while making it compatible with deep learning architectures.

Hugging Face provides an extensive set of pre-trained tokenizers designed for various transformer models, including BERT, GPT, T5, RoBERTa, and more. These tokenizers not only split text into tokens, but also apply additional transformations, such as padding, truncation, and special token insertion to meet the model's input format requirements.

The Role of Tokenization in Transformers

Unlike traditional NLP models that operate on word embeddings (like Word2Vec or GloVe), transformer-based models use subword tokenization to handle Out-of-Vocabulary (OOV) words, morphological variations, and low-resource languages. Tokenization is crucial because:

- It standardizes input text into a numerical format.
- It ensures that unseen words can still be understood by breaking them into known subwords.
- It keeps transformer input sequences consistent, improving model accuracy.
- It helps manage memory and compute efficiency, reducing unnecessary processing.

For example, consider the sentence:

"*Transformers revolutionized* NLP."

A word-level tokenizer might represent this as:

```
["Transformers", "revolutionized", "NLP"]
```

However, if a word is not in the vocabulary, a traditional tokenizer may fail. Instead, subword tokenization ensures robust text representation by breaking words into smaller, known units:

```
["Transform", "##ers", "revolution", "##ized", "NLP"]
```

This allows the model to handle unknown words by leveraging learned embeddings from familiar subwords.

Types of Tokenization Strategies

Different transformer models use distinct tokenization approaches. Hugging Face supports three primary types of tokenization:

WordPiece Tokenization (Used in BERT, DistilBERT, RoBERTa, ALBERT)

WordPiece tokenization splits words into subword units, based on frequency in the training corpus. Frequently occurring words remain intact, while rare words are broken down into smaller components.

For example:

"*Unbelievable results in* NLP!"

would be tokenized as:

```
["Un", "##believable", "results", "in", "NLP", "!"]
```

This strategy ensures that even unfamiliar words can be understood through their constituent subwords, making it ideal for general NLP tasks.

Byte-Pair Encoding (BPE) Tokenization (Used in GPT-2, GPT-3, T5, BART)

BPE tokenization is a compression-based algorithm that merges the most common adjacent character pairs to form subwords. Unlike WordPiece, which is frequency-based, BPE learns merge rules dynamically, making it highly efficient for text generation tasks.

For example, given the word "*unhappiness*", BPE might tokenize it as:

```
["un", "happ", "iness"]
```

BPE is particularly useful for auto-regressive models like GPT because it balances vocabulary size and sequence length, optimizing model efficiency.

Unigram Tokenization (Used in T5, SentencePiece)

Unigram tokenization uses a probabilistic approach, where different subword segmentations are assigned probabilities, and the best segmentation is chosen. This allows more flexibility in determining how words are split, making it well-suited for multilingual and low-resource language tasks.

For example, the word "downloadable" might be tokenized as: `["down", "load", "able"]` or `["download", "able"]`, depending on probability scores.

Using Hugging Face Tokenizers

Hugging Face provides AutoTokenizer that automatically loads the appropriate tokenizer for any pre-trained model. Let's explore how to initialize, tokenize text, and convert tokens back to readable format.

Loading a Tokenizer

To load a tokenizer, simply call:

```
from transformers import AutoTokenizer

# Load BERT tokenizer
tokenizer = AutoTokenizer.from_pretrained("bert-base-uncased")

# Tokenizing text
text = "Hugging Face makes NLP easy!"
tokens = tokenizer.tokenize(text)
print(tokens)
```

Output:

```
['hugging', 'face', 'makes', 'nlp', 'easy', '!']
```

Here, the tokenizer breaks the sentence into WordPiece tokens, based on BERT's vocabulary.

Encoding Text into Token IDs

Tokenized words must be converted into numerical IDs, before being passed into the model.

```
encoded_inputs = tokenizer(text, return_tensors="pt")
print(encoded_inputs)
```

Output:

```
{'input_ids': tensor([[101, 17662, 2227, 4088, 2544, 2015, 3722, 999, 102]]),
 'attention_mask': tensor([[1, 1, 1, 1, 1, 1, 1, 1, 1]])}
```

- **`input_ids`**: The tokenized representation of the text.
- **`attention_mask`**: A binary mask that helps the model focus on non-padding tokens.

This format is necessary for transformers like BERT, GPT, and T5 to process the text properly.

Decoding Tokens Back to Text

To convert tokenized text back to human-readable form:

```
decoded_text = tokenizer.decode(encoded_inputs["input_ids"][0])print
(decoded_text)
```

Output:

```
"[CLS] hugging face makes nlp easy! [SEP]"
```

The **`[CLS]`** and **`[SEP]`** tokens are special markers used in BERT for classification and sentence separation tasks.

Optimizing Tokenization for Performance

Padding and Truncation: Transformer models require fixed-length inputs. In fact, Hugging Face's tokenizers provide built-in padding and truncation options:

```
batch = ["This is a long sentence.", "Short."]
encoded_batch = tokenizer(batch, padding=True, truncation=True,
return_tensors="pt")
print(encoded_batch)
```

This ensures uniform sequence lengths, reducing wasted memory.

Efficient Batching with Fast Tokenizers: Hugging Face supports FastTokenizers that leverage Rust-based implementations for high-speed processing:

```
tokenizer = AutoTokenizer.from_pretrained("bert-base-uncased", use_fast=True)
```

Using `FastTokenizers` can accelerate tokenization up to 10x compared to Python-based tokenizers.

Tokenization is the first and most crucial step in preparing text for transformer-based models. Hugging Face's tokenizers provide an optimized, efficient, and scalable solution for handling diverse NLP tasks. By understanding different tokenization strategies–including WordPiece, BPE, and Unigram models–and leveraging AutoTokenizer, developers can seamlessly integrate tokenized inputs into PyTorch models.

In the next section, we will explore evaluation metrics for comparing Hugging Face models, ensuring that fine-tuned models perform optimally for real-world applications.

Evaluation Metrics and Model Comparison Using Hugging Face Tools

Evaluating the performance of pre-trained and fine-tuned transformer models is a vital step in ensuring their effectiveness for real-world applications. Unlike traditional machine learning models, transformers handle complex tasks, such as text classification, translation, summarization, and question answering, requiring specialized evaluation metrics that go beyond simple accuracy calculations. Hugging Face provides a comprehensive set of tools to automate model evaluation, offering built-in metrics, dataset evaluation pipelines, and compatibility with external libraries like scikit-learn and NLTK.

Model evaluation involves two key aspects:

1. **Performance measurement:** How well does the model perform on a given task?
2. **Model comparison:** Which model is best suited for a specific use case?

A well-evaluated model ensures that fine-tuning and hyperparameter adjustments lead to meaningful improvements, preventing overfitting and optimizing real-world performance.

Choosing the Right Evaluation Metrics for Different Tasks

Different NLP tasks require different evaluation metrics to measure performance accurately. Some commonly used metrics include:

- **Accuracy:** Measures how often the model's predictions match the correct labels (used for classification tasks).
- **F1 Score:** A balance between precision and recall, useful when classes are imbalanced.
- **Bilingual Evaluation Understudy (BLEU)**: Evaluates machine translation by comparing predicted and reference sentences.
- **Recall-Oriented Understudy for Gisting Evaluation (ROUGE)**: Measures overlap between predicted and reference summaries (used for summarization tasks).
- **Word Error Rate (WER)**: Evaluates speech recognition models by calculating how many words were incorrectly transcribed.

Thus, choosing the right metric ensures that we measure model effectiveness in a way that aligns with the specific task requirements.

Using Hugging Face's Built-In Evaluation Metrics

Hugging Face provides an easy-to-use evaluation library which supports a wide range of standard metrics. The evaluate library can be used to automatically compute accuracy, F1 score, BLEU, ROUGE, and many other metrics.

Installing and Loading Hugging Face's Evaluation Module

Before evaluating a model, install the evaluate library:

```
pip install evaluate

Next, load an evaluation metric:
import evaluate

# Load the accuracy metric
accuracy = evaluate.load("accuracy")

# Sample predictions and labels
predictions = [0, 1, 1, 0]
references = [0, 1, 0, 0]

# Compute accuracy
results = accuracy.compute(predictions=predictions, references=references)
print(results)
```

Output:

```
{'accuracy': 0.75}
```

This example demonstrates how Hugging Face automates metric computation, ensuring fast and reliable evaluations.

Evaluating a Fine-Tuned Model Using Hugging Face Pipelines

Hugging Face also provides pre-built evaluation pipelines which allow users to directly evaluate fine-tuned models, without writing custom evaluation loops.

For example, if we fine-tune a text classification model, we can evaluate its performance as follows:

```
from transformers import pipeline
# Load a fine-tuned sentiment classification model
classifier = pipeline("sentiment-analysis", model="distilbert-base-uncased-fine-
tuned-sst-2-english")

# Test model performance
results = classifier(["I love this product!", "This was a terrible
experience."])
print(results)
```

Output:

```
[{'label': 'POSITIVE', 'score': 0.998}, {'label': 'NEGATIVE', 'score': 0.994}]
```

This provides a quick and interpretable evaluation of model outputs.

Comparing Multiple Models on the Same Task

To determine which model performs the best, we need to compare the models, using the same dataset and evaluation metric.

For example, let us compare BERT and RoBERTa for text classification:

```
from transformers import pipeline
# Load models
bert_classifier = pipeline("text-classification", model="bert-base-uncased")
roberta_classifier = pipeline("text-classification", model="roberta-base")

# Define test sentence
test_text = "Hugging Face makes AI easy to use!"
# Evaluate both models
bert_result = bert_classifier(test_text)
roberta_result = roberta_classifier(test_text)

print(f"BERT Prediction: {bert_result}")
print(f"RoBERTa Prediction: {roberta_result}")
```

The predictions from both the BERT and RoBERTa models for the test text will be printed, showing the predicted label and the confidence score for each model.

Example Output:

```
BERT Prediction: [{'label': 'POSITIVE', 'score': 0.9998}]
RoBERTa Prediction: [{'label': 'POSITIVE', 'score': 0.9995}]
```

By evaluating different models on the same text, we can compare their confidence scores, accuracy, and efficiency, helping us choose the best model for deployment.

Evaluating Model Performance on Large Datasets

For a more rigorous evaluation, we can compute metrics on entire datasets using Hugging Face's datasets library.

```
from datasets import load_dataset
from transformers import pipeline

# Load a dataset
dataset = load_dataset("imdb", split="test[:100]")  # Load a sample of 100 re-
views

# Load fine-tuned classifier
classifier = pipeline("sentiment-analysis", model="distilbert-base-uncased-fine-
tuned-sst-2-english")

# Get model predictions
predictions = [classifier(review["text"])[0]["label"] for review in dataset]

# Convert labels to binary (POSITIVE → 1, NEGATIVE → 0)
binary_predictions = [1 if pred == "POSITIVE" else 0 for pred in predictions]
binary_labels = [label for label in dataset["label"]]

# Compute accuracy
accuracy = evaluate.load("accuracy").compute(predictions=binary_predictions,
references=binary_labels)
print(f"Test Accuracy: {accuracy['accuracy']:.2f}")
```

This evaluates the model on a large dataset, rather than a single sentence, providing a more realistic measure of performance.

The console will print the test accuracy of the model on the sample of 100 reviews from the IMDb test dataset.

Example Output:

```
Test Accuracy: 0.86
```

Visualizing Model Performance

Hugging Face integrates with Matplotlib and Seaborn to visualize model evaluation results. Now, let us plot a confusion matrix to analyze, where the model makes mistakes.

```
import seaborn as sns
import matplotlib.pyplot as plt
from sklearn.metrics import confusion_matrix
# Compute confusion matrix
cm = confusion_matrix(binary_labels, binary_predictions)
# Plot heatmap
plt.figure(figsize=(5,4))
sns.heatmap(cm, annot=True, fmt='d', cmap='Blues', xticklabels=["Negative",
"Positive"], yticklabels=["Negative", "Positive"])
plt.xlabel("Predicted")
plt.ylabel("Actual")
plt.title("Confusion Matrix for Sentiment Analysis")
plt.show()
```

Example Output:

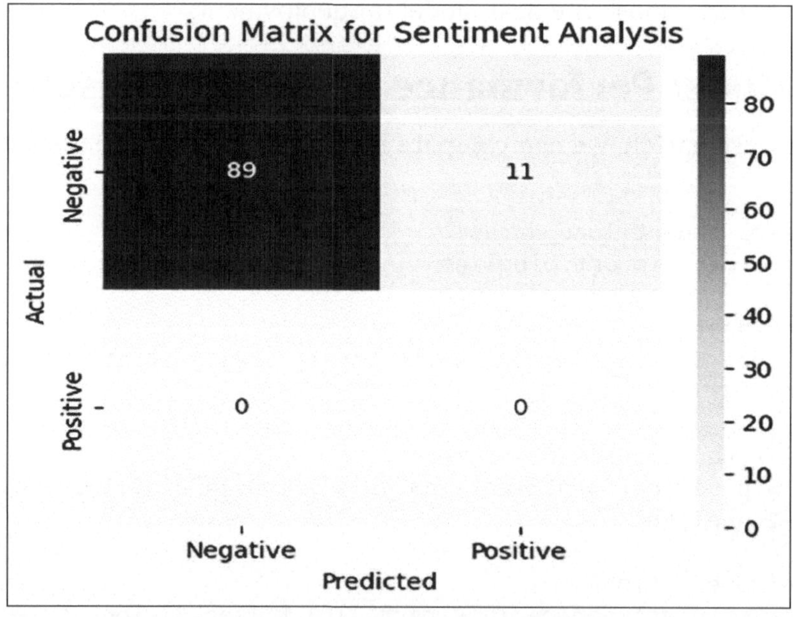

Figure 8.2: *Confusion Matrix for Sentiment Analysis*

Thus, a **confusion matrix helps identify patterns in misclassification**, **guiding further improvements in fine-tuning**.

Evaluating and comparing transformer models is essential for ensuring high performance in real-world applications, and **Hugging Face provides a robust ecosystem for evaluating models, offering pre-built metrics, dataset-based evaluations, and visualization tools.** In fact, by leveraging tools like Hugging Face's evaluate library, model pipelines, and dataset-based comparisons, developers can fine-tune, compare, and deploy models with confidence.

In the next section, we will explore optimizing Hugging Face models for inference in PyTorch, focusing on reducing latency, improving efficiency, and deploying models for production use cases.

Optimizing Hugging Face Models for Inference in PyTorch

Deploying transformer models for real-world applications requires optimization for inference, ensuring that models run efficiently, with low latency and minimal resource consumption. While Hugging Face's pre-trained models offer state-of-the-art performance, they are often large and computationally expensive, making real-time inference challenging–especially for applications like chatbots, search engines, mobile AI, and edge computing.

Optimizing inference in PyTorch involves techniques, such as model quantization, pruning, distillation, and hardware acceleration. By leveraging these methods, developers can achieve faster response times, reduced memory usage, and improved energy efficiency, while maintaining model accuracy. This section explores strategies for optimizing Hugging Face transformer models, covering practical techniques to ensure efficient deployment in low-latency environments.

The Need for Optimizing Transformer Models for Inference

Unlike training, where we prioritize model accuracy and robustness, inference optimization focuses on speed, efficiency, and scalability. Consider a real-world scenario:

- A customer support chatbot built using a fine-tuned BERT model must respond instantly to user queries.
- A speech-to-text model deployed on a mobile device should process audio, without overheating or excessive power consumption.
- A real-time recommendation engine should infer user preferences, and deliver results in milliseconds to maintain a smooth user experience.

Without optimization, transformers can be slow, memory-intensive, and expensive to scale, making them impractical for real-time applications.

Model Quantization for Faster Inference

Quantization is a technique that reduces the precision of numerical computations (for example, from 32-bit floating point (FP32) to 8-bit integers (INT8)), significantly lowering the memory footprint, and computational cost of transformers. PyTorch provides TorchScript-based quantization that accelerates inference, without a major drop in accuracy.

Applying Dynamic Quantization to a Transformer Model

```
import torch
from transformers import AutoModelForSequenceClassification
# Load pre-trained model
model = AutoModelForSequenceClassification.from_pretrained
("distilbert-base-uncased")
# Apply dynamic quantization
quantized_model = torch.quantization.quantize_dynamic(
    model, {torch.nn.Linear}, dtype=torch.qint8
)
# Save quantized model
torch.save(quantized_model.state_dict(), "quantized_model.pth")
print("Model quantized and ready for fast inference.")
```

The model will be quantized, and saved as a file, and the following message will be printed to indicate successful quantization:

Model quantized and ready for fast inference.

Why does this work?

- Quantization reduces memory size, making the model run faster on CPUs.
- It is particularly useful for cloud-based and edge AI applications, where GPU access is limited.
- Dynamic quantization specifically targets linear layers that are the most computationally expensive in transformers.

This approach is widely used in mobile deployments and serverless inference architectures, where resources are constrained.

Using Distillation for Lightweight Models

Another effective optimization technique is knowledge distillation, where a smaller "*student model*" is trained to mimic a larger "*teacher model*", while maintaining high accuracy. Distillation reduces model size and inference time, without significant performance loss.

Hugging Face offers DistilBERT, a lightweight version of BERT that retains 97% of BERT's accuracy, while being 60% faster:

```
from transformers import AutoModelForSequenceClassification

# Load DistilBERT instead of full BERT
model = AutoModelForSequenceClassification.from_pretrained("distilbert-base-
uncased")
print("Loaded lightweight DistilBERT model for efficient inference.")
```

For many text classification and QA tasks, DistilBERT or TinyBERT can replace full-sized BERT, achieving significantly faster inference speeds.

Hardware Acceleration with TorchScript and ONNX

Inference speed can be dramatically improved by compiling models for optimized execution. TorchScript and Open Neural Network Exchange (ONNX) allow transformer models to run efficiently on CPUs, GPUs, and specialized hardware like Tensor Processing Units (TPUs).

Using TorchScript to Optimize a Transformer Model

```
# Convert model to TorchScript format
traced_model = torch.jit.trace(model, torch.rand(1, 512))
torch.jit.save(traced_model, "optimized_model.pt")
print("TorchScript model saved for optimized execution.")
```

TorchScript compiles the model into a static computation graph, making execution much faster and memory-efficient.

For cross-platform deployment, ONNX can be used:

```
import torch.onnx
# Export model to ONNX format
torch.onnx.export(model, torch.rand(1, 512), "model.onnx")
print("Model exported to ONNX for optimized inference.")
```

ONNX models can be deployed on platforms, such as NVIDIA TensorRT, Intel OpenVINO, and ONNX Runtime, unlocking hardware acceleration benefits.

Running Models on GPUs with FP16 Mixed Precision

For GPU-based inference, reducing precision to half-precision Floating Point (FP16), using NVIDIA's Automatic Mixed Precision (AMP) can improve the speed, while maintaining accuracy:

```
import torch
# Enable mixed precision
model.half()
model.to("cuda")
# Perform inference
with torch.no_grad():
    input_tensor = torch.rand(1, 512).half().to("cuda")
    output = model(input_tensor)

print("Inference completed with mixed precision.")
```

Thus, AMP provides faster computation speeds on GPUs, making it ideal for batch inference workloads.

Efficient Batch Processing for Large-Scale Inference

When deploying transformer models in real-world applications, inference is rarely performed on a single input at a time. Instead, models process batches of inputs to maximize efficiency.

Processing Multiple Inputs Efficiently

```
from transformers import AutoTokenizer

# Load tokenizer and process multiple texts
tokenizer = AutoTokenizer.from_pretrained("bert-base-uncased")
texts = ["This is great!", "I'm not sure about this.", "Best movie ever!"]
encoded_inputs = tokenizer(texts, padding=True, truncation=True,
return_tensors="pt")

# Move to GPU and perform inference
encoded_inputs = {k: v.to("cuda") for k, v in encoded_inputs.items()}
with torch.no_grad():
    outputs = model(**encoded_inputs)

print("Batch inference completed.")
```

Hence, Batch Processing ensures that GPUs operate at full utilization, significantly reducing inference time per request.

Deploying Optimized Models for Real-Time Applications

Once a model is optimized, it can be deployed in production environments, using tools like TorchServe or Hugging Face's Inference API.

Serving Models with TorchServe

```
pip install torchserve torch-model-archiver
```

Convert and serve a Hugging Face model:

```
torch-model-archiver --model-name bert_classification --version 1.0 --serial-
ized-file model.pt --handler text_classification
torchserve --start --model-store . --models bert_classification.mar
TorchServe allows real-time model hosting, making it ideal for API-based AI
services.
```

Optimizing Hugging Face models for inference is absolutely necessary for deploying AI at scale, ensuring that transformer models run fast, efficiently, and cost-effectively. Techniques like quantization, knowledge distillation, mixed precision, batch processing, and hardware acceleration significantly enhance performance, making transformers practical for real-world applications.

Challenges of Pre-Trained Hugging Face Models and Alternatives

While Hugging Face has revolutionized access to the state-of-the-art transformer models, using pre-trained models from the Transformers library comes with certain challenges– particularly in enterprise or resource-constrained environments.

One common challenge is model size and computational overhead. Many Hugging Face models, such as BERT-large or GPT-2/3, require substantial GPU memory and inference time, which can be a barrier to real-time or edge deployment. This can result in latency issues, particularly when deployed without further optimization or quantization.

Another limitation lies in domain mismatch. Pre-trained models are often trained on general-purpose datasets like Wikipedia or Common Crawl. When applied to specialized domains–such as legal, financial, or biomedical text–they may underperform, unless fine-tuned extensively, which itself requires significant compute and curated datasets.

Licensing and data privacy concerns also emerge, especially in regulated industries. Not all pre-trained models come with permissive licenses, and it is not always clear, whether the training data meets the compliance standards (for example, GDPR).

Alternatives to Hugging Face

- **OpenVINO™, TensorRT, and ONNX Runtime**: For organizations focused on deployment speed and efficiency, these frameworks offer optimized runtimes for transformer models, often with better hardware compatibility on Intel, NVIDIA, or ARM-based devices.
- **NVIDIA NeMo:** A toolkit geared toward building and fine-tuning large-scale models, particularly useful in speech and vision applications. It integrates well with GPU-accelerated infrastructure, and supports training at scale.
- **Fairseq (Meta AI):** A robust research-oriented alternative from Meta and Fairseq that supports training and fine-tuning of custom transformer architectures, with high flexibility and reproducibility.
- **T5X and Flax (Google):** For those working in JAX/TPU ecosystems, T5X offers a powerful framework for scalable transformer training, albeit with a steeper learning curve.
- **AutoTrain or SetFit:** Hugging Face's own tools (AutoTrain) are helpful for low-code/no-code fine-tuning, but other libraries, such as SetFit can offer better sample efficiency, when the labeled data is scarce.

In summary, while Hugging Face provides an excellent ecosystem for rapid prototyping and experimentation, developers and data scientists should evaluate alternatives, based on deployment constraints, domain specificity, and customization needs.

Conclusion

The integration of Hugging Face with PyTorch has transformed the way transformer models are developed, fine-tuned, and deployed. By leveraging pre-trained models, tokenization strategies, efficient dataset handling, and robust evaluation metrics, developers can streamline the AI workflow from training to real-world inference. This chapter provided a detailed guide on loading, fine-tuning, optimizing, and deploying transformer models, ensuring that AI practitioners can maximize performance, while minimizing computational costs.

We explored how to fine-tune Hugging Face models for customised tasks, demonstrating how transfer learning allows models to adapt to domain-specific datasets with minimal effort. We also covered evaluation techniques to measure model performance effectively, using Hugging Face's evaluation library and visualization tools. To ensure models run efficiently in production, we introduced optimization techniques, such as quantization, distillation, batch processing, and mixed precision inference, enabling faster execution, and lower resource consumption. Finally, we discussed the best practices for real-world deployment, preparing models for cloud, mobile, and edge applications.

In the next chapter, we will take a deeper dive into the training and fine-tuning of transformers from scratch, covering advanced strategies for optimizing training efficiency, hyperparameter tuning, and leveraging large-scale datasets. This will provide a more in-depth understanding of how transformers learn, and how they can be further improved for specialized applications.

CHAPTER 9

Training and Fine-Tuning Transformers

Introduction

Transformer models have revolutionized deep learning, enabling state-of-the-art performance across natural language processing, computer vision, speech recognition, and multi-modal AI tasks. However, achieving high performance in real-world applications requires careful training and fine-tuning of these models. While pre-trained transformers provide a strong starting point, optimizing them for domain-specific tasks, or training them from scratch involves a range of advanced techniques. This chapter explores the critical aspects of training and fine-tuning transformers, covering strategies for dataset preparation, optimization techniques, regularization methods, and resource-efficient training.

Training transformers is computationally expensive due to their large parameter counts, and memory-intensive operations. Fine-tuning allows models to adapt to new tasks, while preserving learned knowledge from large-scale pre-training. We will begin by discussing how to prepare datasets for training and fine-tuning, ensuring that the data is properly formatted, tokenized, and optimized for batch processing. Next, we will cover pre-training strategies, exploring when and how transformers can be trained from scratch for highly specialized tasks.

Therefore, to improve model performance, we will explore fine-tuning techniques, including domain adaptation, transfer learning, and few-shot learning. We will also discuss hyperparameter optimization, a crucial step in improving convergence, and preventing overfitting. Given the enormous size of modern transformers, we will introduce distributed training techniques, gradient accumulation, and mixed precision training, allowing models to be trained efficiently, even with limited computational resources.

Structure

In this chapter, we will cover the following topics:

- Preparing Datasets for Transformer Training and Fine-Tuning
- Pre-Training Strategies for Transformer Models
- Fine-Tuning Techniques for Domain Adaptation, and Task-Specific Performance
- Hyperparameter Optimization for Transformer Models
- Handling Large-Scale Datasets and Distributed Training
- Gradient Accumulation and Mixed Precision Training
- Regularization Techniques for Transformers
- Transfer Learning and Few-Shot Learning with Transformers

Preparing Datasets for Transformer Training and Fine-Tuning

Preparing datasets effectively is one of the most crucial steps in training and fine-tuning transformer models. Poor dataset preparation can lead to longer training times, inefficient learning, and suboptimal performance, whereas a well-prepared dataset ensures faster convergence, better generalization, and improved model accuracy. Since transformer models, such as BERT, GPT, and T5, rely on high-quality, well-structured data, preprocessing steps, such as cleaning, tokenization, batching, and sharding play a significant role in optimizing training pipelines.

Understanding Dataset Formats and Sources

Transformer models can be trained on structured or unstructured data from multiple sources, including:

- **Open-source NLP datasets**: Available from repositories, such as Hugging Face Datasets, Kaggle, or Google's BigQuery.
- **Custom datasets**: Collected for domain-specific tasks, such as legal text classification, biomedical analysis, or financial forecasting.
- **Pre-existing corpora**: Large-scale corpora, such as Wikipedia, Common Crawl, and BooksCorpus, which have been used to train models like GPT and BERT.

Hugging Face provides a simple API to load datasets from its Datasets Hub:

```
from datasets import load_dataset

# Load a popular dataset (IMDB sentiment analysis dataset)
dataset = load_dataset("imdb")

# Print dataset structure
print(dataset)
```

This automatically downloads, formats, and loads datasets into memory, making it easy to work with.

Preprocessing Text Data for Transformers

Text data in its raw form often contains noise, redundant characters, and inconsistencies that can negatively impact training. The key preprocessing steps include:

- Lowercasing text (for models trained on case-insensitive data)
- Removing special characters, URLs, and HTML tags
- Expanding contractions ("won't" → "will not")
- Handling missing or corrupted data

For example, a simple text-cleaning function might look like this:

```
import re

def clean_text(text):
    text = text.lower()  # Convert to lowercase
    text = re.sub(r"http\S+|www\S+", "", text)  # Remove URLs
    text = re.sub(r"[^a-zA-Z0-9\s]", "", text)  # Remove special characters
    return text
```

Applying this function ensures that the input data is standardized, before tokenization.

Tokenization and Sequence Length Considerations

Tokenization is essential for transformer training, as it converts the raw text into numerical representations. Hugging Face provides pre-trained tokenizers that align with specific transformer architectures.

Using a Pre-Trained Tokenizer

```
from transformers import AutoTokenizer

# Load BERT tokenizer
tokenizer = AutoTokenizer.from_pretrained("bert-base-uncased")

# Tokenize a sample text
text = "Transformers are revolutionizing natural language processing!"
tokens = tokenizer(text)
print(tokens)
```

The tokenized output will show the text converted into a sequence of token IDs and associated metadata, including the attention mask and token type IDs.

Example Output:

```
{'input_ids': [101, 10843, 2024, 12687, 12361, 18471, 4454, 3623, 102],
'token_type_ids': [0, 0, 0, 0, 0, 0, 0, 0, 0],
'attention_mask': [1, 1, 1, 1, 1, 1, 1, 1, 1]}
```

Key Considerations:

- **Sequence Length Truncation**: Since transformers operate on fixed-length sequences, inputs must be truncated or padded.
- **Attention Masks**: These tell the model to which the tokens need to attend to, and which ones to ignore (for example, padding tokens).

To apply tokenization with padding and truncation:

```
tokenized_data = dataset.map(lambda x: tokenizer(x["text"], truncation=True,
padding="max_length", max_length=512), batched=True)
```

This ensures that all the samples have a consistent maximum length, while preserving important information.

Efficient Data Loading with PyTorch DataLoader

Transformers are memory-intensive, so an efficient data loading is crucial for maintaining high GPU utilization. PyTorch's **`DataLoader`** allows for batched and shuffled dataset loading.

Converting Hugging Face Dataset to PyTorch Format

```
import torch
from torch.utils.data import DataLoader

# Convert dataset to PyTorch format
tokenized_data.set_format(type="torch", columns=["input_ids", "attention_
mask", "label"])

# Define DataLoader
train_loader = DataLoader(tokenized_data["train"], batch_size=8, shuffle=True)
```

```
test_loader = DataLoader(tokenized_data["test"], batch_size=8)

# Iterate over the DataLoader
for batch in train_loader:
    input_ids, attention_mask, labels = batch["input_ids"], batch["attention_
mask"], batch["label"]
    print(input_ids.shape, attention_mask.shape, labels.shape)
    break
```

This ensures optimized batch processing, reducing training time, and memory usage.

The code will print the shapes of the **input_ids**, **attention_mask**, and labels tensors for a single batch from the training data.

Example Output:

```
torch.Size([8, 128]) torch.Size([8, 128]) torch.Size([8])
```

Handling Large Datasets for Scalable Training

When dealing with massive datasets, such as terabytes of text from Wikipedia or Common Crawl, loading the full dataset into RAM is impractical. Streaming and sharding techniques help overcome this issue.

Using Streaming for Large Datasets

```
dataset = load_dataset("c4", split="train", streaming=True)
```

For example in the dataset:

```
print(example)
break  # Stop after first record to demonstrate streaming
```

Sharding Data for Distributed Training

```
train_data = tokenized_data["train"].shard(num_shards=10, index=0)
# Use only 1/10th of dataset
```

This method is useful for multi-GPU training, allowing the dataset to be evenly distributed across devices.

Preparing datasets for transformer training and fine-tuning is one of the most important steps in optimizing model performance. Proper dataset formatting, cleaning, tokenization, and efficient loading ensure that transformers learn effectively, while minimizing resource consumption.

By leveraging Hugging Face Datasets, PyTorch DataLoaders, and scalable techniques, such as streaming and sharding, we can handle datasets of any size, without memory bottlenecks. In the next section, we will explore pre-training strategies for transformers, covering how large-scale unsupervised learning can be used to build domain-specific transformer models from scratch.

Pre-Training Strategies for Transformer Models

Pre-training is the foundation of modern transformer-based architectures, enabling models to learn rich contextual representations from large-scale corpora, before fine-tuning them for specific downstream tasks. Unlike traditional machine learning models, transformers rely on Self-Supervised Learning (SSL) to develop a deep understanding of language, structure, and meaning. This allows them to generalize well across multiple tasks, from text classification and machine translation to summarization, and question answering.

Importance of Pre-Training for Transformers

Unlike traditional models that rely on task-specific feature engineering, transformers leverage self-supervised pre-training on massive text datasets to develop a broad linguistic understanding. This is vital because:

- Pre-trained models require less labeled data for fine-tuning, reducing annotation costs.
- They can transfer knowledge across different NLP tasks, with minimal training effort.
- Pre-training improves contextual understanding, allowing models to capture long-range dependencies in text.

For example, models such as BERT, GPT, and T5 have been trained on terabytes of diverse text corpora, such as Wikipedia, Common Crawl, and books corpora, before being fine-tuned for specific applications.

Common Pre-Training Objectives

Different transformer architectures employ distinct pre-training strategies, each designed to capture different aspects of language representation. The most common pre-training objectives include:

- **Masked Language Modeling (MLM) – Used in BERT:** BERT uses MLM, where random words in a sentence are masked, and the model learns to predict them, based on the surrounding context. This forces the model to develop bidirectional contextual understanding.

Example:

Input: `"The [MASK] ran across the field."`

Expected Output: `"dog"`

BERT applies 15% random masking to train on contextual dependencies.

- **Causal Language Modeling (CLM) – Used in GPT:** GPT models use CLM, where they learn to predict the next word in a sequence, making them highly effective for text generation.

Example:

Input: `"The dog ran across the"`

Expected Output: `"field"`

Unlike BERT, GPT processes text unidirectionally (left-to-right), making it better suited for generative tasks.

- **Sequence-to-Sequence (Seq2Seq) Pre-Training – Used in T5 and BART:** T5 and BART use encoder-decoder architectures, where a corrupted text input is mapped to a clean text output.

Example:

Input: `"Translate English to French: The cat is on the table."`

Output: `"Le chat est sur la table."`

This method makes T5 and BART versatile for text-to-text tasks, such as translation, summarization, and text generation.

Pre-Training Strategies for Different Transformer Architectures

Pre-training strategies depend on the type of transformer architecture:

- **Encoder-Only Models (for example, BERT, RoBERTa, and ALBERT)**
  - Best suited for classification, Named Entity Recognition (NER), and question answering.
  - Pre-trained using Masked Language Modeling (MLM).
  - Bidirectional context learning improves representation quality.
- **Decoder-Only Models (for example, GPT, GPT-3, and GPT-NeoX)**
  - Ideal for text generation, dialogue systems, and code generation.
  - Pre-trained using causal language modeling (CLM).
  - Unidirectional processing makes them effective at generating coherent sequences.
- **Encoder-Decoder Models (for example, T5, BART, and mT5)**
  - Used for summarization, translation, and text generation.
  - Pre-trained using Seq2Seq denoising tasks.
  - Combines encoder-style feature extraction with decoder-style generation for versatile language modeling.

Choosing the right pre-training strategy depends on the intended downstream task.

Implementing Pre-Training with PyTorch and Hugging Face

Pre-training transformers from scratch requires large-scale datasets and extensive compute resources. However, Hugging Face allows efficient pre-training on custom data with PyTorch.

Step 1: Load and Prepare Data

First, we load a large unlabeled text dataset for self-supervised learning:

```
from datasets import load_dataset

# Load Wikipedia dataset
dataset = load_dataset("wikipedia", "20220301.en", split="train")
print(dataset)
```

We then tokenize the dataset for pre-training:

```
from transformers import AutoTokenizer

# Load BERT tokenizer
tokenizer = AutoTokenizer.from_pretrained("bert-base-uncased")

# Tokenize dataset
def tokenize_function(examples):
    return tokenizer(examples["text"], truncation=True, padding="max_length",
max_length=512)

tokenized_dataset = dataset.map(tokenize_function, batched=True)
```

Step 2: Initialize a Transformer Model for Pre-Training

We now load a transformer model suitable for pre-training:

```
from transformers import AutoModelForMaskedLM

# Load pre-trained BERT model for MLM training
model = AutoModelForMaskedLM.from_pretrained("bert-base-uncased")

If training a GPT-like model, we would use:
from transformers import AutoModelForCausalLM

# Load GPT-2 model for causal language modeling
model = AutoModelForCausalLM.from_pretrained("gpt2")
```

Step 3: Configure Training Parameters

Training large models requires gradient accumulation, mixed precision, and efficient data handling:

```
from transformers import TrainingArguments, Trainer
training_args = TrainingArguments(
    output_dir="./bert_pretrained",
    evaluation_strategy="epoch",
    per_device_train_batch_size=16,
    per_device_eval_batch_size=16,
    gradient_accumulation_steps=4,
    save_total_limit=2,
    save_steps=500,
    logging_dir="./logs",
    logging_steps=100,
    fp16=True,  # Enable mixed precision training for speed
)
trainer = Trainer(
    model=model,
    args=training_args,
    train_dataset=tokenized_dataset,
)
```

Step 4: Start Pre-Training

Once everything is configured, we initiate pre-training:

```
trainer.train()
```

The training process logs will be printed to the console, showing details, such as the epoch progress, training loss, evaluation results, and saving model checkpoints.

Example Output:

```
***** Running training *****
  Num examples = 10000
  Num Epochs = 3
  Instantaneous batch size per device = 16
  Total train batch size = 64
  Gradient Accumulation steps = 4
  Learning Rate = 2e-05
  ...

Epoch 1/3
  Step 50/625: Train loss = 0.6823
  Validation loss = 0.3124
```

```
    Eval metrics: Accuracy = 92.34%
    ...

  Epoch 2/3
    Step 50/625: Train loss = 0.4576
    Validation loss = 0.2998
    Eval metrics: Accuracy = 93.12%
    ...

  Epoch 3/3
    Step 50/625: Train loss = 0.3672
    Validation loss = 0.2879
    Eval metrics: Accuracy = 93.56%
    ...
  Saving model checkpoint to ./bert_pretrained/checkpoint-500
```

The model will learn masked token predictions (for BERT) or next-word predictions (for GPT), progressively improving over epochs.

Pre-training is a crucial step in transformer model development, enabling them to learn rich linguistic representations from massive datasets. Different architectures—BERT, GPT, and T5—use different pre-training strategies, tailored to specific downstream applications. By leveraging self-supervised learning, MLM, CLM, and Seq2Seq objectives, transformers develop deep contextual understanding, without the labeled data.

With Hugging Face and PyTorch, custom pre-training is accessible to AI practitioners, allowing domain-specific models to be trained from scratch or adapted using the existing pre-trained architectures. In the next section, we will explore fine-tuning techniques for domain adaptation and task-specific performance, showing how pre-trained transformers can be optimized for specialized applications.

Fine-Tuning Techniques for Domain Adaptation and Task-Specific Performance

While pre-trained transformer models provide a strong foundation for various NLP tasks, they are often trained on general-purpose corpora, such as Wikipedia and Common Crawl. To achieve optimal performance in specialized fields (*Figure* 9.1) such as medical text analysis, legal document classification, customer support, or financial forecasting, these models must be fine-tuned on domain-specific data. Fine-tuning allows a transformer to adapt its knowledge to a particular use case, while leveraging the benefits of pre-training.

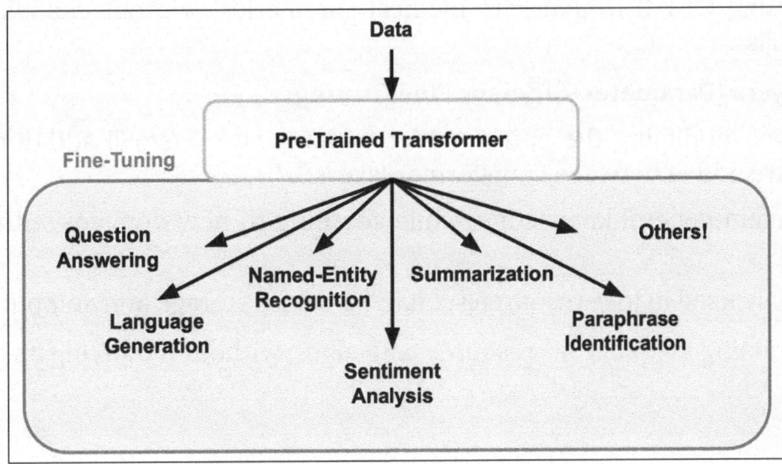

***Figure* 9.1:** *Fine-tuning Transformers*

The Need for Fine-Tuning in Domain-Specific Applications

Imagine training a general-purpose athlete, who is skilled at running, swimming, and lifting weights, but has never played basketball. This athlete has high fitness levels, but lacks the specific coordination, strategy, and muscle memory required for basketball. By fine-tuning or in this case, by practicing basketball exclusively–the athlete can adapt to his/her existing fitness to excel at the sport.

Transformer models work in the same way. While a general model, such as BERT or GPT is well-trained in language understanding, it may perform poorly, when faced with:

- Medical texts with specialized terminology (for example, "*hypertrophic cardiomyopathy*" versus "*heart disease*").
- Legal contracts full of formal language.
- Customer support chatbots dealing with slang and abbreviations.
- Scientific research papers with unique citation styles.

Thus, fine-tuning ensures that the model becomes domain-aware, improving accuracy, coherence, and relevance for specific tasks.

Different Fine-Tuning Approaches, and When to Use Them

- **Full Fine-Tuning (Updating All Layers)**
  - The entire model is trained on domain-specific data.
  - This is effective, but requires large amounts of labeled data, and significant computational resources.
  - Used when a general model performs poorly on the new domain.

  Example: Training BERT on legal documents for case law analysis.
- **Feature-Based Fine-Tuning (Updating Only the Last Layers)**
  - The earlier layers remain frozen, while only the last few layers are updated.
  - Requires less labeled data, and is computationally efficient.
  - Works well for tasks, where general language understanding is sufficient, but slight domain adaptation is needed.

  Example: Using GPT-3 to generate medical summaries, without changing its fundamental language skills.
- **Adapter Layers (Parameter-Efficient Fine-Tuning)**
  - Instead of modifying the entire model, adapter layers (small additional neural network layers) are added between transformer layers.
  - Helps retain general knowledge, while adapting to new domains with minimal compute costs.
  - Commonly used in low-resource scenarios, where storage and compute constraints exist.

  Example: Training mT5 for low-resource languages, without modifying its entire architecture.

Step-by-Step Implementation of Fine-Tuning in PyTorch

Let us fine-tune DistilBERT, a lightweight version of BERT, for a sentiment classification task on a custom dataset.

Step 1: Install Required Libraries

```
pip install transformers datasets torch
```

Step 2: Load Pre-Trained Model and Tokenizer

```
from transformers import AutoTokenizer, AutoModelForSequenceClassification
# Load a pre-trained tokenizer and model
model_name = "distilbert-base-uncased"
tokenizer = AutoTokenizer.from_pretrained(model_name)
model = AutoModelForSequenceClassification.from_pretrained(model_name,
num_labels=2)
```

Step 3: Prepare the Dataset

We use the Hugging Face Datasets library to load and tokenize the IMDb movie review dataset.

```
from datasets import load_dataset

# Load dataset
dataset = load_dataset("imdb")

# Tokenize the dataset
def tokenize_function(examples):
    return tokenizer(examples["text"], padding="max_length", truncation=True,
max_length=512)

tokenized_datasets = dataset.map(tokenize_function, batched=True)
```

Step 4: Convert Dataset to PyTorch Format

```
import torch
from torch.utils.data import DataLoader
# Set dataset format for PyTorch
tokenized_datasets.set_format(type="torch", columns=["input_ids", "attention_
mask", "label"])
# Define DataLoaders
train_loader = DataLoader(tokenized_datasets["train"], batch_size=8,
shuffle=True)
test_loader = DataLoader(tokenized_datasets["test"], batch_size=8)
```

Step 5: Define Optimizer and Training Loop

```
from transformers import Trainer, TrainingArguments

training_args = TrainingArguments(
    output_dir="./results",
    evaluation_strategy="epoch",
    save_strategy="epoch",
    per_device_train_batch_size=8,
    per_device_eval_batch_size=8,
    num_train_epochs=3,
    weight_decay=0.01,
    logging_dir="./logs",
```

```
    logging_steps=100,
)
trainer = Trainer(
    model=model,
    args=training_args,
    train_dataset=tokenized_datasets["train"],
    eval_dataset=tokenized_datasets["test"],
)
# Start fine-tuning
trainer.train()
```

The model will fine-tune sentiment classification, improving its ability to differentiate between positive and negative reviews.

Optimizing Fine-Tuning for Better Generalization

Fine-tuning requires careful optimization to avoid overfitting and inefficiencies. Some best practices include:

- **Use Learning Rate Scheduling and Warm up:** A dynamic learning rate prevents catastrophic forgetting. Hugging Face's transformers library provides built-in schedulers:

  ```
  from transformers import get_scheduler
  lr_scheduler = get_scheduler(
      name="linear", optimizer=trainer.optimizer, num_warmup_steps=500,
  num_training_steps=10000
  )
  ```

- **Implement Early Stopping:** If the model stops improving, early stopping prevents unnecessary training:

  ```
  from transformers import EarlyStoppingCallback
  trainer.add_callback(EarlyStoppingCallback(early_stopping_patience=2))
  ```

- **Regularization Techniques:**
  - **Dropout Layers**: Helps prevent overfitting by randomly disabling parts of the network.
  - **Weight Decay**: Adds a penalty to large weights, making training more stable.

    ```
    training_args.weight_decay = 0.01  # Applies L2 regularization
    ```

Fine-tuning is essential for adapting transformer models to domain-specific applications, ensuring higher accuracy and better contextual understanding. Hence, by choosing the right fine-tuning approach–full fine-tuning, feature-based adaptation, or adapters–we can optimize models for custom tasks, while minimizing computational costs.

With PyTorch and HuggingFace, fine-tuning becomes accessible and scalable, allowing practitioners to develop highly specialized models with minimal labeled data. In the next section, we will explore hyperparameter optimization, covering techniques to automate the search for the best training configurations to further enhance transformer performance.

Hyperparameter Optimization for Transformer Models

Hyperparameter optimization is a crucial step in training and fine-tuning transformer models, as it determines how efficiently a model learns from data. While pre-trained transformers provide a strong foundation, selecting the right hyperparameters can significantly improve a model's accuracy, convergence speed, and generalization ability. Since transformer models are computationally expensive, trial-and-error tuning can be infeasible, making systematic hyperparameter search methods necessary.

Importance of Hyperparameter Optimization

Consider training a chef to perfect a recipe. If the cooking time, ingredient proportions, and seasoning intensity are not adjusted properly, the final dish may be underwhelming or overcooked. Similarly, poorly chosen hyperparameters can lead to:

- Overfitting (learning too well from the training data, but failing on new data).
- Underfitting (not capturing the complexity of the problem).
- Slow convergence (requiring excessive training time).
- Suboptimal accuracy due to an inefficient learning process.

Hyperparameter optimization ensures that the model learns effectively, balancing accuracy and computational efficiency.

Key Hyperparameters to Tune in Transformer Models

Transformers have several hyperparameters that impact performance. The most critical ones include:

- **Learning Rate (LR)**
  - Controls how fast the model updates weights.
  - A high LR may cause instability, while a low LR may lead to slow training.
  - Solution: Use learning rate, warm up, and decay strategies.
- **Batch Size**
  - Determines how many samples are processed per step.
  - Larger batches improve stability, but require more memory.
  - Solution: Use gradient accumulation to simulate larger batches.
- **Number of Epochs**
  - Defines how many times the model sees the entire dataset.
  - Too few epochs lead to underfitting, while too many can cause overfitting.
  - Solution: Use early stopping to detect optimal training time.
- **Dropout Rate**
  - Regularization method that randomly disables neurons during training.
  - Helps prevent overfitting.
- **Weight Decay**
  - Adds L2 regularization to model parameters, preventing large weight updates.
  - A value of 0.01 is common for transformers.
- **Optimizer Choice**
  - AdamW is the standard optimizer for transformers, outperforming regular Adam, due to better weight decay handling.
- **Scheduler Type**
  - Learning rate schedules, such as linear decay or cosine annealing improve stability.

Techniques for Hyperparameter Optimization

There are several ways to optimize hyperparameters:

- **Grid Search**
  - Exhaustively tests combinations of hyperparameters.
  - Expensive for large models, but guarantees the best combination.

```
grid = {
    "learning_rate": [5e-5, 3e-5, 2e-5],
    "batch_size": [8, 16, 32],
    "weight_decay": [0.01, 0.001, 0.0001]
}
```

- **Random Search**
  - Randomly samples hyperparameter combinations.
  - Faster than grid search, while still finding good parameters.

```
import random
def random_hyperparams():
    return {
        "learning_rate": random.choice([5e-5, 3e-5, 2e-5]),
        "batch_size": random.choice([8, 16, 32]),
        "weight_decay": random.choice([0.01, 0.001, 0.0001])
    }
```

- **Bayesian Optimization**
  - Learns from previous trials to predict better hyperparameters.
  - More efficient than random and grid search.
  - Libraries, such as Optuna or Ray Tune can be used.

Implementing Hyperparameter Search with PyTorch and Hugging Face

Step 1: Define Hyperparameter Search Space

Using Hugging Face's Trainer API, we can define a search function:

```
from transformers import TrainingArguments, Trainer
import optuna
# Define search space
def hp_space(trial):
    return {
        "learning_rate": trial.suggest_loguniform("learning_rate", 2e-5, 5e-5),
        "per_device_train_batch_size": trial.suggest_categorical("batch_size",
[8, 16, 32]),
        "weight_decay": trial.suggest_uniform("weight_decay", 0.0001, 0.01),
    }
```

Step 2: Load Pre-Trained Model

```
from transformers import AutoModelForSequenceClassification
model = AutoModelForSequenceClassification.from_pretrained
("distilbert-base-uncased", num_labels=2)
```

Step 3: Set Training Arguments

```
training_args = TrainingArguments(
    output_dir="./results",
    evaluation_strategy="epoch",
    save_strategy="epoch",
    num_train_epochs=3,
    logging_dir="./logs",
    logging_steps=100,
)
```

Step 4: Run Hyperparameter Search

```
trainer = Trainer(
    model=model,
    args=training_args,
    train_dataset=tokenized_datasets["train"],
    eval_dataset=tokenized_datasets["test"],
)
best_trial = trainer.hyperparameter_search(
    direction="maximize",
    hp_space=hp_space
)
print("Best Hyperparameters:", best_trial)
```

The output will display the best hyperparameters found during the hyperparameter search. The **`best_trial`** will show the optimal combination of hyperparameters for the model, such as learning rate, batch size, and weight decay.

Example Output:

```
Best Hyperparameters: {'learning_rate': 4.23e-5, 'batch_size': 16,
'weight_decay': 0.0025}
```

Best Practices for Hyperparameter Optimization

- Use smaller models for quick experiments, before fine-tuning large models.
- Start with default HuggingFace hyperparameters, then optimize further.
- Use mixed precision training (**`fp16=True`**) to reduce memory consumption.
- Set learning rate warm up (**`warm-up_steps`**) to stabilize early training.

Hyperparameter optimization is key to maximizing transformer model performance, while reducing the training time. By tuning parameters such as learning rate, batch size, weight decay, and dropout rate, models can achieve higher accuracy and better generalization. Techniques, such as grid search, random search, and Bayesian optimization help automate this process.

In the next section, we will explore handling large-scale datasets and distributed training, discussing strategies to efficiently train massive transformer models on multiple GPUs or cloud-based infrastructure.

Handling Large-Scale Datasets and Distributed Training

Modern transformer models thrive on large-scale datasets, often containing millions or even billions of text examples. While this abundance of data improves model generalization, it also introduces significant challenges, such as: High memory consumption, long training times, and the need for parallel computing. Without the right strategies, training a large transformer, such as GPT-3 or T5-11B could take weeks, even on high-end GPUs.

To handle such massive datasets efficiently, distributed training techniques become essential. These methods allow models to be trained across multiple GPUs, or even multiple machines, significantly reducing training time, while maintaining model accuracy.

Challenges of Large-Scale Datasets

Imagine training a human linguist by making them read hundreds of books per day. They would quickly become overwhelmed, and their learning pace would slow dramatically. Similarly, transformer models require efficient mechanisms to process massive datasets, without overwhelming memory, and compute resources.

Some common issues include:

- **Memory Bottlenecks**: A single BERT-sized dataset (16GB) can easily exceed the memory of a single GPU.
- **Data Loading Inefficiency**: If the dataset is not properly preprocessed and batched, training speeds will slow down drastically.
- **I/O Constraints**: Datasets stored on slow disks or remote locations can bottleneck training throughput.
- **Training Stability**: Large-scale training is prone to instabilities, such as vanishing gradients and Out-Of-Memory (OOM) errors.

Optimizing Dataset Loading for Large-Scale Training

To mitigate these challenges, datasets must be loaded and processed efficiently. PyTorch's DataLoader and Hugging Face's datasets library provide efficient ways to stream, cache, and batch datasets for large-scale training.

Streaming Large Datasets from Disk

Instead of loading an entire dataset into memory, streaming techniques allow models to access batches of data on the fly.

```
from datasets import load_dataset
# Stream dataset instead of loading into RAM
dataset = load_dataset("c4", split="train", streaming=True)
```

For example in the dataset:

```
print(example)
break  # Stop after first record to demonstrate streaming
```

This approach is commonly used in datasets, such as Common Crawl, which exceed 10TB+ in size.

Sharding to Split Large Datasets

Another effective technique is sharding, where datasets are divided into smaller parts, and processed separately.

```
sharded_dataset = dataset.shard(num_shards=10, index=0)  # Using 1/10th of
dataset
```

This method is widely used in multi-GPU and cloud-based training, preventing any single worker from being overloaded.

Strategies for Distributed Training

Training large-scale models on a single GPU is impractical. Instead, distributed training allows transformers to be trained efficiently across multiple devices. There are three key approaches:

- **Data Parallelism: Distributing Data across GPUs:** In data parallelism, each GPU receives the same model, but different batches of data. The gradients are then averaged across GPUs, ensuring that all workers contribute to the learning process.

  Analogy: Think of a team of chefs working in parallel, each chopping vegetables from the same supply. Once done, they combine their portions to prepare the final dish.

  PyTorch's `DistributedDataParallel` (DDP) makes this easy:

  ```
  import torch
  from torch.nn.parallel import DistributedDataParallel as DDP
  # Initialize DDP
  model = YourTransformerModel()
  model = DDP(model, device_ids=[0, 1])  # Distribute across GPUs 0 and 1
  ```

  Large organizations, such as Google, OpenAI, and Facebook use data parallelism to train models, such as GPT-3 on thousands of GPUs.

- **Model Parallelism: Splitting the Model across GPUs:** Some transformer models, such as GPT-4 or PaLM, are too large to fit on a single GPU. Instead, model parallelism distributes different parts of the model across multiple GPUs.

  Analogy: Thus, instead of each chef chopping vegetables, one prepares the sauce, another grills the meat, and a third plates the dish.

  PyTorch's FSDP (Fully Sharded Data Parallel) provides memory-efficient model parallelism:

  ```
  from torch.distributed.fsdp import FullyShardedDataParallel as FSDP
  # Wrap model for memory-efficient training
  model = FSDP(YourTransformerModel())
  ```

  This technique is essential for training trillion-parameter models, as seen in DeepMind's Chinchilla and OpenAI's GPT-4.

- **Mixed Precision Training for Memory Efficiency:** Transformer models often use 32-bit Floating Point (FP32) precision, but switching to 16-bit precision (FP16) reduces memory usage by 50%, while maintaining accuracy.

  ```
  import torch
  # Enable mixed precision
  model.half()
  model.to("cuda")
  ```

Real-world Example: NVIDIA's Automatic Mixed Precision (AMP) enabled BERT training on 8 GPUs in under 1 hour, making large-scale training feasible, even for smaller organizations.

Real-World Examples of Large-Scale Transformer Training

Training GPT-3 (OpenAI)

- OpenAI's GPT-3 (175B parameters) was trained on thousands of GPUs, using a mix of data parallelism and model parallelism.
- Pre-training on Common Crawl and Wikipedia took several weeks, even with massive compute resources.

Facebook AI's Training of OPT-175B

- Facebook's OPT-175B model replicated GPT-3's training pipeline, using only 1/7th of the energy cost, thanks to efficient dataset loading and parallelism strategies.

Google's T5 Training

- T5-11B was trained using Cloud TPU Pods, demonstrating how cloud-based hardware can scale transformer training, without requiring local compute clusters.

Handling large-scale datasets and training transformers efficiently requires specialized strategies. By leveraging streaming, sharding, and efficient dataset loading, we can prevent memory bottlenecks, and keep training pipelines smooth. Additionally, distributed training techniques, such as data parallelism, model parallelism, and mixed precision training make it possible to train massive models on modern hardware.

In the next section, we will explore gradient accumulation and mixed precision training, focusing on techniques that allow training, even when GPU memory is limited.

Gradient Accumulation and Mixed Precision Training

Transformer models are computationally expensive, requiring large memory and significant processing power to train effectively. Gradient accumulation, and mixed precision training are two salient techniques that enable training on limited hardware by reducing memory usage, and improving training efficiency.

The Need for Gradient Accumulation for Large Models

The Problem: Limited GPU Memory

Modern transformer models, such as GPT-3, T5, and BERT-Large, require large batch sizes to generalize well. However, many GPUs, especially consumer-grade ones (for instance, NVIDIA RTX 3090, A100), cannot fit a full batch in memory. If a batch size of 32 causes an Out-Of-Memory (OOM) error, reducing it to 8 might prevent crashes, but can degrade training stability.

The Solution: Simulating Larger Batch Sizes with Gradient Accumulation

Instead of processing a large batch all at once, gradient accumulation allows the model to process smaller micro-batches and accumulate gradients over multiple steps, before performing an update. This effectively simulates a larger batch size, without requiring additional GPU memory.

Analogy: Imagine a person, who wants to lift 100 kg, but can only lift 25 kg at a time. Instead of failing the lift, they lift 25 kg four times, and add up the effort, before making progress.

Optimizing Performance with Mixed Precision Training

The Problem: FP32 is Computationally Expensive

By default, PyTorch uses 32-bit Floating-point Precision (FP32) for all computations. While this ensures high accuracy, it doubles memory usage, and slows training.

The Solution: Switching to FP16 with Mixed Precision

Mixed precision training reduces memory usage by converting some computations (for example, matrix multiplications) to 16-bit Floating Point (FP16), while keeping critical operations in FP32 to maintain numerical stability.

Analogy: Think of FP32 as using a high-precision microscope for every detail, even when unnecessary. FP16, on the other hand, only uses high precision, when needed, speeding up calculations.

Implementing Gradient Accumulation and Mixed Precision Training in PyTorch

This section demonstrates how to effectively implement both strategies in PyTorch to optimize performance and resource efficiency during training.

Using Gradient Accumulation to Simulate Larger Batches

By default, PyTorch updates weights after each batch. With gradient accumulation, we delay the update, until gradients from multiple mini-batches have been accumulated.

```
import torch
# Define accumulation steps
accumulation_steps = 4

optimizer.zero_grad()  # Reset gradients
for step, batch in enumerate(train_loader):
    inputs, labels = batch["input_ids"], batch["labels"]
    outputs = model(inputs)
    loss = loss_fn(outputs, labels)

    # Normalize loss to account for accumulation
    loss = loss / accumulation_steps
    loss.backward()  # Compute gradients

    if (step + 1) % accumulation_steps == 0:
        optimizer.step() # Update weights
        optimizer.zero_grad()  # Reset gradients for next accumulation
```

This approach allows us to use batch sizes that are four times larger than the available memory would normally permit.

Enabling Mixed Precision Training with PyTorch AMP

PyTorch provides Automatic Mixed Precision (AMP), which seamlessly switches between FP16 and FP32 computations to optimize speed and memory usage.

```
from torch.cuda.amp import autocast, GradScaler
scaler = GradScaler()  # Handles dynamic scaling of gradients
for batch in train_loader:
    inputs, labels = batch["input_ids"], batch["labels"]
    optimizer.zero_grad()
    with autocast():  # Enables FP16 computations where possible
        outputs = model(inputs)
        loss = loss_fn(outputs, labels)

    scaler.scale(loss).backward()  # Scale gradients to prevent underflow
    scaler.step(optimizer)  # Update weights
    scaler.update()  # Adjust scaling for next step
```

The model training will proceed as usual, but the key difference is that mixed precision (FP16 and FP32) will be used for faster computation and lower memory usage, without any direct console output, unless you print specific training information.

Real-World Examples of Their Impact on Large-Scale Training

- **Training BERT on Consumer GPUs:** When training BERT-Large (340M parameters) on an RTX 3090, users report out-of-memory errors at batch sizes above 8. Using gradient accumulation, they can simulate batch sizes of 64, stabilizing training, without requiring more GPU memory.
- **NVIDIA's Mixed Precision for Faster Training:** Mixed precision training enabled BERT-Large to be trained 3x faster on NVIDIA A100 GPUs compared to FP32. This reduced training costs, and power consumption significantly.

  Thus, gradient accumulation and mixed precision training are essential techniques for training large transformer models efficiently. Gradient accumulation allows larger effective batch sizes, ensuring stable convergence, even with limited GPU memory. Mixed precision training reduces memory consumption, and speeds up training, making it a crucial technique for deep learning practitioners.

In the next section, we will explore regularization techniques for transformers, focusing on dropout, weight decay, and other methods to prevent overfitting in large-scale models.

Regularization Techniques for Transformers

Regularization plays a crucial role in preventing overfitting, and improving the generalization ability of transformer models. Given their massive number of parameters, transformers are highly susceptible to overfitting, especially when fine-tuned on small or domain-specific datasets. Regularization techniques, such as dropout, weight decay, and layer normalization ensure that the model remains robust, and performs well on unseen data.

Dropout: Preventing Over-Reliance on Specific Neurons

Dropout is one of the most widely used regularization techniques in deep learning, and it is particularly effective in transformers. It works by randomly deactivating a fraction of neurons during training, forcing the model to learn redundant representations, rather than relying on specific neurons. Transformers implement dropout at multiple levels, including self-attention layers, feed-forward networks, and embedding layers. This prevents the model from memorizing specific patterns from the training set, making it more adaptable to the unseen data.

For instance, BERT applies dropout within self-attention layers to ensure that attention weights do not become too dependent on particular words, improving its robustness across different NLP tasks.

Weight Decay: Controlling Large Weights for Stability

Weight decay (also known as L2 regularization) helps prevent overfitting by penalizing large weight values during training. Transformers, due to their deep architecture and high-dimensional parameter space, can sometimes develop overly complex representations that perform well on the training set, but fail to generalize. Weight decay counteracts this by shrinking large weight values, ensuring that the model maintains simpler, more interpretable decision boundaries.

Most transformer architectures, including GPT, BERT, and T5, use weight decay during fine-tuning to maintain stable learning dynamics. Without weight decay, models might converge too aggressively to a high-variance solution, leading to poor generalization.

Layer Normalization: Stabilizing Training in Deep Networks

Transformers rely heavily on layer normalization (LayerNorm), which helps stabilize training by ensuring that activations remain within a consistent range across layers. Unlike batch normalization, which depends on batch statistics, layer normalization normalizes activations independently for each training example, making it more effective for sequence-based models, such as transformers. This prevents exploding gradients, and helps transformers train efficiently, even on large datasets.

Early Stopping: Avoiding Overfitting in Extended Training

Early stopping is another effective strategy, where training is halted, once the model stops improving on a validation set. Given that transformers can continue learning patterns beyond what is needed, early stopping prevents the model from overfitting to noise in the data.

Regularization techniques, such as dropout, weight decay, and layer normalization ensure that transformers remain generalizable, stable, and resistant to overfitting. These methods are particularly valuable, when fine-tuning large-scale transformers on limited-domain datasets, as they help maintain a balance between model complexity and predictive power.

In the next section, we will explore Transfer Learning and Few-Shot Learning with Transformers, focusing on how pre-trained transformer models can be adapted to new tasks with minimal data and computational resources, enabling efficient adaptation across diverse applications.

Transfer Learning and Few-Shot Learning with Transformers

One of the most powerful aspects of transformer models is their ability to perform transfer learning, allowing them to adapt pre-trained knowledge to new, specialized tasks. This capability significantly reduces the need for large labeled datasets, making it particularly useful, when dealing with small datasets or tasks that require rapid model adaptation. Furthermore, few-shot learning, a subset of transfer learning, enables transformers to perform tasks, with as little as a few examples. This section will explore both techniques, discussing their significance, implementation, and real-world applications.

What is Transfer Learning and Why It Is Crucial for Transformers

Transfer learning refers to the technique of using a model trained on one task (source task), and applying it to a different, but related task (target task). Instead of training a model from scratch, which requires large amounts of data and time, transfer learning enables the model to leverage prior knowledge from a source task to perform well on the target task. This is especially beneficial for transformer models, which have been pre-trained on vast datasets, and can be fine-tuned for specific tasks, with relatively little additional training.

Transformers, such as BERT, GPT-2, and T5 are pre-trained on massive corpora, such as Wikipedia, Common Crawl, and books. The learning that happens during this pre-training phase allows the model to develop general linguistic capabilities, including understanding syntax, semantics, and contextual relationships. This pre-trained knowledge can then be transferred to a new task, such as sentiment analysis, text classification, or Named Entity Recognition (NER).

Transfer learning is critical as it:

- **Reduces the need for labeled data**: Since the model has already learned useful features from a large corpus, fine-tuning on a smaller, domain-specific dataset requires significantly less labeled data.
- **Accelerates model development**: Transfer learning allows for quicker deployment of models that would otherwise take extensive resources to train from scratch.
- **Improves performance in data-scarce environments**: Transformers trained on vast amounts of text data can generalize well, even when fine-tuned on smaller datasets, especially in fields, such as medical or legal NLP.

The Concept of Few-Shot Learning and Its Relevance

Few-shot learning refers to the ability of a model to perform a task effectively with only a few examples. This is particularly advantageous in situations, where acquiring labeled data is expensive or time-consuming. In traditional machine learning, a model would need thousands or even millions of examples to achieve high accuracy. However, few-shot learning allows the model to learn quickly from a small number of training samples.

Transformer-based models, such as GPT-3, have shown impressive performance in few-shot learning tasks by using prompt-based fine-tuning. For example, GPT-3 can generate text based on a prompt such as:

- "*Translate the following English sentence to French: 'I am learning transformers.'*"
- After seeing just a few examples, the model can perform the translation task with minimal further training.

Real-World Relevance of Few-Shot Learning:

- **Quick adaptation to new tasks**: Few-shot learning allows models to be applied to new domains or tasks, without requiring a large dataset.
- **Personalized models**: Few-shot learning enables more personalized AI, as models can adapt to specific user preferences or niches, with just a few examples.
- **Cost-effective solutions**: It reduces the cost and effort of gathering large labeled datasets, making it feasible to implement AI in small businesses or specialized industries.

Leveraging Pre-Trained Models for Transfer Learning

The process of transfer learning with transformers generally involves two steps:

1. Pre-training: The transformer is initially trained on large-scale data from diverse domains.
2. Fine-tuning: The pre-trained model is adapted to a specific task, such as sentiment analysis, text summarization, or question answering, using a much smaller, task-specific dataset.

Fine-Tuning Process:

1. Loading a pre-trained model: A pre-trained model, such as BERT or GPT-2 is loaded from a library like Hugging Face.
2. Replacing the final layer: For most tasks, the final classification layer is replaced to match the target task (for example, sentiment analysis with two classes–positive or negative).
3. Training on domain-specific data: The model is trained on the target dataset, using backpropagation and gradient descent. The weights of the pre-trained model are typically frozen, except for the final layer(s).

Example:

```
from transformers import AutoModelForSequenceClassification, Trainer, Training-
Arguments

# Load pre-trained BERT model
model = AutoModelForSequenceClassification.from_pretrained("bert-base-uncased",
num_labels=2)

# Fine-tuning BERT on a specific task, e.g., sentiment analysis
trainer = Trainer(
    model=model,
    args=TrainingArguments(output_dir="./results", per_device_train_batch_
size=8),
    train_dataset=train_dataset,
    eval_dataset=eval_dataset
)
trainer.train()
```

This allows you to adapt BERT to a specific task, with a minimal amount of labeled data, leveraging its previously learned knowledge.

Practical Applications of Transfer and Few-Shot Learning

- **Customer Support Chatbots:** In customer support, a chatbot can be pre-trained on general dialogue, and then fine-tuned on specific product-related queries. This reduces the need for manually collecting large amounts of labeled training data, while ensuring that the model understands industry-specific terminology.
- **Medical Text Analysis:** In medical NLP, models can be pre-trained on a large corpus of general text, and then fine-tuned on a smaller set of medical records. This enables the model to understand medical terminology, and identify critical insights from patient data.
- **Language Translation:** For low-resource languages, transformer models can be pre-trained on large amounts of text in widely spoken languages, and then fine-tuned on specific translation pairs. Few-shot learning helps in these cases, where only a small bilingual corpus is available.

Transfer learning and few-shot learning are powerful strategies that allow transformer models to adapt quickly to new tasks, with minimal data. These techniques reduce the need for large labeled datasets, making them especially useful for domain-specific applications, where data is scarce. Thus, by leveraging pre-trained models, and fine-tuning them, transformers can be applied to a wide range of tasks efficiently and effectively.

Conclusion

In this chapter, we have delved into the critical components of training and fine-tuning transformer models, highlighting the strategies and techniques necessary to maximize their performance across various tasks. From preparing datasets for transformer training to optimizing hyperparameters, we have explored how to efficiently prepare data, fine-tune models for specific tasks, and ensure that training runs smoothly on large-scale datasets.

We covered essential techniques such as gradient accumulation, which simulates larger batch sizes when memory is limited, and mixed precision training, which speeds up training while minimizing memory consumption. Regularization techniques, such as dropout and weight decay, have been discussed to help prevent overfitting, particularly in large transformers. Additionally, the power of transfer learning and few-shot learning was explored, demonstrating how pre-trained models can be adapted to a wide range of domain-specific applications with minimal data.

Finally, we highlighted the importance of distributed training and how techniques such as data parallelism and model parallelism enable efficient training of large transformer models across multiple GPUs or machines. These methods help overcome the computational limitations of individual machines and ensure that large-scale models can be trained in a feasible timeframe.

As we conclude this chapter, you now have a comprehensive understanding of how to train and fine-tune transformer models effectively. With these techniques in your toolkit, you will be well-equipped to implement cutting-edge AI models and adapt them to a wide range of applications, whether for natural language processing, computer vision, speech recognition, or other domains.

In the next chapter, we will explore deploying transformer models, focusing on the strategies and tools necessary to efficiently deploy these models in production environments and make them accessible to end users.

CHAPTER 10
Deploying Transformer Models

Introduction

As powerful as transformer models are during development and training, their real impact is only realized, when they are successfully deployed into production environments. This chapter marks a pivotal transition from model experimentation to real-world application. Deploying transformer models involves unique challenges that differ from training or evaluation, such as latency constraints, memory efficiency, scalability, and data privacy. Whether you are serving a large language model for customer queries, deploying an image recognition transformer on a mobile device, or integrating a speech model into a call center pipeline, robust deployment strategies are essential to ensure high performance and reliability.

From deploying cloud platforms (AWS, GCP, Azure, and so on) to edge devices and serverless environments, this chapter offers practical insights on how to make transformer models accessible, efficient, and production-grade. Additionally, we will look at critical post-deployment concerns such as monitoring, version control, A/B testing, and ensuring data privacy as well as security. We will also explore PyTorch Serve, a flexible and production-ready solution for model serving, along with Docker-based containerization for reproducibility and portability.

Structure

In this chapter, we will cover the following topics:

- Introduction to Model Deployment Challenges and Considerations
- Exporting Transformer Models for Deployment (ONNX and TorchScript)
- Model Optimization Techniques for Inference (Pruning, Quantization, and Distillation)
- Deploying Models with PyTorch Serve
- Serverless Deployment Options for Transformer Models
- Edge Deployment Strategies for Resource-Constrained Devices
- Scaling Transformer Models in Cloud Environments (AWS, GCP, Azure, and so on)
- Monitoring and Logging Deployed Transformer Models
- Model Versioning and A/B Testing of Deployed Models
- Handling Data Privacy and Security in Deployed Transformer Models

Introduction to Model Deployment Challenges and Considerations

Deploying transformer models is a critical step in bringing cutting-edge machine learning solutions, from development environments into real-world applications. While much of the attention in the AI community is focused on training increasingly powerful models, deployment presents a different set of engineering and operational challenges. A well-performing model in a lab setting may behave differently in production, if not deployed with careful consideration of inference latency, memory usage, infrastructure compatibility, and reliability under scale.

Unlike traditional machine learning models, transformer architectures—especially those with hundreds of millions or billions of parameters—can be resource-intensive and sensitive to inference conditions. Their high computational cost can hinder real-time performance, particularly in environments with limited hardware, such as mobile phones, IoT devices, or edge servers. Additionally, factors such as model size, format, and pre/post-processing pipelines must be considered, when moving from notebook-based experimentation to production-scale inference.

Key Challenges in Transformer Model Deployment

- **Latency and Throughput**: In many production settings, especially real-time applications like chatbots, search engines, and recommendation systems, low-latency responses are vital. Transformer models, especially large ones such as GPT or T5, have complex architectures that can cause high inference times. Ensuring that the model delivers predictions quickly and efficiently requires optimizations at both the software and hardware levels.
- **Memory and Compute Requirements**: Transformers consume significant memory and compute power—both during training and inference. Running a large model on a CPU, or on devices, without sufficient GPU/TPU resources, can cause delays or even crashes. Techniques, such as quantization, pruning, and distillation become critical to making these models feasible in constrained environments.
- **Scalability**: As user demand increases, deployed models must scale horizontally (across multiple machines) or vertically (on more powerful hardware). Scaling introduces its own set of challenges: Managing multiple instances, load balancing, and ensuring model consistency across deployments. For large-scale services like AI-powered search or translation engines, cloud-native orchestration (for instance, Kubernetes) is often used to manage deployment pipelines.
- **Portability and Environment Compatibility**: Models developed in a research environment using PyTorch may not be readily usable in other environments (for example, mobile or embedded systems). Exporting models in interoperable formats like ONNX or TorchScript is often necessary for platform compatibility and performance optimization.
- **Monitoring and Reliability**: After deployment, the model must be monitored continuously to ensure that it performs reliably in production. Issues, such as data drift, input anomalies, or infrastructure failures can silently degrade the model performance. Hence, integration with logging, and monitoring tools (such as Prometheus, Grafana, or custom telemetry systems) become essential for the ongoing health checks and diagnostics.
- **Security and Privacy**: When transformer models are deployed in sensitive applications—such as healthcare, finance, or personalized assistants—ensuring data privacy and model integrity is paramount. Encrypting inputs/outputs, complying with data regulations (like GDPR), and preventing adversarial misuse are all critical considerations.

Strategic Considerations Before Deployment

Before deploying a transformer model, it is necessary to assess the target use case and environment, such as:

- Will the model serve real-time or batch inference?
- Is deployment intended for the cloud, edge, or on-device?
- How often will the model need to be updated, retrained, or monitored?
- What level of fault tolerance and redundancy is necessary?

The answers to these questions shape decisions around model format, serving architecture, hardware requirements, and monitoring frameworks. For instance, deploying a multilingual T5 model on a customer support chatbot for a mobile app requires different trade-offs than hosting a distilled BERT model behind a cloud API for document summarization.

Therefore, understanding the challenges involved helps practitioners build systems that are not only accurate, but also robust, performant, and production-ready. In the sections that follow, we will explore the key components of deploying transformer models, starting with how to export trained models in formats like ONNX and TorchScript that are better suited for inference across various platforms.

Exporting Transformer Models for Deployment (ONNX and TorchScript)

Once a transformer model is trained and fine-tuned, the next critical step is exporting the model in a format that can be easily integrated into production environments. This involves converting the model into a format that is both efficient for inference, and compatible across various platforms–whether running on a server, in the cloud, or on edge devices. Two widely used formats for model export are ONNX (Open Neural Network Exchange) and TorchScript, each offering unique advantages in terms of compatibility and performance.

Understanding ONNX and TorchScript

To facilitate efficient and scalable inference, it's essential to understand the export formats–ONNX and TorchScript–that enable seamless deployment across diverse environments.

Open Neural Network Exchange (ONNX)

ONNX is an open-source format developed by Microsoft, Facebook, and other partners that facilitates interoperability between different deep learning frameworks. It allows models trained in one framework such as PyTorch, to be exported and used in other frameworks like TensorFlow, Caffe2, and MXNet. This makes it highly suitable for deploying transformer models across diverse environments.

Key Benefits of ONNX Include:

- **Cross-platform compatibility:** ONNX models can be run in a variety of environments, such as cloud services, edge devices, and on-premise hardware.
- **Optimized inference:** ONNX provides support for accelerated inference on specialized hardware, such as NVIDIA TensorRT, Intel OpenVINO, and Microsoft DirectML, ensuring better performance.

TorchScript

TorchScript is a PyTorch-specific framework for converting models into a form that can be run independently of Python. It allows for serialization of PyTorch models into a graph representation, which can be deployed and executed in production environments, without relying on the Python runtime. This makes TorchScript especially useful for environments, where Python dependencies might be cumbersome or unavailable, such as mobile or embedded systems.

Key Benefits of TorchScript Include:

- **Python-free execution:** TorchScript allows models to run without the Python interpreter, enabling deployment in production environments, where Python is not available.
- **Integration with PyTorch tools**: Since it is a part of the PyTorch ecosystem, TorchScript integrates seamlessly with the existing PyTorch training pipelines and tools.

Thus, TorchScript models can also be optimized for inference with tools like PyTorch's JIT compiler, which improves runtime performance.

Exporting Transformer Models Using ONNX and TorchScript

One of the most common approaches to model deployment is exporting it to the ONNX format, which ensures broad framework interoperability and optimized runtime performance.

Exporting to ONNX

Exporting a PyTorch model to ONNX involves two main steps:

1. **Export the model:** Use PyTorch's built-in **`torch.onnx.export`** function to convert the trained model into the ONNX format.
2. **Optimize the ONNX model:** Use ONNX runtime, or other ONNX-compatible tools for optimization.

Example of Exporting a BERT Model to ONNX

```
import torch
from transformers import AutoModelForSequenceClassification

# Load a pre-trained BERT model
model = AutoModelForSequenceClassification.from_pretrained("bert-base-uncased")

# Set the model to evaluation mode
model.eval()

# Dummy input for export (batch_size, sequence_length)
dummy_input = torch.ones(1, 512, dtype=torch.long)

# Export the model to ONNX format
torch.onnx.export(model, dummy_input, "bert_model.onnx", input_names=
["input_ids"], output_names=["logits"])
```

After the model is exported, it can be loaded and run using ONNX Runtime, an optimized framework for running ONNX models in various environments.

Exporting to TorchScript

To export a model to TorchScript, we use PyTorch's JIT (Just-In-Time) compiler, which converts the model into a static graph representation that can be optimized for faster inference. There are two ways to convert a model to TorchScript:

- **Tracing**: Suitable for models with static control flow. It records the operations performed by the model given a set of inputs.
- **Scripting**: Suitable for models with dynamic control flow. This method converts the model's Python code into an intermediate representation.

Example of Exporting a BERT Model to TorchScript Using Tracing

```
import torch
from transformers import AutoModelForSequenceClassification

# Load a pre-trained BERT model
model = AutoModelForSequenceClassification.from_pretrained("bert-base-uncased")

# Set the model to evaluation mode
model.eval()

# Create a dummy input
dummy_input = torch.ones(1, 512, dtype=torch.long)

# Use tracing to convert the model to TorchScript
traced_model = torch.jit.trace(model, dummy_input)

# Save the TorchScript model
traced_model.save("bert_model_traced.pt")
```

Example of Exporting a BERT Model to TorchScript Using Scripting

```
import torch
from transformers import AutoModelForSequenceClassification

# Load a pre-trained BERT model
model = AutoModelForSequenceClassification.from_pretrained("bert-base-uncased")

# Set the model to evaluation mode
model.eval()

# Use scripting to convert the model to TorchScript
scripted_model = torch.jit.script(model)

# Save the scripted model
scripted_model.save("bert_model_scripted.pt")
```

Key Considerations and Best Practices, When Exporting Models

- **Model Size and Optimization**: When exporting transformer models, model size can become a significant issue, especially in production environments with limited resources (such as edge devices or mobile phones). Techniques like pruning (removing unimportant weights) and quantization (reducing numerical precision) can help reduce the model's memory footprint, without sacrificing much accuracy. Therefore, it is essential to balance model size and performance, when exporting.

- **Compatibility across Platforms**: ONNX provides great flexibility as it can be used across different frameworks and platforms. However, not all operations in PyTorch are currently supported in ONNX. Therefore, careful inspection of model compatibility with the target deployment platform is crucial. When using TorchScript, be aware that some dynamic operations in PyTorch (for instance, certain loops or conditionals) may not be supported by tracing, and might require scripting.
- **Inference Speed**: Both ONNX and TorchScript are optimized for efficient inference, but specific optimizations–such as ONNX Runtime optimizations or TorchScript JIT compilation–should be considered to ensure that the model performs optimally during deployment. Using hardware acceleration tools like TensorRT, ONNX Runtime, or PyTorch's own TorchScript optimizations can significantly reduce latency.

Practical Examples and Use Cases for ONNX and TorchScript

ONNX

- **Cross-Platform Deployment:** ONNX is particularly useful, when a model trained in PyTorch needs to be deployed on a platform that supports TensorFlow or Caffe2. For instance, a model trained in PyTorch can be exported to ONNX, and deployed in TensorFlow Lite for mobile applications.
- **Accelerated Inference:** ONNX models can be run on NVIDIA GPUs, using TensorRT, significantly speeding up inference for high-throughput applications like real-time translation or search ranking.

TorchScript

- **Mobile Deployment:** TorchScript is ideal for deploying transformer models on mobile devices, such as those running iOS and Android. Using PyTorch's TorchScript API, models like BERT and GPT can be converted into a mobile-compatible format, optimizing them for on-device inference.
- **Edge Devices:** For environments with limited computational resources, such as IoT devices or Raspberry Pi, TorchScript enables efficient deployment, without the need for a Python runtime, making it ideal for low-latency edge applications like real-time speech recognition.

Exporting transformer models for deployment in formats, such as ONNX and TorchScript is a crucial step in ensuring that the model performs efficiently and reliably in production environments. These formats provide significant advantages in terms of platform compatibility, inference speed, and hardware optimization. By leveraging ONNX and TorchScript, developers can easily move from training to production, ensuring that transformer models are accessible across various platforms and devices.

In the next section, we will explore model optimization techniques, such as pruning, quantization, and distillation, which further enhance the efficiency and deployability of transformer models, allowing them to run on resource-constrained environments, such as mobile and edge devices.

Model Optimization Techniques for Inference (Pruning, Quantization, Distillation)

As transformer models continue to grow in size and complexity, deploying them in production environments becomes increasingly challenging, especially for resource-constrained devices, such as mobile phones, IoT devices, and edge servers. These devices often lack the computational power and memory capacity needed to run large models efficiently. Thus, to address these limitations, model optimization techniques like pruning, quantization, and distillation are crucial for reducing the memory footprint, improving inference speed, and ensuring that transformer models can run smoothly on a wide range of hardware.

Why Model Optimization Is Necessary for Efficient Inference

Transformer models like BERT, GPT, and T5 have become standard in various AI applications due to their state-of-the-art performance across tasks such as natural language processing, computer vision, and speech recognition. However, the trade-off for their impressive capabilities is their large model size, and high computational demands. These challenges make deploying transformers on edge devices, cloud services, or real-time applications difficult, particularly in scenarios with limited memory and low-latency requirements.

The Need for Optimization

Model optimization ensures that the inference process is not only accurate, but also efficient. Thus, by reducing the computational cost and memory requirements of transformer models, we can deploy them in real-world applications, without compromising performance. This allows for:

- Faster inference in real-time applications (for example, chatbots, live translation, and so on).
- Reduced power consumption, especially critical for battery-powered devices like smartphones.
- Lower hardware requirements, making it feasible to deploy models on edge devices with limited computational resources.

Optimization techniques such as pruning, quantization, and distillation are commonly used in combination to achieve these goals, without sacrificing the model's ability to generalize and perform well on unseen data.

Pruning: Removing Redundant Weights to Reduce Model Size

Pruning is a technique, where unnecessary weights or parameters in a model are removed to reduce its size, and improve inference efficiency. The goal is to retain the most critical parameters, while discarding those that contribute little to the model's performance. This is particularly effective in transformer models, where a significant portion of the parameters might be redundant or inactive after fine-tuning.

How Pruning Works

Pruning typically involves the following steps:

1. **Identify unimportant weights:** Weights are ranked, based on their importance, often using metrics like magnitude (the absolute value of the weight) or gradient-based methods (weights with smaller gradients during training are less important).

2. **Remove the least important weights:** Weights with lower importance are set to zero, reducing the model's overall size.

3. **Fine-tune the pruned model**: After pruning, the model is usually fine-tuned to recover any potential loss in accuracy.

Benefits of Pruning

- **Reduced model size:** Pruned models have fewer parameters, making them more efficient for deployment on memory-limited devices.
- **Faster inference:** Removing redundant weights reduces the computational load, leading to faster predictions.

Example of Pruning: When fine-tuning a model like BERT, pruning can reduce the number of layers or attention heads in the transformer. For instance, removing attention heads that contribute little to the output can help lower memory requirements, while maintaining accuracy.

Quantization: Reducing Numerical Precision for Faster Inference

Quantization is the process of reducing the precision of the weights and activations in the model, typically from 32-bit Floating Point (FP32) to 16-bit or 8-bit Integers (INT8). This reduces, both memory consumption and computation time, leading to faster inference, particularly in hardware with support for low-precision arithmetic (for example, TPUs and specialized accelerators).

How Quantization Works

Quantization works by mapping a wide range of floating-point values to a smaller range of integers. **For example:**

- **FP32**: A 32-bit representation which uses floating point numbers to represent large ranges of values.
- **INT8**: An 8-bit representation that uses integers to represent a more limited range.

Benefits of Quantization

- **Reduced memory footprint:** With lower-precision values, the model requires significantly less memory.
- **Faster inference:** Lower precision computations require less hardware power, and can speed up inference, especially when running on specialized hardware that supports INT8 operations.
- **Increased throughput:** Quantized models can process more requests per second due to reduced resource demands.

Example of Quantization

Consider a large GPT-3 model: Applying INT8 quantization can reduce its memory usage by 75%, allowing it to run on more accessible hardware, while retaining most of its performance.

Distillation: Transferring Knowledge from Large Models to Smaller Models

Distillation is a technique, where the knowledge learned by a large, pre-trained model (called the teacher model) is transferred to a smaller model (called the student model). The student model is trained to match the outputs of the teacher model, enabling it to achieve similar performance with far fewer parameters. This technique is particularly useful, when working with large transformer models such as BERT or GPT, which can be too slow or memory-intensive for deployment in production environments.

How Distillation Works

1. **Train a large teacher model:** The teacher model is trained on a large corpus, and performs the task with high accuracy.
2. **Transfer knowledge to the student model:** The student model is initialized with fewer parameters, and trained to imitate the behavior of the teacher, often by matching the soft predictions (for instance, the probability distributions over classes), rather than just hard labels.
3. **Fine-tune the student model:** After the initial training, the student model is fine-tuned on the task-specific data to further improve performance.

Benefits of Distillation

- **Smaller and faster models:** The student model is much smaller than the teacher model, leading to lower memory usage and faster inference.
- **Minimal loss in performance:** The student model can perform similarly to the teacher model, even with fewer parameters.

Example of Distillation: For instance, a large BERT-Large model can be distilled into a smaller version like DistilBERT, which retains over 97% of the performance of the original model, but with 60% fewer parameters and faster inference.

Practical Use Cases for Model Optimization Techniques

- **Deploying on Mobile Devices**: Transformer models, such as BERT or T5, are too large to run efficiently on mobile devices. Through pruning and quantization, the models can be optimized for low-latency applications like real-time text classification or sentiment analysis.
- **Edge Computing for IoT Devices**: For IoT and edge applications like smart home assistants or autonomous vehicles, model distillation can be used to deploy lighter versions of transformer models. Quantization and pruning can further optimize these models for devices with limited computational power.
- **Cloud-Based NLP Services**: In cloud environments, large-scale models, such as GPT-3 are often deployed for real-time APIs. Quantization helps improve throughput, while maintaining quality, and distillation ensures that the models are efficient enough to handle millions of requests per second.

Model optimization techniques such as pruning, quantization, and distillation are essential for ensuring that transformer models can be deployed efficiently in production environments. By reducing model size, improving inference speed, and maintaining high performance, these techniques make it possible to run large, complex models on resource-constrained devices, and in cloud environments.

In the next section, we will explore how to deploy optimized models, using tools like PyTorch Serve for real-time applications, enabling the seamless integration of transformers into production pipelines.

Deploying Models with PyTorch Serve

Once transformer models are trained and optimized, the next crucial step is deployment, where they are made accessible for inference in production environments. PyTorch Serve is a powerful, flexible tool designed for deploying PyTorch models at scale. It provides a seamless pipeline for serving machine learning models as APIs, making it easier to integrate into production systems. In this section, we will explore how to deploy transformer models using PyTorch Serve, the benefits it offers, and the key considerations, when setting up a deployment pipeline.

Understanding PyTorch Serve

PyTorch Serve is an open-source model serving framework that allows you to serve PyTorch models as REST APIs or gRPC endpoints, enabling easy integration with web applications or microservices. It offers an easy-to-use interface for deploying models, handling requests, and managing multiple models in production (*Figure 10.1*).

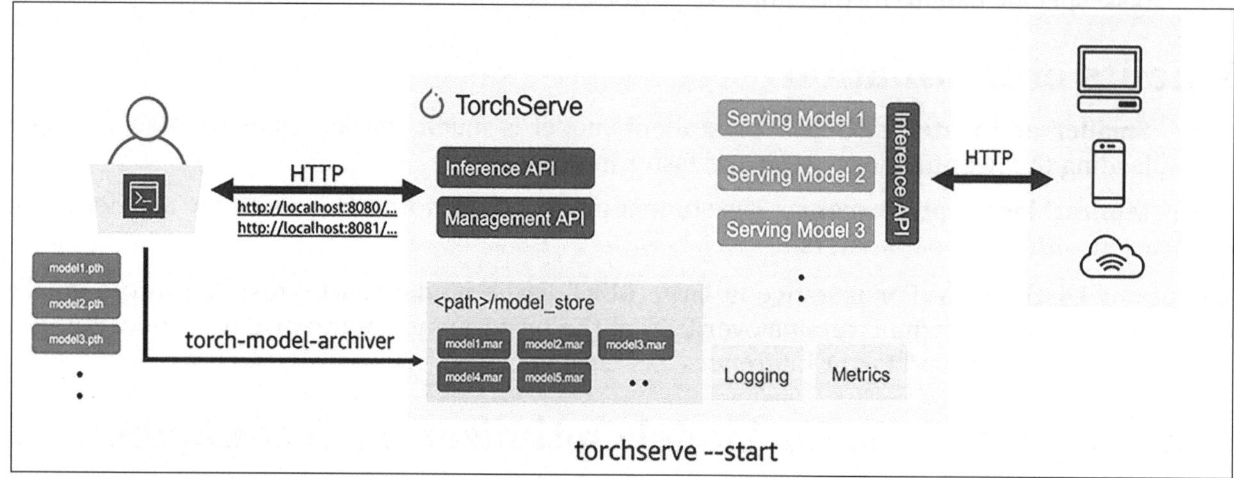

Figure 10.1: *Torch Serve*

Key Features of PyTorch Serve

1. **Model Management:** PyTorch Serve supports dynamic model loading and versioning, allowing you to easily deploy, update, and switch between models.
2. **Scalability:** It supports multi-model deployment, and can handle high-throughput inference with low-latency, making it suitable for large-scale production environments.
3. **Extensibility:** You can easily add custom pre-processing, post-processing, and inference logic, making PyTorch Serve adaptable to different use cases.
4. **Metrics and Monitoring:** Built-in support for metrics logging (for example, inference time, success rates, and so on) as well as integration with monitoring tools like Prometheus.

PyTorch Serve allows developers to deploy their models with minimal effort, focusing on inference tasks, while PyTorch Serve handles all the scaling, monitoring, and request handling.

Setting Up PyTorch Serve for Model Deployment

1. **Install PyTorch Serve**

Before deploying a model, the first step is to install PyTorch Serve and torch-model-archiver (for packaging models).

```
pip install torchserve torch-model-archiver
```

Therefore, TorchServe package provides the server to run the models, while torch-model-archiver helps in packaging the trained model into a format, suitable for serving.

2. **Prepare Your Model for Deployment**

To deploy a transformer model, using PyTorch Serve, the model must be serialized into a format that PyTorch Serve can understand. This typically involves converting your trained PyTorch model into **a.mar** (model archive) file, which includes the model weights, the model's inference logic, and any custom handler functions.

For example, let us say, we have a BERT model fine-tuned for text classification. To deploy it using PyTorch Serve, we need to perform the following steps:

a. Export the model to TorchScript (or any other suitable format) if necessary.

b. Package the model, using torch-model-archiver.

Example of Model Export and Packaging:

```
# Assuming the BERT model is fine-tuned and saved
torch-model-archiver --model-name bert-text-classifier \
                     --version 1.0 \
                     --serialized-file ./bert_model.pt \
                     --handler text_classifier_handler.py \
                     --extra-files "./config.json, vocab.txt"
```

This command creates **a.mar** file that PyTorch Serve can load and serve. The handler file (**text_classifier_handler.py**) is where you define the pre-processing, inference, and post-processing steps, ensuring that the model is served correctly. The extra-files argument is used to include vocabulary files, or any other model-specific resources.

3. **Start PyTorch Serve**

Once the model is packaged, you can start PyTorch Serve to deploy the model. This is done by specifying the model store (where **the.mar** files are stored), and the model to be served.

```
torchserve --start --model-store model_store --models bert-text-classifier
=bert-text-classifier.mar
```

This command starts the PyTorch Serve instance, and loads the BERT model as a web service. The model is now accessible via a REST API or gRPC endpoint for making inference requests.

Handling Requests and Inference

After deploying the model, the next step is to handle incoming requests and generate predictions through inference.

Making Inference Requests

Once the model is deployed, you can make inference requests by sending HTTP requests to the PyTorch Serve API. Here is an example of how to send a POST request to the deployed model, using Python's requests library:

```
import requests

url = "http://localhost:8080/predictions/bert-text-classifier"
data = {"text": "This is an example sentence for classification."}

response = requests.post(url, json=data)

print(response.json())  # Output the model's prediction
```

In this example, the model is served at http://localhost:8080/predictions/bert-text-classifier, and you send a JSON payload, with the text for classification. The model responds with the prediction.

Scaling with Multiple Models

PyTorch Serve supports multi-model deployment, meaning you can deploy several models simultaneously, and expose them under different endpoints. This is particularly useful, when you need to serve different models (for instance, BERT for sentiment analysis, and T5 for text summarization) at the same time.

```
torchserve --start --model-store model_store --models model1=bert-text-
classifier.mar --models model2=t5-summarization.mar
```

This will make two models available at two different endpoints:

- http://localhost:8080/predictions/model1
- http://localhost:8080/predictions/model2

Model Versioning and Updates

With PyTorch Serve, you can easily handle model versioning. If you train a newer version of the model or make adjustments, you can update the model served by PyTorch Serve, without requiring downtime. By specifying the model version during the setup, you can replace old models with new versions seamlessly.

```
torchserve --stop --models bert-text-classifier
torchserve --start --model-store model_store --models bert-text-
classifier=bert-v2.mar
```

Monitoring and Metrics

To ensure the smooth operation of your deployed models, PyTorch Serve includes built-in metrics collection, and monitoring capabilities. PyTorch Serve exposes several metrics via a Prometheus-compatible interface, allowing you to track important parameters, such as:

- Inference time
- Request count
- Error rates

You can also integrate these metrics with popular monitoring tools such as Grafana and Prometheus to get real-time insights into the performance of your deployed model.

Thus, deploying transformer models using PyTorch Serve allows you to efficiently serve models as APIs, ensuring that your state-of-the-art AI is accessible and scalable in real-world production environments. PyTorch Serve simplifies the deployment process with support for multi-model deployments, version control, scalability, and easy model updates. By using REST APIs or gRPC endpoints, it integrates seamlessly with other production systems, enabling the real-time application of transformer models across industries.

In the next section, we will explore containerization of transformer models using Docker, allowing us to easily deploy models across different environments, and manage dependencies more effectively.

Serverless Deployment Options for Transformer Models

The evolution of cloud computing has paved the way for serverless architectures, which have become increasingly popular for deploying machine learning models, including transformer models. Serverless deployment abstracts away the complexity of managing infrastructure, allowing developers to focus entirely on writing and deploying code, without worrying about server management, scalability, or availability. This chapter explores serverless deployment options for transformer models, highlighting the benefits, challenges, and practical approaches to using serverless architectures for serving AI models.

In this section, we will cover:

- What is serverless computing, and why is it beneficial for deploying transformer models?
- Key cloud providers offering serverless options for model deployment (AWS Lambda, Google Cloud Functions, and Azure Functions)
- How to deploy transformer models in serverless environments?
- Considerations for using serverless deployment
- Real-world use cases and examples

Understanding Serverless Computing, and Its Benefits for Deploying Transformer Models

Serverless computing allows you to run applications, without provisioning or managing physical servers. Instead of manually configuring virtual machines or containers, you use a cloud service provider that automatically manages the computing resources for you. Serverless functions are event-driven, meaning they execute only in response to specific triggers, such as an API request or an incoming data stream.

Why Serverless for Transformer Models?

Transformer models, particularly those used for tasks such as text generation, language translation, and speech recognition, often require significant computing resources, making their deployment on traditional infrastructure a challenge. Serverless computing provides several key advantages for deploying these models:

- **Automatic Scaling:** Serverless platforms can automatically scale up or down based on demand, allowing you to handle a large number of inference requests, without manual intervention. This is particularly useful for transformer models that may experience fluctuating traffic.
- **Cost Efficiency:** In serverless architectures, you pay only for the compute time used during the execution of a function, making it more cost-effective than maintaining always-on servers.
- **Simplified Operations:** Serverless abstracts away infrastructure management tasks such as scaling, patching, and load balancing, allowing you to focus on building and deploying your transformer models quickly.

Key Cloud Providers Offering Serverless Options for Model Deployment

Several major cloud providers offer serverless compute services that can be used for deploying transformer models. Here is an overview of the most popular options:

AWS Lambda

AWS Lambda is one of the most widely used serverless computing services. It lets you run the code, without provisioning or managing servers. Lambda is ideal for deploying lightweight models or integrating with other AWS services, such as S3 (storage), SQS (queue management), or API Gateway for API-based interaction.

Use case: Deploying small transformer models or inference services for real-time applications like chatbots or document classification.

Google Cloud Functions

Google Cloud Functions is a serverless execution environment that enables you to run small pieces of code in response to events, such as HTTP requests, Cloud Pub/Sub messages, or changes in Cloud Storage.

Use case: You can deploy transformer models for real-time inference in Natural Language Processing (NLP) or image recognition tasks where cloud-based integration with Google Cloud Storage or BigQuery is required.

Azure Functions

Azure Functions is Microsoft's serverless computing service. Similar to AWS Lambda, it allows you to deploy small, stateless functions that are triggered by events. You can integrate Azure Functions with services, such as Azure Blob Storage or Event Grid for event-driven inference.

Use case: Text-to-speech models or multi-modal AI services that need to be integrated with Azure's ecosystem, such as Azure Cognitive Services.

How to Deploy Transformer Models in Serverless Environments

Deploying transformer models in serverless environments involves a few key steps, such as model export, function creation, and integration with cloud services.

Step 1: Export the Pre-Trained Model

Before deploying your transformer model, it must be exported into a deployable format. Typically, this involves:

- **TorchScript:** Convert the model to TorchScript for PyTorch-based models.
- **ONNX:** Export the model to ONNX for cross-platform compatibility.

Example:

```
import torch
from transformers import AutoModelForSequenceClassification

# Load a pre-trained BERT model
model = AutoModelForSequenceClassification.from_pretrained('bert-base-uncased')
```

```
# Convert model to TorchScript
model.eval()
dummy_input = torch.ones(1, 512, dtype=torch.long)
traced_model = torch.jit.trace(model, dummy_input)
traced_model.save("bert_model.pt")
```

Once the model is exported, it can be uploaded to cloud storage (for instance, AWS S3, Google Cloud Storage) and then accessed by the serverless function.

Step 2: Create the Serverless Function

A serverless function is typically triggered by HTTP requests (via API Gateway) or events (for example, file uploads, and so on). You will define the function to load the model from the cloud storage, and perform inference.

Here is an example of a simple AWS Lambda function for model inference:

```
import torch
import json
from transformers import AutoTokenizer, AutoModelForSequenceClassification

def lambda_handler(event, context):
    # Load pre-trained model and tokenizer
    model = AutoModelForSequenceClassification.from_pretrained('s3://my-bucket/
bert_model.pt')
    tokenizer = AutoTokenizer.from_pretrained('bert-base-uncased')

    # Parse input text from the event
    input_text = event["text"]
    inputs = tokenizer(input_text, return_tensors="pt")

    # Inference
    with torch.no_grad():
        outputs = model(**inputs)
        logits = outputs.logits

    # Return the result
    return {
        'statusCode': 200,
        'body': json.dumps({'prediction': logits.argmax().item()})
    }
```

This Lambda function loads the model from an S3 bucket, performs inference on the input text, and returns the predicted class.

Step 3: Set Up API Gateway (Optional)

To make your transformer model accessible via HTTP, use AWS API Gateway or equivalent cloud service to create an API endpoint that triggers your function. This allows other applications to send requests to the model in real time.

Considerations for Using Serverless Deployment

Serverless deployment brings a spectrum of challenges, making it essential to carefully evaluate these considerations, during the system design phase.

- **Cold Start Latency**: Serverless functions often experience cold start latency, which is the delay that occurs, when a function is called for the first time after being idle. Since transformers are large and complex models, this latency may be noticeable in production environments. One strategy to mitigate this is to pre-warm functions, or keep them warm by periodically invoking them.

- **Execution Time Limits**: Serverless platforms often have execution time limits for functions. For example, AWS Lambda functions typically have a maximum execution time of 15 minutes. This can be problematic for inference, with large transformer models that may take longer than the allotted time for processing.
- **Memory Constraints**: While serverless functions scale automatically, they still have memory limits. For example, AWS Lambda has a maximum memory allocation of 10 GB which may not be enough for large transformer models. Therefore, it is crucial to optimize your models for memory efficiency by techniques, such as quantization, pruning, or distillation to ensure that they fit within the memory constraints.
- **Scalability:** Serverless platforms automatically scale to handle spikes in traffic, but at a cost. If the function is heavily used, the cost can increase significantly. Consider cost implications, when deploying large models, and use auto-scaling tools to balance between performance and cost.

Real-World Use Cases and Examples

Real-Time Speech Recognition: A speech-to-text model (like Wav2Vec 2.0) deployed in a serverless environment can be used to transcribe audio in real time. Serverless deployment ensures that the service can scale based on demand, making it ideal for applications, such as customer service transcription or live captioning.

Chatbots and Virtual Assistants: Transformer models such as GPT-3 or T5 can be deployed serverless to power AI-driven chatbots that generate responses in real-time based on user input. Serverless functions allow for scalability during high user traffic periods, and provide a cost-effective solution as the function is only invoked, when needed.

Serverless deployment offers a scalable and cost-effective solution for deploying transformer models, particularly in production environments, where quick inference and minimal infrastructure management are important. With platforms such as AWS Lambda, Google Cloud Functions, and Azure Functions, transformer models can be seamlessly integrated into production workflows, whether for real-time AI services or batch processing.

In the next section, we will explore edge deployment strategies for running transformer models on resource-constrained devices, allowing us to bring AI-powered models closer to end users for low-latency, and offline applications.

Edge Deployment Strategies for Resource-Constrained Devices

As transformer models grow in capability, the desire to deploy them directly on edge devices, such as smartphones, microcontrollers, embedded systems, and IoT sensors—has grown significantly. Edge deployment allows models to run locally, closer to the data source, enabling real-time inference, offline access, and enhanced data privacy. However, this comes with a set of challenges, primarily because transformers are compute-and memory-intensive, while edge devices are typically limited in processing power, memory, and battery life.

This chapter explores strategies to effectively deploy transformer models on edge devices, discussing optimization techniques, tooling support, deployment flows, and real-world use cases.

Advantages of Deploying Transformer Models at the Edge

Deploying models at the edge brings several tangible benefits:

- **Low Latency:** Since data does not have to be sent to a remote server, response time is faster—critical for applications like voice assistants, object detection, or gesture recognition.
- **Privacy Preservation:** Keeping data on the device ensures that the sensitive user data does not leave the local environment, making edge AI a good fit for healthcare, personal finance, and smart home applications.
- **Offline Functionality:** Models can operate without internet access, ensuring service continuity in remote areas or during outages.
- **Reduced Bandwidth Use:** Since inference is local, edge deployment reduces the need to transmit large volumes of data to the cloud.

Key Challenges in Edge Deployment

Despite the benefits, transformer models pose significant deployment challenges on the edge due to:

- Model size (hundreds of millions to billions of parameters).
- Memory and compute limitations (especially on microcontrollers or mobile devices).
- Energy constraints (battery-operated devices need power-efficient models).

To overcome these challenges, developers must adopt targeted strategies that optimize both the model and the runtime environment.

Use Lightweight Transformer Architectures

Instead of deploying standard transformer variants, such as BERT-base or GPT-2, consider lightweight or distilled versions designed specifically for constrained hardware.

- **DistilBERT:** A compressed version of BERT that retains ~97% of its performance, but is 40% smaller and 60% faster.
- **TinyBERT:** Optimized for mobile and edge use cases, especially suitable for classification and NER tasks.
- **MobileBERT:** A mobile-optimized BERT variant that achieves low latency, without significant accuracy trade-off.

These architectures are ideal candidates for edge scenarios, such as smartphone NLP tasks, voice command interpretation, or real-time translation.

Apply Model Compression Techniques

To further optimize models, three core compression techniques are widely used:

- **Quantization**: Reduces precision of model weights and activations (for example, from FP32 to INT8), significantly decreasing memory, and compute load. Some frameworks even support post-training quantization, which requires no model retraining.
- **Pruning**: Removes weights or attention heads that contribute little to the model's predictions, reducing the computational graph's complexity. This can be done structurally (for instance, whole neurons) or unstructured (individual weights).
- **Knowledge Distillation**: A smaller "*student*" model is trained to replicate the behavior of a larger "*teacher*" model, resulting in a compact model that mimics the accuracy of its full-sized counterpart.

These techniques can be used in combination to shrink model size by 50%–90%, making them deployable on devices with <1 GB of RAM.

Use Efficient Inference Frameworks

Several inference engines are tailored to support optimized transformer models on mobile and edge hardware:

- **ONNX Runtime Mobile:** A lightweight version of ONNX Runtime designed for Android/iOS, supporting quantized models and accelerators (for example, NNAPI).
- **TensorFlow Lite (TFLite):** Offers support for MobileBERT, TinyBERT, and custom transformer models, with optimized execution on ARM CPUs and NPUs.
- **TorchScript:** PyTorch models exported with TorchScript can be integrated into Android/iOS apps, with the PyTorch Mobile runtime.
- **TVM and Apache Tengine:** Open-source compilers that transform deep learning models into optimized binaries for specific hardware like ARM Cortex chips.

These runtimes provide hardware acceleration, support for low-bit operations, and cross-platform portability, helping developers deploy once, and run everywhere.

Optimize for Specific Hardware Targets

Different edge devices support different compute environments:

- **Android Phones:** Use NNAPI for acceleration; integrate models with ONNX Runtime Mobile or TFLite.
- **iPhones/iPads:** Use Core ML and Metal Performance Shaders for optimized inference.
- **Raspberry Pi:** Target ARMv7/v8 CPUs; use lightweight runtimes, such as TFLite or ONNX Runtime with quantized models.
- **Edge TPUs (for instance, Coral):** Convert models to TFLite, and compile them using Edge TPU Compiler.

  Pro Tip: Always benchmark models on actual devices, using profiling tools, such as Android Profiler, Core ML Tools, or Edge TPU Benchmarking Tool to ensure the expected performance.

Real-World Use Cases

- **Smart Assistants (NLP on Mobile):** A quantized version of TinyBERT or DistilBERT is deployed on phones to perform intent classification, or wake-word detection. The model runs locally, offering instant response, and preserving user privacy.
- **Visual AI on Cameras**: Vision Transformers (ViTs) are distilled and quantized to run on smart surveillance cameras for anomaly detection or license plate recognition, without uploading frames to the cloud.
- **Speech Models on Edge Devices**: Lightweight transformer-based speech recognition models (example, distilled Wav2Vec) run on embedded devices such as smart speakers to transcribe voice commands in real time.

Edge deployment of transformer models is no longer aspirational–it is achievable, and increasingly essential. By choosing compact architectures, applying compression techniques, leveraging optimized runtimes, and targeting hardware-aware deployments, developers can bring the power of transformers to the edge.

So, whether you are building offline NLP tools, real-time visual AI, or privacy-conscious speech interfaces, the strategies outlined in this chapter enable you to create low-latency, efficient, and scalable edge AI applications, with the power of transformers.

In the next chapter, we will explore how to scale transformer deployments in cloud environments, enabling you to handle high-demand workloads across distributed infrastructure.

Scaling Transformer Models in Cloud Environments (AWS, GCP, and Azure)

As transformer models become more central to enterprise AI pipelines, scaling them in cloud environments has become essential for handling high volumes of inference requests, training on large datasets, and deploying real-time services across the globe. Unlike edge deployment, which focuses on low-power devices, cloud environments offer on-demand compute power, flexible storage, and global scalability, making them ideal for serving resource-intensive transformer workloads.

This chapter explores strategies to efficiently scale transformer models, using Amazon Web Services (AWS), Google Cloud Platform (GCP), and Microsoft Azure, covering infrastructure options, model orchestration, auto-scaling, and cost-effective best practices.

The Need for Scaling Transformers in the Cloud

Transformer models, particularly large-scale variants, such as GPT, T5, or BERT, require multi-GPU clusters, high-throughput storage, and efficient orchestration to serve thousands (or millions) of users.

Cloud platforms offer:

- **Elastic compute resources:** Spin up GPU/TPU instances, only when needed.
- **Global availability:** Deploy services closer to users for lower latency.
- **Integrated ML tooling:** Use services, such as SageMaker (AWS), Vertex AI (GCP), or Azure Machine Learning to handle training, tuning, and deployment.

Therefore, Cloud Scaling is especially critical for applications like chatbots, document summarization services, real-time translators, and recommendation engines–where response time, availability, and throughput matter.

Infrastructure Options across Cloud Providers

AWS

- **Amazon SageMaker:** A fully managed service that supports training, tuning, and deploying transformer models on GPU-backed instances. It includes features, such as endpoint autoscaling, batch transform, and multi-model deployment.
- **ECS/EKS:** Deploy Dockerized transformer models using ECS (Elastic Container Service) or EKS (Elastic Kubernetes Service), with autoscaling policies.
- **Inferentia/Trainium:** AWS's custom chips for deep learning inference/training–offer cost-efficient scaling for large models.

GCP

- **Vertex AI:** A unified platform for deploying, training, and monitoring models. It supports TPU-backed training, batch predictions, and scaling deployments automatically, based on traffic.

- **Cloud Run and GKE:** Use Cloud Run for stateless containerized inference, or GKE (Google Kubernetes Engine) for more complex orchestration.
- **TPUs:** Exclusive to GCP, TPUs offer fast training/inference for large transformer workloads, such as T5, BERT, and PaLM.

Azure

- **Azure Machine Learning:** Offers endpoints, managed inference clusters, and auto-scaling. It supports transformer model training on NC-series VMs and deployment on AKS.
- **Azure Container Apps:** For serverless deployment, with automatic scaling and cost control.
- **ONNX Runtime with DirectML:** Enables optimized inference on Windows-based virtual machines, and edge endpoints.

Strategies for Efficient Scaling

Strategies for efficient scaling leverage model and pipeline parallelism, auto-scaling with intelligent load balancing, and multi-model endpoints to optimize performance, and reduce infrastructure costs.

- **Use Model Parallelism and Pipeline Parallelism**: For very large transformer models that do not fit on a single GPU, use model parallelism (splitting the model across GPUs) and pipeline parallelism (processing different layers concurrently). Frameworks such as DeepSpeed (Azure), SageMaker Model Parallelism, and GCP's TPU Mesh enable this.
- **Auto-scaling with Load Balancing**: Cloud services support auto-scaling, based on CPU/GPU utilization, request volume, or custom metrics. Combine this with load balancers (for example, AWS ALB and GCP Load Balancer) to ensure reliable routing and failover.
- **Multi-model Endpoints**: Instead of deploying each model on a separate instance, use multi-model endpoints (for example, SageMaker or Azure ML) to dynamically load/unload models, based on traffic, and reducing idle compute cost.

Best Practices for Scalable Cloud Deployment

- Containerize your models, using Docker to ensure portability across clouds.
- Use ONNX or TorchScript formats for optimized inference performance.
- Monitor latency and throughput, using native tools, such as CloudWatch, Stackdriver, or Azure Monitor.
- Cache frequent results, using services like Redis or Memcached to reduce duplicate inference calls.
- Store inputs/outputs in cloud storage (for instance, S3, GCS, Blob, and so on) for traceability and offline processing.

Scaling transformer models in the cloud is no longer a luxury–it is a necessity for delivering real-time, reliable, and scalable AI services to end users. Hence, whether you are using AWS SageMaker, GCP Vertex AI, or Azure ML, cloud platforms offer the flexibility to train, deploy, and auto-scale transformer models, with minimal manual effort. By combining efficient infrastructure, model optimization, and orchestration, developers can ensure that their transformer models are ready for production-level demand.

In the next section, we will explore how to monitor and log deployed transformer models, ensuring that performance, reliability, and security remain intact in live environments.

Monitoring and Logging Deployed Transformer Models

Once a transformer model is deployed–whether in the cloud, on the edge, or via a serverless function–monitoring and logging become necessary. Unlike in training and testing phases, real-world usage introduces a new range of variables, such as: unexpected input patterns, latency spikes, infrastructure failures, or model drift. Without robust monitoring, these issues can silently degrade your model's performance, reliability, and user experience.

This chapter focuses on the why, what, and how of monitoring and logging transformer models, covering key tools and strategies to ensure observability in production deployments.

Why Monitoring Matters

Transformer models often serve mission-critical roles: Powering chatbots, summarizing documents, recommending products, or transcribing voice input. If they fail silently–producing incorrect outputs or becoming unresponsive–the business impact can be significant.

Monitoring helps you:

- Detect issues proactively (for example, latency spikes, failed inferences, data anomalies, and so on)
- Track model performance over time (for instance, accuracy, precision, and recall on live data)
- Ensure uptime and scalability under varying load conditions.
- Enable rollback or retraining, if drift or degradation is observed.

Logging, on the other hand, provides the granular audit trail necessary to debug failures, analyze inputs/outputs, and ensure compliance (for instance, in regulated industries).

What to Monitor

Here are the key aspects, you should monitor in a deployed transformer model:

- **System Metrics**
    - CPU/GPU utilization
    - Memory usage
    - Disk I/O and network latency
    - Throughput (requests per second)

These help ensure that your infrastructure is operating efficiently, and can scale when needed.

- **Inference Performance**
    - Latency per request
    - Success/failure rates
    - Model load time (especially for large transformer models)
    - Batch processing times (if applicable)
- **Model Quality**
    - Prediction confidence scores
    - Distribution of outputs over time (for example, is the model skewed toward certain classes?)

    - Input distribution compared to the training data (to detect drift)
    - Real-time accuracy, where possible (for example, by comparing predictions to the delayed ground truth)
- **User Behavior**
    - Drop-off rates (for example, in a chatbot, users abandoning sessions after poor responses)
    - API usage patterns
    - Region-specific latency or error trends

Key Logging Strategies

Logs serve as the "*black box recorder*" of your model's behavior. Here is what to log:

- Input data (sanitized for privacy)
- Output predictions and confidence scores
- Timestamps and user/request metadata
- Model version and parameters
- Pre- and post-processing steps
- Error messages and stack traces

Thus, to prevent log overload, implement log sampling or rate limiting, especially for high-traffic endpoints.

Tools for Monitoring and Logging

Cloud-native monitoring suites:

- **AWS:** CloudWatch + SageMaker Model Monitor
- **GCP:** Stackdriver + Vertex AI Monitoring
- **Azure:** Azure Monitor + Azure ML Model Monitoring

Thus, these offer pre-integrated dashboards, alerts, and metrics for model endpoints.

Open-source and hybrid tools:

- **Prometheus + Grafana:** For custom metrics collection and visualizations.
- **ELK stack (Elasticsearch, Logstash, Kibana):** For log aggregation and search.
- **OpenTelemetry:** For structured observability data (traces, logs, metrics, and so on).
- **MLflow:** Useful for logging model versions, parameters, and performance.

Real-World Example: Monitoring a BERT-Based API

Imagine deploying a BERT-based API for document classification. You might set up:

- A CloudWatch alarm, if latency exceeds 400ms on average.
- A Grafana dashboard showing live inference throughput and memory use.
- A BigQuery job to periodically sample predictions, and compare label distributions.
- Error logs to capture input samples, where the API fails or returns low-confidence outputs.

Best Practices

- **Version everything:** Always log which model version served which prediction.

- **Monitor inputs for drift:** Tools like Alibi Detect or Fiddler can help catch distributional changes.
- **Use alerts sparingly:** Avoid alert fatigue; use meaningful thresholds.
- **Secure your logs:** Sanitize Personally Identifiable Information (PII), and control access to logs.
- **Correlate with business metrics:** Align model performance with product KPIs (for example, conversions, satisfaction scores, and so on).

Monitoring and logging are the guardrails of reliable AI deployments. For transformer models, which often carry large computational and user-experience stakes, observability is not optional–it is essential. With proper tooling and discipline, you can ensure that your models remain robust, explainable, and performant over time, even as data, users, and infrastructure evolve.

In the next section, we shall explore model versioning and A/B testing, enabling you to experiment safely with new transformer models in production, without disrupting user experience.

Model Versioning and A/B Testing of Deployed Transformer Models

As transformer models evolve rapidly through fine-tuning, retraining, or optimization, managing multiple versions, and evaluating their impact becomes crucial. Without a structured versioning strategy and robust experimentation methods, such as A/B testing, deploying updated models can lead to regressions, unexpected behavior, or missed opportunities for improvement. In this chapter, we explore how to systematically manage versions of transformer models, and implement safe, data-driven A/B testing strategies in production environments.

The Importance of Model Versioning

Model versioning involves assigning unique identifiers to each deployed model, allowing you to:

- **Track model lineage:** from raw data and preprocessing to training configuration and hyperparameters.
- **Audit predictions:** essential for regulated domains like finance or healthcare.
- **Roll back safely:** If a newer model underperforms in production.
- **Compare performance over time:** Using live data to determine real-world effectiveness.

In complex deployments, particularly where multiple models are deployed (for example, language detection, sentiment classification, and NER), versioning ensures traceability, repeatability, and governance across the ML lifecycle.

Versioning Considerations

A good versioning system includes:

- **Semantic versioning** (example, v1.0.3) or timestamp-based IDs.
- **Metadata tracking:** Model architecture, dataset version, training pipeline configuration, and so on.
- **Compatibility tags:** Indicating compatible pre-processing, tokenizer, or downstream systems.

Thus, MLflow, Weights and Biases, including SageMaker Model Registry, and Azure ML Model Management provide built-in versioning support that integrates well with PyTorch workflows.

Deploying Multiple Versions Simultaneously

Most production platforms (for example, SageMaker, Vertex AI, KServe, and TorchServe) support multi-model endpoints or shadow deployments, allowing different versions of the same model to be deployed concurrently.

Deployment Patterns:

- **Blue/Green Deployment:** Two model versions are deployed in parallel; traffic is directed to one ("*blue*") until the new version ("*green*") is validated and promoted.
- **Canary Deployment:** A small fraction of traffic (for example, 5%) is routed to the new version to monitor behavior and performance, before full rollout.
- **Shadow Deployment:** The new model receives the same inputs as production, but its outputs are not exposed to the users–used only for logging and evaluation.

These patterns reduce the risk of releasing underperforming models, and allow validation in a live environment, without disrupting the users.

A/B Testing: Measuring the Impact of New Model Versions

A/B testing is a statistical method for comparing two or more model versions in production by routing user traffic to each variant, and observing the outcomes.

A/B Test Setup

1. **Define a metric:** Choose performance indicators relevant to your task– for example, classification accuracy, latency, revenue per interaction, or customer satisfaction.
2. **Segment traffic:** Randomly assign users or requests to different versions (A and B), with controlled ratios (for instance, 50/50 or 90/10).
3. **Monitor metrics:** Collect and compare real-time metrics, using dashboards or logging frameworks.
4. **Analyze statistically:** Use significance tests (for example, t-test, z-test, and so on) or Bayesian inference to determine if one model is significantly better.

Example

You deploy:

- **Model A (v1.2)**: The current DistilBERT sentiment classifier.
- **Model B (v1.3)**: A quantized version optimized for latency.

Split traffic evenly, and measure:

- Latency distribution
- Classification accuracy (if labels are available)
- User engagement (example, click-through rate, app retention, and so on)

After one week, you observe that Model B reduces latency by 40%, without a drop in classification performance. The A/B test shows statistical significance, and Model B is promoted.

Tooling for Versioning and A/B Testing

- **SageMaker Model Registry and Endpoints:** Automate traffic shifting, rollback, and metric tracking.
- **MLflow:** Manage versions, run comparisons, and log artifacts with UI and APIs.
- **Azure ML and GCP Vertex AI:** Offer version-aware deployment, with built-in A/B testing and monitoring.
- **KServe (Kubernetes):** Allows advanced routing, shadow deployment, and version splitting with Istio.

For custom setups, use:

- Nginx or Envoy proxies to split traffic, based on request metadata.
- Prometheus + Grafana to visualize version-wise performance metrics.

Best Practices

- **Keep version history immutable:** Never overwrite model files; always create new versions.
- **Version pre-processing code too:** A model may depend on specific tokenization or input formatting.
- **Log predictions by version:** Store outputs and confidence scores separately per model to track shifts.
- **Test for regressions:** Always benchmark new versions against previous ones, using production-like data.
- **Monitor fairness and bias:** A/B tests can surface hidden disparities—log metrics across user segments, where applicable.

Model versioning and A/B testing are critical pillars of responsible, scalable machine learning deployment. They allow teams to iterate confidently, quantify improvements, and maintain trust in production models. For transformer architectures, where even small changes in hyperparameters or optimizations can affect outcomes, these techniques ensure a rigorous and user-centered release process.

In the next chapter, we will examine data privacy and security considerations, when deploying transformer models—especially important for industries, dealing with sensitive information or regulatory constraints.

Handling Data Privacy and Security in Deployed Transformer Models

As transformer models become increasingly embedded in real-world applications—from healthcare to banking to personalized virtual assistants—ensuring data privacy and model security, during deployment is not just a best practice, but a necessity. These models often process sensitive information, such as personal messages, voice inputs, medical histories, or transaction data. Mishandling this data can lead to compliance violations, reputational damage, and user distrust.

Thus, this section outlines the key principles and strategies for ensuring privacy and security, when deploying transformer models in production.

Privacy-Aware Data Handling

Transformer models require inputs to be pre-processed and sometimes, logged for monitoring or debugging. However, logging raw user inputs or inference outputs can inadvertently capture Personally Identifiable Information (PII).

To prevent this:

- **Sanitize inputs before logging:** Mask names, addresses, phone numbers, or other PII.
- **Use anonymization and tokenization techniques** to remove identity from stored records.
- **Avoid storing unnecessary data:** Log only what is essential for monitoring or debugging.
- **Encrypt data in transit and at rest**, using protocols, such as HTTPS and AES-256 encryption.

Therefore, for applications in regulated sectors (for instance, healthcare under HIPAA, or finance under GDPR), implement user consent mechanisms, and ensure that your deployment pipeline is auditable and explainable.

Secure the Inference Endpoint

Transformer models are often served via REST or gRPC APIs that must be hardened against misuse:

- **Authentication and authorization:** Use API keys, OAuth2, or JWT tokens to restrict access.
- **Rate limiting and throttling:** Prevent abuse by limiting the number of requests per IP/user.
- **Input validation:** Sanitize incoming text or data to prevent injection attacks.
- **Model sandboxing:** Run models in isolated containers or serverless environments, with limited permissions to minimize the blast radius of any exploit.

Prevent Model Inversion and Data Leakage

Transformer models are known to memorize patterns from their training data, which can be exploited via model inversion attacks–where attackers probe the model to reconstruct sensitive training examples.

Mitigation strategies include:

- **Differential privacy training:** Introduce controlled noise during training to mask individual contributions.
- **Limit response verbosity:** Avoid returning full attention maps or confidence scores that could aid adversaries.
- **Monitor for anomalous query patterns:** Use logging and detection tools to identify scraping or probing behaviors.

Secure Model Artifacts

Transformer models, once exported and deployed, become assets that must be protected:

- Store models in secure artifact registries with access control.
- Digitally sign models to ensure integrity, and verify authenticity during deployment.
- Avoid embedding hardcoded secrets or configuration files, within serialized model objects.

So, as transformers scale across industries, protecting data and models becomes paramount. By combining privacy-preserving techniques, secure infrastructure, and robust access controls, teams can ensure that their transformer deployments remain trustworthy, compliant, and resilient. Privacy and security are not one-time checkboxes–they are ongoing responsibilities that evolve with your users, data, and threat landscape.

Conclusion

This chapter covered the essential journey of deploying transformer models, from development to real-world production. We began by examining the key deployment challenges, such as resource constraints, latency, and scalability, and explored tools like ONNX and TorchScript for efficient model export. To enhance performance, we discussed optimization techniques, including pruning, quantization, and distillation, making large models viable in limited-resource environments. Deployment methods, using PyTorch Serve and serverless architectures were introduced, along with strategies for edge deployments and cloud scaling across platforms like AWS, GCP, and Azure.

We then shifted our focus to the ongoing responsibilities after deployment, such as monitoring, model versioning, and A/B testing to ensure reliability and adaptability in live settings. Emphasis was placed on the importance of data privacy and security, recognizing the ethical and legal implications of working with sensitive information. Collectively, these practices offer a robust framework for deploying transformer models effectively and responsibly. In the next chapter, we will explore real-world applications of transformers, across industries such as healthcare, finance, education, and entertainment.

CHAPTER 11
Transformers in Real-World Applications

Introduction

Transformer models are no longer confined to research labs or NLP-specific tasks–they now power some of the most innovative systems across healthcare, finance, education, entertainment, robotics, and customer service. Their ability to handle complex, context-rich data has unlocked new possibilities in everything, from drug discovery and fraud detection to art generation and autonomous decision-making.

In this chapter, we explore how transformers are being applied across diverse industries, highlighting practical use cases, integration strategies, and real-world challenges. From legacy system compatibility to emerging trends like multi-modal AI, this chapter provides a grounded perspective on the transformers' role in solving real business problems and shaping future technologies.

Structure

In this chapter, we will cover:

- Overview of Transformer Applications Across Industries
- Transformers In Healthcare: Medical Diagnosis and Drug Discovery
- Transformers in Finance: Market Prediction and Fraud Detection
- Transformers in Social Media: Content Moderation and Recommendation Systems
- Applications in Creative Industries: Art Generation and Music Composition
- Robotics and Autonomous Systems: Transformers for Decision Making
- Transformers in Education: Personalized Learning and Automated Grading
- Transformers in Retail and Manufacturing: Enhancing Efficiency and Customer Experience
- Integrating Transformers with Legacy Systems and Databases
- Future Trends and Emerging Applications of Transformer Models
- Challenges and Limitations of Transformers in Practical Scenarios

Overview of Transformer Applications across Industries

Since their introduction in 2017, transformer models have rapidly evolved into one of the most influential architectures in artificial intelligence. Initially designed for natural language processing (NLP), transformers have demonstrated remarkable versatility, enabling them to power a wide range of applications beyond text–from image recognition and audio analysis to molecular modeling and recommendation systems. Their strength lies in their ability to model long-range dependencies, capture contextual information, and scale efficiently with data, making them a natural fit for data-rich, pattern-driven domains.

In healthcare, transformers are used for medical image interpretation, clinical decision support, and even drug discovery, where they analyze chemical sequences to predict molecular behavior. In finance, they drive market forecasting, portfolio risk analysis, and fraud detection by modeling time-series data and spotting subtle anomalies in transactional patterns. In the media and entertainment industry, transformers power content moderation, personalized feeds, and automated summarization–key to platforms like YouTube, Twitter, and Netflix.

The creative sector has embraced transformers for music composition, AI-generated art, and text-to-image synthesis, while education platforms use them for adaptive learning, automated grading, and intelligent tutoring systems. Meanwhile, in customer service, transformer-based chatbots have raised the bar in handling complex queries with human-like fluency and emotional awareness.

Transformers are also at the core of innovation in robotics, where they are used for vision-language navigation, action planning, and sensor fusion, enabling more autonomous and intelligent machines. Across industries, transformers are being deployed both in the cloud and at the edge, integrated with traditional systems and APIs to deliver real-time, scalable AI capabilities. This widespread adoption signals not just a technical shift, but a paradigm change–one in which transformer models are redefining the boundaries of what machines can understand, generate, and act upon.

Transformers in Healthcare: Medical Diagnosis and Drug Discovery

The healthcare industry is experiencing a transformative shift, driven by artificial intelligence–and transformers are at the forefront of this revolution. Their ability to model complex relationships, handle multimodal data, and learn from vast, unstructured information makes them highly suited for some of healthcare's most demanding challenges, such as: accurate diagnosis, personalized treatment, and accelerated drug discovery. From analyzing radiology images and clinical notes to predicting molecular properties, transformers are enhancing both clinical workflows and biomedical research at scale.

Transformers in Medical Diagnosis

One of the most promising applications of transformers in healthcare is in aiding medical diagnosis. Traditional diagnostic tools rely heavily on human interpretation of medical images, structured data, and physician notes. Transformers bring a new capability to this space–understanding context-rich, cross-modal information across text, image, and sensor inputs.

- **Analyzing Clinical Text and EHRs**: Electronic Health Records (EHRs) are a goldmine of patient data, yet much of it is unstructured–consisting of free-text physician notes, discharge summaries, and pathology reports. Transformer-based language models like BioBERT, ClinicalBERT, and MedPaLM are fine-tuned on medical corpora to extract symptoms, identify comorbidities, and suggest differential diagnoses. For example, ClinicalBERT has been used to predict patient deterioration in ICUs by modeling temporal sequences in clinical narratives.
- **Medical Imaging and Multimodal Learning**: Transformers have also made inroads into medical imaging. Vision transformers (ViTs) and their hybrids are now being used to classify tumors in MRI scans, detect anomalies in chest X-rays, as well as segment organs in CT scans. Unlike CNNs, which focus on local patterns, transformers can capture global dependencies across image regions, leading to more nuanced diagnostic outputs.

In multimodal setupslike combining CT scans with patient history–transformers are uniquely capable of integrating textual and visual information, improving diagnostic accuracy. Models such as UNITER and BioViL-T are being adapted to align radiology images with textual reports, enabling cross-modal search, automated report generation, and error reduction in radiological interpretations.

Transformers in Drug Discovery

Drug discovery is a time-consuming, resource-intensive process involving the exploration of millions of molecules. Transformers are changing this by helping researchers predict molecular behavior, optimize compound structures, and even generate novel molecules–dramatically speeding up the preclinical phase of development (*Figure 11.1*).

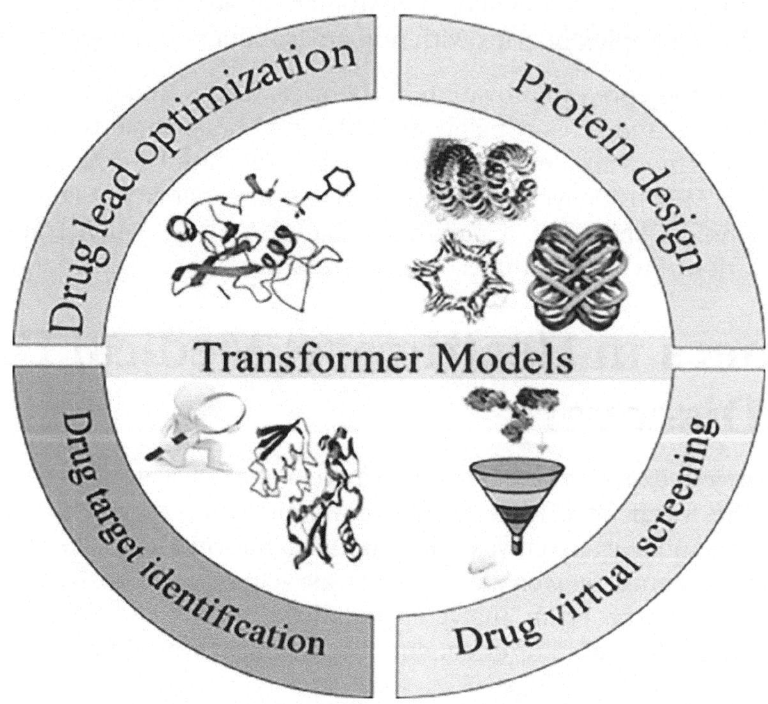

Figure 11.1: *Transformers in Healthcare*

- **Molecular Sequence Modeling**: Similar to how transformers process language, they can be trained to understand chemical languages like SMILES (Simplified Molecular Input Line Entry System), where a molecule is represented as a sequence of characters. Models such as MolBERT and ChemBERTa are pre-trained on large molecular datasets and fine-tuned for tasks like property prediction, activity estimation, and toxicity classification.

  For instance, given a molecule in SMILES format, a transformer can predict its binding affinity to a target protein, helping eliminate unsuitable candidates, early in the discovery pipeline. These models significantly reduce the need for expensive and time-consuming wet-lab screening.

- **Protein Folding and Structure Prediction**: One of the most groundbreaking applications of transformers in healthcare is protein structure prediction. DeepMind's AlphaFold 2, while technically a hybrid of multiple architectures, uses transformer-based attention mechanisms to predict 3D protein structures, with atomic-level accuracy–something that traditionally required years of experimentation.

  This has profound implications not only for understanding diseases, but also for designing targeted therapies. For example, during the COVID-19 pandemic, structural predictions helped identify viral protein targets for vaccine and drug development in record time.

- **Generative Chemistry**: Transformer-based generative models, such as GPT-like architectures adapted for molecules, are now capable of generating novel compounds with desired properties. These models can be guided to design molecules that are, for instance, lipophilic, non-toxic, and have high bioavailability–creating a new paradigm in silico-drug design.

Challenges and Considerations

Despite their promise, deploying transformers in healthcare is not without obstacles:

- **Data privacy and security** are paramount. Patient records must be anonymized, and access to models should comply with the regulations like HIPAA and GDPR.
- **Model explainability** is critical in clinical settings. Physicians require interpretable outputs, not just raw predictions. Tools, such as attention visualization and SHAP values are being explored to make transformer decisions more transparent.
- **Domain-specific training** is required. General-purpose transformers often underperform on medical data, unless fine-tuned on large, domain-specific corpora.
- **Integration into clinical workflows** is non-trivial. Models must align with the existing systems (EHRs and PACS) as well as meet the hospital-level reliability standards.

Thus, transformers are driving a paradigm shift in healthcare–enhancing diagnostic accuracy, accelerating drug development, and enabling a more personalized and efficient medical system. By leveraging their unique ability to process complex, high-dimensional data across modalities, transformers are helping clinicians and researchers make faster, better-informed decisions. While challenges remain in terms of interpretability, regulation, and workflow integration, the momentum is clear: transformers are fast becoming indispensable tools in modern medicine.

Transformers in Finance: Market Prediction and Fraud Detection

The financial industry thrives on information, such as: Patterns in time-series data, nuanced text from regulatory filings, customer behavior, and transactions happening in real time. With their ability to model sequential dependencies, understand contextual relationships, and process multimodal data, transformers are increasingly being adopted in finance for tasks, such as market trend prediction, portfolio management, and fraud detection. These applications demand not only high accuracy, but also interpretability, low latency, and robustness–areas where transformers are proving to be highly effective.

Market Prediction with Transformers

Transformers can be leveraged to uncover hidden patterns and trends in sequential financial data, enabling more accurate market predictions.

Understanding Sequential Financial Data

Financial markets generate massive volumes of time-series data–stock prices, trading volumes, and technical indicators–that are inherently sequential, and often noisy. Traditional models, such as ARIMA or LSTMs have been used for decades, but transformers offer several advantages:

- **Self-attention mechanisms enable the model to focus on important time steps**, capturing long-range dependencies that LSTMs might struggle with.
- **Unlike RNNs, transformers process entire sequences** in parallel, allowing for faster inference–critical for real-time trading systems.

Thus, Time-series transformers, such as Informer, Autoformer, and Temporal Fusion Transformer (TFT) have been fine-tuned for market forecasting. They are used by quantitative analysts, and hedge funds to model trends, detect volatility shifts, and even identify potential arbitrage opportunities across assets.

Multi-Modal Market Signals

Financial decision-making also depends on unstructured data, such as news articles, analyst reports, earnings calls, and social media sentiment. For instance, Transformer models, such as FinBERT and Financial-RoBERTa, trained on domain-specific corpora, extract valuable insights from this data:

- Sentiment analysis on earnings calls or CEO statements.
- Entity recognition in filings (for example, identifying mentioned competitors or regulatory risks).
- Event extraction (for instance, mergers, lawsuits, and bankruptcies).

When combined with numerical time-series data, these multi-modal transformer pipelines enable more holistic and accurate market prediction systems.

Fraud Detection Using Transformers

Financial institutions process millions of transactions daily—each a potential vector for fraudulent activity. Traditional rule-based systems or tree-based classifiers can detect known fraud patterns, but transformers bring a new layer of intelligence by learning subtle, contextual relationships that indicate emerging or disguised fraud tactics.

Modeling Transactions as Sequences

Fraud often manifests in behavior over time: A sudden spike in transfers, location anomalies, or deviations from past purchasing patterns. Transformers are adept at modeling such sequences:

- Each transaction can be treated as a "*token*" with features, such as merchant code, amount, device ID, location, and time.
- Self-attention allows the model to capture irregularities across the full transaction history—not just the most recent activity.

Research has shown that transformer-based models outperform traditional approaches in recall and precision, especially in detecting low-frequency, and high-impact fraud events.

Anomaly Detection at Scale

Transformers can also be used for unsupervised or semi-supervised anomaly detection:

- Train a transformer to predict the next transaction or reconstruct past sequences.
- Flag deviations from the predicted behavior as potential anomalies.

This is particularly useful in detecting money laundering, identity theft, or transaction spoofing, where the fraud does not fit known patterns, but deviates subtly from the learned norms.

Deployment and Regulatory Considerations

Explainability and Auditability: In the financial sector, regulatory compliance requires those AI decisions—especially related to fraud flags, loan approvals, or trading signals, and are explainable.

Hence, Transformer Models must be equipped with tools, such as:

- **Attention visualization:** Which features influenced the decision?
- **SHAP or LIME explanations:** Local feature importance for each prediction.

Without such interpretability, even high-performing models may face rejection by auditors or compliance officers.

Latency and Infrastructure: Financial applications often require low-latency responses–especially in High-Frequency Trading (HFT) or real-time fraud prevention. To meet these constraints, transformer models may be:

- Distilled or quantized for inference efficiency.
- Deployed using ONNX Runtime, TorchScript, or serverless endpoints.
- Combined with edge computing in point-of-sale terminals or mobile banking apps.

Thus, transformers are rapidly reshaping how financial institutions process, understand, and act on vast streams of structured and unstructured data. By bringing together sequence modeling, contextual understanding, and multi-modal integration, they provide a powerful toolkit for tackling complex problems like market prediction and fraud detection. As these models continue to evolve–with better interpretability and deployment efficiency–they are all set to become a cornerstone of AI-driven finance, improving both the accuracy of predictions, and the security of financial ecosystems.

Transformers in Social Media: Content Moderation and Recommendation Systems

Social media platforms operate at an extraordinary scale–processing billions of posts, comments, likes, and media uploads, every day. The dynamic, unstructured, and often sensitive nature of this content poses complex challenges for moderation, personalization, and user engagement. Transformer models, with their ability to understand language, context, and sequence at scale, have become central to managing these challenges. Therefore, from filtering harmful content to powering personalized feeds, transformers are increasingly the engine behind safer and smarter social media experiences.

Content Moderation with Transformers

Social platforms must balance freedom of expression with user safety, legal compliance, and brand integrity. As shown in *Figure* 11.2, this requires automatic detection of:

- Hate speech and abuse.
- Misinformation and fake news.
- Nudity or graphic content.
- Spam and phishing attempts.

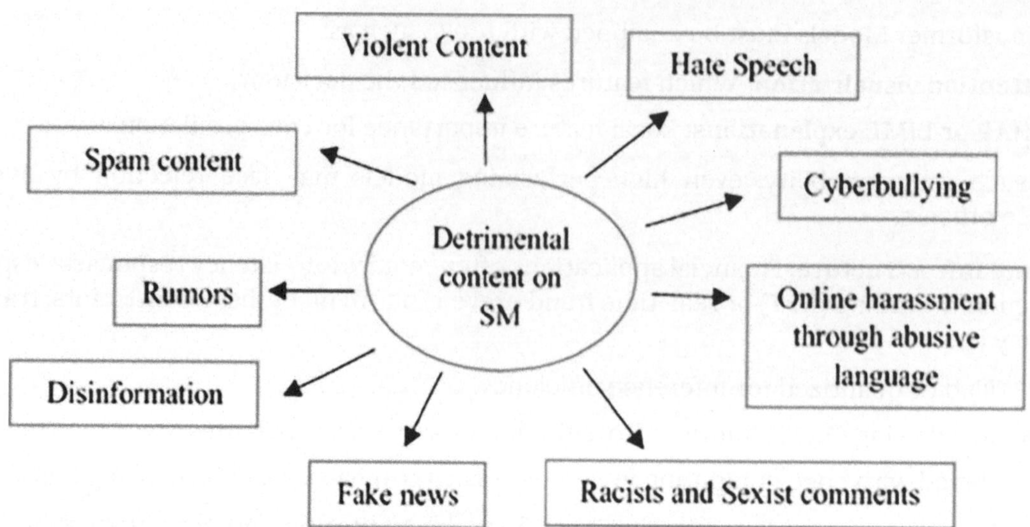

Figure 11.2: *Types of Detrimental Content on Social Media*

Natural Language Moderation

Text moderation is one of the earliest and most mature use cases for transformers. Models, such as BERT, RoBERTa, and XLM-R–fine-tuned on platform-specific data–can identify toxic or policy-violating content across multiple languages and dialects. They offer several advantages, such as:

- **Context-awareness:** Transformers understand subtleties like sarcasm, code-switching, or implied threats better than older keyword-based or RNN-based systems.
- **Multilingual support:** Pretrained multilingual transformers can moderate content across diverse user bases, without training a separate model for each language.

Platforms like Facebook and Twitter use transformer-based models to automatically flag or remove posts that violate community guidelines, with additional human review for edge cases.

Multimodal Moderation

Many harmful posts are not purely textual–they combine text, images, and videos. Recent transformer-based architectures like Contrastive Language-Image Pretraining (CLIP) and Flamingo can analyze and align visual content with text captions, detecting harmful memes, deepfakes, or visually encoded hate symbols.

Some platforms are also experimenting with real-time moderation during live streaming, using vision-language transformers to assess video content and subtitles simultaneously, enabling proactive intervention.

Transformers for Recommendation Systems

Personalization is the backbone of user engagement in social media. Platforms aim to deliver relevant, timely, and engaging content in every user interaction–whether it is a post, video, ad, or friend suggestion. Transformers are now playing a pivotal role in re-ranking feeds, predicting user intent, and optimizing long-term engagement.

Sequential and Contextual Modeling

Transformer architectures, such as YouTube's Reformer, Facebook's DLRM-T, and T5-based recommenders model user behavior as sequences– for instance, scrolls, clicks, likes, watch time–and learn rich representations of user preferences as well as content interactions.

These models:

- Capture temporal dependencies (for example, recent interests vs. long-term interests).
- Adapt to contextual signals, such as time of the day, location, or trending topics.
- Enable next-item prediction, and personalized ranking for feeds, stories, and video playlists.

Multi-Task Learning in Recommendations

Transformers are well-suited for multi-task learning, allowing platforms to train a single model to optimize for multiple objectives, such as:

- Maximizing Click-Through Rates (CTR)
- Improving session duration.
- Reducing content fatigue or filter bubbles.

By jointly optimizing for short-term engagement and long-term user satisfaction, transformer-based systems can balance commercial goals with platform health.

Real-World Applications and Scaling

- **Facebook and Meta**: Meta uses transformers extensively in their content understanding and moderation stack. Their XLM-R models operate across languages and geographies, while custom architectures, such as TimeSformer are used to process video data for proactive moderation and recommendations on platforms like Instagram and Reels.
- **YouTube**: Google has developed deep transformer-based ranking models that personalize recommendations for billions of users. These models incorporate both watch history and real-time signals, continuously retraining on user feedback to improve prediction quality, and minimize harmful recommendations.
- **TikTok**: TikTok's algorithm—renowned for its uncanny accuracy—is believed to use transformer-inspired architectures to model, not just content but user behavior across sessions, capturing subtle engagement signals to surface highly personalized short-form video content.

Ethical and Practical Considerations

- **Bias in moderation:** Transformer models trained on biased data may over-censor certain dialects, cultures, or communities. Hence, fairness audits and human-in-the-loop systems are essential.
- **Transparency:** Users and regulators increasingly demand explainability. Platforms must invest in interpretable transformers or provide transparency into moderation and recommendation decisions.
- **Latency and scaling:** Social platforms require inference at low latency and high throughput. Therefore, optimizations, such as distillation, quantization, and dynamic routing are crucial for deploying transformers at this scale.

Transformers have today become a cornerstone of modern social media infrastructure—enabling more accurate content moderation, and more engaging, personalized experiences. Their ability to understand context, model complex behavior patterns, and handle multimodal data makes them uniquely suited to address the evolving challenges of digital communication at scale. As social media platforms strive to build safer, smarter, and more inclusive environments, transformer models will continue to play a central role—powering not just what users see, but how they interact, engage, and connect.

Applications in Creative Industries: Art Generation and Music Composition

While transformers were originally designed for language modeling, their capacity to understand and generate structured sequences has made them a powerful tool for creative applications–particularly in art, music, and design. By learning from vast datasets of creative works, transformer models can emulate, remix, and even innovate upon human artistic expression. As a result, they are now being used by artists, musicians, designers, and filmmakers to co-create content, automate production workflows, and push the boundaries of creativity.

Visual Art Generation

Transformer models such as DALLE-2, Stable Diffusion, and Imagen can generate high-fidelity images from text prompts–a capability known as text-to-image synthesis. These models use transformer backbones trained on massive datasets of paired text and image data to understand nuanced semantic relationships. For example, a prompt like "*a surreal cityscape painted in Van Gogh's style*" can yield visually coherent and stylistically aligned outputs in seconds.

In commercial design, these tools are being used for:

- Advertising concepts and storyboards.
- Game environment prototyping.
- Fashion design and virtual try-ons.
- Album art and editorial illustrations.

By adjusting prompt structures and seeds, artists can rapidly explore stylistic variations, iterate concepts, and even create interactive generative art experiences.

Music Composition and Audio Generation

In music, transformer-based models, such as Music Transformer, Jukebox (OpenAI), and MuseNet generate compositions in multiple styles, genres, and instrumentations. These models treat notes, chords, and dynamics as tokens, much like words in a sentence, allowing them to learn patterns in rhythm, harmony, and structure over long sequences.

Applications include:

- Composing background scores for film and games.
- Generating melody accompaniments or basslines for musicians.
- Real-time improvisation tools for live performance.
- Stylistic transfer, where a melody is rendered in a different genre.

Some models even generate raw audio directly, enabling the synthesis of expressive vocals or instrument timbres in high fidelity.

Collaborative Creativity and Accessibility

One of the most exciting developments is the emergence of human-AI collaboration tools, where artists can guide generative models through prompts, sketches, or partial melodies. Tools like Runway ML, Google's Magenta Studio, and Adobe Firefly embed transformer models into intuitive interfaces, enabling non-programmers to explore AI-generated creativity.

Moreover, transformers are making artistic creation more accessible–empowering individuals with no formal training in drawing or music to express themselves through AI-augmented tools.

Transformers are opening new frontiers in the creative industries–not by replacing human artists, but by expanding the palette of creative possibilities. So, whether generating striking visuals, composing symphonic music, or enabling real-time artistic interaction, transformer models are redefining how we imagine, create, and collaborate in art and music. As these models continue to evolve, they are not just tools–they are becoming creative partners in the digital age!

Robotics and Autonomous Systems: Transformers for Decision-Making

In robotics and autonomous systems (*Figure* 11.3), decision-making often involves integrating diverse sensory inputs, modeling sequential actions, and adapting to dynamic environments–tasks well-aligned with the capabilities of transformer architectures. Traditionally dominated by rule-based control systems and recurrent models, the field is increasingly adopting transformers for high-level perception, planning, and control, bringing new levels of context awareness and adaptability to machines.

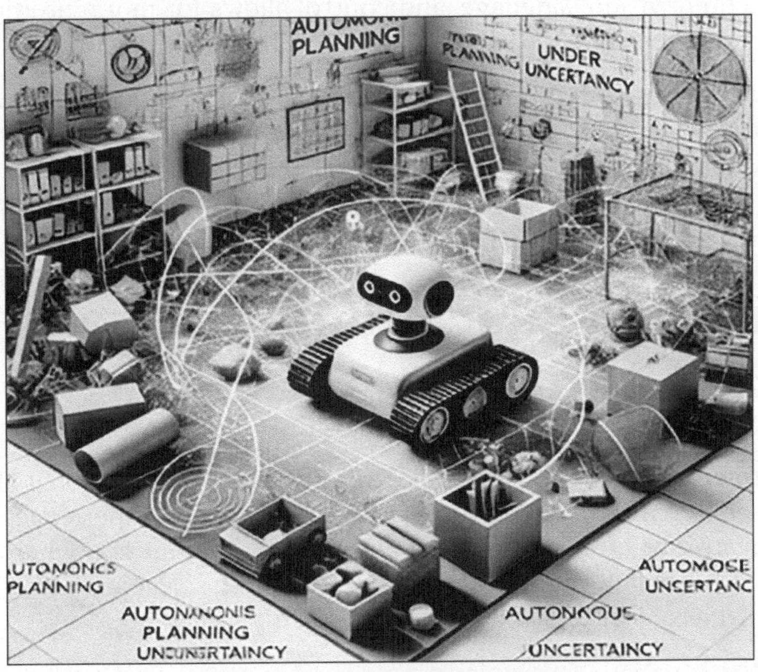

Figure 11.3: *Autonomous Systems*

Transformers for Perception and Sensor Fusion

Robots rely on multiple sensors–cameras, LiDAR, radar, GPS, and more–to understand their surroundings. Transformer models, such as Perceiver, BEVFormer, and UniFormer are used to fuse this multimodal data into coherent representations. Unlike traditional models that process each modality separately, transformers can attend across sensor types, making them ideal for tasks like:

- 3D scene reconstruction
- Object detection and tracking
- Depth and motion estimation

For instance, in autonomous vehicles, transformer-based perception stacks help create real-time semantic maps by integrating camera views, LiDAR point clouds, and road metadata.

Sequential Decision-Making and Policy Learning

Robotics often involves taking actions in a sequence–moving a robotic arm, navigating a room, or interacting with objects. Transformers, such as Decision Transformer and Trajectory Transformer frame reinforcement learning as a sequence modeling task, where past states, actions, and rewards are encoded as tokens. These models excel in:

- Learning from offline datasets, without explicit reward shaping.
- Generalizing across multiple tasks, with minimal retraining.
- Predicting long-horizon outcomes in complex environments.

Applications range from robotic manipulation (for example, stacking blocks, and assembling parts) to path planning in drones and warehouse robots.

Human-Robot Interaction and Language Understanding

Transformers also enhance human-robot communication through natural language interfaces. Models such as SayCan and Palm-E combine language transformers with real-world robotics, enabling systems to understand commands like "*Bring me the blue cup from the table*", and plan actions accordingly. This fusion of vision, language, and control allows for more intuitive and generalizable robot behavior in homes, hospitals, and manufacturing settings.

Transformers are redefining how robots perceive, plan, and interact with the world. By unifying diverse modalities and modeling long-term dependencies, they enable more intelligent, flexible, and human-aligned autonomous systems. As the robotics field embraces large-scale pretraining and foundation models, transformers will play a central role in powering the next generation of versatile, real-world-ready machines.

Transformers in Education: Personalized Learning and Automated Grading

The field of education is undergoing a quiet transformation, powered in part by advances in AI–particularly transformer models. These models, known for their exceptional ability to understand and generate language, are now being used to personalize learning experiences, support educators, and automate administrative tasks like grading and feedback. In an era, where remote and hybrid education models are becoming the norm, transformers offer scalable and adaptive solutions that cater to the diverse needs of learners and institutions alike.

Personalized Learning at Scale

Every student learns differently, but traditional classroom models often follow a one-size-fits-all approach. Transformer-powered systems are changing this by enabling adaptive learning platforms that tailor content based on a learner's pace, knowledge level, and engagement.

Using student interaction data–such as quiz responses, written submissions, and click patterns, transformers can model learning trajectories and recommend next-best lessons, flagging where a student might need remediation or where they are ready to advance. Models such as BERT, GPT-4, and T5 fine-tuned on educational data can power real-time tutoring systems that provide explanations, solve problems, or even simulate Socratic questioning to deepen understanding.

Automated Grading and Feedback Generation

Grading essays, assignments, and open-ended responses is time-consuming, and prone to subjectivity. Transformer models, particularly those fine-tuned for natural language understanding and generation, are being deployed to automatically evaluate student work–offering not just scores, but detailed feedback.

For example:

- **Short answer grading:** Models assess correctness, completeness, and coherence.
- **Essay scoring:** Transformers evaluate organization, grammar, and argument strength.
- **Code assessment:** Models like Codex can review student-written code, offering suggestions and identifying logical errors.

Some systems go further by suggesting alternative phrasing, offering personalized revision tips, or summarizing common mistakes, across a class–empowering teachers with actionable insights, while saving time.

Ethical and Practical Considerations

As with any AI-driven application, care must be taken to avoid bias, ensure explainability, and maintain student data privacy. While transformers can support instruction, they must not replace the human empathy and judgment that are essential to effective teaching. Transparent model behavior, clear boundaries, and teacher oversight remain the key.

Transformers are rapidly becoming valuable allies in education–helping scale personalized instruction, lighten educator workloads, and improve the learning experience. As these models continue to evolve, they hold the potential to bridge the learning gaps, support lifelong education, and make high-quality instruction accessible to learners around the world.

Transformers in Retail and Manufacturing: Enhancing Efficiency and Customer Experience

While transformers have made headlines in domains, such as healthcare, finance, and social media, their applications in retail and manufacturing are equally transformative. These industries, traditionally driven by supply chains, logistics, and customer behavior, now benefit from the predictive and generative capabilities of transformer-based AI systems.

Retail: Personalization at Scale

In modern retail, the key to customer loyalty is personalization. Transformer models enable hyper-personalized product recommendations, leveraging historical purchase data, browsing patterns, and user reviews. For instance, Large Language Models (LLMs) can power intelligent shopping assistants that guide users through online stores via conversational interfaces, dynamically updating suggestions in real time.

Transformers also enhance inventory forecasting. By analyzing sales trends, seasonal shifts, and regional behaviors through sequential modeling, retailers can avoid both overstocking and stockouts. Walmart and Amazon have adopted transformer-driven forecasting engines that outperform traditional time-series models in predicting demand surges.

Another key area is customer service automation. Retailers deploy transformer-based chatbots trained on company-specific data, capable of understanding nuanced customer queries, handling returns, and upselling with contextual sensitivity. These chatbots can perform multilingual support, and even code-switch between languages in real-time, critical in global markets.

Manufacturing: Smarter Operations with Predictive Insights

In manufacturing, transformers are being applied to predictive maintenance, quality control, and supply chain optimization. By ingesting time-series sensor data from machinery, transformer models like Time Series Transformers or Informer can predict failures before they occur, minimizing downtime, and reducing repair costs.

For instance, a transformer model can analyze vibration, temperature, and voltage readings from CNC machines, and flag anomalies indicative of wear or malfunction. When paired with Vision Transformers (ViTs), manufacturers can detect surface defects in assembly lines with precision–improving quality assurance in sectors, such as automotive and electronics.

Transformers also support automated documentation and reporting in manufacturing. Technical logs, operator notes, and maintenance manuals can be parsed and synthesized into actionable insights, using LLMs, saving time and reducing manual errors.

Integrating Transformers with Legacy Systems and Databases

While transformer models have revolutionized AI capabilities, most real-world enterprises–including those in healthcare, finance, government, and education–rely heavily on legacy systems and traditional relational databases. Integrating the state-of-the-art transformer models with these long-standing infrastructures is a critical step in enabling AI-driven decision-making across organizations. However, this integration poses unique challenges that require thoughtful engineering, system compatibility, and workflow design.

Why Integration Matters

Transformer models are typically deployed via Python-based frameworks (for example, PyTorch, TensorFlow, Hugging Face, and so on), and often reside in containerized or cloud environments. On the other hand, legacy systems may be written in Java, .NET, C++, or COBOL, and operate within rigid, regulated IT architectures. Bridging this gap ensures that:

- AI models can consume real business data in real time.
- Model outputs can be actioned through the existing business logic.
- AI becomes a seamless part of the existing workflows, not a parallel or siloed solution.

Common Integration Patterns

- **API-Based Access:** The most common approach is exposing transformer models via REST or gRPC APIs. This allows legacy systems to send requests to a model server (for example, via PyTorch Serve, FastAPI, or Flask), receive predictions, and integrate them into downstream processes.

  Example: A legacy insurance platform calls an NLP model to classify customer complaints, and update the CRM database accordingly.

- **Database Adapters and ETL Pipelines:** Transformers can be connected to structured databases (for instance, PostgreSQL, MySQL, and Oracle) via ETL (Extract-Transform-Load) processes. Batches of customer queries, transactions, or medical records are periodically extracted, analyzed by a transformer model, and written back to the database with predictions or annotations.
- **Model Inference within SQL Workflows:** Modern SQL engines, such as BigQuery ML, Snowflake with external functions, or AWS Athena, now allow AI inference calls from within SQL. This enables analysts and developers to run transformer-based predictions on tabular data, without leaving their data environment.
- **Embedded AI Services:** For high-performance scenarios, some organizations embed quantized or TorchScript versions of transformer models directly into legacy applications, using wrappers or language bindings (for example, via Java-Python bridges or ONNX Runtime).

Challenges and Considerations

- **Data Formatting and Compatibility:** Transformers expect tokenized text or structured input tensors. Legacy systems often store data in flat tables or verbose logs, requiring careful preprocessing.
- **Latency Sensitivity:** Older systems may not tolerate model inference delays. Model optimization, caching, and batch inference are often needed for acceptable performance.
- **Security and Governance:** Transformers must adhere to the existing enterprise security policies, including access control, audit logging, and PII redaction–particularly, when interfacing with sensitive databases.
- **Version Control:** Model updates should be versioned and synchronized with legacy system releases to prevent inconsistencies, and ensure explainability.

Integrating transformers with legacy systems is not just about retrofitting new tech into old frameworks–it is about unlocking value from the existing data and workflows with the intelligence of modern AI. Thus, by leveraging APIs, database connectors, and containerized deployments, organizations can embed transformers into everyday operations–bringing advanced NLP, classification, and prediction capabilities to even the most traditional IT environments. Done right, this integration offers a practical and powerful path toward enterprise-wide AI transformation.

Future Trends and Emerging Applications of Transformer Models

Transformer models have already redefined natural language processing, computer vision, and cross-modal AI–but their evolution is far from complete. As research advances and computational tools improve, transformers are set to play a foundational role in next-generation AI systems that are more generalizable, multimodal, and interactive. This section explores the key trends shaping the future of transformer models, and the emerging domains, where they are poised to have a transformative impact.

Multimodal and Foundation Models

A major trend is the rise of multimodal transformers–models that simultaneously process and reason over text, images, audio, and video. Pioneering models, such as CLIP, Flamingo, PaLM-E, and GPT-4V illustrate how a single architecture can handle inputs from various modalities, enabling use cases like:

- Image captioning and visual question answering.

- Video summarization and sentiment analysis.
- Speech-guided robotics and AR/VR content synthesis.

These models act as foundation models: Massive, pre-trained architectures fine-tuned for downstream tasks with minimal data. They promise zero-shot and few-shot generalization across an expanding range of real-world applications.

Real-Time and On-Device Transformers

Another emerging frontier is running transformer models locally on edge devices. Thanks to advances in quantization, distillation, and efficient architectures, such as MobileBERT, TinyViT, and FNet, as it is now feasible to deploy transformers for real-time tasks on:

- Smartphones (for instance, translation, summarization, and so on)
- IoT sensors (for example, anomaly detection)
- Wearables (for instance, health monitoring)
- Autonomous vehicles (for example, sensor fusion and planning)

These developments unlock privacy-preserving and latency-critical applications in healthcare, smart homes, and automotive systems.

Scientific Discovery and High-Impact Domains

Transformers are beginning to show promise in scientific fields, once dominated by physics-based models and human expertise. Notable trends include:

- **AI for code:** Models such as Codex and Code LLaMA automate software development, debugging, and documentation.
- **Materials science and chemistry:** Transformers help predict molecular interactions, generate synthesis pathways, and design new materials.
- **Climate modeling:** Early work is applying transformers to long-term weather prediction and environmental simulations, with fine-grained spatial awareness.

These use cases extend transformers' utility beyond automation and language into knowledge creation and discovery.

Societal Integration and Human-Centric AI

As transformers become embedded in public life, we will see more focus on human-centered design, including:

- **Explainable AI:** Integrating interpretability directly into transformer outputs via attention visualization, causal modeling, or natural language rationales.
- **Ethics and fairness:** Tools to mitigate bias, control harmful generation, and ensure responsible use–especially in healthcare, finance, and education.
- **Collaborative AI:** Systems where humans and AI co-create, such as educational tutors, creative assistants, and decision support tools.

Transformers will evolve not just as tools for automation, but as partners in cognition, helping humans extend their reach across domains of thought and creativity.

Thus, the future of transformers lies not just in scaling parameters, but in broadening application contexts, improving efficiency, and deepening their integration into human workflows. As these models grow more adaptable, interpretable, and multimodal, they will form the backbone of AI systems that are domain-agnostic, collaborative, and impactful across science, industry, and society. In fact, the age of the transformers is only just beginning!

Beyond: Additional Industry Applications

- **Telecommunications:** Transformers are used for network traffic forecasting, optimizing resource allocation, and even predicting outages. Models trained on past call data and network logs can identify patterns of congestion and self-heal systems, before failure.
- **Legal and Compliance:** In the legal industry, transformer models streamline document review, contract analysis, and regulatory monitoring, helping legal teams process high volumes of information, with minimal oversight.
- **Agriculture:** Transformers aid in crop yield prediction, pest detection, and satellite imagery analysis, offering farmers AI-driven decision support for sowing, irrigation, and harvesting.

Challenges and Limitations of Transformers in Practical Scenarios

While transformer models have achieved remarkable success across domains, deploying them in real-world, production-grade environments comes with significant challenges. These limitations often arise not from model performance on benchmarks, but from the practical demands of scalability, interpretability, cost, and context. Understanding these hurdles is essential for making informed decisions about when and how to use transformers effectively in applied settings.

High Computational and Memory Costs

Transformers, especially large-scale models like GPT-4 or T5, require immense computational resources to train and run. Their self-attention mechanism scales quadratically with input length, making long-sequence tasks prohibitively expensive. Even inference for moderately sized models can be resource-intensive, limiting their deployment in:

- Real-time systems with strict latency requirements.
- Edge devices with limited compute and battery power.
- Budget-constrained or sustainability-conscious organizations.

Thus, while techniques like quantization, pruning, and distillation help mitigate this, significant trade-offs in accuracy or flexibility may occur.

Data Hunger and Domain Adaptation

Transformers perform best, when trained on massive datasets. However, many real-world domains (such as legal, tech, healthcare, or manufacturing) lack large, high-quality, labeled datasets. Even with transfer learning, fine-tuning transformers on small, domain-specific datasets can lead to:

- Overfitting or catastrophic forgetting
- Instability in fine-tuning (especially in low-resource languages or tasks)
- Performance degradation in out-of-distribution settings

This makes their use in specialized applications challenging, without robust pipelines for data curation and augmentation.

Lack of Interpretability and Explainability

Transformers are often considered "*black boxes*," making it difficult to understand why a model made a specific prediction–a serious drawback in domains, requiring transparency, such as:

- Healthcare diagnoses
- Financial decision-making
- Legal risk assessment

While attention weights offer some interpretability, research has shown that they do not always correlate with feature importance. Without clear explanations, trust and adoption among end-users and regulators may be hindered.

Ethical Risks and Bias Amplification

Pretrained transformer models often inherit and amplify biases from their training data which can manifest in:

- Stereotypical or offensive outputs
- Skewed recommendations or classifications
- Discriminatory behavior in hiring, lending, or law enforcement use cases

This poses significant ethical, legal, and reputational risks, particularly when deployed at scale. Mitigating these biases requires auditing, debiasing techniques, and ongoing monitoring–all of which add operational complexity.

Infrastructure Integration and Legacy Compatibility

Integrating transformer models into the existing business systems is rarely seamless.

Certain common challenges include:

- Differences in data formats and pipelines.
- Incompatibility with monolithic architectures.
- Deployment across heterogeneous environments (cloud, edge, on-premise, and so on)

Organizations often struggle to productionize transformers due to these integration bottlenecks, leading to pilot project stagnation and AI deployment delays.

In fact, transformers offer state-of-the-art performance across many tasks, but they are not silver bullets. Their practical limitations–ranging from compute intensity and data demands to ethical concerns and operational complexity–must be carefully managed. Future progress in efficient architectures, robust fine-tuning, and transparent decision-making will be essential for transformers to fulfill their full promise in real-world applications. But, for now, success depends on balancing innovation with cost, compliance, and context-aware deployment.

Conclusion

In this concluding chapter, **we explored the diverse and ever-expanding impact of transformer models across real-world industries.** From revolutionizing healthcare diagnostics and drug discovery to enhancing financial forecasting and fraud detection, transformers have demonstrated their versatility in solving complex, high-stake problems. Their influence extends to social media, where they support content moderation and user engagement; the creative arts, where they co-create images, music, and narratives; and robotics and autonomous systems, where they empower intelligent perception and decision-making.

We also examined how transformers are used in education, providing personalized learning experiences and automating assessment. Recognizing the gap between cutting-edge models and traditional infrastructure, we looked at ways to integrate transformers with legacy systems and databases. We then turned our attention to the future of transformers, highlighting trends, such as multimodal AI, on-device deployment, and scientific discovery–while also acknowledging the real-world limitations around compute, bias, explainability, and system compatibility.

As transformer models continue to mature, their success will depend not only on architectural innovation but also on practical deployment, ethical foresight, and the ability to align with human values and needs. Their power lies not just in accuracy or scale, but in their capacity to reshape how we learn, decide, create, and interact.

Throughout this book, we've journeyed from the foundations of neural networks to the most advanced transformer architectures, learning how to build, fine-tune, optimize, and deploy these models with PyTorch 2.0. Along the way, we've emphasized not just technical implementation but also real-world utility, scalability, and responsibility.

Transformer models are more than just tools–they're becoming foundational infrastructure for knowledge, automation, and interaction in the 21st century. Whether you're a data scientist, developer, researcher, or educator, your ability to harness transformers will define your impact in the evolving AI landscape.

As you move forward, continue to explore, experiment, and ask critical questions–not just about what transformers can do, but what they should do, and how they can be used to build systems that are intelligent, ethical, and truly human-aligned.

Congratulations on reaching the final chapter–and best of luck in shaping the future with transformers.

Index

D

E

F

L

M

N

Q

R

S

T

V

W

Z